Comb Ridge and Its People

Courtesy of Kay Shumway

Sunrise over a Butler Wash ruin on the eastern slope of Comb Ridge.

Comb Ridge and Its People

THE ETHNOHISTORY OF A ROCK

Robert S. McPherson

Utah State University Press
Logan, Utah

Utah State University Press
Logan, UT 84322–7800
www.usu.edu/usupress

Publication of this book was supported by a subvention from the Charles Redd Center for Western Studies at Brigham Young University.

Manufactured in China

ISBN: 978-0-87421-737-7 (cloth)
ISBN: 978-0-87421-738-4 (e-book)

Library of Congress Cataloging-in-Publication Data

McPherson, Robert S., 1947-
Comb Ridge and its people : the ethnohistory of a rock / Robert S. McPherson.
p. cm.
Includes bibliographical references and index.
ISBN 978-0-87421-737-7 (pbk.) -- ISBN 978-0-87421-738-4 (e-book)
1. San Juan County (Utah)--History, Local. 2. Comb Ridge (Ariz. and Utah)--History. 3. Indians of North America--Utah--San Juan County--History. 4. Indians of North America--Comb Ridge (Ariz. and Utah)--History. I. Title.
F832.S4M37 2009
979.2'59--dc22

2008053907

To Winston Hurst—friend, scholar, and guru—without his assistance, this book would not be.

Courtesy of Kay Shumway

Comb Ridge has a rich legacy from its people. Ancestral Puebloan dwellings are among the most visible elements.

Contents

Courtesy of Kay Shumway

Rugged ravines compartmentalize much of the eastern slope of Comb Ridge.

Acknowledgments

As an author, this is the best part of a book—the opportunity to thank people who have shaped my thinking and assisted with the project. Foremost in this category is Winston Hurst, field director of the Comb Ridge Archaeological Survey Project. He has been intimately involved with the writing of this manuscript from its inception and has provided expert opinion. To his credit, he desires none. In spite of his insistence that he be left out of the final product, I have insisted more forcefully that he be included, since by his own admission, Comb Ridge has played and does now play a major role in his life. His writings bring a perspective that spans from boy to man, from uninitiated to professional, from observer to advocate.

John Holiday, Navajo medicine man from Monument Valley, shaped much of the ethnohistorical perspective from his traditional background. He not only herded his sheep and lived in the area surrounding Comb Ridge, but his clear and vibrant understanding of its role in Navajo practices added insight about a geographic feature that is unparalleled in many accounts of Native American geographical sites. His willingness to share this information with future generations insures that his understanding will not be lost. Marilyn Holiday, as usual, did an excellent job in translating John's complex Navajo ideas into understandable English concepts.

Other Navajo and Ute elders, most of whom have passed on, also informed this work. Their willingness to share their knowledge of local geography adds a depth and breadth of experience that could not otherwise have been attained. Clayton Long of the San Juan School District Bilingual Program assisted in standardizing spelling of Navajo names and words; Ron Maldonado of the Navajo Nation Historic Preservation Office provided initial guidance, read the manuscript, and commented on the draft; and Edward Dutchie, Sr. (deceased), Stella Eyetoo, and Lola Mike shared Ute teachings.

Agencies and their representatives include Cathy Cameron, Comb Ridge Project director, from the University of Colorado at Boulder, and Nick Sandberg and Paul Curtis from the Monticello Bureau of Land Management Office. The Charles Redd Center for Western Studies, whose director is Brian Cannon, provided monetary assistance for publishing the color photographs. As for the photographers, thanks go to Andrew Gulliford and Lloyd Kartchner with a special thanks to L. Kay Shumway for sharing their artistic eyes on Comb. Such a dramatic monolith requires people like them to capture its essence as well as its physical properties. John Alley, editor of Utah State University Press, with whom I have worked before, has again brought the finished product to a pleasing conclusion.

A final thanks to my wife, Betsy, for listening to my incoherent babbling at the dinner table about Ancestral Puebloan roads, Navajo beliefs, Ute practices, old Bluff, and contemporary issues. Perhaps now that she can read this book, it will all make more sense.

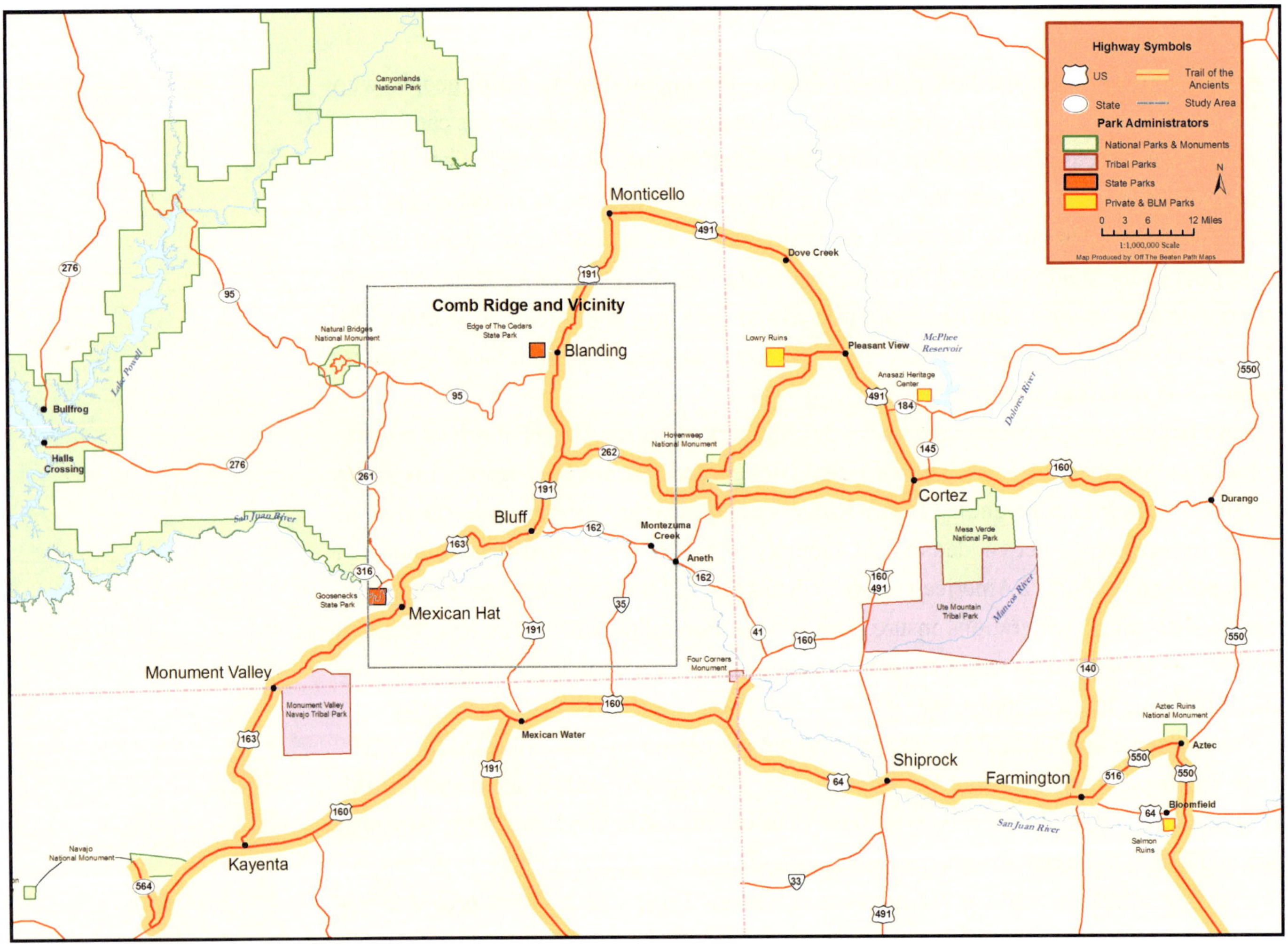

Four Corners Region

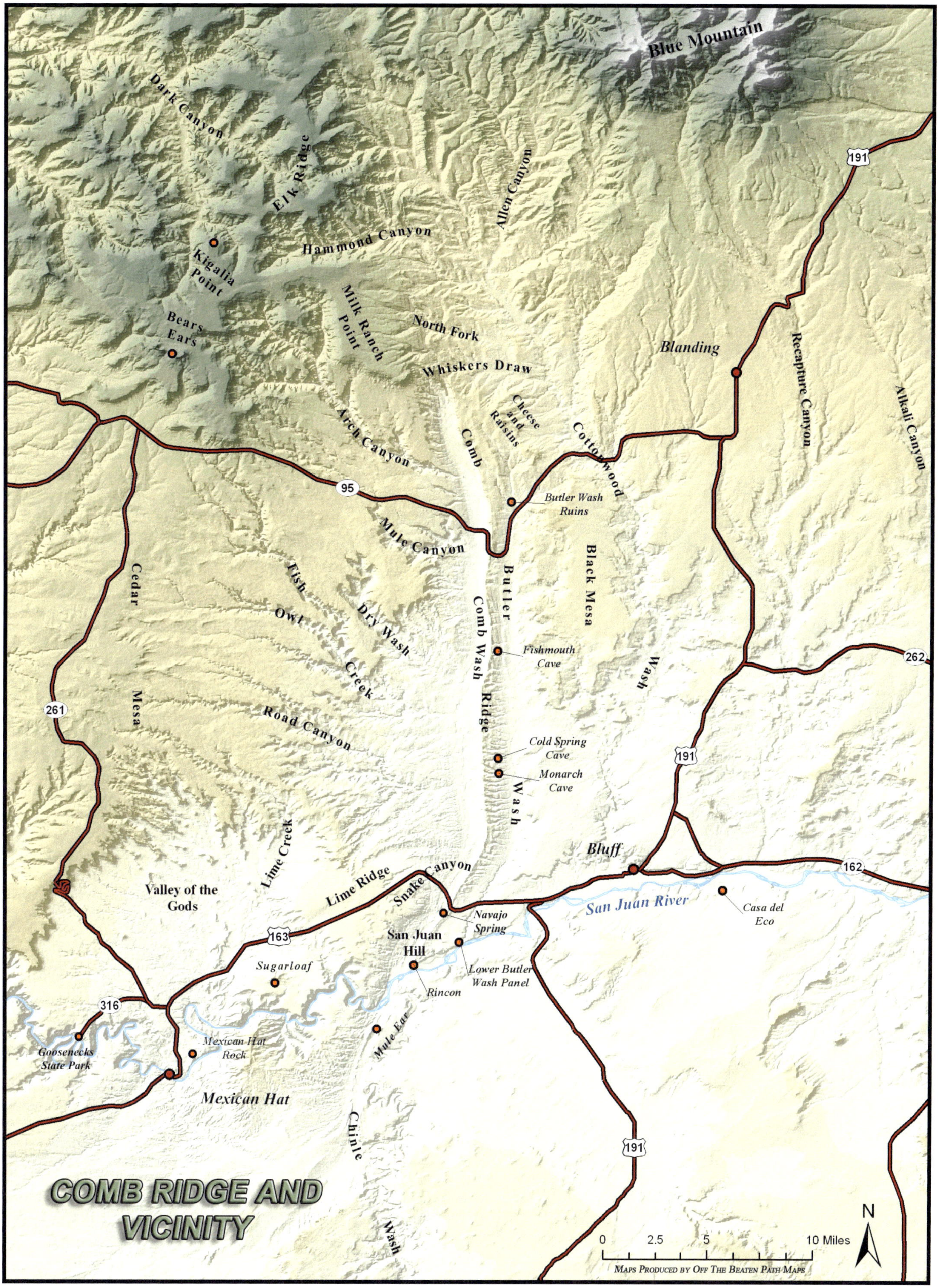

Blue Mountain
Dark Canyon
Elk Ridge
Allen Canyon
Hammond Canyon
Kigalia Point
Bears Ears
Milk Ranch Point
North Fork
Whiskers Draw
Blanding
Recapture Canyon
Alkali Canyon
Cheese and Raisins
Arch Canyon
Comb
Cottonwood
Butler Wash Ruins
95
191
Mule Canyon
Butler
Black Mesa
Cedar
Fish
Owl
Dry Wash
Comb Wash
Fishmouth Cave
Creek
Wash
262
261
Mesa
Road Canyon
Ridge
Cold Spring Cave
Monarch Cave
Wash
Lime Creek
Bluff
Snake Canyon
Lime Ridge
Valley of the Gods
162
San Juan River
Casa del Eco
Navajo Spring
San Juan Hill
163
Lower Butler Wash Panel
Sugarloaf
Rincon
316
Mule Ear
Goosenecks State Park
Mexican Hat Rock
Mexican Hat
Chinle
Wash
COMB RIDGE AND VICINITY
0
2.5
5
10 Miles
N
Maps Produced by Off The Beaten Path Maps

Courtesy of Kay Shumway

A portion of the knife-like Comb Ridge that cuts across the desert of the Colorado Plateau.

Introduction

Comb Ridge

A Rock, A View, Some Thoughts

I stood and turned to look at Comb Ridge, still a couple of miles away. From this vantage it had the appearance of an ice palace—its white sandstone slick with rain—and canyons melted out of its face. . . . Usually bone-dry, Comb Ridge was inhaling the previous night's storm, and now it slowly let water back out through its porous sandstone, dribbling from seeps and springs where maidenhair ferns grow.

— Craig Childs, *House of Rain*[1]

Comb Ridge is unique. The rock's massive serrated edge jabs the blue sky with knife-like points, prodding the clouds for rain. Heated in the summer and doused with snow in the winter, this tempered blade stretches for one hundred miles, cautioning people to cross its sharp two-hundred-foot cliffs carefully. A barrier, a place of protection, a sentinel, the rock has figured significantly in the prehistory, history, and current events of the region. Just how significant is the story of this book?

The other day, a friend asked what project I was working on. I mentioned that there was a five-year archaeological study around Comb Ridge and that I had been asked to write the history portion. His response: "Is there really that much history? I wouldn't think you could even squeak a pamphlet out of that." I have since ruminated over his query and need to thank him for crystallizing in my mind why this type of work is necessary. Here is a man, born and raised in the area, who has traveled on and flirted with Comb Ridge all of his life. He is a college graduate, an educated soul, who loves the land and spends his free time hiking or riding to many of the far recesses of the county. He loves the country and works well with its people. Yet he does not know even a pamphlet's worth of information about one of the most dominant historic landscapes in his backyard. He is not alone but represents the vast majority of people who have set foot at the base of Comb Ridge, not to mention those who have scaled its heights.

Next, one has to ask which height. From each of its knobs, pinnacles, and points comes a different perspective. If one does not like the view, slip north or south a mile for a different scene. To the east, Butler Wash twists its way along Comb's striated slopes. At the foot of the ridge rest cottonwood groves, alcoves, desert flats, and a ribbon of dirt road. Depending upon where one stands, one might see the Procession Panel of Ancestral Puebloan rock art at the north end, Bluff City with its unnatural nest of trees, Sleeping Ute Mountain in Colorado, or the sinuous curves of the San Juan River to the south. Facing west, one can sight up the knife edge and see Blue Mountain in the distance, Comb Wash (a parallel, dry creek bottom), gray sagebrush covering Lime Ridge, the Bears Ears peering over the edge of Elk Ridge, and, on the horizon, part of Monument Valley pointing its buttes and mesa tops to the heavens.

There are just as many different types of views, metaphorically speaking, of the people who have lived upon the land. Here, the shift is not north or south a mile, but through time. The panorama is just as varied, just as enlightening. A brief glimpse of PaleoIndians hunting mastodons, Archaic groups adapting to the changing environment, Ancestral Puebloans (Anasazi) leaving riddles for archaeologists, Navajos and Utes intensely loving and depending on the land, and the newest, briefest occupants, white men, exacting change. For those unaware of these "vistas," the land appears as a tabula rasa, waiting to be used for contemporary needs and desires. To many people, the past is as muted and intangible as a fading sunset over the Bear Ears. But this is not true for all.

In 1953, a six-year-old boy stood with his father on Comb Ridge and watched explosions of dynamite raise clouds of dust and debris into the air; large chunks of sandstone slid from the west side of the cliff. The boy, Winston Hurst, was witnessing the construction of Highway 95, a new route that opened the Grand Gulch Plateau and points west to routine automobile traffic. Repeated visits spread over his primary and adolescent years, bonding him to this massive rock, which served as both an escape and a mentor for the growing youth. The contemplative self blossomed as he "learned to breathe deeply and to slip open the windows of [his] soul, first just a crack then more widely."[2] The landscape became a powerful force that spoke to him, but he did not yet understand what it had to say; he has since learned. In his words:

> I didn't yet know that I was looking down on the faint trace of an ancient roadway connecting ruins of long-abandoned Indian ghost towns whose inhabitants had once lived here since time immemorial and had adorned themselves with objects from as far away as Mexico and the Pacific Ocean. I didn't know that just over there stood the collapsed remnants of a hogan built by one of the last free-living Navajo Indians; or that here Hastiin Nez once escaped a ledge on the cliff face by tying himself to a tree and committing himself to a thrilling toboggan ride to the bottom; or that this great rock on which I sat had once been known to my pioneer ancestors as "The Highland Lady" but was really part of the great ridge known by the Navajo and Ute Indians to be the literal backbone of the living Earth. I had no idea that, just over there, my Great Grandfather Bayles had survived an outlaw's ambush and helped carry home the body of

> a good man of lesser fortune who wanted to recover his favorite horse; or that that faint faraway scratch in the land marked the very road by which my ancestors, driven by religious zeal and almost incomprehensible audacity and bullheadedness, had brought a great wagon train through an impassable (to reasonable people) wilderness to pioneer the town of Bluff and later Blanding. I didn't know that by the same road, wagons and pack trains of ancient artifacts freshly disturbed from the slumber of centuries had long ago been hauled out by characters like Richard Wetherill and Charley Lang and my own Great Grandfathers Lyman and Bayles, to be sold and distributed to great and greedy museums across the country; or that I would someday help in the retracing of those collections and the successful effort to reestablish their links to places on the land.[3]

There were other things the boy did not know. In the not-distant future, he would become an archaeologist, giving sprout to the seeds of wonder planted in his youth. He would learn more than a pamphlet about the land, becoming an expert in the region's prehistory and history. Indeed, Winston has spent his entire adult life studying the Ancestral Puebloan, reading pioneer oral histories, mapping and photographing sites, sharing what he has found, and protecting what he loves. No one has done more to preserve the prehistoric past of San Juan County. His greatest fear is that what he has worked so hard to understand and protect could be trampled under the feet of unsuspecting, uninformed enthusiasts who share similar interests. The conundrum now is how does one educate the public while avoiding evisceration of the "teacher."

Given Winston's background, it is not surprising that in 2005 he became the field director for the Comb Ridge Survey Project. The objective established by the BLM, partly in celebration of the one-hundreth anniversary of the Antiquities Act (1906), was to implement a five-year cultural resource inventory of Comb Ridge and its environs, encompassing approximately sixty-six square miles. Contracting and overall supervisory responsibility for the project lay in the hands of Professor Catherine Cameron, University of Colorado at Boulder. A four-person team of archaeologists and volunteers provided much of the onsite labor, with other assistants handling the clerical work of Geographic Information System (GIS) data entry. One lone historian assumed the responsibility of gathering the ethnographic and historical documentary background of the survey area. The end result of all this was to be a well-researched survey, based in varying levels of intensity, that identified prehistoric and historic cultural resources spread throughout the length of Comb Ridge, as bounded by Highway 163 in the south and the old Highway 95 in the north.[4]

On the ground, this translated into a myriad of sites—an estimated four thousand at the time of writing—that ranged from a lithic scatter of fifteen flakes to the great houses and great kivas of the Ancestral Puebloans. In terms of time depth, the survey considered everything from PaleoIndian points and sites hearkening back to 12,000 BC to contemporary site degradation and preservation in 2008. Six different cultures (PaleoIndian, Archaic, Ancestral Puebloan, Ute/Paiute, Navajo, and Anglo) played across the landscape, leaving remains of their lifestyles. The types of sites they left included habitation, food processing, resource procurement, ceremonial, roads, and trails. Many of these archaeological remains are quickly disappearing, given the intense use of the land by those pursuing recreation and economic development.

Historic regional patterns become subject to change because of environmental variation, cultural innovation, ethnic migration, technological shifts, and happenstance. So, while the relation of the Puebloan people of Chaco Canyon to those in southeastern Utah is considered, as is the tourist industry to isolated Mormon communities in the twentieth century, one should not lose sight of what happens on the micro level. Just as Hurst started with his own forebears then moved back in time to an interest in broader ancient and historic cultures, so too does this study depend heavily on individual experience and belief. Joseph Amato, in *Rethinking Home*, reminds the reader that "all history is local."[5] His study, set in southwestern Minnesota, is just as relevant in southeastern Utah when he posits that intimate detail on a micro level has power to connect a reader to place. Hence, the eyewitness account of a Bluff cattleman in the 1880s can be just as telling as an examination of the regional livestock market. More important, it provides a mental image of experience as it moo-ved around, in this case, Comb Ridge. Landscape plus people plus culture provides immediacy.

But there is more. This study is invested in anthropology as well as in the past. Ethnohistory is defined as "a kind of historical ethnography that studies culture of the recent past through oral histories, through the accounts of explorers, missionaries, and traders; and through analysis of such data as land titles, birth and death records, and other archival materials."[6] The story of Comb Ridge cannot be told without drawing on this discipline. Thus, there are two tracts that course throughout the book. The first is an examination of what happened, while the second is what the land and events mean to the different cultures that experienced them. Some chapters are derived almost entirely from what Navajo and Ute elders believe. Their views of an intangible, spiritual world are given as much credence as the scientific, measurable reality of the Anglo. The connection of snakes, arrowheads, lightning, and wind to Comb Ridge holds as much truth in Native American thought as the geological explanation of vanished seas and mechanical cleavage and the buckling of the earth's surface found in scientific views.

A quick perusal of the endnotes will show just how dependent this book is upon oral history. Native American elders, cattlemen, road builders, miners—the list goes on—have contributed their views derived from experience. From their understanding has sprung the action of events around Comb Ridge. Navajo prayers offered at its foot and crest, the Ute explanation of the origin of the wedding basket, cattle grazing on the Barton Range, four-wheelers (ORVs) splashing up Arch Canyon Creek all speak to values held by society but that are played out through the individual. More than just a rock, Comb Ridge has been central in evoking the principles of those who come to live, work, and play on its slopes.

How unique, then, is Comb Ridge? As a single rock formation, it is most likely the longest of its kind. Native American teachings surrounding it are at least as prevalent as some of the better-known sites such as Devil's Tower, Bear Butte, and Chimney Rock.

All of these sacred sites, and hundreds—more likely thousands—of others, hold sacred powers for traditional ceremonial practices. In terms of complexity of teachings, the Navajo, who have an intricate system of chantways and stories, offer for Comb among the most varied and largest number of explanations surrounding a single rock formation. John Holiday, practitioner of the Blessingway, is particularly interested in seeing these teachings passed on to future generations. He worries that much of them is now disappearing. Other elders added their voices to expressing the importance of a rock which has long outlasted their existence.

On the other end of the philosophical spectrum stands John Wayne. Not noted for deep introspection but as a man of action, he has come to typify the rugged individual in his movie roles. Much of the action of those films occurred across the sands and between the mesas of Monument Valley, bordered by Comb Ridge on the east and the San Juan River in the north. Wayne and film mogul John Ford fell in love with the landscape and befriended the Indian people they worked with. The scenery became stereotypically clichéd; movie after movie used the same settings, shot from different angles. Little wonder that Wayne, when speaking of the area, is said to have quipped, "This is where God put the West."[7] His reference, of course, was to the Wild West of the mid- to late nineteenth century.

Comb Ridge was very much a part of that frontier, an unsettled period of drama. Here, facts surrounding this rock support the cliché. There were Indians living on the land, wagon trains of settlers, traders and missionaries, the cattle industry using the open range, gunfights between cowboys and Indians, shootouts with rustlers, and a gold rush. The twentieth century had its own dramatic flavor—the boom-and-bust oil industry, the pillaging of Indian remains, road building, uranium mining, tourism, and environmental conflicts. Through it all, Comb sat as mute witness. Wayne's perception, regardless of how clichéd or magnified it may have become, is made manifest in the following pages.

More than a pamphlet full of adventure and insight is here for the reader. Comb Ridge is a place that, once a person has been there, is not easily forgotten. By understanding more about its history, it becomes a memory-jogger that speaks to the soul of those who have lived their life in its shadow. Different cultures, different views, different events are united under the brow of a magnificent rock.

A Personal Note

I have never felt the necessity of sending a letter to the editor or of making a personal position statement in any book that I have written. As in this work, I have always aimed for balance, showing both sides of an argument. Thus far, no one has accused me of being prejudiced or lopsided, though I am sure that joy probably lies ahead. It is difficult to write about Native American, environmental, and contemporary issues and avoid the barbs. In this particular work, because of the controversy that swirls around Comb Ridge today (see chapter 9) I felt a short explanation of my position, which, I hope, does not come through in the text, might be wise. For those not interested, skip to chapter 1.

Boxes are helpful. A person puts things in them that appear similar in function and form, labels them, and stores them on a shelf until just the right tool is needed, then rummages through until the tool is found and used as seems best. Labels may change, items may be shifted into other containers, but the tool remains as part of the collection. So it is with polarizing contemporary issues—boxes with labels place people and ideas in handy packages. It simplifies issues: locals versus out-of-staters, pot hunters versus feds, environmentalists versus ORVers, wilderness versus multiple use, cattlemen versus tree huggers, Navajos versus Utes, etc. Simplification through labeled boxes denies the complexity of a situation and pigeonholes an individual or group so that they do not have to be listened to. One already knows what is in the box, what it is about, and so gives little thought to it.

I live within sight of Comb Ridge, take both the local papers, and closely follow current controversies. A constant dialogue erupts from opposing caves, each person sprinting into the sunlight to yell what is right, then returning to the acceptance of the rest of the tribe waiting in the shadows. Most are dedicated, well-meaning people from both sides of the ridge who share comparable but opposite forms of steadfast beliefs. On one side are those who claim their forefathers' perception of "right of discovery" and first come, first served; others personify the role of those who are too old to otherwise enjoy the beauties of nature and promote "open entry, open access" at whatever cost; another says, "I fought for my country and I have my rights"; and the last asserts that all environmentalists are extremists and will use every trick in the book to snatch away god-given privileges. These arguments generate more heat than light and snatch away any common ground for the opposing side to share.

The other camp on the ridge is just as adamant. Tinged with a strong anti-Mormon flavor, they shout from the cave that the local populace has no concern for the environment. A redneck approach is pinned on the opposition, who are seen as abusing the land, wasting resources as if there were no tomorrow, lacking respect for antiquities, disregarding scientific land management, fostering a closed local society that dislikes out-of-towners, and promoting a Wild West attitude that rapes the land and thrives on truculence. Each side makes very little effort to bridge the gulf. I straddle both slopes, glimpsing into each alcove to the fire that burns inside. By explaining my position, I hope to start building a bridge. This is difficult because it may come across as rooted in condescension or advocating for a particular side. Neither is my intent. I will be brief and hope that my words may be helpful.

I arrived in Blanding in 1976 and have lived here ever since. I cannot claim Hole-in-the-Rock ancestry or that my forefathers settled the land, though I did have a distant family member who came over on the Mayflower. Maybe that trumps everybody else's hand (except for the Native Americans), but I doubt it. More relevant is the fact that my wife and I have raised our family of six children here; we love San Juan County and intend to be buried in its soil—not in Salt Lake City or Colorado. I wholeheartedly believe in multiple use, spent eight years as a scout leader with monthly camping trips as part of the regimen, heat my home with wood that comes from public lands, and depend upon access to water and roads on Blue Mountain. I served in the military (active and parttime for thirty-eight years), hold a Purple Heart, and am just as concerned about federal and state rights as anyone else. Having crossed the great divide of sixty, my knees and ability to get around limit my hiking, hence how much country I can see.

So what am I willing to accept? I accept that I do not have to demand the ability to travel anywhere I want on public lands, given the extent of damage done by ORVs. The land is fragile, and yes, vegetation grows back when given a chance, but there have never been bigger and more powerful machines—and more of them—than have come to San Juan County recently. Their tires do not tread lightly on the landscape. Increased access does not equate to fewer off-road incidents, but more. Nine riders may be conscientious, law-abiding citizens, but the tenth one opens an unauthorized path that suddenly moves from beaten trail to road to thoroughfare. I watch it happening often out my office window. I do not want to see the landscape locked up into a designated wilderness with more law enforcement officers from the BLM and Forest Service and less personal freedom. However, given what is happening in the heavily trafficked areas of Utah, the region is heading in that direction. Self-policing could delay it somewhat, but eventually enough damage will be done that it becomes a necessity.

Other issues rest for those in the "liberated" environmentalist box. I am always amazed at how they quickly hang the Mormon tag around the necks of local people involved in some kind of environmental infraction. It is not as if the LDS Church encouraged its members to ride ORVs, plunder ruins, or fight for multiple use. Some of the offenders may be Mormons, but to bring up a religious denomination in arguments about environmental policy makes no more sense than to say that the Catholic Church sponsored the Italian Front in World War II. In the same respect, I have concerns about how information, particularly that of Native Americans, in this book will be used in lawsuits for personal agendas to close the lands. Also, there are many local people, Winston Hurst and myself to name two, who are very concerned about what happened in the past as well as the present to Ancestral Puebloan sites and remains. Disturbing any prehistoric site—especially desecrating graves—is wrong and stems from insensitive, personal greed. I believe much of this has greatly slowed because people are realizing that there is a spiritual and sacred responsibility as caretakers of the land that has been ignored in the past. The educational value associated with sites is also more apparent. Most local people understand that archaeology, science, and land management join hands in preserving what everyone loves. Finally, I have seen time after time when local people have opened their arms in friendship to the "outsider." Letters to the editor in local papers often bear this out. Many good people who live in San Juan County are loving, kind, and friendly. It will take building the bridge from both sides to meet in the middle.

In summary, a greater effort is needed to bring opposing views together in harmony. I am not so naïve to think that my sharing of thoughts will close the gap. What I do hope is that as you read the following pages, you will evaluate what is and is not acceptable, then recommit to working with others to insure that all points are considered. It will take everyone to create a brighter, more sustainable future that all can enjoy.

1

Creating the Comb

In Mind and Matter

At the end of the creation, God took all of the left-over rocks and dirt then built the canyons and mesas of San Juan. He must have been tired.
—Karl Barton, local cattleman

What can be written about a rock? In the case of Comb Ridge, it is big and it is there. In reality, Comb Ridge (or Reef) has a fascinating prehistory and history to share. It is part of a dramatic landscape that has both beckoned and stymied some of its most determined visitors. Nestled in the far southeastern corner of Utah and northeastern Arizona, Comb Ridge is one more defining feature in an already visually crowded part of the Colorado Plateau. It is not just the mesas, buttes, spires, and rocks that give this impression. The thin clear air of a high desert climate, laccolithic mountain ranges, thin, sandy soil with its xerophytic plants, and unobstructed vistas—in some cases for over one hundred miles—give a feeling of immensity in space.

Yet, each person who comes here has a different experience, a different understanding, a different view. Nature writer Joseph Wood Krutch, with strong ties to the Sonoran Desert near Tucson, felt dwarfed by the Colorado Plateau landscape. Describing his feeling as "terror," he viewed southeastern Utah as "a country where the inanimate dominates and in which not only man but the very plants themselves seem intruders. We may look at it as we look at the moon, but we feel rejected. It is neither for us nor for our kind."[1] Krutch, however, turned this sense of immensity into a philosophical nugget. His acceptance of canyon country lies in how he glimpsed eternity. Krutch warned that man should not contemplate either this land or the stars too long, but rather take "refuge from them with the small and the familiar." Otherwise, one dwells on the "platitude that man is small and that life is precarious. . . . Such truths are among those which no one should either totally forget or be too constantly aware of."[2]

The story of Comb Ridge proves, in part, Krutch's point: Man is small against this landscape; life is precarious; terror may result from both animate and inanimate forces; and the land has certainly done its share of rejecting. But the philosopher has missed

Courtesy of Lloyd Kartchner

Eons of sand deposition and erosion give the one hundred miles of Comb Ridge distinctive formations that change hues as sunlight and shadows shift.

some points. From the Paleo-Indian searching for game along Comb and neighboring Lime Ridge to the Ancestral Puebloans living in alcoves to the winter camps of Ute tepees or Navajo hogans bathed in reflected warmth to the Mormon settlers and cattle companies grazing livestock on Comb's adjacent pastures, to the awestruck tourists of today, this ridge has been a place of power. Here power resides in religious, cultural, economic, and political senses that inform people's views. How that power has been captured and utilized, shared and disputed, is the story of the rock. Its lesson is not one of cowering individuals dwarfed by the landscape but the struggle and triumph of those who made this their home. Each group that has faced this "stone" has shown that in their own way it was for "us and our kind."

In the beginning, there was Comb Ridge, or at least the elements from which it was derived. To many people that occurred in both a physical and spiritual sense. Science offers one view, lending itself to a physical interpretation of how this massive rock hove into existence. Careful analysis of physical evidence and compilation of data explain the history of the formation and the evolution of animal life that roamed around it. Based on natural and universal processes and properties, science excludes God, gods, or spiritual forces from the mechanistic world.

Much could be said of the complex geologic processes that spanned an incomprehensible period.[3] Geologists explain that 600 million years ago or earlier, the earth entered its first geologic period known as the Precambrian. This era laid the bedrock foundation upon which all other strata rest and saw the first in a series of shallow seas that covered what is now Utah. Faulting, shifting, and drying trends merged as part of a pattern during which eleven seas or fresh water lakes or swamps covered the land then receded from it. Shifting of continental plates; erosion from wind, water, and mechanical forces; deposition of silt and sand; and climate change led to the layering of more than two-dozen different types of sandstone and limestone on the Colorado Plateau. Add to this the bending, folding, faulting, and differential erosion of these layers, and one can see why canyons and rock formations in this region offer such striking variety in color, shape, and texture.

Comb Ridge, a product of these processes, is a monocline rock strata tilted over a considerable distance, in this case from the foot of Elk Ridge in Utah to Kayenta, Arizona, approximately one hundred miles to the south. The ridge is the eastern edge of the Monument Upwarp, which extends as far west as Lake Powell, as far south as Kayenta, and as far north as the Needles District of Canyonlands National Park. Uplift aside, Comb Ridge has been subject to extensive erosion which has cut washes—Comb on the west and Butler on the east—and pealed away layers of sandstone on top of the 800- to 900-foot-high prominence.[4]

The Utah portion of Comb Ridge is particularly fertile in prehistory and history. For this reason, the geographic limits of the area under consideration will range from the base of Blue Mountain in the north to the San Juan River in the south. This north-south boundary encompasses a variety of landscapes and some intensely inhabited, utilized, and documented pieces of ground. The roughly thirty-five-mile long area includes the twenty-eight-mile northern end of the ridge. Below, on the south side of the river, lies the Navajo Reservation, an equally important but less developed region, that assumes an entirely different historical aspect. For this book's purpose, the reader will stay primarily north of the San Juan.

The east-west boundaries for this study are more problematic—less clearly defined by geography and more clearly delineated by culture and history. For instance, the chapter on Navajo beliefs associated with Comb Ridge would be less powerful if I did not consider the surrounding area to the west. At the same time, to ignore Bluff on the east side would be just as improper. Cattle ranges, trading posts, a gold rush, and the road system were all linked to this town's experience and had significant impact on how others saw, used, and avoided Comb Ridge. Thus, on both sides of the reef, enough territory is included for context to develop a fuller view without diluting the significance of this dramatic feature.

What comprises this twenty-eight-mile long piece of rock? Looking west from the crest of Comb Ridge, a geologist will recognize exposures of the Pennsylvanian Hermosa Formation capped by various members of the Permian-age Cutler group of formations,

Deposited by single drops of water in a cave on Comb Ridge, some of these limestone stalagmites have grown to be six feet tall and fourteen inches in diameter. Algae and minerals provide contrasting colors.

including Cedar Mesa Sandstone. Alluvial deposits on the floor of Comb Wash obscure the Triassic-age Moenkopi Formation, cut by the meandering channel of the intermittent Comb Wash stream. A steeply eroded exposure of Upper Triassic-age Chinle clay and shales littered with talus rubble from the sandstones that cap Comb Ridge flank its east-side alluvium. Rising even more steeply above the talus-strewn Chinle clays are cliffs of the Early Jurassic Wingate Formation, dominating the steep western scarp of the Comb Ridge monocline. Early Jurassic Kayenta Formation sandstones and shales overlaid by remnants of the massive Navajo Sandstone deposited during the Early Jurassic period crown the top of the ridge.

Slickrock exposures of Navajo Sandstone dominate the more gently sloping eastern side of the formation. Looking east from Comb Ridge crest, one views a series of ever younger Jurassic and Cretaceous rocks flanking the alluvium-filled valley of Butler Wash. These surface rocks are sedimentary, ranging from shale and clay deposited by the ancient inland seas and tidal flats to massive sand deposits left by ancient desert dunes. The Mule Ear diatreme is a prominent example of a volcanic dike formed by igneous gasses that broke through to reconfigure the sandstone surface. It is located near the mouth of Chinle Wash on the east side of Comb Ridge approximately four miles (straight-line distance) west and south of where Comb Wash enters the San Juan River. Small volcanic plugs and dikes of volcanic rock are visible south of the river, while other igneous rocks are exposed to the northeast in the Pliocene laccolithic complex known to locals as "Blue Mountain" and on government maps as the "Abajo Mountains."

The topography in and around Comb Ridge consists of steeply tilted rocks sandwiched between extensive regions of more horizontally bedded, flat-topped mesa landforms to the west and east. In general, these landforms descend from the Elk Ridge-Abajo highlands in the north to the San Juan River in the south. West of Comb Ridge, flat-topped landforms rise northward in a series of steps from the lower and more xeric limestone benches bordering the San Juan River. The highest landforms in the immediate area are the twin buttes known as Bears Ears, remnants of Chinle shale capped by Wingate Sandstone, which rise from the platform of Elk Ridge Plateau.

These upland mesas are dissected by a complex series of impressive canyons that head at the foot of the Elk Ridge scarp and cut deeply through the Cedar Mesa Sandstone. Several of these canyon systems, that drain southeastward into Comb Wash and are substantial enough for official names, include (from north to south) Arch Canyon, Mule Canyon, Dry Wash, Fish Creek, and Road Canyon. Comb Wash, itself, heads near Whiskers Draw at the eastern foot of Milk Ranch Point on the southwestern edge of Elk Ridge. East of Comb Ridge, flat benches and mesas rise in fewer steps from the broad, Bluff Sandstone of Tank and Bluff Bench to the upland mesas flanking Blue Mountain in the Blanding area and east.

A meteorologist brings a different view to the land. Speaking of the weather in this region, he or she would note how dry it is. Classified under various systems as "midlatitude dry," "dry-to-arid continental," and "dry sub-humid continental," there is no missing that all who live here keep an eye on the weather with its potential for moisture.[5] Precipitation comes in two forms—warm-season convectional thunderstorms that build over high elevation and cool-season storms that derive from Pacific frontal disturbances in the late fall, winter, and early spring. The month of July averages ten degrees warmer in the south near Bluff than on Elk Ridge or Blue Mountain to the north. Drier intervals in late May–June and October generally separate this seasonal pattern. Temperature and precipitation vary with elevation. The farther north one goes toward Blue Mountain and Elk Ridge, the more moisture there is—thirteen inches annually in the north compared to seven inches along the San Juan River.[6]

The growing season for crops is also longer near the river. In the south, farmers receive anywhere from 131 to 254 days per year between hard frosts, with 70 percent of the years having at least 180 consecutive days without freezing. To the north, the frost-free days range from 115 to 240 with an average of 165 per year. Maize horticulture, which averages 120 days to mature, is feasible in both zones and greatly aided by spring snowmelt and spring and summer rains. In both Comb and Butler washes, the western valley slopes offer extensive slickrock sandstone inclines that shed runoff and funnel it into natural catchment drainages, thence into sandy fans at the edge of valley bottoms. This environment offers deep terraces and occasional springs and seeps.

Natural plant communities also respond to varying amounts of moisture. The northern area is higher and a bit more mesic, supporting a vegetation community of piñon-juniper, sagebrush, rabbitbrush, and upland shrubs. Higher up Elk Ridge and the Bears Ears, forests of aspen and ponderosa pine occur. To the south, where elevation drops toward the San Juan River, the plants are more xeric and dominated by blackbrush, shadscale/saltbush, greasewood, and other species associated with a lower, drier climate.

Courtesy of Kay Shumway

Dramatic proof of the necessity of water in a high desert environment is provided by this ponderosa pine. Growing from a crack in a rock, one side of the tree received sufficient water and nutrients while the root system on the other side died, causing the tree to "twist."

Predictable and controllable water for crops affected settlement patterns for land users. Except for the San Juan River, there are no perennial streams in or immediately near the Comb Ridge area. The most dependable source of water other than the San Juan is Arch Canyon Creek, the northernmost of the major tributaries of Comb Wash. With its head deep in the Elk Ridge Plateau near the Bears Ears, Arch Canyon boasts a flow that runs some water through most months of a normal year. It persists throughout many wet years but in dry years is dependable only in the spring when Elk Ridge snow melts, the water running intermittently during the summer and fall. All drainages are subject to prolonged periods of dryness interrupted by occasional floods that can be torrential, impressive, and destructive, but generally short-lived.

Comb Ridge offers other views. Religion, while not disputing the facts of the physical world, has different explanations about how that world derived. Creation and the creative process, in both the scientific and religious sense, are laden with values filtered through the cultural and personal understanding of an individual. In terms of the spiritual creation

Courtesy of Kay Shumway

Every January and February, weather permitting, the "Ice Angel" appears in these crevices found up Arch Canyon three miles from its confluence with Comb Wash.

of Comb Ridge and its surrounding area, a variety of interpretations speak of unseen forces. Moving beyond those of science, which is quantifiable and reproducible, one enters the less measurable and indistinct world of Holy Beings, supernatural and spiritual power, divine intervention, the efficacy of prayer, and humanity's dependence on these forces. Highly qualitative, the results of religion in our lives can be just as powerful and real as the physical forces that govern it. Both define their own reality.

Take, for instance, the Navajo (Diné) view of the creation of Comb Ridge. Traditional Navajo beliefs say the gods created everything spiritually before forming it physically. The Holy Beings, before entering this world, existed in a spiritual form and created spiritual things—prototypes—prior to emplacing the objects in their physical forms. During the creative process, these spiritual forms of humans, animals, and insects shared a variety of experiences as they passed through three (and, in some versions of the creation, four) worlds beneath this one. All of these beings learned lessons and gained powers to assist each one's life in this world. Principles of government, the role of the sexes, cures for sickness, respect for the environment, elements of witchcraft, the power of songs and prayers, as well as crafts and skills, had their origin in these beginnings. But each world ended with the people emerging into the next because of some wrongdoing that destroyed their present world by water and forced them above. Each world, however, was better and more sophisticated than the one left behind. In the third (or fourth) world beneath this one, the glittering world, exact replicas of the mountains and other topographical features created the pattern to be reproduced in the world we live in now.[7]

In the world beneath this, the animals and people were in trouble. Many versions of the story tell how Coyote, the Trickster, stole and hid in his garments Water Monster's baby. The mother longed for its child, so to put pressure on the mysterious thief to return the infant, she caused the waters to rise. Many of the beings below questioned who had the child and how it could be returned to Water Monster. No one came forth. Climbing to the highest mountain beneath this world and then climbing through a reed to the sky, the animals eventually reached the under-layer of the world above. Bear, Mountain Lion, Wolf, and Badger took turns digging through the hard, glossy roof, but it was Locust who finally broke through. Locust also passed a number of trials with various birds living above before being allowed to lead the Holy Beings into the next world. Eventually the people and animals discovered Coyote's deception and forced him to give the Water Monster's child back. The encroaching flood receded.

Initial impressions of this new world were unfavorable. "At this time, there were no ducks, no animals, no creeping nor walking things on the earth, for they were to be brought there from below. Neither were there any trees, grasses, nor plants. These, too, were brought up. In fact, there was only water covering the earth."[8] Narratives of the creation vary in detail, but all talk of a large expanse of water. Washington Matthews recorded the earliest detailed version of these events. In it, the hole entering the Fifth World was on an island in a lake surrounded by high cliffs beyond which lay a large plain.[9] Other stories speak of a vast ocean, which held all kinds of creatures. The Gishin Biyé version of the emergence describes these creatures: "And there were seen the Water Monster, Monster Fishes, Water Horses, the White Nostrils, Children of the Water Monster and White Septums, Children of the Water Horses."[10] To drain the water, make room for terrestrial life, and remove these dangerous beings, various animals and the Holy Ones used supernatural powers.

> The noise and rush of the water above lasted something like four days—after which it ceased. The Spider Man and Spider Woman then inhaled their webs again [which had covered the hole above] and the light shone through the opening. And again they sent the Locust up to investigate. "There is quite a change up there, but it is very muddy," he said. "Here and there you can see lakes and pools of water, and in the distance some objects which are the young of the Water Monsters, Water Horses, and Monster Fishes which they left behind on their way to the ocean. Therefore, today these are in the ocean.[11]

Mud puddled everywhere. Holy Beings summoned the Black, Blue, Yellow, White, and Speckled Big Winds to dry the earth's surface so that the people beneath could emerge and begin their new world experience. The rocks, still soft, held the tracks of the animals as they moved across the land and can still be seen on the hardened surface today as fossils.

Another version of the same events tells of a Holy Being named Blue Body taking four stones from the world beneath and throwing them in the four cardinal directions to break passageways through the cliffs surrounding the body of water. One narrative tells of him "cut[ting] the cliffs with his knife shaped like a horn."[12] In either case, the penetrated cliffs released the waters to the four directions, allowing the Winds to dry the land.

The creation story of the Navajo is as malleable as the mud left behind the draining waters. Those living in a certain locale often interpret these stories geographically because

Courtesy of Kay Shumway

This prehistoric burrow, one in a cluster found on Comb Ridge, was exposed by differential erosion, where the softer sandstone washed away.

the tales are full of wisdom and explain the physical world of the Diné. The teachings become embedded in the land, empowering it, giving religious immediacy to geographical features, and providing concrete evidence to the teachings. The San Juan River/Comb Ridge area exemplifies this practice. Medicine man John Holiday from Monument Valley understands the power of specific ties to landforms.[13] He tells that when the gods created the earth, they gave it different markings.[14] It is said that the ocean was as narrow as a blade of grass. Beneath the land's crust, which is a "thin layer of sand," are the three worlds through which the Navajo people emerged. These are now filled with water, so humans will never run short because of their ability to dig or drill wells.

Twelve Holy Beings were among the first to arrive on the surface, then came the spiritual predecessors of the Navajo. Once the people entered this world, the Holy Beings implemented their spiritual plans by creating a tangible space for the Five Fingered People (humans) to live. First Man, "who always had the sacred arrowheads in his possession for ceremonies," cut deep into the earth toward Alamosa, Colorado, in the east, to create a passageway for the water to drain. Today, this arrowhead rests as a block of volcanic rock outside Pueblo, Colorado. Next, First Woman carved the earth to the south, toward Albuquerque, New Mexico, with a "twisted metal" arrowhead-shaped volcanic rock now found near the Rio Grande. First Boy then tore the earth just outside of Bluff, Utah. The arrowhead, now seen as Designs on the Rock or Decorated Rock (Tsénąąshch'ąąii—Mule

Courtesy of Winston Hurst

Mule Ear or Designs on the Rock rests near the San Juan River (lower left) as it passes through Comb Ridge, where the giant knife slashed the rock. In the foreground lies the Mormon pioneer trail that ascends San Juan Hill.

Ear; another, less well-known name is Béésh Yist'ogii Naazhjaa'—Decorative Metal Arrowhead), is a sharply prominent feature resting near the slit it cut through which the San Juan River passes today. First Girl took a red arrowhead and sliced the ground to the north, placing the point outside of Naturita, Colorado. All four of these cuts drained the water to the cardinal directions while the arrowheads, beacons of protection, surround the Navajo Reservation.

At first, the cuts were small, but they have grown into what they are today. Following the draining, the Holy Beings stretched the earth and the ocean until they reached their present size. The rocks, while made of mud, were stretched out with the rest of the earth but still show signs of the effects of water. The gods created the mountains, on the other hand, from materials brought from beneath this world before placing them on the surface. This is why one does not see watermarks or levels on the sacred mountains and their sides are smooth, unlike the sandstone mesas with their strata. The stretching of the earth pulled the mountains farther apart and, with the help of the Holy Beings, were expanded to their present size.

As the waters drained in the four directions, deep canyons and gorges formed. The water level dropped, leaving mesas and large rocks standing in their places. The plants growing under the water dried and left their impressions as fossils, while the creatures that once lived in the waters were either flushed to the ocean—where they are today in the form of whales, sharks, octopuses, and other sea creatures—or died and left their remains as dinosaur bones. Suzie Yazzie's grandfather, Hastiin Atine, a medicine man, said that in the early twentieth century, some of the animals became buried in the mud, and are minerals today such as uranium and are still dangerous. Suzie, who was seventy-five at the time of the interview, explained:

> These water creatures were huge. Some were like giant lizards and fish. Some were like cockroaches, but they were big. They'd run on top of the water, many of them. There were a variety of different insects and creatures as big as boats that ran on the water. Some creatures looked like donkeys, but they lived underwater. He [Hastiin Atine] also mentioned another animal he called "Bił Hajooltsoii" (Yellow Coming Out), which had a horn. These animals traveled around in the water, floating and swimming around in groups. But once the water drained out, it left pillars of rock standing, like the mesas and spires in Monument Valley.
>
> The creatures made paths as they swam in the water. It was said that they came from the east and went through here [the canyon called Tségiizh—Path between the Rocks—next to Goulding's Trading Post, Monument Valley]. It was their pathway under the water—a trail for them. As the water drained out, these animals fell into the mud and left tracks behind. That's what my grandfather told me. He said no one is to make their home on these trails, but today we see many homes on these sites. This is the trail of the huge reptiles (Tł'iish Tso—Big Lizard or dinosaur). The trail is called Tł'iish Tso Bitiin (Large Lizard Trail). There used to be dinosaur tracks on the rocks close to where the [Seventh Day Adventist] hospital was. These were large footprints, too. . . . These rocks were dynamited—blasted when they were making the road.[15]

Martha Nez, who has lived in sight of Comb Ridge most of her life, tells of a box canyon near her home. Found in the rock is a trail of what she identifies as horse hoofs. "Some have big footprints and some are very small. It seems like they went through there when there was mud. . . . It is these water horses that left their tracks behind."[16] Medicine men have scraped the surface of these tracks for powdered sand to make medicine to put on horses to improve their qualities. Dinosaur tracks, because they came from powerful creatures, are used by healers for protection. Offerings made at the site evoke power. Witchcraft can be turned away from the person being witched and placed back on the bewitcher by using ceremonial procedures and the creature who made the tracks. As with many types of power, unless an individual knows the specific way to control it, they should avoid the object.[17]

Dinosaur tracks or remains are found in a number of places near Comb Ridge—Upper Butler Wash, Eagle's Nest Canyon, Casa del Echo Mesa, near Saint Christopher's Mission in Bluff, the Nancy Patterson site in Montezuma Canyon, and Monument Valley. Interestingly, many dinosaur bones and fossilized remains are found on the east side of Comb Ridge, from whence the water was drained, in the Morrison Formation. On the west side, few bones but a lot of petrified wood and sea fossils are present. The Jurassic and Cretaceous layers with dinosaur bones have eroded away until one reaches the high plateau country beyond Lake Powell.[18]

Courtesy of Kay Shumway

This three-toed dinosaur print is one of a number found in Butler Wash near Highway 95. Fossils hold power that can be used by Navajo medicine men, who understand how to control it.

Other stories exist about the creation of Comb Ridge. Ada Benally, a resident of Bluff who has lived all of her life in the shadow of Comb, tells that once the waters drained and the Winds were drying the mud, a large bird, "Táshchozhii" (Swallow), flew about tearing the earth in several directions.[19] This created ridges near Shiprock, Kayenta, Bluff, and elsewhere. The soft ground, fanned by the bird's feathers, held the impressions of the wings as the ground pushed skyward. The crenellated top of Comb Ridge remains as proof of the powerful bird's flight. The water continued to drain down the San Juan, the earth solidified, and vegetation began to grow. Today, smaller relatives of this bird are seen flying about the water, while the Diné have settled around San Juan and other rivers.

Many Navajo elders refer to Comb Ridge as the backbone of the earth.[20] John Holiday teaches that in each of the four worlds that the Navajos have inhabited, there has been a backbone. As a living, sentient being, the earth has a backbone as part of its makeup, just as everything in the Navajo world has a male and female counterpart. When the Holy Beings stretched the world, so too, was Comb Ridge.

Comb Ridge, as backbone of the earth, is said by some Navajo people to stretch far beneath the surface once it disappears from view. Others specify its head and foot.

> The bones protruding out of the earth were stretched southward. Then the ridge that extends into the San Juan River near Farmington, New Mexico [The Hogback], goes to the north. That is the female. It is said that the two ridges lay side by side, male and female. That is what our forefathers used to teach about long ago. It is from this special area that our people exist today. The male and female combination, the birthing of the five fingered [humans] derived from this. It is said that long ago, when the mountains were being set in place, one of them [Blue Mountain] was set on the feet of Comb Ridge that extends to the north, just as the one that extends to the south looks as if the head is tucked under Black Mesa [near Kayenta]. They are holy and sacred, with songs and prayers attached to them.[21]

Coyote, the Trickster, is said to have been the one to have given the formation its name of Tséí K'áán or "Rocks Standing Up" instead of "Backbone of the Earth" (Tségháán) by which it should be known.

Comb Ridge plays yet another role during the creation of the earth, this time with the sun and moon. The Holy Beings originally planned that these heavenly bodies would follow the course of Comb Ridge that lies generally north–south. As they tried to obtain their celestial orbit by following this path, the sun, then the moon, returned to the earth to rest on the east side of Comb Ridge. The large circular alcoves interspersed between Blue Mountain and Kayenta are these resting places, alternating one for the sun, one for the moon. But the plan just did not work. The Holy Beings next tried to have the sun and moon travel in an east–west direction, but found the journey too long, with the heavenly bodies remaining at a standstill midway in their course. Coyote solved the problem by offering to be in all four directions to keep the earth and heavenly bodies in motion. The gods agreed and that is how it is today.[22] A precedent for this local teaching is found in the Blessingway story in which the sun and moon are directed by the Holy Beings on a journey to their place in the sky. Before reaching this place, they rested on the landscape.[23] Other Navajo beliefs about Comb Ridge will be discussed in chapter 3.

What of the creation stories of the Ute and Paiute who live in this area? Unfortunately, many of their traditional teachings have been lost. There is little available about the formation of the earth, and that which does exist is general. Edward Dutchie, Sr., a Ute elder born around 1913, tells a story from his grandfather of how all of the large canyons, including Comb and Butler washes, began. Hawk had a nest high in the cliffs and was a very successful hunter. At the time of creation, he had contests with the Creator but always came in second. He became angry and retreated to his home to sleep and recuperate. A beautiful woman fell in love with Hawk despite his shortcomings. She fashioned a ladder and climbed into his nest, startling him. The sleeping Hawk awoke with a scream so loud it shook and cracked the earth, forming the major canyons in the Four Corners region.[24]

Another account, heavily entwined with Christianity, tells of the wanderings of the Ute and Paiute people in an area centered on a "Spiritual Cross." The crux of this cross is formed at the junction of the San Juan River with Comb Ridge (called by the Utes Mother Earth's Backbone—Tűwűpű Őav). "This giant cross represents the center of both the temporal and spiritual migrations of the People . . . and was made by Jesus Christ as a guidepost for the Utes to return to their Motherland or 'Avikan,' meaning 'The Homeland Where the People Rest.'"[25] No other mythological teachings have been recorded about Comb Ridge's creation or significance.[26]

This should not be interpreted as a lack of Ute or Paiute interest in this feature. In the Numic language, it is called "Slick Rock Mound" and was a favorite camping place in the winter. The San Juan cuts through Comb Ridge at a place called "Coming Together" (Naváču Nikyet), a place "where all nations will come together, much like what is happening today."[27] The lower altitude, access to the San Juan River and various springs, and the reflection of the sun's heat off the rocks, provided ideal cold-weather campsites.[28] In other seasons, Comb Wash was a favorite place to gather Indian ricegrass and herbal tea (west side), and Butler Wash (east side), a favorite source of willows and sumac for basket making. Lola Mike, an eighty-year-old basket weaver, claimed that the design of the traditional Navajo Wedding Basket (manufactured by both Navajos and Utes) was inspired

Courtesy of Winston Hurst

While evidence of Spanish or Mexican presence in southeastern Utah is will-o'-the wisp, this recently discovered Navajo or Ute petroglyph in Comb Wash suggests an Hispanic lancer mounted on either a horse or mule. The Bears Ears appears on early Spanish maps as for Orejas (the Ears), which Comb and Chinle washes provided a feasible pathway for travelers.

by the broken skyline of Comb Ridge, which she believes gave rise to the design as the birthplace of the basket.[29]

Some elders mention the presence of Little Dark People (Turúúkčičin), who are small but powerful supernatural beings having the ability to change into different forms. One leaves offerings of cloth or food to obtain their assistance. These beings are found wherever there is a site that holds power and not surprisingly, "they live along Comb Ridge in the side of the hills, and early in the morning you can see their smoke fires, but no one sees them because they have medicine."[30] Lola Mike suggested there could be a connection between these little beings and the Ancestral Puebloans as perhaps their children.

Courtesy of Kay Shumway

By 1880, Comb Ridge had received its name, some suggesting that its serrated edge looked like a rooster comb or an object to tame hair. A Navajo creation story says the flapping of a bird's wing in mud formed it.

Placing names upon the land is another creative way of viewing the world. Keith Basso, in *Wisdom Sits in Places*, gives an excellent example of how the White Mountain Apache, close relatives to the Navajo, use names on the landscape to instruct and promote values.[31] At other times, names may appear because of a historic incident or a landform's resemblance to something. The area around Comb Ridge offers many interesting possibilities. Four advance scouts of the Mormon Hole-in-the-Rock group first applied the name in 1880, when they saw the massive barrier stretched in front of the approaching wagon train. The rock resembled a huge reef or comb and was known by that time as Comb Ridge.[32] That same year, the settlers gave Bluff its title because of the high sandstone cliffs surrounding the nascent community. Butler Wash received its name from John Butler, who, a year earlier as part of an advanced scouting party, was the first individual recorded to explore it.[33] Butler and Comb washes feed into the San Juan (Saint John) River, named sometime after 1776 when two Spanish padres, Fray Atanasio Dominguez and Fray Silvestre Vélez de Escalante crossed what they called Navajo River further upstream in Colorado.

Courtesy of Kay Shumway

As the Holy Beings placed the sun and moon in a north–south orbit, the heavenly bodies needed to rest and so returned to earth. Along the length of Comb Ridge are found these resting sites, created when the earth was soft.

There are other place names on the map that seem mundane yet mask interesting nuggets of history. In 1892, the Illustrated American Exploring Expedition, comprised of amateur archaeologists bent on revealing the mysteries of the Ancestral Puebloans, floated the San Juan River ending up in Bluff. From there, they traveled up Butler Wash along Comb Ridge, visiting its alcoves and carving their identity into the sandstone. They also named some of the sites they left behind, such as Giant's Cave for what is now known as Fishmouth Cave, Cold Spring Cave, Monarchs Cave, and Eagle's Nest Cave. Long Fingers Canyon is named for an Ancestral Puebloan petroglyph carved into the rock.

During the 1880s, Mormon settlers gave the names First Valley and Milk Ranch to the forks of a drainage where they established a dairy operation to supply milk, butter, and cheese to Bluff. The heads of those forks are on a prominent point of Elk Ridge, which came to be known as Milk Ranch Point. Stevens Canyon, most likely named for Joshua Stevens, offered grass for cows producing milk for the industry. First Valley's name was changed to Whisker's Draw when a cantankerous Ute named Whiskers arrived in Willard Butt's camp and demanded a meal at gunpoint. The Milk Ranch tributary came to be known as Whisker's Draw or North Fork. There is also The Highland Lady, a name recorded by archaeologist T. Mitchell Prudden, for a prominent landmark on Comb Ridge, when he passed along the Salt Road in Butler Wash. This rock is located near the top of the Posey Trail and was most likely named by John Allan, a Scotsman with a thick brogue who missed the old country. He traveled this trail numerous times on the way to the Milk Ranch. The livestock industry added two other names—(James B.) Decker Cove to the east of Butler Wash and the (Amasa and Joseph) Barton Range to the west of Comb Ridge. These early settlers, with other stockmen in Bluff, grazed their herds on this pasturage.

As mentioned previously, many of the teachings and names of the historic Utes have been lost. Those that remain are more descriptive and have few recorded stories or teachings associated with them. Stella Eyetoo, a Ute elder from White Mesa, when asked to name specific sites replied, "I don't know what they call it, because mostly they would name a place by the plant that grew near the spot. For instance, that area is known for its different herbal plants of yucca or green tea or rabbitbrush. These plants thrive when there is good moisture."[34] Comb Wash is to the Utes "Slick Rock Wash" (Pihkééviyaagat), Butler Wash "Yellow Knoll," Arch Canyon "Rock Canyon" (Tüpwi Wiyagat), Posey's Trail "Horse Trail" (Gava Pöö), The Highland Lady "White Rocks" (Sagar Tüpwič), the camp area where Highway 95 enters Comb Wash "Tall Cottonwood" (S̱ügav), while the Bears Ears is a direct translation (Kwiyagat Nügavat).[35] This last site is said to be the first place that bears come out of hibernation in the spring and is where the Ute people held their first Bear Dance. Other landmarks in the area include Blue Mountain "Water Mountain" (Paa Gauv) or "Soaks up Water" (Paa Čáágarür), the San Juan River "Big River (Paa Saagat) or "River Flowing from the Sunrise" (Paa Tükwi Tavači Mowisi Mamanuq), Elk Ridge "Big Bridge of Land" (Avaughta Paa Saagat), and Bluff, before the white man settled there, was "Down by the River" (Pah saw gut).[36]

While the memory of Ute place names is dwindling, Navajo elders have retained much of what existed in their culture. The oral tradition and ceremonies serve as a repository that links the landscape to a rich history of places and events. Just how rich is illustrated by John Holiday, who lived and herded livestock along both sides of Comb Ridge during the early twentieth century when many of the older stories were still being told. Unless otherwise noted, John provided the following information on place-names during a daylong drive to these sites.[37]

Like the Utes, Navajos name some places descriptively, just as a street sign indicates where a traveler might be. Oak Bush Canyon (Cháchil Bił Nástł'áhí), near the head of Comb Ridge; Yellow Rock Ridge Coming Out (Tsé Łitsoi Haat'i'ii), a home site with a number of hogans; Short Stubby Mountain (Dził K'ik'ęę'ii); Rock Point (Tsé Deez'á) a prominent point on Tank Mesa; Between the Rocks (Tsé Giizh), a small canyon between Monarch Cave and Long Fingers Canyon; Red Rock Sloping Down (Tsé Yaaniichii'), a long, low ledge of sandstone; Long Gray Hill/Ridge (Łibáí Yilk'idí—Black Mesa); and Setting White Rocks (Łigai Sinilii), a series of white rock knobs west on Comb Wash road, are all examples of this type of identification.

John pointed out five sun-and-moon sites on the east side of the ridge and mentioned there were a half-dozen more clustered around Kayenta, with others dispersed along the entire length. A rounded crescent-shaped alcove north of Highway 163 is named "Setting

Comb Ridge offers numerous cisterns that fill with water, in this case, six feet deep. Prehistoric and historic Native Americans built dwellings, trails, and garden plots near some of the larger potholes.

Moon" (Tł'éhonaa'áí Si'áanii) because it is round, just like the full moon. Farther up Butler Wash, the huge alcove, popularly known as Fishmouth or Giants Cave, is identified as one of the resting places for the Sun. Canyons and rock formations serve as other landmarks. "Under the Rock" (Tsé Yaa') provided shade for sheep during the warm summer months, "Sumac Gathering Place" (K'įį' 'Ál'íinii) is a popular place for basketry materials with both Utes and Navajos, and Little Black Mesa (Bii iłushii—no translation) was a favored place for hunting cottontail rabbits. "Small Amount of Water Coming Out" (Tó 'Ałch'įdí) is a little canyon with a spring on the eastern slope; it could not rival the flow at "Sweet Water Coming Out" (Tó Łikan Háálíinii) on the west side of Comb Ridge, next to the old road called "Trail Coming Down" (Adah 'Adeetiin) that went to Bluff. The spring and an associated hogan owned by the local Navajo leader, Jim Joe, was a favorite stopping point for weary travelers. Today both have been covered with blocks of talus blown from the side of the ridge during the construction of the Highway 163 dugway.

Some Navajo place names require visual acuity and imagination. John indicated that when looking at Pointed White Rock (Tsé Łigai Deez'á), "If you look very hard, you can see a person riding a donkey. It is dark shaded and then close to that, you can see three people walking" on the rock cliffs up in the canyon. In another small canyon called Bobcat's Trail Coming Down (Náshdóí 'Adabitiinii), one finds lots of bobcat tracks traversing the path. John shot a bobcat there and sold the skin to a government trapper. Somewhere between Monarch Cave and Long Fingers Canyon rests White Horse Lying Down (Łį́į́łigai Sitíinii), a white rock that is a prominent landmark for Navajo travelers. "People used to say, 'The sun went down just when I reached the lying white horse' as they returned from visiting the stores in Blanding. . . . People used to say that in the early morning, the white horse seemed to be standing because of the mirage, then it would lie down as the sun moved upward." On the other hand, Navajos reduced the visual imagery of the dramatic Highland Lady of John Allan's fantasy to The Rock that Peaks Higher than the Rest (Tsé 'Aghá Haa'áí) or The Big Bump Rock (Tsé Tso Dahyisk'idii).

Long Fingers Canyon, in addition to having a water hole used by the Navajo, held plants important for healing. Known as "Where the Cottonwood is Green," this canyon has a rock formation in its opening that is shaped like a woman's vulva. Navajo medicinal teachings often associate similar-looking objects or places with the sickness or the cure.[38] Like begets like. The narrow declivity of the canyon appears as the female reproductive part of the body, and so medicine men and women come to this spot to gather herbs associated with healing women who have any type of internal uterine ailments including cancer. John remembers, "My maternal grandmother Asdzáán Bikinii (Woman Who Owns the House) came here to gather such herbs. This time it was to treat a man by the name of Aching Stomach (Tsą́ Dinihii), who had a 'near rotten' ailment, having contracted venereal disease. [She gave him] probably the worst herbal mix I have ever seen, because it is combined with the big lizard's intestines." He did not remember the specific names of the plants his grandmother gathered, but "there were several and you can find them only around that area."

Names also became affixed to the land because of historic events. The valley through which Highway 95 wends its way before passing through Comb Ridge to the wash below is called "I Want Sheep Fell Down." Like many Navajo names on the land, if the story is unknown, unraveling the meaning is anyone's guess. In this case, Harry Goulding, who opened a trading post in Monument Valley in 1925, sent employees out to buy sheep from the Navajo. One of his men became known as "I Want Sheep."[39] According to John, this person "used to go from home to home with three pack mules and a donkey, hauling groceries to the people. He delivered food to the Navajos, saying, 'I want sheep and I'll trade food for them.' The man's name became 'I Want Sheep' (Dibé Nisin). The people would say, 'Here comes I Want Sheep again.'"[40] He also worked on a road project that went from Navajo Mountain to Navajo National Monument and then continued into this area. He apparently fell into a wash in this valley, which the ever-observant Navajos immediately dubbed upon the land.

Cedar Mesa to the northwest is known as Hanging Meat Mesa ('Atsį' Dahididlo'ii). This landmark obtained its name from a hunter who tied his deer meat in a tree to cool and dry before cutting it into smaller pieces. His hunting party killed all the game they wanted and departed, leaving his deer meat suspended. The man never went back to retrieve it. In that same area, in the eastern corner of Valley of the Gods, lies "Cornering Rock Ridge" ('Adah Tsé Naa'ígi). Here, because of the steep canyon walls on both sides of this formation, hunters chased, cornered, then shot the deer they pursued.

In another part of Valley of the Gods, the Holy Beings left a saddle, which is now a rock formation (Tsé Łį́į' 'Ayélii). One Holy Being turned to stone and sits nearby. This and other formations are said to be Navajo warriors frozen in place, who can be appealed to for protection. They are guardians whose power and strength aid young men going to war. By placing ntł'iz, a male offering of precious stones and shell, at one of these pinnacles, the spirit becomes a protective guardian, providing supernatural help to the one whose name is spoken.[41] The Navajo Twins, a rock formation in Bluff, serves a similar function. The Man Raised Underground, also known as Monster Slayer, left behind these two prayersticks (k'éét'áán). One is called "The One You Pick Up" (Dah Nídilyéí) and the other "Naalyéí" ("To Handle"), and they are used by medicine men in ceremonies and considered very sacred. Around the corner of this rock formation to the north is a cove with an echo. Prayers petitioning Monster Slayer to protect servicemen going to war are amplified in their transmission by this echo.[42]

The entire length of Comb Wash is called Mountain Sheep's Testicles (Naaghású Bicho'). Sometime before the Navajos went to Fort Sumner during the Long Walk Period (1860s), a hunting party camped at the mouth of Arch Canyon where the water passes through a grove of cottonwood trees. Two hunters, Dinilchíí (One Who Is Reddish) and Ta'neeszahnii (Tangled People [clan]) bickered over the testicles of two mountain sheep killed nearby. A wrestling match broke out over who should keep the prize, each hunter demanding that the "mountain sheep organs are mine." The other men separated the scrappers and cautioned them to settle down. Someone tossed the testicles in the fire, causing them to explode because of the moisture within. When the dispute ended, the hunters packed their meat and belongings and went home. Some Navajos claim that a white rock formation near the campsite also looks like a sheep's organ. The wash, a trail, and one of the canyons that meet at that site share this name.[43]

Another trail that feeds into Comb Wash is "The Place Where the One Who Spreads Anger Hauled up the Meat" (Hashkéneiniihii Ha'ashjidii). It received this name when Hashkéneinii (The One Who Spreads Anger), from the Monument Valley-Navajo Mountain area, killed three deer in what is now called Arch Canyon. The steep cliff walls proved no barrier to him. He cleaned his kill, placed one over his shoulder and climbed out of the canyon, then repeated this feat two more times. "He was a very strong man," John assured me. Additional Navajo names of features in the Comb Ridge area will be discussed later.

A final means of viewing the land is as a storehouse of nature's goods—its flora and fauna. Native Americans used the land intensely, harvesting the plants, animals, and minerals for various purposes. What follows is not an exhaustive list but an overview of some of the material wealth the area around Comb Ridge provided. While there are obvious

Comb Wash was a favorite place for collecting Indian ricegrass, where it grew in abundance. Processed by either burning off or winnowing the chaff, the seeds were ground and added to stews or mush.

differences between the Ancestral Puebloan culture (even within its own various stages of development during the Basketmaker and Puebloan periods) and the Ute/Paiute and Navajo cultures, certainly all three used much of the wild flora and fauna in similar ways. Each group also may have emphasized certain plants and animals to a greater or lesser extent, depending upon availability and cultural beliefs. For instance, bones of rodents such as mice and kangaroo rats are found in Ancestral Puebloan sites showing distinct evidence of having been eaten. Navajo beliefs associate these rodents with burial of the dead and so are avoided as part of the diet. The Ancestral Puebloan and Navajos generally did not eat fish while the Utes did. These examples of acceptance and rejection were culturally, not physically, determined.

Chapter 2 will discuss the evolutionary stages of Ancestral Puebloan existence in the Southwest in general and the Comb Ridge area specifically. Their use of the high desert environment depended on what was either naturally available or could be introduced through trade and domestication. The Basketmaker culture introduced corn, squash, and gourds into the San Juan region about 1000 BC. These cultigens, originally domesticated in Mesoamerica, supplemented indigenous plants and moved the precursor of the Ancestral Puebloans from strictly hunting and gathering to a more sedentary lifestyle. Early Basketmaker culture is characterized by "successful farming with a robust foraging effort. . . . Perhaps the most salient aspect of wild plant use in the San Juan Basin was its consistency from one era to the next."[44] A brief examination of the archaeological record illustrates how intensely these people used everything in their natural habitat.

Indian ricegrass rested at the top of the shopping list. This plant prefers dry, sandy soil, intense summer heat, and intermittent moisture. Found in the vast piñon and juniper zone throughout San Juan County, Indian ricegrass (*Oryzopsis hymenoides*) was easy to collect and to separate the seed from its chaff. By beating the seeds with a stick into a basket then cracking the outer husk with a mano, the kernel was freed from the refuse, which was blown away by winnowing. Since the plant could be harvested by mid-June, before most wild plants bore fruit and corn had not matured, it was a welcome addition to the diet. Plant specialists have studied Ancestral Puebloan dietary habits and conclude, "Indian ricegrass was probably the most valuable wild cereal harvested in our study area during prehistoric times."[45] The historic Navajos and Utes recognized Comb Wash as being particularly fertile for obtaining ricegrass.

The Ancestral Puebloans depended on four other plants that appeared in the disturbed soil of their gardens where they were encouraged to put down roots. Goosefoot or lambsquarter (*Chenopodium spp.)* offered as high a caloric content as ricegrass, thrived with summer rain, and grew in disturbed areas where man had built camps, created gardens, or consistently traveled. Three of its neighbors blossomed in similar conditions. Amaranth or pigweed (*Amaranthus spp.*) was eaten as a type of spinach. Its leaves and stem are rich in amino acids and vitamin A. Rocky Mountain beeplant (*Cleome serrulata*), also called wild spinach, needed to be boiled in fresh water several times to remove the acid before being consumed. The plant could either be devoured fresh or formed into cakes and stored. Ancestral Puebloan pottery is decorated with a black paste made from the distilled residue and then fired, causing the plant to oxidize and color the design on a pot black. Purslane (*Portulaca spp.*) rendered seeds that went into mush or bread; its stems offered high concentrations of vitamins A and C. These foods—ricegrass, goosefoot, amaranth, and purslane—characterized as the "Big Four" of wild plant greens—grew along Comb and Butler washes and near Ancestral Puebloan sites.[46]

Both moisture from the sky and warm temperatures could decrease, leading to crop failure and starvation. Some wild plants offered a lifeline to survival. Prickly pear cactus (*Opuntia phaeacantha*) was one of the "starvation foods" that thrived during extremely dry periods and whose sweet fruit could be picked and eaten well into the winter. The seed pod or banana of the yucca (*Yucca baccata*) contains high-energy nutrition while the plant itself can be used to fashion baskets, cordage, paintbrushes, and sandals. Its roots, when crushed and swished in water, provide a powerful soap and shampoo. Indians ate chokecherries (*Prunus virginiana*) fresh, dried them to concentrate their sugar before adding them to soups and mush, or ate them plain. Juniper berries (*Juniperus scopulorum*) were

Two Navajo women are collecting sumac to make wedding baskets. Some Ute basketmakers suggest that Comb Ridge inspired the crenellated design on the outer part of the basket.

another persistent crop that grew regardless of weather. Harvesters picked the young berries and ate them fresh, put them in stews, brewed them to make a diuretic tea, or cached them for later use.[47] Archaeological evidence in San Juan County suggests that when corn and squash yields decreased, these plants as well as dropseed, ricegrass, and currants increased in the Puebloan diet.[48] All of them, like corn, were capable of being cached in dry rock shelters and overhangs.

Trees, in addition to the juniper, bore useful nuts and seeds. The most important one for food was the piñon (*Pinus edulis*). When ripe, Indians knocked the nuts out of the cones with a stick, then ate them raw or baked, added them to mush, stew, and bread, or stored them. "When there was a good yield of piñon nuts, only about once every six years, food value from the harvest of this plant would probably have exceeded that from all other wild species combined."[49] Acorns from the Gambel oak (*Quercus gambelii*) had to be leached several times to remove the tannic acid before being ground and added to cakes and mush; they contain lysine, an amino acid that assists in breaking down corn and releasing nutrients that would otherwise simply pass through the digestive tract. Acorns played an important nutritional role before the introduction of beans, which also have lysine.[50] All of these plants are found around Comb Ridge and its environs.

Wood played a vital part in Ancestral Puebloan home life. Wattle and daub construction, vigas or roof beams, and tools all derived from wood. Large timbers that spanned the great kivas along Comb Wash and in Bluff required tall pines such as ponderosa (*Pinus ponderosa*), found on nearby Elk Ridge or Blue Mountain. Firewood was essential for cooking and heating homes in winter. The removal of trees, especially those of the piñon-juniper forest, fostered erosion and created a need to either range farther for more or burn less desirable types of fuel. As wood depleted, inferior substitutes like greasewood (*Sarcobatus vermiculatus*), saltbush (*Atriplex spp.),* and cornstalks, cobs, and husks warmed their shelters.[51]

The Ancestral Puebloans obtained animals for food, clothing, and other products in four different ways—local hunting and trapping, long-distance hunts, trading, and domestication. Deer, bighorn sheep, and elk comprised some of the largest game, while rabbits, mice, gophers, prairie dogs, porcupines, and beavers were some of the smaller species taken. Ducks, geese, hawks, eagles, jays, and cranes added variety to a diet dominated by corn, beans, and squash. Another benefit to planting fields was their ability to attract animals. Once animals neared a garden, hunting and trapping them became easier. As deer, bighorn sheep, and other wild game became increasingly scarce during the Pueblo I period (AD 750–900), smaller animals and rodents increased in importance. The Puebloans raised turkeys, originally domesticated in Mesoamerica, around their dwellings as early as the Basketmaker III period (AD 450–750).[52] Their feathers provided warm blankets and robes; turkeys did not become a staple in the diet until the Pueblo III period (AD 1150–1300). By 1300, the Ancestral Puebloans departed the San Juan Basin and assumed residence at the eastern pueblos along the Rio Grande and at the western pueblos of Acoma, Zuni, and Hopi where they remain today.

Possibly two hundred years (AD 1100) before the abandonment of San Juan by the Puebloans, Ute and Paiute people migrated from the west, employing a primarily hunting and gathering lifestyle, supplemented occasionally by small patches of corn.[53] Their food-collecting activities followed much the same pattern as the deer, moving to higher elevations such as Elk Ridge and Blue Mountain in the summer and lower elevations within the canyons, desert floors, and along the San Juan River where cold is less intense and winters generally milder. The east side of Comb Ridge, along the fans of dirt that splay out onto the flats of Butler Wash, contained desirable camping spots because of the reflected sunlight and heat off the rocks. The deer, a primary source of food, clothing, and shelter, also sought a warmer clime, less snowfall, and browse. The men trapped them, formed drives into canyons or enclosures, shot them from blinds, or chased them on horseback. They used everything in some way except for the eyes, which were removed following the kill—the hide for clothing or shelter, the meat and entrails for food, bones and antlers for implements, and the hoofs for glue. The women dried, pounded, and mixed the meat with grease then packed it in parfleches or rawhide bags for trips or stored it in alcoves such as those found along Comb Ridge.[54]

In addition to the plants and animals harvested by the Ancestral Puebloans, the Utes and Paiutes used other resources. They peeled off the outer bark of young cottonwood and pine trees, scraping the sap into a container to use as a sweetener. Cottonwood sap did not have as noticeable a taste as pine, was sweeter, and preferred. Weavers fashioned willows, sumac (also called squaw bush) into "Navajo" wedding baskets and other containers. Women and children also harvested currants, gooseberries, chokecherries, and rose hips, which they ate fresh or dried, then stored them for the "starving time" around February, when preserved food supplies diminished and game and plants were scarce.[55] Unlike the Navajos, Utes ate fish, snakes, bird eggs, mice, rats, and grasshoppers, the latter having their legs plucked off, then heated in a campfire and turned into a paste, said to be very rich.[56]

Navajos also have an extensive understanding of the environment and its uses. Much plant use is derived from ceremonial knowledge for medicinal practice.[57] Physical ailments, whose origin took place during the period of creation, have an equally powerful cure obtained from herbs provided by the Holy Beings. As illustrated in the appearance and use of Long Fingers Canyon in curing venereal disease, certain plants in specific places have curative powers. John Holiday mentioned that Elk Ridge, named Mountain Sheep Mountain by the Navajos, was also a place to obtain dirt from where a mountain sheep fell or landed from a cliff to protect someone from injury sustained by falling or in wrestling contests. Along Comb Wash and the eastern side of Lime Ridge are deposits of minerals that taste sweet, which can be put in stews with grass seeds as food extenders. Various clays are fashioned into pottery or used as body paint. Sand from Comb Ridge, because of its association with lightning, is used by medicine men to heal sickness brought about by electrical storms; they also use different colored sands for sandpaintings.[58] Thus, resources from Comb Ridge play vital physical and spiritual roles in both Navajo and Ute well-being.

From the creation of Comb Ridge has come a geographic phenomenon that provides a geological account of millions of years of activity. The rock formation offers resources used by the earliest inhabitants to the present day. Wood, soil, stone, and water form the basis for man's interaction with the land in a continuing quest for survival. But man does not live by bread alone. Comb Ridge is as much a spiritual entity, whose existence hearkens back to the creation of the world. Viewed as a product of the Holy Beings and other supernatural forces, the lands surrounding this monolith are imbued with power. They stand as concrete evidence of the beliefs and teachings of Navajo and Ute people. More than just historic sites and place names on a map, this formation is a focal point for those who wish to connect the natural and supernatural worlds through a landscape created long ago.

2

Discovering the Comb

Early Inhabitants—From Hunting to Farming

I, Utset [Holy Being], will soon leave you; I will return to the home whence I came. You will be to my people as myself; you will pass with them over the straight road. I will remain in my house below and will hear all that you say to me."

—Zia Teaching[1]

The world—whether created by Holy Beings or geologic and climatic forces—evolved from a gigantic slime ball to today's landscape. Humans stood in the wings, preparing for millennia to stride upon different parts of the stage. The earliest evidence of humans are not found on the American continent, but prehistoric Native Americans certainly are. Their story, based on material remains, provides a fascinating glimpse of what life was like in the Comb Ridge area, beginning around 12000 BC. Fragments of stone, bone, skin, and wood, when pieced together by archaeologists, weave a sometimes vague, sometimes sharp image of life for these people. A constant unfolding and revising of their story comes from newly discovered facts and informed conjecture, illuminating knowledge of early Indian life in southeastern Utah. What follows draws on recent thinking about who these people were, how they lived, and what they felt was important as they existed in the lands surrounding Comb Ridge.[2]

Earliest evidence of inhabitants, the Paleo-Indian (12000–6000 BC), emanates from the final ice age of the Pleistocene epoch. Traveling as hunters and gatherers in groups of fewer than forty people, they targeted now-extinct animals such as mammoths, camelids, horses, tapirs, and species of bison that roamed the cool, verdant lands. Forests of spruce and limber pine, and grassy savannahs covered the land where today only sagebrush and cedar grow. The San Juan River and its drainages created a swampy morass rich in vegetation, likely a favored feeding place for large game. Not only has Butler Wash yielded a mammoth femur, found by rancher Clyde Barton in the 1950s, but packrat middens from Fishmouth Cave provided environmental information that

Ice age hunters, looking at the confluence of Comb Wash with the San Juan River, would have seen a more densely vegetated landscape with mammoths and other extinct creatures roaming below. Close to three hundred Clovis artifacts were found in this site.

goes back to over 12,000 years ago.[3] Plant communities that dominated the area then are now found several thousand feet higher in the mountains or hundreds of miles further north.

Paleo-Indian cultures made effective tools to work this environment, most prominent being the weapons to kill large game. The earliest spearhead associated with these people is the finely crafted, lance-like, fluted Clovis point. The flintknapper chipped the cutting edges then hafted the point with sinew and pitch into a wood or bone foreshaft. The hunter either launched the three- to four-foot dart with an atlatl or thrust it as a spear. The projectile proved highly efficient in killing large game, as was borne out in experiments on contemporary African elephants. Only nine isolated Clovis points have been documented in San Juan County (several more have been reported by collectors), all of which were surface finds. One of these was at the Goodwin Site located at a trail crossover on the crest of Comb Ridge. The Clovis point base found at this traffic point suggests the trail could have been used since the late Pleistocene.

Isolated Clovis points identify a presence, but atop Lime Ridge, a Clovis site yields a greater perspective. Archaeologists in 1985 identified a Clovis hunting stand on a ridge that overlooks the confluence of Comb Wash with the San Juan River. These drainages, filled with water and lush vegetation, were prime territory for animals feeding on plants and hunters feeding on animals. Ideally situated to observe the river bottom, this campsite held six Clovis point fragments among 294 stone artifacts that included knives, scrapers, and wedges. This is the only analyzed Clovis tool assemblage in southeastern Utah.[4]

As the climate shifted, creating a drier, warmer, more desert-like environment similar to that of today, the Paleo-Indian changed and adapted. Many species of large mammals became extinct, and the Clovis and Folsom cultures gave way to successive cultures marked by evolving tool kits and projectile point styles. Identified archaeologically by their tool types, this shift started with the displacement of the Clovis culture by the Folsom (9000–8000 BC), then by a series of cultures known collectively as Plano (8000–6000 BC). Archaeologists identified bits of Folsom points in the Blanding area and lower Recapture Wash and a distinctively spurred Folsom implement for scraping on a rocky bench between lower Butler Wash and Comb Ridge. Plano points are extremely rare in southeastern Utah, but a few fragments have been found. By about 6000 BC, a population of foragers collectively known as "Archaic" evolved from the Paleo-Indian cultures.[5]

The Archaic people appear to have been all business, preoccupied with survival, capturing and consuming everything edible from lizards to prickly pears to mice to grasses to bighorn sheep. Their increasingly broad emphasis on wild plants and small game gave rise to a modified and diversified tool kit. Milling implements (simple basin metates and one-hand cobble manos) became an important addition and could grind everything from rodents to grasshoppers to grass seed. Where the preceding Paleo-Indian points emphasized style and sophistication, the distinctive Archaic points are often utilitarian and relatively crude but still effective. The last of the true hunters and gatherers before corn and squash arrived, these people sometimes used rock shelters for seasonal residences, built cists to store seeds and other plant materials, and wove sandals and baskets from yucca fiber. The Archaic era lasted for over 5,000 years, the longest of any of the various periods of prehistory.

Archaic materials are scattered widely over the Comb Ridge/Wash and Butler Wash areas. There are an estimated twenty sites containing elements of this culture, on two of which archaeologists have performed limited test excavations. Old Man Cave is located in a slickrock canyon that drains the northeastern edge of the Grand Gulch Plateau and empties into Comb Wash. The cave is ten meters deep and fifteen meters wide at its mouth; Archaic peoples lived in it beginning 7,800 years ago and continued to use it for the next 1,000 years. Inhabitants abandoned it for four thousand years until Puebloan Basketmaker II occupants arrived around 200 BC. Although modern looters have disturbed a good portion of the site, there were sufficient materials—two Elko points (Archaic-type), an open-twined sandal, bark, burned bone, chaff from dropseed, coprolites (feces), and hearths—to indicate Archaic lifestyle. Two findings from this excavation suggest that, one, the arrival of the Basketmakers came through migration and was not developed in situ, and, two, that archaeologists struggle to piece together the story from these older eras, especially when sites are heavily disturbed.[6]

A second Archaic site is Boomerang Shelter, located in Long Fingers Canyon on the Butler side of Comb Ridge. This site also held a distinctive open-twined sandal fragment and a layer of Archaic materials located beneath five successive layers of later Basketmaker II storage cists.[7] As with Old Man Cave (and virtually every sheltered site in San Juan County), looters disturbed this alcove. Other issues—the relatively small, ephemeral, and easily obscured character of sites left by mobile peoples; the tendency of later cultures to rework the larger tools of their predecessors; and the resultant ease with which such elements can be lost or obscured among the more intense and substantial remains left by later sedentary peoples—compound the problem. The final message from both Old Man and Boomerang is that much is still unknown about the Archaic period and that the archaeological record, when scrambled and vandalized, becomes increasingly difficult to decipher.

Copyright by Andrew Gulliford

Archaic and Ancestral Puebloan peoples used sandstone rock to sharpen implements ranging from arrowheads, spear points, and awls to axes. Archaeologists are not sure how the small depressions in the bottom of some of these worn grooves were used.

Although the Archaic lifeway may have persisted in some areas for a considerable time, the Archaic period in the Four Corners region ended with the appearance by 1000 BC of a culture with corn and squash and a means to store them. This marks the beginning in southeastern Utah of the Ancestral Puebloan or Anasazi cultural tradition. The first identifiable Ancestral Puebloan era starts with the Basketmaker II tradition (1000 BC to AD 450). The Basketmaker I phase is an undifferentiated period of time during the Late Archaic and so is dropped from the sequence of Basketmaker II and III, and Pueblo I, II, III, and IV found in southeastern Utah. When these Indians first appeared, they were dependent on corn and squash, primary staples in their diet, supplemented with big game such as deer, elk, and bighorn sheep and small game such as rabbits, mice, and prairie dogs. Still, an estimated 70 percent of their food derived from what they grew, buttressed with wild plants.

Basketmaker occupation north of the San Juan River, beginning at about 1000 BC, focused first on rock-shelter habitations in canyon areas and floodwater farming from the moisture that descended from the washes and off rock slopes. Significant concentrations of this early Basketmaker II lifestyle are found in and among the canyons of Comb Ridge, Butler Wash, and the Grand Gulch Plateau. Their homes in the alcoves were simple shelters, ranging between eight and thirty feet in diameter with extensive cists for storage and burial. Indeed, storage cists lined with upright slabs under these rock overhangs hold some of the best-preserved remains of Basketmaker II culture.

By around 100 BC, the Basketmaker II people were building open-air sites with relatively substantial pit houses in more upland areas with floodwater farming potential such as the Bluff Bench and Cedar Mesa. The pit houses built on the mesas have a partially excavated bottom approximately a foot deep with enclosed sides of wood covered with dirt and an entryway on one side. Alcoves were now used primarily for storage. By the third century AD, there were neighborhoods of loosely clustered pit houses in groups of from one to three families in the upland divides such as the Grand Gulch Plateau mesas, an area more suited to dry farming than floodwater irrigation. The entire Basketmaker II culture is the longest of all of the phases of Ancestral Puebloan culture, lasting for a period in excess of fifteen hundred years.

Artifacts from this period include fringe-toed and straight-toed sandals; striped, seamless twined bags; atlatls with darts; side and corner notched dart points; nets made of cordage to snare small game; digging sticks for planting crops; and manos with distinctive trough metates for grinding seeds and corn. Clothing consisted of breechcloths for men, woven yucca or cedar fiber aprons for women, and the ubiquitous turkey feather or rabbit fur blankets woven into a warp and weft of yucca fiber. Basketmaker II people enjoyed wearing ornaments and jewelry, such as necklaces, ear pendants, hair combs, and labrets made of bone, a variety of stones, and olivella and abalone shells traded in from the Pacific coast, and in one Basketmaker II site (dated ca. 100 BC) near Bluff, pounded copper pendants similar to those found in the contemporary Great Lakes region.

Ceramics were absent during this period of prehistory, and these people became noted for their finely woven sumac or yucca handiwork, creating baskets for many uses. Some were for winnowing seeds, others were burden baskets with tumplines that went across the forehead or shoulders, others were for burial of bodies often in a tightly flexed prenatal position and accompanied by a new pair of sandals. Some baskets were so tightly woven that they held water in which heated rocks boiled food. Indeed, one of the diagnostic elements for a Basketmaker II site is the presence of limestone used in cooking. Corn, when boiled with limestone, releases lysine, an amino acid that is highly desirable in a maize-dependent diet. Until beans, containing readily assimilated lysine, became part of the Basketmaker III diet, limestone filled the need. Butler Wash, Cedar Mesa, the upwarp of Comb Ridge, and, of course, Lime Ridge, have rich strata of limestone rock used for

Courtesy of San Juan County Historical Commission

Tightly woven baskets, skillfully knapped arrowheads and knife blades, and drilled pendants are some of the artifacts made by Ancestral Puebloans that came from sites in Butler Wash.

cooking. Hundreds of years later, Mormon settlers availed themselves of this resource in Butler Wash by creating a kiln in which they processed lime to mix with mortar in adobe construction.

Basketmaker II sites in the Comb Ridge area include the already mentioned Old Man Cave and Boomerang Shelter as well as the Bent Oak Shelter in the Long Fingers tributary of Butler Wash. There are many others. The most famous Basketmaker II site in southeastern Utah is Cave 7 in Whiskers Draw on the east side of Milk Ranch Point near the north end of Comb Ridge. This site is important for a number of reasons.[8] Excavated in December 1893 by Richard Wetherill, leader of the Hyde Exploring Expedition (discussed in chapter 7), this alcove was the first place where Basketmaker remains were found to be stratigraphically underlying, and therefore, older than, those of the later puebloan "cliff dweller" peoples. Within months of the Cave 7 discoveries, the term "Basketmaker" became a neologism for this group of Ancestral Puebloans. The cave also produced the largest series of Basketmaker skeletal remains ever recovered: more than ninety individuals from a single site. These bodies also dispelled the notion of an idyllic agricultural society living a peaceful existence in picturesque canyon country. Instead, they reveal evidence of a prehistoric massacre.

On top of the Basketmaker II site is a three-foot-layer of Pueblo II two-room masonry structures with cultural material from that and the Pueblo III era. Six feet below is the Basketmaker II layer where Wetherill made his "great discovery." Excerpts from the expedition's field notes describe what they saw:

> We have now taken 90 skeletons from one cave. . . . Several skeletons were three feet under the lower foundation of the cliff house. We have backbones with stone spear points still sticking in them and several breast bones shot through with [spear points] and many broken heads and arms. With these we have not less than seventy stone spear heads. . . . We found one interesting group, a mother with an infant on each arm, and another lying on her breast with its head under her chin. There are warriors, "mighty men of valor," with ten or twelve spear points lying near; younger men with bone tools near them, and the unwarlike counselors or priests, with decaying baskets originally filled with food, or possibly tools of trade. These latter have left little trace save a dark stain in the sand.[9]

Recent analysis (1990) of the remains by a group of professional and avocational archaeologists, as part of the Wetherill Grand Gulch Project, provided information on this burial alcove. Statistically, of sixty-one corpses examined, forty (65 percent) were male, fifteen (25 percent) female, nine (15 percent) non-adult. Twenty-four (60% percent) of the males were damaged (i.e., with imbedded points or injury to bone, with no way of determining what happened to soft tissue); 27 percent of the females, with a little under 50 percent showing signs of a violent death.[10] Hyde Expedition field notes give cryptic descriptions such as, "a group of six skeletons apparently thrown in a pile," "three of ten dart points found along the right arm" of a particular skeleton, and "large dart point found with ten dart points 'upon the right arm' of a person." Buried with one middle-aged adult male were twenty-four blades, a red cloud blower pipe, chunks of red ochre, a round stone, and a bone awl.[11] Many of the other victims had distinctive elements concerning either their death or burial. All appeared to have been buried shortly after dying, since there is no sign of animal scavenging, even of dismembered parts interred separately from the bodies.

A final means that gives a glimpse into Basketmaker culture is its rock art, found in the form of either pecked petroglyphs or painted pictographs. The San Juan River corridor, which encompasses Comb Ridge, lies at the heart of the richest concentration of pre-pottery rock art in the United States. San Juan anthropomorphic-style forms dominate classic Basketmaker II art with large, frontally depicted, rectangular-or-trapezoid-bodied human figures that include details of adornment and facial features.[12] They are found in association with a wide array of other motifs, many of which occur with such frequent repetition that they were likely imbued with formal symbolism. These elements include lobed circles, bags, head scalps or masks, humans with bird-shaped heads or bird forms on their heads, crooked staffs and staff bearers, humans with one spread hand raised and the other lowered, and humans with fountain-like headdresses. The highest concentration of this

Copyright by Andrew Gulliford

Lower Butler Wash Panel is one of the best examples of Basketmaker rock art in the Four Corners region. Trapezoidal torsos; necklaces, earrings, and belts; and markings above the head speak of cultural values not always easy to interpret.

style of art is along the San Juan River between Bluff and Lime Ridge; the best-known example is the Lower Butler Wash Panel. Rock art is difficult to both date and interpret, but these elements, found in association with Basketmaker II sites, are assigned as characteristic of this era.

Around AD 450, Basketmaker culture underwent rapid changes: the bow and arrow, introduced by neighbors to the north, replaced the atlatl; beans became an important addition to the diet, completing the triad of what the Iroquois called the "three sisters" (corn, beans, and squash); simple, plain gray and crude black-on-white pottery joined basketry as standard containers in the household; hard, wooden cradleboards replaced the flexible cradleboards of the Basketmaker II period, resulting in the universal flattening, broadening, and shortening of the skull, formerly long and undeformed; pit houses became much more substantial and formal; and settlement arrangements were standardized in layout with a pithouse lying between a group of storage cists to the north/west and a midden to the south/east. Households frequently clustered into villages of a dozen or more structures, often boasting an extraordinarily large pithouse that may have served either as a community center or as the home of a very prominent personality or family. All of these innovations characterized the Basketmaker III (AD 450–750) period.

The people of Basketmaker III modified or expanded upon many of the qualities of the Basketmaker II period. For instance, during the latter time, large populations settled in the mesas, canyons, and washes east of Comb Wash that feed into the San Juan River. What had been small clusters of pithouses now expanded into full-fledged communities. One, located west of Bluff, held a series of homes and a single larger edifice that served as a community center and contained the burial of a golden eagle. There was also a community gravesite with at least eighteen bodies. A similar find in Recapture Wash held the largest Basketmaker III pithouse excavated in southeastern Utah. This structure and a nearby smaller pithouse contained burials of raptors, in this case, Red-tailed hawks.

Regular family pithouses also were modified. The pit became deeper (two to five feet) and larger (nine to twenty-five feet), with exterior storage cists clustered to the north of the pithouse. Four corner poles provided a more substantial frame that allowed not only a larger structure but also an entryway in the roof with a ladder to descend to the hard-packed clay—or very rarely—stone-lined floors. Mats, brush, and mud overlaid the roof and side materials were built on a supportive frame of wood. A greatly reduced side entrance assisted with the draw of the fireplace while a deflector stone prevented strong breezes from extinguishing the fire. Beyond this was a small hole in the floor, said by today's Pueblo Indians to represent a sipapu or place of emergence discussed in creation stories. From these architectural innovations came the profile of future kivas. Stockade walls surrounded some excavated Basketmaker III clusters of pithouses, but none have been identified in southeastern Utah.

With the marriage of the "three sisters," another innovation arose in garden plots. A more sedentary lifestyle that flourished because of the high water table in this era, the use of various types of drainage systems, and an increased population drove the people to more efficient means of agriculture. Based on contemporary ethnographic comparison, the Puebloans most likely dug basins in the soil to catch the water then planted six to ten corn seeds in the bottom, maximizing use of moisture while clustering the plants in a way that protected them from the sand-blasting winds of the desert. Flood irrigation and pot irrigation capitalize on this technique. Add to this beans that entwine themselves on the stalks and add nitrogen to the soil that the corn removes, and the squash plants at the base that spread over the ground providing shade and maintaining water, and one has an efficient system of production in a dry environment. Cotton was not grown for clothing until Pueblo I times.

The start of Puebloan characteristics (Pueblo I— AD 750–900) followed next. Sites of this era are rare in lands west of Comb Wash such as in the canyons and on the mesas of the Grand Gulch and Red Rock plateaus. But on the east side of the Grand Gulch region, remains of medium-to-large communities are present in Comb, Butler, and Cottonwood washes, along the benches of the San Juan River, and South Cottonwood's major tributaries. Pueblo I times witnessed the full suite of Puebloan culture patterns, where populations

Courtesy of Kay Shumway

Attempts to interpret rock art usually leave room for discussion. While some designs are standardized and clearly depict certain objects, the story behind these objects often escapes clear understanding.

tended to concentrate into larger and more compact settlements of above-ground contiguous house blocks of rectangular rooms with pit structures in front. The only excavated Pueblo I site in the Comb Ridge area is Cholla Knoll, north of Highway 95 in Butler Wash.[13] This C-shaped room block, with its storage cists and pithouses, is a solid representation of this era in Puebloan construction.

Pueblo I homes are characterized by thin walls built in various ways including adobe, rough stone masonry, and jacal, a type of adobe construction also called wattle-and-daub. Jacal buildings are framed with a latticework of interwoven sticks with a heavily applied coat of adobe on each side of the frame. In some cases, coursed stone masonry is also set into the adobe. By the late decades of this period, surface room blocks were sometimes constructed of uncoursed or semi-coursed stone masonry involving unshaped or edge-shaped slabs set in thick mortar beds. A typical residential surface room block consists of two or three adjoining rooms fronted by a larger residential room. These blocks may be joined end-to-end to form curving or L-shaped room blocks in a unified communal structure. Pueblo I settlement layouts typically conform to the unit pueblo pattern with surface room blocks, pit structures, and middens arrayed in series from north or northwest to south or southeast.

The kiva—a semi-subterranean ceremonial chamber with architectural antecedents from Basketmaker times—arrived full-blown during the Pueblo I era. Based on contemporary ethnography, these circular structures have deep religious significance, tying the Pueblo story of emergence into the architecture. These rooms have a sipapu or entryway from the world beneath, a compacted floor—representing the next world, a bench approximately two to three feet above the floor—and a ladder that bisects the roof to the daily world outside. The firepit in the floor has a deflector stone between it and a ventilator shaft to decrease air currents coming down the shaft so that the smoke can rise through the ceiling/doorway. This architectural phenomenon will be ubiquitous by Pueblo II.

Early in the Pueblo I period, the people lived in communities dispersed across different landforms and environments. By about AD 885, in apparent response to a warm, dry climatic episode, they abandoned the mesa interior areas, concentrating settlements in highland foothills and along major drainages. This allowed the people to use the water from canyon confluences or to live in proximity to reliable springs. Most of these settlements were not defensive in nature, but a few clearly capitalized on protective qualities. In Comb Wash, overlooking the mouth of one of its tributary canyons, sits an early-to-middle Pueblo defensive site. It is marked by numerous postholes carved into the sandstone bedrock, outlining a complex of round and rectangular structures made presumably of jacal.

The Comb Ridge area is also providing new information about Puebloan multi-story room-block construction, which until recently had been associated only with the Pueblo II era. At the Moki Steps Site, Monarch Cave, and Arch Canyon Ruin, distinct evidence is apparent that during Pueblo I times, the Indians were building at least two-story structures supported in the back by the alcove wall.[14] All three of the sites are located near a significant source of water, have pecked butt sockets for jacal room blocks in the cliffs, and remnants of construction that indicate at least two levels of the building.

At the Moki Steps Site, on the gravel terrace overlooking the San Juan River floodplain, there are surface remains that include elements of two substantial room blocks, an array of slab cists, extensive and rich middens, and a significant amount of rock art. In the cliff directly above the end of one of the early room blocks are four pecked butt sockets, defining roof levels of a two-story structure. At Monarch Cave, which overlooks a perennially productive pour-off pool, there are five butt sockets pecked into the cliff that clearly define the second- and third-story levels of a Pueblo I structure. A geometric pictograph resembling late Basketmaker–Pueblo I ceramic design elements is painted on the cliff above the sockets, likely by someone standing on the third-story roof. And at the Arch Canyon Ruin, overlooking the creek, there are pecked sockets that attest to architecture rising as high as four stories. Although the visible architectural remains are from

Pueblo II and Pueblo III, the sockets predate the surviving architecture and the associated midden is dominated by Pueblo I ceramics. The new evidence emerging from these three sites associated with Comb Ridge will prompt a re-evaluation of Pueblo I construction.

Pottery, by this time, was evolving into better, more refined, and stylistically more complex forms. Local deposits of clay in Comb Wash, White Mesa, and elsewhere provided the raw material for a burgeoning art. Cookware, decorated bowls, ladles, jugs, and novelty images sprang from the hands of potters experimenting with this medium. While baskets continued to meet certain needs, pottery was less time consuming to make, made the transport of water more practical, allowed for the slow cooking of beans, which were now a significant part of the diet, and encouraged greater artistic expression. Most pottery derived from the coil method. The potter placed the coils one on top of the other, then smoothed the concentric circles with a piece of broken pottery, wood, or a stone. The artist added decoration by using an implement to depress or raise the surface or by covering the piece with slip, a liquid form of clay that when heated by a wood fire, produced a particular color or smoother surface for decoration. Plants such as beeweed were boiled, applied with a yucca brush to the ceramic surface, and fired. Other pottery was decoratively painted with minerals of iron or manganese. The result was a wide variety of designs—parallel lines, zigzags, triangles, checkerboards, interlocking frets, or animal representations.

Copyright by Andrew Gulliford

This Puebloan rock art ladder, located in Butler Wash below the Eagle Nest site, shows a willow-tied ladder similar to the ones used to descend into kivas or climb into a homesite perched in a crevice or alcove.

Pueblo I ceramic developments include the appearance and rise to dominance of neck-banded grayware, the proliferation of boldly decorated, mostly unslipped redware, and the stylistic and technological refinement of whiteware. The west-central reaches of the northern San Juan area, between Comb Wash and Montezuma Canyon, appear to have been a center of production of both redwares and White Mesa Black-on-white. The redwares were in wide demand and circulated throughout the southern Colorado Plateau, whereas White Mesa Black-on-white, despite a distinctively elegant and well-executed design system, was apparently produced almost entirely for local consumption.

The Pueblo II period (AD 900–1150) encompasses two distinct trends. Beginning roughly about AD 920 and lasting for eighty years, there appears to have been a depopulation or abandonment of many of the previous Pueblo I haunts. Those who did remain continued where stable water sources provided what was needed for crops, but the number of sites decreased. The reason for this population shift is unknown, but it was during the time when Chaco Canyon in New Mexico swelled in both numbers of people and architectural development. Large structures such as Pueblo Bonito, Casa Rinconada, Chetro Ketl, and Pueblo Alto reached their height in both size and function. Their impact in the entire San Juan drainage, to include the Comb Ridge and Bluff areas, is unmistakable. Indeed, archaeologist Stephen H. Lekson has titled this period the Pax Chaco, in comparison to the Pax Romana, or two hundred years under Roman rule that saw a type of controlled peace over the Mediterranean world, enforced by leadership from Rome. Exactly what type of relationship Chaco Canyon had with Puebloan settlements north of the San Juan River has not yet been determined, but there is no doubt as to its architectural connections. Around AD 1000, a large influx of people repopulated the area, establishing many of the technological and architectural elements prevalent in Chaco.

Early Pueblo II architecture continued the trends found in the late Pueblo I era with unit pueblos, earthen-walled pit structures, and surface rooms in connected block structures, but also with a marked absence of defensive structures or citadels. Following the depopulation, the middle-to-late Pueblo II saw a proliferation of relatively small unit and double-unit pueblos loosely clustered into neighborhoods or communities. West of Comb Wash, these sites often exhibit ceramic and architectural properties characteristic of the Kayenta region to the south, with an abundance of imported southern pottery and the prevalent use of jacal construction. On the other side of Comb Wash, however, a more pronounced adherence to Mesa Verde architecture, with its stone masonry and ceramics, is found. There is no explanation as to why this regional, permeable boundary exists, but it is interesting to note that Comb Ridge somehow became a part of the division.

Following the repopulation of the area in the late eleventh or early twelfth century, people lived scattered across the landscape in residential hamlets, many of which clustered into loosely nucleated communities centering around public architecture. While small kivas and separated room blocks continued, the people living in the Pueblo II era embraced three forms of architecture that extended into Pueblo III times. All of these—the great house, great kiva, and roads—were contemporary with what developed in Chaco on a much larger, grander scale. Archaeologists have performed much more excavation on and studied such features in New Mexico compared to the relatively nascent studies in Utah, but general patterns of similarity between the areas are evident.

Clearly identified great houses are scattered about the Comb Ridge area. There is one in Comb Wash near Highway 95, another in Arch Canyon, three in Cottonwood Wash, another on White Mesa, and one on Mustang Mesa. An additional fourteen potential great houses lie between Grand Gulch and Montezuma Canyon, inviting further investigation. The great house at Arch Canyon, for example, boasts robust Pueblo II architecture with

Copyright by Andrew Gulliford

This Pueblo II and III ruin in Butler Wash shows remaining paint on the adobe wall and soot on the ceiling of the alcove from cooking and heating fires. The Wetherill brothers had their picture taken here in the 1890s, and the site shows relatively little damage since then.

large-scale vertical walls that provide a high ceiling for the rooms in this two-storied pueblo.[15] The structure is fifty yards long and approximately fifteen feet high. Rooms in many great houses have living facilities or domestic features such as the prevalent Pueblo II grinding bins, laid side by side with upright slabs of rock to separate each metate.

The size of these structures suggests that each was much more than one family would use, given Puebloan living standards of the day, and so has been labeled as public architecture. They could have served as housing space for a dominant lineage, whose power and influence over the people in the area called for impressive architecture. Perhaps they were meeting places that required sufficient space to entertain community leaders. Another possibility is that, as in Chaco, some of the rooms served as storage areas for an expansive trade network. At this point, no one knows the exact function of a great house, and in the case of Arch Canyon, until the structure is excavated, it will be difficult to determine.

The second element of the Chacoan triumvirate is the great kiva. Starting in Basketmaker III, these structures appeared long before the construction of great houses but became a

The bottom room in this block illustrates a Pueblo II form of masonry in which the rocks in the wall are edge-flaked on exposed sides while the upper room of Pueblo III construction has more carefully shaped and squared rocks embedded in adobe.

common (but not universal) element in later great house sites. With most great houses there appears to be a great kiva in direct association. In some instances, great kivas occur in isolation without a great house. Examples are found in Cottonwood Wash (late Pueblo I) and at Rincon (late Pueblo II–Pueblo III). How these two architectural structures compliment each other in Puebloan thought is unknown. Based on excavation at the Bluff Great House and Great Kiva, the only Pueblo II–Pueblo III great kiva yet excavated in Utah, it appears that elements found in Chaco great kivas are repeated in Utah. These buildings have a circular wall construction with a floor-to-roof height of about nine feet. Diameters vary between thirty to forty feet with stone masonry-lined walls, which, with four large posts/columns, supported the roof. Smaller sticks filled in the beam framework as part of the roofing material before being covered with adobe. Inside the kiva is a firebox, a bench that runs around the circumference, foot drums, subfloor enclosures, peripheral rooms, a circular trench, and two low vaults. Without access to contemporary beliefs, it is impossible to say with surety what each element of this religious architecture means. Certainly, they reflect values associated with the creation story and lend themselves to its being retold and re-enacted.

The third leg of the triumvirate is the system of roads. While the difference between roads and trails can become murky, roads are defined here as wide, formal, excavated thoroughfares that follow a distinct pattern, while trails are smaller and informal. Currently there are at least fifteen known prehistoric constructed trails over Comb Ridge. Four of these appear to be components of roads.[16] Where archaeologists have traced four hundred miles of roads in or emanating from Chaco Canyon, only fifty to sixty miles of road (if all of the missing or "undiscovered" pieces are connected) have thus far been identified between Cedar Mesa and Cottonwood Wash.[17] In Comb and Butler washes, there are ten to twelve miles of road.

While people have only recently started to trace the outline of these structures and study their characteristics, they have known of their presence for some time. Utes like Jim Mike, at the turn of the twentieth century, were aware of them, commenting to Mormon settlers about these "irrigation ditches." Albert R. Lyman, who had been raised on the range in the livestock industry but was also a local historian, took note. In studying the relationship of a great house and great kiva to Puebloan roads, he recalled:

> Right north of Bluff on the hill there west of the graveyard, there was one time quite a house, with a kiva at the east end of it. . . . When I was a youngster, there was quite a deep hole west of that; it's been filling up with sand all the time since then. But if you go by there, you'll see that that was quite a prominent house on the hill there, just west of the graveyard. There was an old roadway that went right up from Bluff and over the hill right in front of that house and down the hill on the other side and into the mouth of Cottonwood. . . .
>
> There's one other thing in this country. . . . [A] Ute came down into Bluff and asked us about a ditch. There was an old ditch up there. Some of us went up there and looked at it; made a special trip to go and see it. It was an old graded

Courtesy of Winston Hurst

The swale where this woman stands is an unusually prominent section of a Puebloan prehistoric road. Most such road sections are difficult to see, even with proper lighting, and can easily be destroyed by vehicular traffic.

> road. It had been cut through the hills with cuts in the hills to show that that road was there, and it looked as if it might have been made for heavy traffic—cars. But I'd say it was three thousand years old! That's the oldest thing I know of in San Juan County, and it went over into Cottonwood.[18]

Other Puebloan road networks also exist in Colorado and Arizona, making the Four Corners region a well-traveled prehistoric crossroads.

While there is much to be learned about great houses, great kivas, and roads, much has already surfaced. Aerial and ground reconnaissance has helped identify six miles of segments in a twenty-five mile stretch of Cottonwood Wash associated with great house complexes. Archaeologists have found others between Cedar Mesa and Montezuma Canyon, some of which began at the San Juan River and headed north; yet none has been specifically tied to roads emanating from Chaco Canyon. Some of the Utah roads appear to follow routes in use at least as early as AD 900, or the end of Pueblo I, but their formalization into constructed roads may not have occurred until the 1000s or later.[19]

The roads were actually highly developed footpaths, since there were no wheeled vehicles until after the white man arrived. The width of the roads is fairly constant at seven to eight meters (about twenty-five feet). Their course is evident as a subtle linear swale or a

Courtesy of Owen Severance

A bedrock groove near the San Juan River marks a section of Puebloan road similar to marking found in Chacoan roads. The purpose of this linear feature is unknown.

series of aligned notches in crosscutting ridges. When descending or traversing a grade, the swale is typically defined by a cut on the uphill side and a low berm on the downhill slope. The roads run in straight lines or in sweeping curves, with course corrections often occurring on ridges or high points.[20]

The Puebloans constructed the roads using a number of different means. Removal of surface rock, when practical, maintained the straight alignment. A certain amount of excavation displaced the topsoil, bringing the roads down to a firm rock or clay base layer. This gave the trail its dish-shaped cross section with debris added to the sides for more depth. There are suggestions of filling and possible bridgework in some areas where the roads cross low spots or washes. Prehistoric roads tend to be wider and more weathered than historic ones or bulldozed mineral exploration trails and use stairs or pecked hand/toeholds instead of ramps for steep ascents. At least two, and probably four, road segments climb up and over the steep west face of Comb Ridge. As in the Chaco area, bedrock sections are sometimes marked by pecked grooves from four to six inches in width and of variable length.

Around one of the great house-great kiva settlements in Comb Wash is a beltway or "business loop" that encircles half of this Pueblo III settlement before heading off toward

Comb Ridge. Like the grooves in bedrock, there appears to be no other explanation for this beltway other than it served some type of ceremonial function. The Chacoan roads had parallel sections that might be separated by one hundred yards of open space. This certainly could not have filled an economic or utilitarian function either. While this phenomenon has not yet been identified in southeastern Utah, the loop in Comb may have served some type of ceremonial necessity.[21]

Architectural features along the roads are scarce, the only consistently related element being shrine-like masonry enclosures from four to nine meters in diameter. These *herraduras* (horseshoes) are most often found at the crest or base of an escarpment, generally where the road makes a dramatic shift in direction. Six of these features—three on Comb Ridge and three in Comb Wash—create a definite pattern, but exactly how they functioned is unknown. The fact that they exhibit deliberate construction, some two-to-three foot walls having been dry laid and others wet laid in difficult, unproductive stretches of terrain, suggests that their functions were at least as symbolic as economic.

There is little ethnographic literature concerning the relevance of these herraduras.[22] Frank Waters offers a tantalizing bit of information. Waters is a writer noted for excellence with the finely turned phrase but also given to sweeping interpretations that may not be carefully buttressed by fact. He tells of a time, probably in the late 1950s or early 1960s, before the archaeological community had paid much attention to the Chaco road system. Waters spent the day with John Lansa, a "Hopi informant," looking at pictographs interpreted as clan symbols. John was convinced that a shrine would be in the immediate vicinity, and he found one after an hour's search. From there, he sighted a pile of rocks and discovered a second shrine with three circular stones; from these two shrines, he sighted a third across Escavada Wash. Even though he had never been to any of these places before, he revealed their location then followed with an interpretation.

> These three shrines, he told us later, marked the courses of three race tracks. The one to the west he believed had been used by the Flute Society during the Flute Ceremony. Ceremonial races are still held during the Flute and Snake-Antelope Ceremonies—the only Hopi ceremonies which include races. The pohoki [Prayer Standing House or tutuskya—shrine in the open] to the east where the three circular stones were found, was a shrine of the sun; the three stones symbolizing the three previous worlds to which life was imparted by the sun. It was the southern terminus of a long race track that extended northward to the sun temple at Mesa Verde, some three or four days' travel by foot, a faintly discernible trail is still visible by plane.[23]

While Lansa's understanding offers interesting possibilities, there may be other explanations that answer why so much time and effort was put into constructing the road system and why the shrines are such an integral part.

What can be said with a degree of certainty is that the roads connected well-developed communities that had great houses and great kivas. The settlement in Arch Canyon was a significant node in a road complex that stretched from Bluff to upper Cottonwood Wash, linking several great house communities in the Comb and Cottonwood drainages and possibly connecting some of those sites to farm areas in the uplands of the Cottonwood drainage.[24] How these great houses in Cottonwood and Comb washes tie to two potential great houses on Cedar Mesa is not clear, but all have sections of roads associated with them. Another unknown is the relationship of the isolated great kiva found at Rincon at the mouth of Comb Wash to the various great house sites. There is no related identifiable road, possibly due to periodic flooding and channel adjustment of the San Juan River floodplain. Unlike the other nodes on the roads, there are few habitation sites and no great house associated with this site; it appears to be an anomaly—a lone shrine at the geographically dramatic space where ridge intersects river at a right angle.

Puebloan towers were closely associated with a Mesa Verde influence.[25] In southeastern Utah there does not appear to be a strong connection between the roads and the towers, which appeared during Pueblo III times. More often, towers were built around the heads of canyons or perennial sources of water such as springs. At the Comb Wash Great House there were four towers clustered near where the loop diverges from the road coming up the wash. They are not in close proximity to significant habitation structures, near a spring or source of water (though they are clustered around a seep), and do not appear to have a utilitarian function. Towers also exist in other parts of Comb Wash—probably totaling eight to a dozen—with the same number in Butler Wash— and others in nearby Mule Canyon and Fish Creek. Exactly why they were built in those locations is a mystery. There is still much to learn about Puebloan thought and practice.

Archaeologists debate various interpretations today. Some emphasize the secular/economic perspective, arguing that the great houses and great kivas connected by roads represent administrative integrated structures in communities linked by a road complex that facilitated movement of commodities including food, building materials, and exotic goods. Others have felt that most of the roads do not join in an integrated system but are more localized, public architectural phenomenon converging on community ceremonial centers, with religious and symbolic significance.[26] It is very likely that both of these interpretations are correct: different roads may have served different functions; the same road may have served diverse functions at different times; and road construction for any purpose would have certainly served to organize and reinforce the community's social order.

The Pueblo II period is generally characterized as a time of social order. Its rise and decline parallel the Chaco developments to the southeast, which cast their light over much of the southern Colorado Plateau. With the decline of the great centers in Chaco Canyon came the rise of dominance of other communities north of the San Juan River such as Aztec and Salmon, New Mexico, and Mesa Verde, Colorado, around the start of the twelfth century. The growth of these centers and the proliferation of northern great houses may have been associated with social stresses, causing further fracturing of the communities in southeastern Utah. Where the Pueblo II period is fairly free from defensive settlements and documented acts of violence, the opposite is true of both the Pueblo I and Pueblo III eras that surround it. By about AD 1150, the peaceful Pax Chaco had ended.

The Pueblo III Period (AD 1150–1300) has historically been viewed as "the stage of large communities, great development of the arts, and growth of intensive local specialization."[27] While this is certainly true, it was also a time of social ferment and conflict that culminated in the abandonment of the Four Corners Ancestral Puebloan domain and movement to areas that are today inhabited by the Eastern and Western Pueblo peoples. The height of cultural development in the San Juan area continued to blossom further south in the region of historic pueblo settlement. The reasons for these changes are not clearly defined, the physical remains telling only part of the story.

Pueblo III times expanded a number of the traits started in Pueblo II. The roads, great houses, and great kivas remained in use while towers proliferated. The general move within the culture was an abandonment of scattered smaller communities with a concentration of the population in large defensive sites often located in protective alcoves or on precarious canyon rims and mesa tops with controlled access. Residential room blocks rose two and three stories high. Numerous kivas, courtyards, and plazas with sometimes exquisitely dressed masonry characterize this era. Prominent examples north of the San Juan River include Cliff Palace and other sites on Mesa Verde, Yellow Jacket and other large towns in the Montezuma Valley of Colorado, and late components of the old great house towns at Aztec and Salmon, New Mexico. As one moves further west, the size of the communities diminish. In the Comb Ridge area, the largest sites barely boast fifty surface rooms, compared to hundreds and even thousands in some Colorado sites. By late Pueblo III, the people constructed major settlements in direct proximity to, and often enclosed, permanent water sources, something that had not occurred in previous sites.

Most of the communities in southeastern Utah assumed a Mesa Verde style of architecture, the Pueblo II Kayenta influence west of Comb Ridge now giving way to this epicenter's dominant forms. A profusion of different types of ceramics developed in various regions fostering their own distinctive styles. In southeastern Utah and southwest Colorado, prominent types included Dolores and Mesa Verde Corrugated, Mancos Black-on-white, and McElmo Black-on-white. Fine craftsmanship prevailed and the exchange of wares with local groups was common. Long-distance trade that had characterized the PII period, showing a Mesoamerican influence—particularly evident in the barter of macaws and products made from their feathers—declined. Domesticated turkeys, which had been part of Puebloan culture since Basketmaker III times but had not been a significant part of their diet, now replaced deer and other large game as a primary source of protein. The villages became increasingly territorial and defensive while areas between the large settlements depopulated. All of these developments illustrate social defensiveness and stress, consistent with clear evidence of warfare in several of the latest Pueblo III sites in Colorado.

Archaeologists have excavated only two Pueblo III sites in the immediate area of Comb Ridge. Performing site mitigation for road construction of Highway 95, they unearthed a small Pueblo III unit pueblo named Alternate Village in Comb Wash. There was no apparent sign of violence. Nearby, the Comb Wash Great House complex, the largest ruin in

Copyright by Andrew Gulliford

This defensive pueblo in Long Fingers Canyon is characteristic of Late Pueblo III sites, which were built in places difficult to access. One reason that it is so well preserved today is because it is hard to reach.

Comb Wash, was another Pueblo III community. This fifty-room block structure, compacted into a twenty-five to thirty-meter diameter space, had at least two stories and five kivas. Occupied until the middle 1200s, the ruin's two converging roads and belt loop, may have been in use until abandonment of the region. Here also, based on limited excavation testing, there is only slight indication of violence before the inhabitants departed.

Butler Wash has several notable late Pueblo III ruins, two of which may have been linked to the Comb Wash Great House complex by roads. The Butler Wash Indian Ruin, located on a pullout off Highway 95, is perched in a high alcove on the backside of Comb Ridge, in line with the northeast road out of Comb Wash and an old Comb Ridge crossover trail. Sitting on a mesita northeast of the Butler Wash Ruin rests a small complex of rooms with two towers. There is direct line-of-sight signaling capability between the two sites so that each could communicate with the other. Two miles to the south, the late Pueblo III O'Grosky Site lies directly on the projected route of the road that extends southeast from the Comb Wash Great House toward another ancient crossover trail. It also has two towers, perhaps as many as fifty rooms, and is located beside a seep. Other nearby sites of similar style and age include Ruin Springs and Radon Point complexes on White Mesa, and the Cave Towers and Dry Wash Ruin complexes on the Grand Gulch Plateau.

A different kind of Pueblo III site, a purely defensive citadel, sits atop a knob of rock on Comb Ridge. This is one of the best-selected defensive sites in the region. Two walls built across the site's only access protected the ten- or twelve-room pueblo, as did the steep cliffs on three sides with anywhere from a 50- to 100-foot sheer wall above the talus slope. The occupants looked down on a major trail sporting a herradura located on traces of the road that continued on the flat below the escarpment of Comb Wash.

There are a variety of explanations why the entire Puebloan population departed from the Colorado Plateau prior to AD 1300, leaving behind their dwellings, implements, and some of their cultural and social institutions. Because archaeologists deal with physical remains, many of their explanations hinge on identifiable and measurable effects of physical events. Accumulating paleoclimatic evidence testifies of an unusually cold and dry period during the late 1200s. While some sources of water would dry up during this drought, there were other sources that did not. In some areas, arroyo cutting is credited with forcing abandonment because the water could no longer be pushed onto the crops for irrigation. In the Comb Ridge area, so much of the farming depended on runoff from alluvial fans and some floodplain irrigation that this is not a very satisfactory answer. Some archaeologists blame the exodus on internal disputes while others look to pressure from non-sedentary neighbors—possibly ancestors of the Utes/Paiutes or Navajos. There is very little clear evidence to support this view, but certainly there would eventually be a new influx of people.

Another way of viewing this period—entirely unprovable because of its intangible nature—is to look through Native American eyes at the difficult physical events and place the blame for them on religious reasons. Failure of snow and rain for crops, dried-up sources of water, cold temperatures for a shortened growing season, generally diminishing food resources, and internal and external conflict can all be associated with witchcraft, antisocial behavior, revenge of the gods, and the curses of natural forces. Ekkehart Malotki's translation of stories embodied in *Hopi Tales of Destruction* gives an excellent introduction into one Pueblo tribe's oral tradition of social and cultural decline through warfare and supernatural means.[28] While not all-inclusive and indicative of individual settlements and the tribal culture as a whole, the pattern established throughout the varying Hopi stories is unmistakable—displeasure by the gods sealed the fate of transgressors. Whatever the reason, whatever the explanation, by AD 1270, all Puebloan sites in the Comb Ridge area and throughout the Colorado Plateau were abandoned. Most of their occupants moved south to form new groups or augment others along the Rio Grande (Eastern Pueblos) in New Mexico or other locations to the west—Zuni, Hopi, and Acoma (Western Pueblos).

Some cultural historians argue that the ancestors of today's Navajos (Athabaskan speakers) and Ute/Paiutes (Numic speakers) were in the area and helped force the withdrawal. The defensive posturing during Pueblo III times could be part of a strategy to protect the limited resources the pueblo peoples held. Unfortunately, there is no real evidence

The historic Ute camp shown in this picture illustrates why so few such sites are easily identified by archaeological means. After a few years, little would remain to distinguish it as a habitation.

of an invasion from outside and a land wracked by war. Violence—yes—perhaps caused by internal instead of external forces. There is also no evidence of the Puebloans returning to inhabit southeastern Utah, although there is proof of occasional visits. The Pueblo IV period (AD 1300–1600) did not have much, if any, impact on the Comb Ridge area other than for the inexplicable appearance of some Hopi pottery—mostly service (decorative) ware but also occasionally utilitarian ware. Archaeologists have recorded two separate finds of Jeddito Yellow Ware in association with crossover trails on Comb Ridge. Hopi pottery has also been identified at a small shrine or temporary shelter on Lime Ridge, as well as on White Mesa, in Cottonwood Wash, and in Whiskers Draw. What is not clear is if these sporadic finds of more recent Hopi materials represent occasional revisitation to the area or importation of Puebloan artifacts by non-Puebloan peoples involved in trade.

An accurate date of arrival for the Navajos and Utes/Paiutes is subject to debate for a number of reasons. Primary among them is the fact that hunters and gatherers have a small impact on the land, leaving little trace of their presence. Very few sites occupied prior to 1800 are identified as belonging to early Utes or Navajos. The problem of documenting their early presence is compounded by the tendency for a site to have multiple occupations by all peoples who depend on finite resources in a given area over time. Take Navajo Spring, for instance, at the foot of Comb Ridge west of Bluff. There can be little doubt, considering the importance of water in this area, that people from every era of prehistory and history used that source and the associated trail until rubble from road construction covered them in 1953. Concrete proof, however, is not readily available. Also, Navajo and Ute ceramics can be easily overlooked by archaeologists who are not attuned to searching for them. This has undoubtedly served to exaggerate their rarity. Likewise, prehistoric and historic rock art left by these people prior to EuroAmerican contact is poorly known and may be difficult to distinguish from generic, older Puebloan art.

Many scholars believe that today's Utes and Paiutes wandered from their homeland in the Death Valley area of southern California. Fanning out from this location, these two groups, both Southern Numic speakers, separated perhaps four hundred years ago as they settled in the Four Corners area.[29] Southeastern Utah represents the furthest eastern extension of the Southern Paiute in the form of the San Juan Band and the furthest western extension of the Southern Ute Weeminuche Band. The material culture of the two groups is hardly distinguishable; there was a great deal of intermarriage and, in the historic record, there is a lot of confusion between the two. Differences become a matter of degree, so for present purposes, the two will be simply referred to as Utes. On the other hand, literature credits the Navajo with migrating from Alaska and Canada, where other Atahabascan-speaking Indians live. Many scholars accept their arrival in the Southwest around AD 1300 and no later than AD 1500.[30]

Starting in the late 1700s, the Navajo and Ute archaeological records become more clearly recognizable in San Juan County. Navajo hogans and sweat houses made from rot-resistant juniper logs remain identifiable and have been widely reported throughout the area. Several "forked stick" (male hogan) sites in Butler Wash appear to date to the 1800s with rare examples of Navajo ceramics appearing on some of these sites.[31] The oldest identifiable Navajo site in the Comb-Butler area may be an ancient collapsed hogan located in Butler Wash south of Long Fingers Canyon; archaeologists have identified nineteenth-century Navajo pottery in both Butler and Comb washes, with equal amounts in each. Ute/Paiute presence is more difficult to pinpoint, continuing to be maddeningly elusive, even where historic accounts specify Utes camped. Wickiups and tepee rings leave ephemeral traces.

Ute and Navajo rock art is somewhat kinder, although distinguishing between the two, plus dating it, can be difficult. Navajo rock art is usually more formal, depicting

Among the oldest Navajo archaeological remains in southeastern Utah, this colapsed forked stick hogan near Long Fingers Canyon dates back to before the time of the Long Walk (1860s).

supernatural yé'iis (Holy Beings), elements reminiscent of sand paintings, or stylistically distinct horses. Ute rock art is often drawn with charcoal or pecked more casually, depicting bison, stick figures, and sometimes Ute-style clothing with attributes such as braids, fringed attire, and in some cases, plains-style headdresses. Rock art panels that appear to represent Ute work from the nineteenth century include the "Big Rock" site near Arch Canyon, a panel associated with a cliff dwelling in a tributary of Butler Wash, charcoal drawings in the Arch Canyon Ruin alcove, and various sites along the San Juan River corridor. As with the periods of Puebloan prehistory, there is still a lot to learn about the early presence of the Navajo and Ute inhabitants of the Comb Ridge area.

Probably no period of time and human activity captures the imagination of visitors to San Juan like that of the Ancestral Puebloan. Their life, culture, and technology speak of a people at home in a difficult environment. Their abandonment of the area is equally intriguing. As we learn more about their times, we desire to better understand them and why they lived as they did. The Comb Ridge area saw all phases of the rise and decline of this culture, playing its part in sustaining these people and preserving what they left behind.

Inside and Outside the Comb

Power, Prayers, and Protection

Lightning lives on top of those peaks. It comes down to earth from the dark storm clouds above. I have seen lightning in its physical form on the ground. It probably lives in pocket-like areas in Comb Ridge. The rocks talk. When we lived or herded sheep near the rocks, we could hear the wind talk through the rocks. The sacred winds dwell along the ridges of rock, too.

—John Holiday, Blessingway singer

John Holiday ate his pan-fried tortilla and canned mixed fruit with gusto, washing it down with strong black coffee. After fortifying himself for a day of travel, he reached for his crutches and moved slowly to the door and car beyond. Navajo moccasins, green and black plaid pajama bottoms, blue striped shirt, and a white/blue/red headband covered with Southwest designs spoke of casual yet traditional attire. There was no missing the large turquoise bracelet and bolo tie, and the headband, by which the Holy Beings recognized him. In contrast, the clothing of archaeologist Winston Hurst, with his baseball cap, and translator Marilyn Holiday, in her striped shirt and jeans, hinted of a different culture. A quick stop at a convenience store to get John some fig bars, "what used to be around before candy came in," and a strawberry drink, then we were off to spend a day visiting Comb Ridge.

Stories flowed. Filming movies with John Wayne, playing tricks on unsuspecting white crew members, the friendship of people now departed, were part of his banter as we drove thirty miles before leaving the highway. John, however, was also intent upon teaching us and imparting information for future generations. In a previous interview, he offered his feelings about such an undertaking.

> Once upon a time, we used to have a lot of medicine men who knew all the different types of sacred ceremonies and stories, but when you asked them about their knowledge, they would say, "What are you going to do with it? You are crazy and ill-minded."

Courtesy of Stan Byrd

John Holiday, Blessingway singer from Monument Valley, lived and worked in the vicinity of Comb Ridge and shared his extensive knowledge of traditional Navajo beliefs concerning the importance of this rock formation.

> Here's what I think. This is not so. It is a shame. All of these wise, knowledgeable teachings, sacred songs, prayers, and wisdom—everything there is to sustain life—they have taken to their graves. Nobody has that kind of knowledge to carry on these days. As for me, I will not do that. I refuse to do that. Whatever I have, my sacred songs, prayers, my voice, my wisdom, my acquired gift of knowledge, I want to share with anyone—young or old, male or female—who is wise and interested in learning. They can live by these sacred teachings and make it their beliefs. The wise ones who learn these teachings can pass it on for many generations to come. That is why I share it with those who want to learn just the way you are recording it now. I do not hide it.[1]

For the next nine hours, with the exception of a brief picnic lunch, the three of us remained under the tutelage of this master teacher who had lived, herded livestock, and traveled around Comb Ridge for many years. His recall was remarkable, his insight impeccable.[2]

Once the car stopped on top of Lime Ridge, the land began unfolding its stories. John pointed to rock features, naming them and sharing a bit of information about each. His teachings came from the narratives behind the ceremonies he conducted. In John's case, it was primarily the Blessingway. Elements of this ceremony accompany other rituals because it adds harmony and protection at the end of the healing process. Since the land figures in many of the stories, giving concrete relevance to sacred events, no single body of lore contains all of the teachings about a specific site. Rather, there is a multiplicity of meanings. The Blessingway, so familiar to John, derived from a different narrative with accompanying lessons than that of the Evilway. When I asked him if he had ever heard about a particular teaching associated with Comb Ridge, he emphatically said no, explaining that it was contrary to what he had learned. Other people, however, were very familiar with this understanding.

Our group stood upon Lime Ridge and looked to the east. Visualize Comb Ridge looming in the distance with Comb Wash at its foot; they parallel Lime Ridge in a north-south orientation for approximately nine miles. To the south run the brown turbid waters of the San Juan River while to the west lies Valley of the Gods. As John began teaching in earnest, the landscape transformed into a series of dominant themes. Supernatural forces lay ready to be summoned on behalf of mortal man. Stories of Holy Beings empowered the hills, rocks, river, and mesas with unseen forces. Complex Navajo thought and imagery united in a rational explanation, springing from chantways, of how to ward off evil. Indeed, the entire landscape was a series of sentient beings. Those who know the stories understand how to properly control and utilize these powers; those who do not can be seriously harmed. John focused on wind, lightning, snakes, bears, arrowheads, the San Juan River, and boundaries. By the end of the day, these seemingly unconnected things melted into a cohesive perception anchored in power, prayers, and protection.[3]

John began by teaching about snakes, a particularly powerful entity. During the creation of this world, Big Snake, a Holy Being, performed a number of tasks. When the Twins, Monster Slayer and Born for Water, visited their father, Sun Bearer, they found Big Snake, Bear, Thunder, and Wind guarding the entrance to this god's home. Big Snake and Bear also protected Changing Woman, wife of Sun Bearer and mother of the Twins. She, in turn, gave these two protectors as pets to the Navajo people as they traveled about. Big Snake became both a help and a hindrance. He hunted game for the travelers, who fed him from a basket of corn pollen, but became increasingly tired and had to be carried. He rested at a number of places, one of which is El Capitan (Aghaałą́—"Much Wool") in Monument Valley, where one can still see the coil marks around the southern exposure of the rock. He became so heavy that his transporters left him behind.[4]

Big Snake appears in other stories. One tells of him crawling into a deerskin with all of the other deer coming to him as pets. A hunter showed disrespect to him and so he hid all of the game animals by having the winds drive them into seclusion. Black God eventually restored the animals and sat with Big Snake in a ceremony to heal the now sickened but repentant hunter. W. W. Hill suggests another connection to hunting through what he called the Big Snake Huntingway. Although much of the information concerning this rite is now lost, Navajo informants familiar with the practice described the hunters as

With a head shaped like an arrowhead and coils like the entrenched meander of the Goosenecks, this rattlesnake is a powerful relative to the Navajos' Big Snake.

"attack[ing] like snakes from ambush."[5] Big Snake uses magnetic powers to lure the game into striking distance and then envelops his prey.

A number of stories apply the motif of a beautiful woman marrying a snake, disguised as a handsome man, only to awaken to the real situation. Narratives associated with the Plumeway, Navajo Windway, Big Starway, and Shootingway feature Big Snake or snakes in some aspect. The Flintway, Windway, Small Windway, Shooting or Lightningway, and Starway provide effective elements to counter the illness caused by snakes.[6] According to Gladys Reichard, "The Shooting Chant is armor against diseases caused by snakes, lightning, and arrows, but the Wind Chant features snakes as extensively; it protects against their power and the harm of storms."[7] Types of illness may include leg and neck pain, crippling disease, urinary or reproductive tract sickness, and unnatural swelling of the stomach.[8]

Traditional Navajo belief suggests that snakes have great wisdom. Father Anselm Weber from the Saint Michaels Mission in Arizona noted that snakes are associated with luck in gambling and "believe them to understand human languages, to be good listeners, and to be able to turn to evil account what they have heard."[9] Because they are sentient beings who control power, snakes should not be killed but only removed from one's presence. If they are destroyed, the person who dispatched them needs to have a ceremony performed to drive the snake spirits out of the body. Also, certain stories are not told until the frost is in the ground and snakes, spiders, and other warm-weather creatures are asleep so that they will not listen and be offended.

In August 1994, Navajo women using the restrooms in an administration building in Window Rock, Arizona, spotted a snake in a bathroom stall. The incident created a large stir, and the reaction to it was widely publicized and studied both on and off the reservation. Maureen Trudelle Schwarz, an anthropologist living in New York, analyzed the cultural reaction to the event.[10] Summarizing her findings, she determined that snakes are powerful beings that need to be treated with respect. The appearance of the snake was an omen for all concerned, and medicine men needed to interpret the message. All snakes are descended from Big Snake and hold part of his power. Snakes affect humans particularly through body secretions but also hair, nail clippings, etc.; when a snake comes in contact with these elements, it may gain control or influence over the individual. And in the time of the myths, snakes assumed the role of inflicting certain types of disease on humans. A final point is that in the Navajo universe, everything is either male or female, but within an individual, animal, or object, there are both male and female powers. The male power (naayéé'jí) exerts the ability to harm and destroy while female power (hózhǫ́ǫ́jí) is peaceful and benevolent. These forces can either help or harm. Yet male power can be as much for protection for good as for offensive action to destroy.

This positive power is also seen in fire pokers, used to stir ashes and coals, but which also symbolizes protection for the home. Often referred to as a "home-sitter," a poker carved from piñon wards off evil as a common object of home defense. In curing ceremonies, four fire pokers represent bull snakes that turn the effects of witchcraft away from the injured. During the time of creation, mythological snakes selected how they wished to be represented. "'A dark big reed must be my prayerstick, my Grandchildren,' said Big Snake. Jet is his sacrifice, with tobacco. Endless Snake has no prayerstick, 'but I wish to appear in sandpaintings, and this shall be my prayerstick.' He usually furnishes the border around sandpaintings. . . . [The prayerstick] of Bull Snake is made of reed and painted yellow."[11] Snakes have special names used only in ceremonies. A male rattlesnake is "The Youthful Chief Reared in the Earth with Dark Moss," a female is "The Maiden Chief Reared in the Earth with White Moss," and a bull snake is "The Youthful Chief Whose Body is of Pollen and Who was Reared in the Earth with Yellow Moss." [12]

By now, it should be apparent that Big Snake and his earthly offspring control significant power. Comb Ridge and its environs represent that power. A half-dozen sites connected to Big Snake and his ability to protect lie within a ten-mile radius; there are undoubtedly corresponding sites on other parts of the reservation. Some Navajo elders suggest that Comb Ridge is a frozen part of Big Snake, with its head pointing towards Blue Mountain.[13] Known as Arrow Head Big Snake (Tł'iish K'aa') or Big Snake, this reptile is said to have been able to fly through the air. Breathing for this creature transpired through the alcoves found along the ridge's side, the air passing in and out of these "vents". "Comb Ridge was not a rock when it was created, but was alive and moved around. The air pockets were created to give it air to breathe and to keep it alive. They are a part of its body like lungs through which it breathes. These air pockets were placed along its rib cage. When it was created it was little, like a baby, then it grew. It became very big. All the rock formations were alive at one time."[14] Falling rocks indicate the snake's "backbone" is injured, in part because of the highways that cut through it. The

Alcoves found along the length of Comb Ridge, primarily on the Butler Wash side, are said to be breathing holes that allow Big Snake, personified by this formation, to breathe.

snake cannot heal itself and feels disrespected. "It is still alive and can hurt people because it is never given any offerings."[15]

A snake becoming a solid rock formation is not novel to Navajo thought. Monster Slayer traveled the land searching for evil creatures to kill to make the earth safe. When he reached the Chuska Mountains in New Mexico, he found two huge snakes. He walked along the back of one, then stepped from one to the other and went on. "Since that time, the two snakes lie there, having turned to stone."[16] No specifications exist for the exact location of these two formations, but Comb Ridge (male) and the Hogback (female), its paired mate, lie within sight of the Chuska Mountains.

Elder Martha Nez tells of a place near Comb Ridge called Tó Adinidahaskaní (Place Where Water Collects). It is part of Big Snake, whose rattle is nearby. "They say that the tongue of the snake is at the other end, where it is smooth on the rock. Where the black rock ends, people say that is its hole. . . . The snake was returning to its hole, but was turned into stone before it reached home."[17] Lime Ridge shares strong ties with Comb Ridge and its connection to Big Snake. On both flanks of this massive hill are wavy

Snake-like undulations on the east and west sides of Lime Ridge warn that Big Snake is present, as a protector of this land, and that his home on top of this ridge (not seen) is a sacred site.

patterns of variegated sand that look like a snake in motion. The horned snake on the western side of the hill is male and its mate on the eastern side female. They reside within the ridge and are in concert with Big Snake and his power.

On the surface of the hill, chert (commonly called flint) is scattered about, said to be the scales or skin of Big Snake.[18] At the top of the hill, facing Valley of the Gods, sits Sugarloaf rock formation. One story tells of it being a male hogan with disobedient children trapped inside by Sun Bearer. Others say that it is the forehead of Big Snake, his home, or a shield that protects him.[19] Most agree with John that "this ridge, where all the snakes once lived, is our shield against all bad and evil things. We bring our offerings in prayers and songs to this ridge when we need to. Recently, a man and his son came to me from Navajo Mountain to ask for a blessing of protection. His son left for the war in Iraq. Later his parents came to me and told of how their son wanted to thank me for saving his life. . . . That is how sacred and holy this ridge is to the Diné."

Behind Mexican Hat Rock lies "Mountain That Is Coiled" (Dził Na'neests'ee'ii), also known as Navajo Blanket. The pattern on the hill reflects the same design of the giant bullsnake that lives inside. Large puffs of air hiss at people who have tried to uncoil this snake. Bad luck accompanies those who trespass in this area and do not show proper respect. For instance, some people have drowned in the river below, said to have been killed by the snake that slips down to the water. Big Snake can also wriggle over the ground without touching it and can harm a person mentally just by being near. When people disappear in this area, the serpent receives the credit; and when an oil company could not drill successfully at a site nearby, it was because the snake kept pushing the drill bit out of the earth. Even white men have died here because of its power. Downstream two miles lie the Goosenecks, an entrenched meander formed by Big Snake's coils creating the river's sinuous path.[20]

Other places hold similar power and are just as dangerous. A hole on the east side of El Capitan once was the home of Endless Snake. This creature traveled on the rainbow and the wind.[21] Joe Manygoats, a medicine man from Navajo Mountain, describes the home of another huge serpent:

> It is a large hole with a bare entrance way. The vegetation around it is all dead or dying. People are forbidden to go near this place. This creature is capable of retrieving objects from far away. Long ago a man living near Navajo Mountain lost his horse. He searched and searched until he found his tracks leading up to the creature's home; there were no tracks going out. Evidently, the creature got his horse. They say this animal lures its prey from a distance of a mile, by way of electrical magnetic current or something like that.[22]

Other sites with similar phenomena are found in Kane Valley near the old VCA mine and Tsegi (Tséyi,' meaning Canyon), west of Kayenta.

Comb Ridge and its surroundings are places of power. Following traditional Navajo thought, Big Snake and those related to him have given the landscape identifiable, spiritually energized sites for healing and protection. John insists that whenever influenza or other sicknesses ravage the people, Navajos go to this location to make offerings and recite songs and prayers. Each place has an inner form, a spiritual essence that is human in form and communes with the person praying. Pollen and sacred stones, or nt'łiz, are accepted by this being.[23] The belief in an inner form extends to many natural phenomena including the four cardinal directions, wind, thunder, lightning, and water.

The power from these sites heals colds, especially those that are fatal. In time of war, combatants or their relatives come here to say prayers for safety. The first time this was done, prior to the Long Walk (1860s), a group of medicine men came to Comb Ridge and Navajo Blanket to create a supernatural, spiritual shield based in the power of Big Snake to protect the People. "That (Comb Ridge) is where the Diné language of protection came from—the sacred language of the code talkers used against the enemy. The prayers and sacred offerings were given to the mountain because that is where the sacred "'shake offs' were derived from Thunder, Bear, and Air (Níłch'i). It is all very sacred."[24] And that is why Slim Benally is assured through prayer that from Navajo Blanket, "beauty will come [his] way."[25]

Closely associated with snakes are lightning and arrowheads. Looking along the ridge in a panoramic side view, one sees serrated edges of rock that cut the sky. John believes that lightning could live in the points of the ridge or in pockets of rock along it. These pockets are also home to various types of wind. He described the lightning like a bird whose dark green is the color of algae found in water. The electricity goes to the clouds and returns to earth just as a bird does. When asked if ceremonial songs mention Comb Ridge, he answered yes and that reference is made to illnesses caused by harmful things that come from the heavens.

Suzie Yazzie described an experience related by her grandfather Hastiin Atine. This occurred in Mystery Valley, in close proximity to Comb Ridge. Lightning repeatedly struck a large oak brush-covered hill over the course of three days. The electricity became trapped in the roots of a large bush.

> He [Hastiin Atine] said it was a very small round object that was very shiny. It was covered with tiny lightning currents, like electricity, and made a sound each time it lifted the mound. Some people were observing it from a distance. Everyone was questioning what would happen to it and what they should do. "I know what to do," he replied. He prayed and prayed as he dressed like a Yé'ii Bicheii dancer, then walked up to the mound. He laid down a deer hide and spread it on the ground. The hide he used was not from a gun-or-weapon killed deer. . . . He then sprinkled some sacred corn pollen and ground white corn powder, yellow corn powder, mixed corn powder, and blue corn powder all over the spread deer hide on the ground. Then he prayed and talked to the lightning object, which later came out of the mound of roots and fell on the deer hide. He scrambled over and quickly wrapped it up in the hide. Within the next few seconds, lightning struck the hide and took the object away.[26]

Many people there wanted the "shake offs," or residue, from the captive lightning. Not until after medicine men performed a day-long ceremony was the powder given to those who wanted its protective power.

The Shootingway cures people who have come in contact with lightning-struck objects and other illnesses. Lightning, arrows, and snakes are central imagery in this story about Monster Slayer and Born for Water, who traveled about making the earth safe for humans. Armed with various kinds of lightning received from Sun Bearer, the Twins set about protecting the People. At one point in the narrative, Monster Slayer visits the home of the Rattler People, outperforms their chief, and receives different types of bows and arrows and sandpaintings with cures. Soon, he goes to Striped Mountain, home of the Arrow Snake People, and then Coiled Mountain.[27] He does not specify geographic locations, but one could make a case for the area around Comb Ridge as the latter site. Snakes, arrows, and lightning provide a complimentary mix threaded throughout this chant. The Shootingway philosophy integrates the three "'concerning-the-shooting-of-objects-that-move-in-zigzags.' Lightning, snake, arrow, or indeed any one of many other names might have been chosen; all indicate what the chant stresses."[28]

Whether cloud-to-ground or ground-to-cloud, this "male" lightning is said by the Navajos to have been used by Monster Slayer and Born for Water to kill the monsters that roamed the earth. Female heat lightning is not as destructive.

John believes this ceremony was "passed down through generations—only by the Holy Ones—it is not a man-made ceremony." While he does not practice it, he knows that it and other sandpaintings include special sand taken from Comb Ridge. The sand does not come only from here, but it is one of a number of sites that provides materials. In addition to the complex practices of the Shootingway, medicine men leave offerings at lightning-struck trees and other places associated with it. Herbs and powerful songs, so powerful that one should never sing them while riding in a car or on a horse, are other ways of addressing lightning and thunder. When doing so, offerings and prayers are used, or else lightning will strike. "Lots of lightning prayers are said to calm it in some way. It is told to keep up in heaven as is the wind. This is why they are sung."[29]

At the creation of this world, Decorated Rock, one of four giant arrowheads, released water covering the earth. Through this connection, Comb Ridge becomes another protective symbol. John, speaking of the giant arrowheads, says, "They are all related, just as we people are. We are one. They all live like we do altogether as one." Martha Nez believes that Comb Ridge itself is one of the four arrows that provide protection around the borders of the land of the Navajo. Billy Yellow, a medicine man from Monument Valley, and Mary Blueyes from the Bluff area agree. They view Comb Ridge as an arrowhead that extends all the way to Blanding, but it also is a ridge made out of arrowheads lined in a row. The undulating serrations caused by its peaks are separate arrowheads, each providing individual and collective power and protection.[30] Mary suggested it was made of flint, a word synonymous with arrowhead and identified with armor used by Monster Slayer.

The belief for this extends back to the protective flint armor and arrows given to the Twins by Sun Bearer. Before returning to earth to kill monsters, the boys received arrows made of chain lightning, sheet lightning, sunbeams, and rainbows as well as protective clothing of flint. Thus prepared, they were ready to destroy the evil creatures, each of which had its own qualities and means of protection. Yé'iitsoh (Big God) wore armor, which, once pierced by Monster Slayer's arrows, shattered and scattered. That is why one finds flint strewn about the land. Then Monster Slayer said,

> "Let us gather those flint flakes. Our people can use them for knives. They can use them for arrowheads. They can cut with them and hunt with them."
> "Yes they can," replied the other.
> "That way we can turn Yé'iittsoh's evil into something good."[31]

Arrowheads, knives, and other objects made of flint are synonymous with protection and safety.

Another monster, Walking Rock (Tsé Naagáí), had to be killed in a different way. He crushed those who came close. "Monster Slayer made a trail of arrowheads for him. The series of points went from Dennehotso through Kayenta and on top of Black Mesa. Today they call these arrowheads Comb Ridge and El Capitan. Some are black lava. Luckily, this monster ran into these arrowheads which chipped off his body, killing him. Monster Slayer collected the broken rocks that were its body and took them home as his trophy."[32]

Manmade arrowheads flaked from flint hold special ceremonial powers to cure and protect. Just as snakes are related to Big Snake, so too, are arrowheads connected to the world of the sacred. Monster Slayer gathered flint and learned arrowhead's protective prayers; medicine men invoke this power on behalf of a patient. Flint's hardness, the sound as it rattles, and reflected light representing lightning, give it power. Horned toads use it as protection against lightning and are able to fashion their own points. As mentioned previously, arrows are an integral part of the Shooting Chant, the theme of which highlights "things that move in a swift, squirming fashion; it is a chant in which lightning, snakes, and arrows are closely identified." [33]

A person finding an arrowhead says a small prayer and inhales over it four times. The finder offers words such as, "From behind this arrowhead bad ailments will not go" or "In the four directions black arrowhead will protect me."[34] This keeps harm away. The recipient feels, "This is a very sacred, holy thing that came into my possession."[35] Fred Yazzie explained the thinking behind these protective powers. In his view, Ancestral Puebloans made these points. "The Navajo collect these arrowheads, which have already killed off enemies or dangerous animals. So the people think that because they have already killed these things, that power will ward off disease. They use them to shield the patient and others involved in a ceremony. When this protection is used, the unseen evil force goes back to where it came from."[36] S. P. Jones summarized just how important arrowheads are in healing and protecting. When talking about Ancestral Puebloans and the things they left behind, he was not overly concerned, until he considered chipped points. "The arrowheads are ours. In ceremonies we hold them against our joints or put them with herbs and water to drink. They are sacred to us. . . . Lightning has an arrowhead. We are built as an arrow—our body is the stick part and our head an arrowhead. . . . May I walk in harmony, being shielded by my arrowhead. May I live a few more days."[37]

Winds blow rain clouds across Sugarloaf near Comb Ridge. This rock formation is the home of Big Snake, a shield that protects him, and a male hogan, within which disobedient children are confined.

Just as arrowheads protect, so too, can Wind. As one of the four guards stationed outside Sun Bearer's home, Wind can take many different forms and hold various powers. Gladys Reichard provides an extensive list of its functions. Wind gives life—the whorls on a person's toes, fingers, and top of the head are proof that it is a life-giving force within the body. It is personified as a holy being and as a group of holy beings who assist but do not require an offering from man. Wind mentors and can forewarn of approaching danger; it also reports events and thoughts, be they good or bad. And Wind has both a helpful and destructive side.[38] The interconnectedness of Wind with life begins with birth and ends with death. When a child is born, the winds argue as to which one is entering the body; once it does, this determines how long a person will live. "The wind will already set a day that it will leave your body and a person does not live any longer than that."[39]

There are two different types of wind. The first is níyol or the wind that one feels blowing against the skin. This is a physical manifestation of the second type, nílch'i, which is the spiritual force or being behind níyol and which acts in much the same way as the Christian deity, the Holy Ghost. Both are powers designed to aid, instruct, and warn. It is also something that man can appeal to and through. James McNeley's extensive study *Holy Wind in Navajo Philosophy* examines many of nílch'i's functions.[40] In relation to Comb Ridge, it is important to understand that there is a large body of teachings concerning Wind, and that only part of it is discussed here.

The alcoves and potholes found along Comb Ridge are Wind's home, and when the wind blows, it is moving inside. The round holes on top of the ridge are called "[Wind's] Tracks on It" and the alcoves on the side are "Tracks Along Side of It."[41] John tells of hearing the winds blow within the ridge. Wind is present throughout. Anywhere along this 100-mile stretch of rock, a person appeals to Wind's power, giving offerings and prayers to prevent Wind's harm. One time a group of people from Kayenta and Black Mesa came to John fearing the onslaught of a destructive gale. He went to the head of Comb Ridge near Tonalea.[42] There, he placed his offering of ntł'iz, uttered a prayer, and the clouds, wind, and storm dissipated. The Twins were the ones who accepted the offering of "sacred stones" and calmed the elements. John's prayer asked his "big brother [Monster Slayer] to have mercy on the people, to not come this way again," and to recognize, "I am here below among these people."

During this ceremony he "prayed from 'head to toe,' because it is said that it (Comb Ridge) is full of holy wind spirits of all kinds. . . . These days nobody does the sacred offerings. Back in our ancestors' day, one would ride, ride, and ride their horse to Comb Ridge, just to say their prayers and place their sacred offerings."

Lack of respect can result in death. John told a short story of how fourteen Ancestral Puebloans ascended Comb Ridge with an object that allowed them to bore holes in its alcoves and the surrounding mesas. The tool went against "nature," the winds became angered and "sucked out all the living Anaasází from their dwellings and killed them. But the Diné were put inside the mountains—way, way, way inside the mountains and were not brought out until the destruction was over."[43]

The destructive power of wind has been a force to be reckoned with since the creation of the earth. In the beginning, First Man formed four different types of wind—White (east), Blue (south), Yellow (west), and Black (north)—then placed them in his garment to make them holy. He next stationed four young men, each one in a cardinal direction, to watch over these winds, then created Striped Winds to the east and west and Twisted Winds to the south and north. "And they all are things to be feared."[44] Big Wind is the tornado and comes in the four colors. This wind can be a messenger of future bad news and may pick up belongings. The small whirlwind that circles about an open fireplace is called the Gossiping Whirlwind. It collects bad conversation from the earth and brings it back to the Holy Beings. These and other types are holy wind people.[45]

Navajo Blanket or Mountain That Is Coiled is said to be the home of the Wind. In Gilmore Graymountain's mind, it has been "set aside" for this purpose and should be treated with great respect, just as it is for Big Snake.[46] Ada Black agrees. Speaking of Navajo Blanket, she recounts that it, too, is the home of different winds, which made the swirling marks on its exterior. There are big winds and small ones, but either one can be

Courtesy of Kay Shumway

Navajo Blanket, or Mountain that is Coiled, is said to be the home of the Wind. Its swirling patterns and variegated rock formations are visual representations of the invisible forces of wind.

approached because "it is right there [Navajo Blanket] that prayers are offered."[47] After Ada and her husband asserted again that the winds live there, she explained how they act and are handled.

> Wind takes the lives of people and their homes. The big wind (tornadoes and hurricanes) are very strong. When everything goes haywire, the big wind is given the right to take our lives. This is why it is very feared. The small ones, like a twister, are messengers. Sometimes it moves clockwise and other times counter-clockwise. They are like spies it is said. It also has a way of casting a spell. This type is called Young Female Twister (Ch'ikę́ę́ Naayisí) when giving it an offering. If it ever goes over you and takes a possession, you just let it go. Do not take the object back. You sprinkle the corn pollen after it and say that the thing you took from me will have no meaning now, however, if you put a spell on me it is no more. The curse is given when the wind takes the sweat and dirt from your body. By taking it, the wind is able to steal your thinking and you become confused. Sometime, in the days that follow, when the people go in deceitful ways where it looks like there is no more hope, Big Wind has been given the right to take up their lives, just as he did with the Anaasází. . . . If

> there is nothing wrong with your place, it won't come to your home or bother your livestock. Only when something is bothering your household will it do this. This is what was said.[48]

Wind has homes in other places. At Navajo Mountain, there lies a barren spot where all of the sand has blown away. Thunderous noises come from this area called "Where the Wind Blows It Out" (Hahwiiyoołii). Two days before violent weather sets in, Wind warns, through sound, what is to happen. On the south side of Navajo Mountain on the old trail to Rainbow Bridge is a large hole that descends into a rock. A whirlwind attacks those who get too close. One man threw a rock down the hole to test for depth. It finally hit the bottom, but immediately a powerful funnel of air rose and came out of the hole and scared the Navajo away. It is forbidden to go near these kinds of places unless the site is approached after using Wind's sacred name. There is another large hole on the north side of the mountain that is also home of Wind.[49]

The Comb Ridge area is filled with power. Different aspects of Big Snake and snakes, lightning and thunder, arrowheads and flint, winds and nilch'i have been discussed thus far. The relationships amongst these different elements are apparent, yet to truly see their integration and how this plays across the land, one needs to return to the myths. A brief paragraph from the Wind Chant illustrates how all of them tie together and are manifest through ceremonial objects and religious sites. Briefly, a hunter near Cabezon Peak in New Mexico killed a deer, ate some of its intestines, turned into a blue racer snake then crawled into the cave of Big Snake. His family became concerned and searched for him. Big Fly, a mentor, sent the father to the curly-headed Wind People, who instructed him about how to redeem his son through ceremonial means. The family gathered all that they needed and met the Wind People at the mouth of Big Snake's cave where they could hear him moving about. The Winds made four hoops and set them nearby.

> The Wind People and Thunder People were all dressed in flint armor and they prepared offerings to the Great Snake, and the boy's father was told to present these to the Snake, and that even if he was frightened, he must not run away. So he approached, lightning flashed, but he put down the offering in spite of his fear, and as he did so, a quantity of fighting snakes approached him, among them the blue snake which he knew was his son. The father caught the blue snake and threw him outside the cave to the Wind people and they passed him through the hoops, one after the other, and as he passed through them the snake skin split off his head, body, and limbs and he finally emerged in human form again and the people rolled the hoops toward the east.[50]

These same symbols and powers are a part of the Comb Ridge landscape and imbue it with potency.

Bear is another powerful symbol that ties into Comb Ridge through Elk Ridge. The Bears Ears is not only the home of bears but is an important site in a rich body of lore. Bears' sacred names—Reared in the Mountains, Roaming in the Mountains, and Roaming in the Woods—reflect the connection to high-forested areas that sit above the desert floor.[51] Navajo mythology tells of how Bear joined Wind, Thunder, and Big Snake as one of the protectors at the entryway of Sun Bearer's home. Bear and Big Snake served as guardians of Changing Woman, Sun Bearer's wife and mother of the Twins. And when the Navajo people traveled about after their emergence, these two animals protected them from enemies.[52]

On one occasion, The Arrow People attacked the travelers. Bear roared a warning then sang a song called "My-Home-is-in-Danger." He next performed a protective ritual, circled the People four times, bit the enemy as they advanced, and chased the remainder away.[53] Once the Navajos were safe, Bear took plants and arrowheads and placed them on the ground as he sang:

> *I make a mark, they won't cross it.*
> *Monster Slayer I am, they won't cross it.*
> . . . .
> *Black obsidian zigzag lightning darts four times from me stream out.*
> *Where it goes dangerous missiles will be scattered.*
> *I make a mark they won't cross.*
> *I come back with lightning streaming out from me in four places.*
> *I come back, dangerous things and missiles being scattered.*[54]

Thus, arrowheads, marked barriers, lightning, and the bear form a powerful protective force behind which Navajos live free from fear.

There are other protective qualities. When the People completed their travels, Bear became increasingly irritable and bothersome, so they sent him to the mountains. Each version of this story specifies which mountains, but for people living near Blue Mountain and Bears Ears, these two places are connected as one and the home of bears. Speaking of the future, Ada Black believes that when bears vanish, there will no longer be harmony in life. This is one reason why Navajos don't kill these animals. "They should be left alone so that there will be life in the future. Then, when the world is not right, they will become our shield. We will go behind them. We will walk the life path with these stories as our shield in the future."[55] She went on to say that servicemen going to war left prayers and offerings in these mountains and returned home safely; they were shielded from death.

Flint and arrowheads (béésh) are associated with bears. In prayers the two are linked—"With this arrowhead the bear will guard me"—meaning that the arrowhead will be the bear's armor that will protect him as he encircles the patient and guards him or her.[56] The song of the bear is protection also. "Even if you only knew this one song, you can be protected if you are staying by yourself. With that, it keeps the enemies away. The Bear's song is where the song of protection begins."[57]

The Female Mountainway tells the story of two sisters who visited various locations in their quest to become reunited. One woman wandered to the Bears Ears and spent the night. There she met some bears, played with them, and then sat upon a bluff and sang a song of loneliness. The next day she moved on, but her example is still followed today.

Bears figure prominently in the ceremony resulting from this story. It explains why bears of all kinds are associated with mountains and what to do when a person suffers from loneliness, sadness, or excessive weight loss. A medicine man may bring his patient to the Bears Ears, where he sings songs of comfort. Before and after a Blessingway ceremony, people may go there for a short prayer and dispose of yucca suds and materials from sandpaintings.[58]

Bears not only protect but can harm people. This powerful being is connected to evil, sickness, and death. The roots of the Evilway ceremony (Hóchxǫ́íjí) lie in the lengthy narrative of Changing Bear Maiden.[59] Despite small variations in the story that arise from the oral tradition, its main events tell of a young virtuous woman who lives with her brothers. She denies many suitors but through Coyote's wily trickery, marries him and begins to change. She learns how to transform through witchcraft into an evil powerful bear then tracks down and kills all of her brothers, except for the youngest one.

Wind (Níłch'i), who understands the wicked intent of her heart, whispers instructions to the brother and warns of her plans. He hides underground, but she discovers him. She offers to comb his hair and as she does, he watches her shadow turn from a kindly woman to a ferocious bear. Younger brother shoots her with his bow and arrows but Wind warns him that her life force (the element that prevents her from dying no matter how "destroyed" she may appear) is hidden in the brush. He shoots the life force. From it comes a liquid that runs across the ground and toward her blood that is also spreading. Wind warns that if the two liquids combine, not only will Changing Bear Maiden come back to life, but she will be even harder to kill. Younger brother takes his knife and draws a trench in the ground, creating furrows on each side. He then carves up the body, gives each part an injunction to become something good for the Navajo people and tosses them away.

This is the crucial part of the story. The body parts are scattered about today's landscape. When he cut off her vagina and threw it in a tree, it became a porcupine. He did the same with her left nipple, and it became piñon nuts; the right one became acorns, the glands within the breasts yucca fruit, and her entrails sorrel, dock, and other plants. He dragged her paunch to the water, which became alkali, while her limbs became various types of bears that he sent off with a strict warning to behave. The head he threw away is now the Bears Ears, while the furrow dug with his knife is Comb Ridge and Wash.[60] By these actions good triumphed over evil, and the slain brothers came back to life. Awareness of this account shields those who know it. Oscar Sloan said, "It is behind this [story] I have seen life. Now I have gray hair. It is because of this I have seen gray hair."[61]

The Bears Ears is also a male guardian, one of a pair, that protects Dibé'Ntsaa (Mount Hesperus in Colorado, mountain of the north) one of the four sacred mountains. The female counterpart to the Bears Ears is in the Carrizo Mountains, though no exact location is specified. It is said they talk to each other, one facing out, the other in.[62] Discussion of this being is found in the story of the Twins, who killed various monsters to make the earth safe for humans. Tracking Bear, one of these evil beings, lived in the Carrizos and was destroyed in much the same way as Changing Bear Maiden.[63] Bears as paired

Courtesy of Kay Shumway

The Bears Ears is an important landmark in southeastern Utah. Navajo ceremonial lore associated with Changing Bear Maiden and other narratives say that it is a place to rid oneself of depression and evil influences.

guardians are a common motif in the sandpaintings of the Mountainway, where they protect an entrance from evil.[64] Florence Begay explains:

> When the two bears are brought together, they take care of the mountain. For this reason, they have the shashchíín—miniature bears made out of special stones such as turquoise and jet, which are used when prayers are offered. The ones who have these are the ones who hold special prayers to ward off evil. . . . It is like this within the Navajo boundaries. The bear is standing to guard and another bear is guarding the opposite side. For that reason, when a prayer is being offered, there is a part that says the Great Dark Black Bear will stand guard, you will walk to protect or shield me.[65]

A different-colored bear may be called from each of the directions, bringing with it flint points to keep harm from the patient.[66]

Changing Bear Maiden is often associated with evil and mental illness. For instance, "when a person loses his mind or becomes insane . . . [or starts] to rattle their teeth or gnash them," a figurine of her as well as prayersticks are carved and placed with offerings at a sacred site.[67] An individual may have nosebleeds, crazy thoughts, and dreams about mountains. The Mountainway ceremony stops this.[68] Plants used to cure witchcraft and incest are picked on the Bears Ears. Once gathered, they are crushed and sprinkled around the home in a clockwise manner, the person being careful never to complete the circle, a protective barrier, and trap the evil in.[69] As with every power in the Navajo universe, that of the bear can help, cure, and protect, or curse and destroy.

Witchcraft is a malignant power feared by the Navajo, and not surprisingly, Comb Ridge is connected to it. Navajos, even medicine men, do not usually discuss this force, since to know too much is to indicate the possibility of practicing it. Indeed, medicine men and those who are wealthy are often accused of using this power for their own aggrandizement. Admission of practicing it leads to being outcast with the power turned against the person using it. There are extensive studies on this topic explaining the various forms witchcraft can take.[70] Here is only a brief glimpse.

Wherever there is power for good, there is also the potential for evil. Metaphorically, supernatural power is comparable to electricity—which can be both helpful and harmful—depending on its use and control. Snakes, wind, arrowheads, dinosaur tracks, water, bears, and a multitude of plants, animals, places, and objects have power for good and bad. The user is the one who determines how it is applied. John told of how he went to the head of Comb Ridge near Kayenta to perform a protective ceremony. In that same area, people say that witchcraft is powerful. Caves or cracks in the rocks may be entrances that open into an anit'į́įh báhoogan, or witch's home and meeting place. Incest, the murder of close relatives, the making of corpse poison, and witches' Sabbaths occur in these rooms, which are inaccessible to normal humans.

Skinwalkers, or people who control supernatural evil, are said to travel a route near Sand Island Bridge very close to Comb Ridge. The trail passes by the white-tipped bluffs to the south on the way to a place where the San Juan River joins a side canyon stream. Not far from there is a home for the practitioners of evil.[71] A few miles from this trail sits Designs on the Rock (or Decorated Rock), the arrowhead that carved a path through Comb Ridge. On one side of the top of the rock is a thin flat spot where witches hold meetings. Another site called Tsézhiin'íí'áhí, or Standing Black Rock, has strong powers used against people. The rock is witched and can cause starvation.[72]

In John's view, witchcraft sites are also connected to the Anasazi and their ruins. Again, studies on the Navajo perception of the Puebloans show that there is an extensive lore concerning these people.[73] The Navajo see them as gifted and blessed by the gods. They became complacent, ignored religious responsibilities, held nothing sacred, misused their powers, flaunted their knowledge, and became evil. The Holy Beings, shocked at this behavior, destroyed them by wind, fire, and other means. What is left on the landscape for today's inhabitants are the remains of a blessed people who forsook their beliefs and were punished. Additional Navajo beliefs concerning the Anasazi and witchcraft will be discussed in chapter 7.

A final place of power is the San Juan River that cuts through Comb Ridge. Viewed as a northern boundary of Navajo land, the river is one of four bodies of water that protect where the People live. Just as each of the Four Sacred Mountains has distinct

Copyright by Andrew Gulliford

The San Juan River cuts through Comb Ridge at this site called the Rincon. With Raplee Ridge in the background, the remains of the Amasa Barton Trading Post in the foreground, Chinle Wash around the river bend, and San Juan Hill nearby, this is an important nexus of historical events.

characteristics, so do the San Juan, Colorado, Little Colorado, and Rio Grande rivers. The San Juan is male with the female Colorado River its mate. At one time, the two met near Navajo Mountain, where the San Juan flowed over the Colorado, but today it is no longer possible because of Lake Powell.

The San Juan River is known as Old Age River (Są́ Bitooh), Male Water (Tooh Biką'ii), Male with a Crooked Body (Biką'ii Bitsíís Nanooltł'iizhii), Decorated with Abalone Shells (Bikáá' Hodiichíłí), and One with a Long Body (Bits'íís Nineezí). It is a powerful river described as an older man with hair of white foam, as a snake wriggling through the desert, as a flash of lightning, and as a black club of protection to keep invaders from Navajo lands.[74] To some, the sparkle on the surface represents the shine of lightning. Prayer and pollen invoke the spirit within, which may be connected to protection through "singing the ways of the snake."[75] Certainly, its holiness is called upon to help the traveler obtain goods and enjoy safety. To Tallis Holiday, leaving an offering on the shore of the river helped him achieve his goals after he crossed.

> When a person comes to the river, he offers his corn pollen for a good journey and prosperity. "I will receive many things with this small amount of money or trading items." The people pleaded with the river's holy being. A long time ago, the river was the boundary to keep the enemy out.[76]

Crossing to the north side of the San Juan River places the traveler in enemy territory. Before going to the far shore, a person offers a prayer asking the spirit of the river to wrap its protective shield about him before he enters the land of the Utes and the white man. Florence Begay recalls how Navajos prayed against their enemy. "The prayers were a tool to defeat evil or to hide behind for a safe journey."[77] In addition to protection, rain, grass, and other good things come to the person who beseeches. Now that this practice of prayer for protection and assistance is no longer being performed, the land is dry, rain has decreased, accidents have increased, vegetation is short and withered, livestock is dwindling, drowning is prevalent, and harmony is scarce. When people paid respect to Navajo boundaries, life was safe and happy.[78]

Boundaries separate sacred from profane space.[79] The land bounded on the south by the San Juan River, on the north by Elk Ridge and the Bears Ears, on the west by Navajo Blanket and Lime Ridge, and on the east by Bluff, holds tremendous meaning for the Navajo people. Snakes, lightning, arrowheads, wind, bears, Puebloan sites, witchcraft, and the river are not unconnected physical entities but powerful religious and philosophical things that lead directly to sacred teachings. Power, prayers, and protection are their theme.

Do the Navajo, then, look at Comb Ridge and its environs as a physical barrier that is a spiritual boundary of power? Definitely. Ada Black, among others, recalls, "Comb Ridge became a shield and boundary at the time the monsters were killed. The rocks were red and made into a ridge. It starts close from the Bears Ears. My maternal grandmother said a long time ago the boundary was made here."[80] When asked why there was a need for a boundary, she explained that after the monsters were killed, the People still feared they might be harmed. The Holy Beings created the boundaries to be shields through ceremonies. These shielding powers "will probably be used in the future. These are very powerful and when a person makes a prayer offering there, it will serve as a shield."[81] No single power dominates; they are all connected, each stemming from a different ceremonial belief and practice.[82]

John referred to Butler Wash on the east side of Comb Ridge, or the side where the Utes and white men live, as "outside" and Comb Wash as "inside." When Navajo people crossed the ridge heading toward Bluff, they left prayers and pollen at its height before descending. Travel is an important aspect of Navajo life, both in the past and present. Crossing from a safe haven to a place of potential danger requires spiritual precautions and supernatural help. Returning to the Twins traveling to see their Father, a motif of travel, danger, and protection continues to this day. Joe Manygoats, in recounting this tale, included many of the forces connected to Comb Ridge.

> The Twins came to two large bears guarding the entrance to the Sun's home. They laid crisscross at the door. Again the boys used the sacred feather [with supernatural powers] to cross over these dangerous animals. On they went and came upon two huge snakes and they used the sacred feather to cross over the top of them and went on. Next they came to two thunder-beings who lay crisscross guarding the entrance. The boys spoke to the two thunders and used the feather to cross over them, too. Then they came to two lightning-beings that killed by flashing back and forth. They also guarded the entranceway. Once again, the boys spoke to the lightning and used the sacred feather to cross over them. Next they came upon two wind beings. It was Black Wind and Blue Wind. They lay crisscross guarding the entrance. Once more the boys crossed over. When they arrived at the door of the Sun, they encountered another guard. It was black flint. It made a "swooshing" sound as it mashed together like a pair of scissors. Once again, the boys used the sacred feather to cross over the flint stones. The two boys then reached their destination.[83]

These same types of creatures guard part of the northern boundary of Navajo land. Undoubtedly, there are other areas surrounding the reservation that have their own protective sites and powers. For the Utah Navajo, Comb Ridge is a special place of power for protection through prayer.

As our SUV climbed onto the pavement after a day of dirt, we headed west. The sun, already low on the horizon, bathed the landscape in late afternoon light, accentuating the yellow, orange, red, and gray of the sandstone. Comb Ridge glowed in the rearview mirror as we glided up, over, and down Lime Ridge, passed Valley of the Gods, then on to Monument Valley. John shared more experiences. The depth of teachings clung to our thoughts. None of us could look at the land with the same eyes that we had started with that morning. San Juan River, Navajo Blanket, Bears Ears, Lime Ridge, Sugarloaf, Comb Wash, the ridge, alcoves, and Butler Wash, were now not just names on a map but places of power. Identified in narratives and through teachings, this area held significance far beyond the rocks, blue-green sagebrush, and a few stories. It was a portal of protection and a place to pray for the good things of life. As John said earlier that day, as he talked about a place on Comb Ridge:

> You make sacred offerings here when you are in need of special blessings. It has the "forces" of the earth, the universe, the mountains, waters, rocks, mesas, and all the land that exists to the ends of the earth. We pray for peace, "hózhǫ́ǫgo" beauty, and harmony for all living things on this earth and the universe. We pray for the environment. We pray for our protection and to live without harmful obstacles getting in our way. These were the sacred prayers of our forefathers and we still pray the same.

So may we all.

4

Navajos, Utes, and Mormons

Settling Comb Ridge and Its Environs, 1860–87

This country is mine and I feel like it is my mother because it has hidden me, hidden my relatives in times of conflict, and saved them.
—Eddie Nakai, San Juan Navajo

If ever there was a need for Navajo power, prayers, and protection it was during the "Fearing Time" (Náhonzhoodą́ą́') that began in the late 1850s and continued to 1868. While on a national level the westward movement, including Mormon settlement, continued, the government displaced eastern Indian tribes, and the Civil War (1861–1865) raged, the Southwest had its own bed of conflict. Broken treaties and cultural misunderstandings between the U.S. military and the Navajos led to open conflict. The general population of Navajos went to war not only with the government but also with New Mexican and Native American groups such as the Hopi, Zuni, and other pueblo tribes. For those Navajos living in the Utah region, the most feared enemy was the Utes, who were particularly effective in aggressively ferreting out, killing, and capturing their enemies. The great roundup of the People (Diné), the Long Walk from places like Fort Defiance, and the eventual incarceration of over eight thousand prisoners at Fort Sumner on the Pecos River are milestones in Navajo history.[1] For many of the People living in the Four Corners region, the area's isolation offered a place of protection.

The Utes were the primary salient of the military's campaign in the northern part of Navajo lands. Having shared a bittersweet relationship of peace mixed with hostilities, the Navajos and Utes finally broke friendly ties over a series of tit-for-tat incidents. Since the U.S. military sought an economical way to bring in a widely dispersed foe, the Utes became one of the "weapons" of choice. Highly mobile, skilled in fighting, and knowledgeable of the terrain, they prosecuted a scorched-earth policy that caused thousands of Navajos to either surrender or scatter to peripheral hiding places. That is why in 1860 Colonel T. F. Fauntleroy requested the use of three hundred Utes to serve against the

H. S. Poley, courtesy of Denver Public Library, Western History Collection

Utes in the Four Corners region were extremely effective in hunting small groups of Navajos and either capturing or compelling them to surrender and move to Fort Sumner. Armed by the military, knowledgeable of the land, and highly mobile, the Utes helped force Navajo dislocation from traditional territory.

Navajos "as they do not require pay as soldiers but only to be supplied a short time with provisions until they can get well into the Indian country. . . . It will at once have the effect to get the cooperation of a most valuable force and at the same time employ these restless people, who otherwise must foray upon our own settlements."[2] Once set in motion, the plan proved highly effective.

For the Navajos inhabiting the San Juan region located in or near Ute territory, events took a frightening turn. Wolfkiller, a Navajo living in the Oljato area, left a chilling account of what it was like to live during this time.[3] He tells of seeing signal fires lit on prominent terrain features to warn of hostilities, feeling helpless with uncertainty and having to be ever vigilant, moving constantly to avoid detection by Ute raiders, surviving in winter weather without permanent shelter, building fires near large rocks that acted like a chimney to dissipate smoke, and of surrendering his family to the soldiers to avoid any contact with enemy Utes.

The Comb Ridge-Bears Ears area received a number of Navajo families like his seeking to avoid detection. Old Man Bob or People Lying Down at the Spring (Hastiin Tó Bitsíigiisitíinii) recalled that, "There were no permanent homes because there were Utes raiding in this country in those days so we were afraid to stay in one place too long."[4] His mother told him that her family used to inhabit the area between the Dolores River and the

Bears Ears long before the conflict began. Once the Utes started attacking Navajos, her family stayed more in the Bears Ears area, living in fear of a warrior called "Ute Warrior with White Hair" or Cabeza Blanca. Old Ruins, born in 1871, shared his family story of his mother, Woman Who Walked Like She Was Crippled (Asdzáán Jidii), and his father, also called Old Ruins (Kints'iilnii), living north of the Bears Ears. Crippled Woman's mother remained west of the Bears Ears and north of the San Juan River. A raid by the Utes pushed her group across the river, which then doubled back to the Bears Ears, joining a noted headman named K'aa Yélii.[5]

Not all Navajos were as fortunate. Woman Who Had Her House Burned (Asdzáán Kin Díídlii) was born at the Bears Ears, but with the start of hostilities she ended up on Black Mesa, Arizona. The enemy, under the leadership of White Haired Ute, raided her camp, captured her, and sold her as a slave to a Mexican; she did not return home for two years until the soldiers released the Navajos from Fort Sumner. "It was told by the Navajos that this leader [White Haired Ute] looked for Navajos who had sheep, horses, or young girls that he could capture and sell to other people such as the Mexicans."[6] Her great grandfather, Man who Regained and Lost Horses (Hastiin Bilį́į́' Nádláhí), received his name when Utes and Mexicans stole his large horse herd. After he obtained more livestock, the Utes again stole a large portion of them. Finally, his camp, comprised of many hogans located on Long Point near the Bears Ears, came under attack. Utes from the Dolores River area raided the settlement, killing him and others.[7]

These types of occurrences are typical of the well-known events of the time. Less known are the stories of those who were not detected and did not go on the Long Walk. Estimates vary as to their number, perhaps as few as two thousand or as many as eight thousand; no agent stood on the periphery of Navajo lands, counting those who escaped and refused to surrender.[8] Close to Comb Ridge, the canyons, mesas, ridges, and hills offered hiding places from bands of marauders seeking targets of opportunity. The Bears Ears, as a prominent terrain feature, served as a general descriptor for an area that included Elk Ridge and canyons feeding from there used by the Navajos. Many of these features parallel part of Comb, known by the Navajos at this time as White Ridge.[9] While the region north of the San Juan is generally accepted as being Ute territory, there is no doubt that the Navajos inhabited many of its isolated corners. Oral history accounts suggest that there were fairly peaceful relations between some members of the two tribes and that it was the Utes living farther to the east who actually hunted for those in hiding.[10]

Piecing together the story of those who either already lived in or fled to this region is detective work dependent primarily on oral history. What emerges is a fascinating story of perseverance in the face of fear and uncertainty. A number of Navajos lived along Comb and Butler washes before the conflict began. White Sheep (Dibé Łigai) tells of his family in this area, providing a sense of time-depth. His mother, Yellow Woman (Asdzáán Łitsoi) was born at Sweet Water (Tó Łikan at the foot of Comb Ridge where Highway 163 passes through today) and was a mature woman when she went to Fort Sumner. Her husband, Mister Heavyset (Hastiin Díil), was born in Allen Canyon at a place called

Copyright by Andrew Gulliford

The remains of old Navajo structures, such as this sweat lodge in Butler Wash, are silent remains of an active presence in this area from before the Long Walk to the 1950s and a final Navajo relocation.

White Spotted Reeds (Lok'aahagi) but did not go on the Long Walk, remaining with his family in upper Comb Wash, where he is buried today. His mother, Blue Coat Woman (Asdzáán Biéétoh Dotł'izhí), was born at the mouth of Comb Wash at a place called Beautiful under the Cottonwoods (T'iis Yaa Hózhónii) where she lived before and after her return from Fort Sumner. White Sheep's paternal grandfather, Mexican Clan People (Naakaidine'é), died at White Rock Point along Chinle Wash. Other friends and relatives that lived in the Bluff–Comb Ridge area before the Long Walk included Giving Out Anger (Hashkéneinii), White Sheep's paternal uncle; another uncle, Mister Rope, or Ropey (Hastiin Tł'óół), named because he made braided ropes; two brothers, Mister Wife Beater (Hastiin Be'asdzáán 'Atííłíinii) and Owl (Né'ash jaa'), the latter of whom acted funny and did not worry about things; and Small Man of the Tótsonii Clan (Tótsonii Yázhí) and Old Man of the Tótsonii Clan (Tótsonii Sání), who were friends with White Sheep's father.[11]

Paul Goodman tells of his family group and their association with the Bears Ears. His maternal grandmother named Shoot or Dragging Something was born on the south

Stewart Malcom Collection, Cline Library, Northern Arizona University

Hashkéneinii, photographed here in 1909, found refuge at Navajo Mountain during the 1860s. A frequent visitor to K'aa Yélii's camp on Elk Ridge, he was a powerful leader who gained wealth and respect as other Navajos returned after hostilities.

side of the Bears Ears, fifteen or twenty years before the People went to Fort Sumner. As a younger sister of Hashkéneinii, she remained north of the San Juan River during the Fearing Time. Her mother, Uses Club Downward (Yaago 'Adiłhaałii), and father, Very Small, were both born near the Bears Ears. His maternal uncle, Giving out Anger, married a woman of the Bitterwater (Tódích'íinii) Clan, making him an in-law by clan to K'aa Yélii (One with Quiver), the most famous of headmen living on Elk Ridge at what is now the Kigalia (anglicized name for K'aa Yélii) Ranger Station. Five or six hogans comprised his settlement located near a spring (K'aa Yélii Bitó) named after him.[12]

A pattern begins to emerge from these oral testimonies. The first is the importance of relationships. Extended families shared a general area of resources; intermarriage was common. The Bears Ears, known as a good place to hunt deer, herd livestock, collect berries, and obtain seeds and nuts, served as a magnet that drew Navajos to its resources.[13] Plants such as salt berry, three-leaf sumac, sacaton, and sand grass and piñon nuts, juniper berries, wild cherries, wild potatoes, and yucca fruit were plentiful.[14] Other places for collecting plants included Blue, La Sal, Henry, Navajo, and Sleeping Ute mountains, the area around Bluff, and the canyons along Comb Ridge.

Navajo clans, although usually not a corporate group focused on economic concerns, played a part in social organization. The Folded Arm People (Bit'ąhnii), Many Goats (Tł'ízí łání), Bitter Water (Tódích'íinii), Towering House People (Kin yaa'áanii), Salt (Áshįįhí), and Water's Edge People (Tábąąhá) were among the most prominent in this area of the people who did not go to Fort Sumner. Leadership by local headmen (naat'áanii) fostered another means of social control. Giving out Anger of the Red Running into the Water People (Táchii'nii) Clan moved away from the Kayenta area when soldiers with Ute scouts passed through the region. His small band of seventeen followers escaped to Navajo Mountain where they remained for four years in relative isolation before hostilities ceased.[15] Oral testimony suggests that Giving out Anger maintained ties with groups living around the Bears Ears even after he moved to the west. He is also said to have resided at Wooden Shoe

Butte and traveled as far north as Green River.[16] His wife, Black Goat (Tłizi Łizhinii), and brother, Gentle Man (Hastiin Doo'át'íní), also shared relations with Navajos in this area.

The most prominent leader around Comb Ridge was K'aa Yélii (One with Quiver). Born near Shonto, Arizona, about thirty years before the Long Walk, K'aa Yélii belonged to the Within-his-Cover People (Bit'ahnii) Clan. As a naat'áanii, he established his camp near the Bears Ears. He had at least two brothers, Manuelito, a famous war chief who was among the last to surrender at Fort Sumner in 1865, and Abaa'ade (a Ute name—no translation) who lived in Montezuma Creek.[17] The people accepted K'aa Yélii as their leader, adopting his policy of not provoking the enemy to avoid conflict. At the same time, he had an uncanny ability to escape raids and ambushes. He also was skilled in hunting and working with livestock. "These headmen . . . were good horse trainers. They trained their horses for hunting deer. They could ride these horses all day long and they would not play out. These old Navajos used to hunt in the Monticello area [Blue Mountain] when they did not have anything but bows and arrows, but they used to get the game they wanted."[18]

K'aa Yélii's sister, Woman with a Burned House (Asdzáán Kin Díídlii), lived in his camp behind the Bears Ears with other Navajos at Place to Escape from the Enemy (Naznidzoodii), a canyon that facilitated disguised movement off Elk Ridge.[19] Her husband, Mexican Man (Naakai Diné), was born in the vicinity of the Bears Ears, where the couple stayed during the Fearing Time. Her maternal grandmother (no name) was not as fortunate. The Utes captured and sold her to Mexicans, guarding her in a log cabin. She found a ladder inside and escaped, making her way to the mountains where snow covered her tracks. She eventually reached the San Juan River, recognized Shiprock, followed the south side of the river to Douglas Mesa, then wended her way back to Naznidzoodii and K'aa Yélii's band.[20]

West of the Bears Ears is a site called "Lonely Tree" or "Navajo Woman gave Birth to a Child." The family of Warrior Woman (Deezbaa'), who was born and raised on Elk Ridge, identified this spot where a pregnant woman was traveling. Wolves pursued her so she climbed a lone tree to escape and did not descend until she had given birth while resting in the branches of the tree.[21]

Navajo accounts often give an impression that few Utes and Paiutes lived in the area of the Bears Ears and Comb Ridge during the Fort Sumner period. Ute testimony is not as plentiful but is just as certain that their groups were in the same places at the same time. Anderson Cantsee remembers his mother, Paana (Bread), and his father, Čiyu̲'a (Combing Hair), who is buried in Butler Wash, living together in Allen Canyon during the Fearing Time. His maternal grandmother and grandfather are buried there too, indicating a lengthy acquaintance with the area. All of them hunted on Blue Mountain and the Bears Ears, shared the same camps with Navajos, traded buckskins for Navajo rugs, spoke both languages, and built hogans and shade homes similar to those of the Navajo. At the time of the interview, Cantsee was ninety years old, placing his birth shortly after the Long Walk. He recalls that as a boy living in Allen Canyon, there were ten Ute families subsisting on corn, beans, squash, and wild foods.[22]

Jim Mike, of Ute/Paiute ancestry, was five years younger than Cantsee, born west of Bluff, but has little family recollection of interaction with Navajos. His mother and father remained in the area where Blanding is now located, living in wickiups and tepees during the Long Walk period. There was never any mention of meeting Navajos while hunting or of even a presence north of the San Juan River, though Jim Mike had heard of K'aa Yélii.[23] Mary Jelly and her mother hunted on Blue Mountain and the Bears Ears, and although they met Utes in the vicinity, she insists they did not have homes or live in the area.[24] There is, however, other Navajo testimony that clarifies this seeming dichotomy of presence and relationships between the two groups.

At least in the Bears Ears and Navajo Mountain areas there were strong ties amongst some of the San Juan Band Paiutes, local Weeminuche Utes, and Navajos. Trade was an important element. For example, Giving out Anger was an "outstanding" trader, visiting many Utes and Paiutes who had moved around the Bears Ears. From this, friendships grew.[25] Items traded by the Utes included buckskins, buckskin clothing, elk hides and elk storage sacks, buffalo robes, saddlebags, horses, bandoleers, beaded bags, beaver skins, buffalo-tail rattles, pitch for ceremonial whistles, and baskets. The Navajos traded woven blankets, silver, and agricultural products.[26] Navajo Mountain provided red earth paint sold by Paiutes to the Utes.[27] Paiutes worked for wealthier Navajo families with large herds of livestock that required tending. Navajo informants also tell of using Paiutes to provide early warning of danger. George Martin says that his father first met the Paiutes in the Bears Ears country, and they became his "watchers."[28] Others mention Paiutes hiding Navajos from Ute raiders, of intermarriage, and of sharing resources. K'aa Yélii "had men posted to watch for the approach of enemy tribes," so that his group could flee.[29] Giving out Anger practiced the same technique at his camp near Navajo Mountain.[30]

Perhaps the most dramatic, documented proof of Ute, Paiute, and Navajo cooperation occurred in September 1866. A group of Capote and Weeminuche Utes and a few Mexicans organized a ruse to trap a group of Navajos living in northern Arizona. The plan was to send word that the Utes wanted to live in peace and in close proximity to them. After the Navajos arrived, the Utes would kill the men, enslave the women and children, and capture the livestock. Upon hearing this, White Haired Ute refused, saying that he had friends among those Navajos whom he did not want to kill. A fight ensued; the Capotes killed him then fled. Following retaliatory strikes, White Haired Ute's sons went with other Utes to "the neighborhood of Rio Dolores, Sierra Salir [La Sal Mountains], and Sierra Orejos [Bears Ears]" to "join as is supposed the [Weeminuche] and Pah Utes who had made friends with the Navajos."[31] Even with this slight leavening of apparent friendship, intertribal conflict with its fear and mistrust dragged on for another two years before the Treaty of 1868 ended hostilities.

The Navajos returned to the region they had lived in before the war, although many were slow to resume activities close to the Utes. The frontier quieted until Euro-American miners, cattlemen, and settlers began eyeing the region for economic development. Southeastern Utah, because of its formidable terrain, slowly entered the peripheral vision of land seekers during the late 1870s. Among the first groups of players to walk upon the stage were the Mormons.

On April 13, 1879, The Church of Jesus Christ of Latter-day Saints (Mormons) sent its first tentacles of exploration into the San Juan River area of southeastern Utah. The exploring party, in advance of planned settlement, was comprised of twenty-seven men, two women, and eight children all loaded into twelve wagons. They departed Parowan in southwestern Utah for the San Juan River.[32] Their travels took them into Arizona, across Navajo lands, and through a series of adventures that convinced them that this was not the best route for the main contingent of pioneers to take. They reached the San Juan River on June 1 then spent the next seventeen days establishing Fort Montezuma near Montezuma Creek and mapping the area between McElmo Creek and Butler Wash. The latter received its name from John Butler, who was among the first to explore this area east of Comb Ridge.[33] The group, with the exception of the Henry H. Harriman and James L. Davis families, departed north to explore a different route back to southwestern Utah via today's Spanish (Moab) Valley, Green River, and Salina.

Seven months later, roughly 250 men, women and children with eighty-three wagons and over one thousand head of livestock stood at the precipice known as the Hole-in-the-Rock above the Colorado River wondering if their newly carved road would suffice. Neither the southern or northern route of the exploring party was acceptable in the face of a supposed shortcut that took six months instead of the planned six weeks to complete. Blazing a trail down the twelve hundred-foot deep Colorado River gorge, ferrying families and equipment across a three hundred-foot wide river, moving the wagon train out of the canyon, traveling across slickrock and through a piñon-juniper forest, and wending their way another hundred miles to the San Juan River created an epic tale of sacrifice and hardship.

One of the key elements for success was route selection. Four men—George Hobbs, George Sevy, George Morrell, and Lemuel Redd—accepted the responsibility to find the best route to Fort Montezuma. They promptly got lost in the maze of canyons and wooded areas. Christmas Day 1879, found the four men out of food, wading through snow, and shrouded in a bank of clouds on the side of Elk Ridge without bearings. Hobbs, the only one who had previously been to Montezuma, climbed a mound given the name of Salvation Knoll and spied Blue Mountain to the northeast. The group identified its location but now faced a new reality—Comb Ridge. On the twenty-seventh, the party entered Comb Wash, exploring as they went. Hobbs recounts:

> The next day we came to a break in the cliff where the cliff dwellers had previously done a vast amount of work in making a trail [later known as Navajo Spring Trail] leading up the side to the top.[34] After repairing the trail in places and pushing and pulling our animals up jump offs that spanned the trail, we arrived at the top towards night. Going but a short distance further east we encountered another gulch now known as Butler Gulch, paralleling Comb Wash. Brother Sevy remarked that we might have to go up this wash 50 miles in order to get across, as the walls were perpendicular and obstructed our passage

Courtesy of Kay Shumway

The Hole-in-the-Rock party faced the daunting spectacle of Comb Ridge stretching as a barrier before them. Taken from the "Twist" (part of the route), the trail crossed a landscape dotted with sagebrush and juniper.

> going to the east. Night overtaking us, we camped in this small canyon, this being the third night out of food. I cut my name in the rock with the date I was there, not knowing that I would survive the journey.[35]

One wonders if this group ever saw the inscription "Louis Clift, 1870" carved in a boulder near Navajo Spring.[36] Perhaps a wandering miner or hunter, Clift may have been the earliest person to leave his name in Comb Wash, but he was not the last.

On another night of snow, a group of Navajos traveling south lost mounts, and a sense of entrapment in Butler Wash added to the party's discomfort. They eventually found a means across and headed to where Bluff would soon be established then on to Fort Montezuma. During the return trip, the four men rode with two prospectors, Ernest Mitchell, whose father operated a trading post in Aneth, and James Merrick. They parted company at Comb Ridge, the prospectors crossing the river there and heading south in search of Navajo silver mines, while the Mormons sought a glimpse of the wagon trains approaching Comb Ridge. The scouts entered one box canyon then shifted to a trail near what came to be known as Road Canyon, identifying it as the most feasible route, before returning to the main group.[37]

In the meantime, men with the main party built dugways and chopped a road through the piñon-juniper forest toward the east. A few weeks after returning to the wagon train, Hobbs left again for Fort Montezuma to bring supplies. He packed his mules, led them through the forest alone, and broke trail through the snow. He reached Comb Wash on February 22, noting, "I got out of this deep snow into a branch of the Comb Wash where the ground was bare. Here my mules would eat a little grass and then roll in the sand, which seemed to give them much pleasure, after being in the snow so long. The next day was good traveling down the Comb Wash."[38] For his return trip, Hobbs had prearranged a signal of three fires in a triangle from a prominent height to guide the wagon train in the proper direction. The answering signal came from Elk Ridge. Between the signal and the time that Hobbs rejoined the group, a party of Utes went to the main camp, received clothes and food, and told the Mormons that they had not seen anyone behind them on the trail. A short while later Hobbs entered the camp, allaying fears that he had been killed.[39]

Courtesy of San Juan County Historical Commission

Platte D. Lyman, a member of the Hole-in-the-Rock party, Bluff settler, active participant in the San Juan Co-operative Company, and San Juan Stake president, played a crucial role in establishing a Mormon presence in southeastern Utah.

By the end of March, the main party descended near Road Canyon and into Comb Wash. Platte Lyman recorded in his journal, "The road is dry but rough and rocky and very sandy. The water is very bad and feed pretty good." A day later he penned, "Drove 10 miles down the wash through very bad sand to the San Juan River where the company is camped and at work on the road. We cannot follow up the river, so we have to do some work to get up over the bench."[40] The trail carved out of the rock up a steep incline leading to the "bench" is known as San Juan Hill. Blocked by the river to the south and not ready to tackle the lengthy task of forging a route up Butler Wash, the pioneers opted for a short but steep sandstone road up to the more level east side of Comb Ridge with Butler Wash as the only major obstacle standing between them and the founding of Bluff. For five or six days, workers hacked and smoothed the rock surface so the wagons could ascend. They were not so busy, however, that William H. Hutchings and J. Smith could not take time to inscribe their names at the base of San Juan Hill, with the date of March 28, 1880.[41]

Within a few hours of the first day, the animals had "slicked off every spear of grass in sight."[42] Men drove the herds of horses and oxen across the river to graze on the sand hills to the south, drying their clothes in the sun as they guarded the animals. This area and all the way down to Chinle Wash would soon become a major crossing point because of the gravel bottom that offered more sure footing than much of the muddy streambed along the San Juan.

The challenge of ascending San Juan Hill became a defining moment for many who had already endured the Hole-in-the-Rock and other points of impossible terrain. The slick sandstone, steep slope, tired teams, exhausted people, and discouraging distance combined to persuade the travelers that Montezuma Creek was too far and that the flood plain where the city of Bluff now stands was the place to establish their community. San Juan Hill cast the final vote that convinced the travelers to end their highly memorable trip. Albert R. Lyman, a local historian who lived with many who made the journey, wrote: ". . . The horses and oxen trembled and fell and skinned their bony knees reaching the top [of the hill] with the expression of having just come out of a terrible convulsion. But San Juan Hill, with the slippery humps of its solid roadbed smeared and splattered with hair and blood, was serving then the only purpose it ever served. Not long after, a better way was found. . . . 'My horses were so poor and weak,' said L. H. Redd, Jr., 'that when I reached Cottonwood [Wash, that roughly parallels Butler to the west], they could hardly drag along. I was five days coming from San Juan Hill.'"[43] At the top of the hill, someone etched a heartfelt sentiment appropriate for all who made the ascent: "We thank thee oh God."

For a very short time, the settlers of Bluff maintained their ties with the people of Escalante and southwestern Utah, using the Hole-in-the-Rock Trail for primarily personal travel. Supplies came from southwestern Colorado and northwestern New Mexico, making the Hole-in-the-Rock Trail obsolete almost as soon as it was finished. This is true of the San Juan Hill section also, although a trading post, cattle range, and later, an oil field near Mexican Hat, demanded some type of access to the lands west of Comb Ridge. To meet this need, the people of Bluff widened an old Indian trail that wound through Butler Wash and up onto the eastern slickrock slopes of Comb, south to the San Juan River and Rincon, then up Comb Wash to the sandy grasslands west of the ridge.[44] Freight wagons trundled down this route by late 1883 and continued to use it for roughly thirty years before another road sliced through the lower end of Comb Ridge at Navajo Spring.

The establishment of Bluff dramatically transformed the history of Comb Ridge, moving the area from one inhabited solely by Navajos and Utes to a prominent landmark encountered on a daily basis by white settlers. Stories from both sides of the cultural fence record some first encounters. Lyman tells of when an older Ute man rode up to the advancing wagon train and asked where it had come from. "He dropped his jaw and raised his hands in surprise" when the settlers pointed in the direction of the Hole-in-the-Rock Trail and the Colorado River.[45] "'No!' he grunted in disgusted unbelief, they couldn't cross there; they might have crossed farther up, but there was no place to cross at the Hole-in-the-Rock. 'And the old man was perfectly right, affirmed one of the company, there never was and never will be a place for crossing at the Hole-in-the-Rock.'"

Navajo recollections of their first encounters with the settlers created vivid impressions. Men like Hastiin Joe, Old Man of the Big Water People, and Tall Man of the Mexican People met them as they cut the trail near the Bears Ears. The Mormons approached the Indians and asked if they had clothing or shoes. "We traded them some stuff for green coffee beans and sugar. Then they asked the Navajos where they could find a level place to plant corn, melons, and squash." Later, White Sheep, who was describing this event, noted that the "Mormons 'crowded' the Navajos out. 'They said, 'This is Mormon country.'"[46]

Courtesy of San Juan County Historical Commission

The Peter Allen home, established in early Bluff, is typical of what the pioneer settlers lived in for the first ten years. Many buildings served multiple functions but only this one was the first courthouse in San Juan County.

Hetty Nepah recalls Navajos living at Ledge Hewn Out (Bitát'a Íítsélii) where road builders blasted rock for the wagon route between the mouths of Comb and Butler washes.[47] This was a short, steep dugway up a cliff from the floodplain to the first bench above the river. The future held further displacement for the Navajos and Utes, leading Black Horse to tell his people that "the Bears Ears was Navajo country; that they should hold this country by all means because they had lived in this country long before Fort Sumner, and it has been Navajo country from the beginning."[48] Albert R. Lyman agreed, saying that, "If I had been a Paiute or Navajo, I'd have helped myself to everything the invader had."[49] The clash between cultures commenced soon after the establishment of Bluff, not only with the Mormons but with everyone who depended upon the land to survive.

The story of Comb Ridge now becomes inextricably connected to Bluff. As isolated as this small town was, there is a surprisingly well-recorded history of its first twenty years that came from the pen of Albert R. Lyman, born the same year the settlers arrived. His intimate knowledge of the land and its people provide a wealth of information that would otherwise have been lost. He lived in Bluff for twenty-five years, then in Blanding for another sixty-seven years, recording oral histories of those who lived through the events of this era. One cannot write the history of this town or Comb Ridge without resting in Lyman's shadow.

After laying out city blocks and drawing homestead lots, the pioneers embraced a three-pronged approach to economic development. The first two—agriculture and freighting—did not have a direct impact on Comb Ridge. Five years of fighting the San Juan River with its floods and low water, shifting channels, heavy silt content, and erosive qualities convinced the settlers that large-scale agriculture was impossible.[50] Freighting between the railroad and mining camps in Colorado required traveling long distances, removed men from the community for extended periods of time, and supported—but did not really build—the economy until other business, such as mining and oil, brought outsiders with money and industry to Bluff. At this point, the potential for growth lay in the livestock industry and the related operation of trading posts. The town soon accepted this reality and shifted from an agrarian emphasis to one of ranching.

Conflict followed. The high desert environment offered land with a limited carrying capacity. The Utes, as hunters and gatherers, depended on a wide-ranging cycle of travel to summer and winter areas to obtain different resources. Following the same pattern as the deer, one of their primary sources of food, they stayed in the mountains during the summer and the lower regions along the river and in the canyons during the winter. The livestock industry of the Mormons, non-Mormons, and Navajos depended on good summer and winter ranges and called for keeping competitors off. The Navajos' cultural agenda, while not unified like the livestock companies, encouraged expanding herds of sheep, goats, cattle, and horses. From sheep came wool and blankets, which were shipped to the East. The Utes reacted against this rising pressure and competition for the livestock ranges; for over fifty years, the jousting persisted, fostering animosity amongst all four groups.

The areas west and north of Bluff were favored grazing sites. Relatively close to town, making them within reach of assistance, the Bluff herds grazed under the watchful eyes of young men. Their numbers were relatively small compared to future herds, but cattle and sheep were the start of an ever-growing problem. Like many men who came through the Hole-in-the-Rock, Hanson Bayles arrived with only a handful of what he started out with. His holdings had shrunk from 21 cows to 6 when he settled in Bluff.[51] But it did not take long for Mormon herds to grow. Seven years later, there were three thousand head of cattle grazing the summer range on Elk Ridge.[52]

Reaction against this and the herds belonging to non-Mormons spawned intense retribution from the Utes. In 1881, a posse of Mormons traveled beyond the head of Butler Wash in pursuit of cattle taken by the Indians and viewed, for the first time, the lush pastures in the valleys below Elk Ridge. Shortly after, at the head of Butler, the white men intercepted a group of Utes coming from the Pinhook Draw fight on their way to Elk Ridge. The Indians had helped themselves to part of the Mormon herd but allowed the settlers to peacefully retrieve their stolen horses. As they returned to Bluff, however, the white men found many of their cattle dead or mutilated and left to die. Later, a similar incident repeated itself, with the Navajos returning stolen horses obtained from the Utes. That September, some men from Bluff crossed the river at Rincon and retrieved stolen cattle taken by a Navajo named "Hoskay."[53] Events of this nature were repeated numerous times. Accounts indicate Butler Wash and the Rincon were active thoroughfares for all concerned.

First Valley, known today as Whiskers Draw, and its vicinity enticed the settlers to greener pastures. Moving closer to Elk Ridge with its summer range, the advance of the cattle industry ran into four Navajo families living in the area with their flocks of sheep.

Courtesy of San Juan County Historical Commission

Prime grazing lands, as characterized by the Twin Springs Cattle Camp northwest of the Bears Ears on Elk Ridge, became contested territory between Mormon and non-Mormon livestock operations. The Utes and Navajos were equally slow to relinquish it.

Most likely one of these families was K'aa Yélii's, since in 1884, Lyman noted that this Navajo was there with his livestock when the first Mormons explored Elk Ridge.[54] While the settlers worked at persuading the Navajos to remain south of the river, the Utes were not ready to forsake their homeland. Mancos Jim and others killed more cattle, stole more horses, and refused to accept the loss of prime hunting lands. Moencopi Mike, however, softened his angry attitude when fed and encouraged by the explorers to grant permission to use Elk Ridge.[55]

Whiskers Draw and Elk Ridge were soon annexed as part of Mormon ranching operations. Platte Lyman and two other men made improvements in a spot near Whiskers Draw at a place that came to be known as the Milk Ranch. This first stake in claiming this area for the people of Bluff began as a dairy operation that produced milk and cheese sold in the town of Bluff and in the markets of Colorado. Access to this business and the ranges on Elk Ridge was by a trail that went up Butler Wash and over the Cheese and Raisins divide into Whiskers Draw. By the late 1890s, workers had forged a wagon road up Butler and into Whiskers and from Whiskers onto Elk Ridge.

In 1884, Bluff residents obtained a large flock of sheep from New Mexican herders; non-Mormon cattle companies to the north, Navajo herds pushing from the south, and

William Hyde, entrepreneur along the San Juan River, owned three trading posts, one of which was at Rincon, which had a water wheel for agricultural purposes and a flat-bottomed ferry capable of transporting fifteen customers at a time.

growing Bluff herds of cattle and sheep placed environmental strain on the ranges. Grazing land came at a premium. Kumen Jones, a missionary to the Indians, hoped to overcome the land issues by holding open discussions. "There was a big powwow held with all of the Utes and Paiutes that were come-at-able at that time and a treaty or contract was entered into with them, by which on our part were to pay the Indians two or three hundred dollars in flour, merchandise, and ponies. And with the exception of Posey and one or two others, the Indians lived up to their part of the contract very satisfactorily."[56]

Another spot that became increasingly important for the welfare of Bluff was the gap in Comb Ridge, where the San Juan River flows. This highly important crossing point was a check on traffic heading in both directions. The gravelly cobblestone bottom, the break in the ridge, the Indian trail in Comb Wash and Chinle Wash on the other side of the river, the accessibility of Butler Wash with its road, and the rock shelves and floodplains on both sides of the river encouraged a steady flow of people and animals through this choke point. Navajo herds forded the river heading north for summer pasture while Mormon herds went south for winter range. Known to the settlers as the Rincon (Spanish for "Corner"), this nexus became a natural place to establish a trading post.

William Hyde arrived in Montezuma Creek in 1880, opening a store and building a large waterwheel for his agricultural endeavors; both appeared highly successful. Wishing to replicate this success, he established a trading post near Comb Wash around 1883. Oral accounts from his two sons, Frank and Ernest, give conflicting information, with dates, place names, and historical events difficult to pinpoint.[57] Given the lay of the land, documented events, and information contained within their testimonies, the following scenario gives a plausible picture of what developed at Rincon, and Comb and Chinle washes in the 1880s and 1890s.

Exactly where the first of two posts sat is difficult to determine, but it was approximately 150 feet back from the river. A floodplain large enough to fit this description is upstream just around the corner from the Rincon and big enough to warrant a waterwheel for crops. The San Juan played a major role in both opening and closing this enterprise. The characteristics of this river varied with the seasons. During the months of May, June, and the first part of July, the water ran high, sometimes reaching flood proportions, overflowing its banks, covering the river valley with silt, and changing the course of its channel. Melting snow provided spring runoff with intense spring and summer storms adding a high volume of silt to the flow. During this period, boats at trading posts along the San Juan were essential. The months of July through January saw the river subside at the Comb Wash–Chinle crossing, reaching an average level of two to three feet and sometimes dipping to a foot during drought conditions. The Indians rode or swam their horses while wagons trundled their way over the gravelly, cobblestone bottom that provided sure footing for their teams.[58]

To accommodate his trade in horses and goods for Indian sheep, cattle, wool, and blankets, Hyde built a flat-bottomed boat with a shallow draft. Its dimensions, thirty feet long by twelve feet wide, allowed "the Indians to [ride] with their loads on their ponies, sit there, fifteen to twenty of them at a time and come over."[59] A cable anchored on both shores kept the boat from drifting and allowed for retrieval from one side of the river to the other. This large ferry operated for an estimated eighteen months before the river claimed it as its own. Starting on December 22, 1883, the area received the first of many prolonged dousings of rain and snow, lasting forty-eight hours.[60] One storm followed another. Heavy showers in February 1884, continued into March, raising the river seven feet above normal. Cottonwood Wash added to the melee, spewing forth a torrent of water "loaded with drift and stinking loud with filthy sediment."[61] Doubtless, Comb and Butler washes matched the flow and filth.

By May, the San Juan, swollen by continuing heavy showers, gained more momentum from the melting snows of Colorado. The flood peaked on June 18, sweeping everything except the settlement of Bluff in front of it. The river washed out the homes in Montezuma Creek, flooded parts of Bluff, and, in the Rincon post, left four feet of water. The waterwheels along the river flowed toward the Gulf of California, as did Hyde's flat-bottomed boat, joined by its cribbed cable post. All became subject to the flood and waves.[62] Hyde went in the opposite direction, returning to the Montezuma Creek–Aneth area to rebuild his fortunes.

Still, the Comb Wash–Rincon area remained an important location in the trade business. Frank and Ernest joined in partnership with brothers Joseph and Amasa Barton to restart the Rincon post in November 1884.[63] Amasa had married the Hyde brothers' sister, Harriet Parthenia (Feen or Feenie), and assisted in running the newly built store. Realizing the river was unpredictable, the Hyde and Barton Trading Company moved to a new location on a rimrock shelf twelve feet above the water. Instead of the large ferry capable of transporting wagons and livestock, they decided to do away with that system and rely on an oar-propelled skiff that was half the size. To stock the post, supplies came from Santa Fe in six to eight weeks during the winter, and Alamosa, Durango, or Animas, Colorado, in the summer, which took two to three weeks round-trip.[64]

Agriculture at the post continued, most likely on a reduced scale. Frank's testimony indicates that he was probably the one who built a second waterwheel. It was located on a sandstone ledge that protruded twelve feet above the river. The men fashioned a

This cottonwood log and rock cribbing served as the anchor for a waterwheel at the Barton Trading Post. Built by William Hyde, his sons, or Amasa Barton in the mid-1880s, this wheel and others like it were first introduced on the San Juan by William. The picture, taken in the 1950s, shows the extended beam that supported the wheel.

> cottonwood log pier, notched up hog-pen style about twelve feet high and filled that with rock; then over that they put a big, heavy cottonwood, extended it over the river channel beyond the edge of this cliff, built a waterwheel so the wheel would hang in the river current at the face of this cliff. They got it going; started to raise a little garden with it; and went out one morning and the river was over one hundred yards the other side of it, a sand bar filled in up to eighteen inches deep on the lower paddles; quit them entirely.[65]

Eventually the river swung back into its previous channel, and the wheel again performed its function.

The post, in addition to attracting Navajo trade, also owned a herd of sheep that grazed in Comb Wash, on Lime Ridge, and down to Mexican Hat, the land assuming the title of the Barton Range. Frank described the summer range as going back "forty to fifty miles from the river in the vicinity of Blue Mountain; in the winter the stock drifted back into the sand flats nearer the river."[66] Joseph, Ernest, and Frank took care of the sheep while Amasa watched after the post. Since Ernest spoke Navajo and Spanish fluently, he supplemented his income by interpreting for miners and law officers. He made good friends with Utes and Navajos, receiving the Navajo name of Night Singer (Tł'éé'jí Hataałii) because of his singing and whistling around the campfire or while watching the herd at night.[67] Many respected him for his ability with firearms.

Amasa Barton was not quite as fortunate. Although he was industrious, resourceful, and a physically powerful man, he and his wife, Feenie, had the difficult task of meeting Navajo and Ute customers' needs. On June 9, 1887, a Navajo named "Bad Eye" or "Old Eye" visited the post with a friend. Bad Eye received his name after his eye was put out when struck by a gad. He was well known to the Hydes, working for them on Amasa's farm on the floodplain east of the rock shelf where the post sat. So that morning, it was not surprising that the two Navajos ate breakfast with the Bartons before stepping into the post to conduct business. Bad Eye wanted to retrieve some jewelry that his wife had previously pawned. He offered an old pistol in exchange and demanded a reduced price of two dollars. An argument ensued with Barton ordering the two men out of the store. As he stooped under the counter to enter the "bullpen," Bad Eye slipped a rope around his neck, jerked him to the floor, and began a tussle. The other man joined in wrestling, strangling Barton with the rope and attempting to pin his arms. Encountering a tough opponent, the unnamed Indian drew his pistol and fired at Barton, but the shot went wild hitting Bad Eye close to the heart. He ran outside, taking his last breaths behind the store. The next shot entered Barton's head as he lay on the threshold of the door. After the assailant learned that he had killed Bad Eye, he returned and placed another round in Barton's head, the brains oozing from the holes.[68] The trader clung to life.

Feenie and her mother-in-law, Angeline Harris Hyde, and two children watched the horror unfold. Amasa, still alive, warned his family to stay away until the Indian left; he knew there was little they could do for him. The Navajo carried Bad Eye to the skiff, rowed across the river, left the body under a blanket, secured the boat, and went to tell others. Feenie prepared for the worst. She implored three Utes—Cheerpoots, Posey, and another man, all of whom were innocent bystanders—to move her husband to a shed where he could rest more comfortably, then offered one of them fifteen dollars to go to Bluff nine miles away for help. Cheerpoots, Posey's father, accepted the task, returning with Kumen Jones and Platte Lyman in a little over an hour. This represented a third of the men present in town at the time. Word of the incident reached Joseph Barton at Recapture Canyon where he was returning with freight. Other men were at the Milk Ranch or in the valleys herding livestock. All made an effort to return to Bluff.[69]

Before any assistance arrived at Rincon, seven armed Indians crossed the river. Barton played dead, convincing them that there was no need to shoot him again or to molest the women. Instead, they demanded from Feenie the keys to the post and helped themselves to what they wanted. Warning shouts from nearby cliffs told of riders in the distance. The Indians gathered their plunder and rowed the boat to the far shore then disappeared. Jones and Lyman assessed the situation. Rather than move Amasa to Bluff at that time, a group of five or six men cared for him but remained vigilant of the Navajo camps now established out of sight on the opposite side of the river. There was no hope for Barton's recovery. On June 16, he died, was brought to Bluff, and buried in the cemetery. Shortly after,

Navajos constantly came to Bluff to trade and visit. During the Amasa Barton affair, relations became fragile as both sides blamed the other for the two deaths. Open communication and the threat of military intervention eventually cooled the situation.

a band of sixty Navajos came to town ready for a fight. Diplomacy on both sides averted further bloodshed, and the incident came to a close. Although Feenie returned to the post for a short time, as a store, the Rincon site was soon abandoned.[70]

Comb Ridge witnessed a similar tragedy just a year before—this time involving outlaws. The L.C., or Lacy Cattle, Company arrived around 1880 and established its headquarters at the confluence of Recapture and Johnson creeks in the canyons near Blue Mountain. Its winter range was on White Mesa, where Blanding and the Ute community are today. Contemporary estimates indicate that the outfit had seventeen thousand cattle on the southeastern slopes of Blue Mountain and Recapture and Cottonwood washes.[71] This was one of several such operations grazing herds in San Juan County at the time. In the spring of 1886, four men received room and board from the L.C. Company with a promise of future employment. They worked under the guidance of foreman Bill Ball long enough to hatch a plan to steal horses from the outfit then make their way out of Utah. They implemented the plan, heading south to Bluff and beyond.

Bob Allan, a settler from Bluff, was riding in Butler Wash one Sunday morning when he saw four men with a herd of horses.[72] They waved him off with their guns and continued on their way to Rincon then up Comb Wash to Navajo Spring. Allan rode to Bluff and alerted the men attending church that he had probably seen some horse thieves attempting to melt into the wilderness. Just as an impromptu posse of eight to ten men prepared to leave, Ball and three other riders from the L.C. arrived and identified the thieves. The Bluff men knew of the Navajo Trail shortcut that went over Comb Ridge and hoped that the outlaws did not. The posse reached the top of the ridge and was pleased to see the thieves camped at the spring at the foot of the trail with weapons stacked and horses browsing beyond. This was an opportune moment to end the affair quickly.

Unfortunately, Ball, the appointed leader of the posse, had a different plan. Leaving two men at the top of the ridge in a commanding position and five men holding horses, he took the rest down the trail to get closer. The thieves detected movement above, mounted, and drove the stolen herd up Comb Wash toward Road Canyon. Night fell, both groups halted and waited for light while the posse enjoyed a meal brought to them by two of their party from the Bartons at Rincon. The morning found the outlaws following a trail south of Road Creek, heading for what is called Dead Bull Flat within the cover of the piñon and juniper forest. At one point, the pursuers encountered a heavily lathered horse but did not spy a rock displaying a sheepskin with the charcoal-scrawled words, "For God's sake don't follow us any farther. We'll have to kill you. Our horses are about played out."[73] The outlaws proved good to their word.

The thieves separated, encouraging the pursuers to divide forces. Hanson Bayles and Joseph Barton took the group to the right, and the rest followed the ones who went to the left. The latter trail eventually led up a slope to an Ancestral Puebloan dwelling. Shots rang out from the ruin, Ball falling with a bullet in his lung. The remainder of his group caught up to the foreman but could not see his predicament because of the unevenness of the terrain. In the meantime, one of the outlaws walked down from the ambush site and talked to Ball, asking who and how many men were following them. Bill groaned, "By God, I was one of them." The rest of his party moved to a position and exchanged shots with the fleeing outlaws, wounding one. They all made good their escape. This was enough for the pursuers, who placed Ball on a horse, hoping to get him to Bluff for medical attention. It was too late. He knew he was dying and riding a horse was too painful, so he requested they take him down to die in peace, which he did. The two separated parties rendezvoused that night at Rincon, returning to Bluff the next morning to bury Bill in the cemetery.[74]

In spite of the hardships of eking out an existence in San Juan, the livestock industry burgeoned far beyond its initial forecast. Throughout the American West, this was the time of the open range, the growth of transportation networks, and large business enterprises. The cattle industry in the Four Corners region was part of this national movement. What played out around Comb Ridge was one small part of this larger picture. Non-Mormon as well as Latter-day Saint efforts were successful, but the Mormon approach assumed a communal as well as individual role. On March 24, 1882, the San Juan Co-op (Cooperative) Store began operation. President Platte D. Lyman, Vice President (Bishop) Jens Nielson, and Directors Kumen Jones, Charles E. Walton, and Hyrum Perkins—all Hole-in-the-Rockers with strong church commitments and experience in working with

Courtesy of San Juan County Historical Commission

The San Juan Co-operative Company or Bluff Co-op built this structure to serve as a trading post, business headquarters, social hall (upstairs), and symbol of its economic prosperity. The group sitting or kneeling soon left for a trip to Elk Mountain.

Indians—charted the course of the new enterprise.[75] Selling shares to town members, the business specialized in Navajo wool, pelts, and blankets as well as its own produce from its sheep flock and cattle herd. Supplies came from the railhead in Durango where co-op members freighted on a rotational schedule of stockholders working in pairs for protection and assistance.[76] From the beginning the log store and, later, the two story rock building, provided a profitable source of income from the Navajo and Ute traffic as it competed with other posts along the river.

On December 18, 1884, Francis A. Hammond, newly appointed stake president for the Saints living in southwestern Colorado and southeastern Utah, arrived in Bluff to begin his stewardship. Aggressively promoting the livestock industry in San Juan, he evaluated the ranges and the competition then went to work—in both an economic and ecclesiastical sense. Loss of livestock from Indian depredations, decreasing amounts of open range, as well as growing competition from three large cattle companies called for unified action. In 1886, the co-op established a rotating guard on what Hammond considered his "eastern border along the White Mesa" to keep "all of the stock west of White Mesa." The Butler and Comb Wash drainages sat in the heart of this Mormon-claimed territory. Two men, each receiving two dollars a day, held the task of constantly riding the range and protecting co-op interests against interlopers.[77]

The plan was valiant but did not deliver the intended results. A week after the committee adopted the plan, Nielson and Redd contacted Hammond warning that 5,000 Navajo sheep from the south were on the north side of the river, "some of them near the town." Redd and Jones received the task of encouraging the Navajo owners to move this flock to the south side of the river. A week later Hammond had discussions with a Mr. Brooks, supervisor of a large herd that he wanted to move to San Juan to use Mormon range. This prompted Hammond to be "somewhat concerned about it for we need that range very much." Pickings were slim on the winter ranges. The stake president reported that the co-op herd had moved from Recapture to Cottonwood to Butler drainages looking for feed, and there was not a lot to be found. Although he felt solace in being in the good graces of Mancos Jim, who expressed concern with sheep herds overgrazing the ranges and was a "terror to the cowboys but a fast friend of the Mormons," this friendship did not stem the flow of outsiders.[78]

A year later, Mr. Brooks was en route. Hammond fitfully penned, "Brooks, cattle man, has about 7,000 head of stock on the way to turn loose on our range which will make some three thousand or four thousand owned by outsiders now on the range near Bluff besides some forty thousand head of sheep. It appears as though we could be overrun with stock."[79] Hammond fashioned a defensive strategy. Members of the co-op council received assignments to establish outlying ranches or settlements to serve as buffers against encroachment. After referring to a speech about "[setting] a good example before our gentile neighbors and Indian allies and preach the Gospel by our daily works," President Hammond called eighteen missionaries to locate at strategic locations near and far from Bluff. Some of these sites included North Montezuma (today's Monticello) to counter the Kansas and New Mexico Land and Cattle Company under the direction of Harold and Edmund Carlisle; Indian Creek Valley north of the Elk and Blue mountains; the head of Butler and Cottonwood washes at the foot of Elk Mountain (or Ridge); and the Moki Crossing on the Colorado River. The money to pay for these efforts would come from "church appropriations." The meeting ended with a caution to the men "to be careful of what they write about the mission," but "all the brethren received their appointments with willing hearts and hands."[80]

Hammond notified church leaders in Salt Lake City about his plan. John Taylor, president of The Church of Jesus Christ of Latter-day Saints, responded in January, congratulating him for his initiative and agreeing with his assessment. Hoping to send new settlers to "strengthen the places which need help and to enable you to form the new settlements which you consider necessary," Taylor was impressed with the "importance of maintaining control of that country and pointed out its advantages as a place of refuge for any who are in jeopardy here," referring to the intense anti-polygamy campaign underway in the north.[81] Bemoaning the fact that so many large herds of livestock grazed the ranges near Bluff, Taylor encouraged Hammond to make sure that the Indians knew the difference between the Mormon herds and tenders and those of the non-Mormon cowboys. John Taylor died July 25, 1887, while in hiding during the federal government's hunt for polygamists. Wilford Woodruff, the next president of the church, took up the cudgel where Taylor dropped it. He urged Hammond not to abandon Bluff for Mancos,

Colorado, or settlements in New Mexico. Woodruff understood that "the families who are there are making means more rapidly than double the same number of families in any other settlement."[82] Whether or not this was true, there was no budging the Saints from the Bluff settlement.

The following week, W. J. Forham took pen in hand to recruit for the Mormons in Bluff, writing a promotional piece published in the *Deseret News* in Salt Lake City on October 12, 1887.[83] Putting his best hoof forward, he painted a telling picture of the pooled efforts of the livestock industry under the control of Hammond and the Bluff Co-op as well as the competition they faced. A part of this article reported that the co-op had: "a capital stock of $150,000, of which $20,000 is paid up. . . . 11,000 head of sheep, cost $1.40 per head. . . . 1000 acres of land under cultivation. . . . [and] about 32,000 head of cattle upon the ranges in this county, mostly owned by large companies, some by foreigners . . . [and] about 100,000 head that come down into our county from Colorado for winter range and to be taxed. . . ." The environmental impact of this onslaught from both sides of the barbed wire was severe. Butler Wash and the Barton Range figured heavily as a grazing area and collecting point for this livestock.

The Indians' situation, especially the Utes and Paiutes, became increasingly untenable. Starvation stood at their doorstep, a major change from twenty-five years before. Hammond easily identified why, on November 28, 1887, when he wrote:

> A few Utes and Paiutes are camped near our house, just down in the bottom. They are constantly begging, poor creatures. They have a hard time as since the white man has come with his immense herds of stock. The game which was formally plentiful is now very scarce and the poor Indian is hard pushed to obtain a living.[84]

Hammond assigned Thales Haskell, interpreter and accepted ambassador to the Navajos and Utes, to establish an Indian farm at the southeast base of Elk Mountain. The potential of raising fruits and vegetables was good except for the fact that agricultural undertakings were anathema to the Utes, who for the most part, also did not get along with many Navajos. They did not come.

With the death of Amasa Barton and its unsettled aftermath, there was not much chance of the Navajos being involved either. Hammond's terse, "They will move away from Rincon where the murder was committed" refers not only to Navajo avoidance of a place where death has occurred but the general tenor of relations. Seven months after the incident, Hammond discussed the situation with members of the council, noting that the Indians had been "very cool and quite distant for some months past" because of threats made by Frank and Ernest Hyde. The council agreed that relations needed mending and that the Navajos who plundered the store would be left alone. The co-op also reviewed its entire Indian policy. Some members felt that an Indian caught in a wrongful act should be whipped. After some discussion the vote passed that such a person would be brought to an interpreter or bishop, who would appeal to the miscreant's better nature.[85]

A year later, the co-op remained in the doldrums with only an occasional breath of good news to energize it. In April, Hammond reported that the cattlemen were driving livestock into Comb Wash to get them ready for sale. Fletcher and Joseph Hammond established a horse and cattle ranch at the head of Comb Wash and fenced in twenty acres, part of which had been planted in crops. Feenie Barton and her mother wished to withdraw $4,000 of co-op stock and move away. And the Indian trade had fallen sharply because "Brother Joseph Barton, Superintendent, is not qualified to win the Indians' good feelings."[86] Life in Bluff and around Comb Ridge, like the San Juan River, had its ebb and flow, torrents and droughts. When one considers how the entire landscape and economic use of the land had shifted over a period of roughly twenty years, it is not surprising that there was so much social upheaval between the different cultures. Moving from an isolated Navajo refuge during the Fearing Time to a highly publicized and sought after rangeland with permanent settlements, San Juan County, in general, and the Bluff-Comb Ridge area, specifically, became a destination on the map. But few could guess exactly how much of a destination lay in the future.

5

Who Owns the Comb?

Ute, Navajo, and Anglo Disputes

The United States officers and posse here will probably adopt the plan of starving Old Polk and his band of outlaw Piutes fortified in Butler Wash into submission. . . . Any attempt to 'rush' the Piutes in Butler Wash would result in the loss of many whitemen. . . .
—*Salt Lake Herald Republican*, March 1, 1915

During the spring, when winter snow melts and April showers bring May flowers, Comb Ridge rests between flowing streams in Butler and Comb washes. The muddy water cascades over sandstone rocks and ledges, wends its way around bends and corners, and flows smoothly on top of the sandy desert floor, making its way to the San Juan River. Here it joins the melee and is swept downstream with even greater force. In a sense, Comb Ridge is a metaphor for the events that played out around it between the 1880s and the 1920s. The Utes remained on one side, the Navajos on the other, with Anglos in between, each having a separate role to play, each affecting the other. And like the water tumbling over the stones, conflicts peaked, demanding all the energy the cultures could muster while at other times events flowed smoothly. All three groups arrived at the general flow of mid-twentieth century American society, having run the gamut of a difficult past, now poised to be swept along with events in mainstream society. This chapter looks at the three separate cultures during this period of intense conflict and social change in preparation for the future.

In the 1880s, the Utes struggled the most. White encroachment in the form of Mormon (Bluff, 1880; Monticello, 1887) and non-Mormon (Aneth/Montezuma Creek, 1879) settlers as well as ranchers from both groups and cowboys from Colorado (1880s) greatly curtailed the Indians' hunting and gathering practices. Friction increased, the Utes resenting particularly the cattlemen from Colorado and the Carlisle spread with their huge herds that decimated the landscape. In addition to these problems, the Southern Utes in Colorado were squeezed onto a reservation 15 miles wide and 110 miles long that offered few resources. Those Southern Utes, Paiutes, and Navajos that had coalesced into an

Courtesy of San Juan County Historical Commission

These corrals on Elk Ridge were two of many that held cattle grazing on range the Utes considered theirs. As part of the public domain, this land beckoned ranchers from other parts of Utah as well as Colorado.

amorphous group locally known as Paiutes, or "renegades," refused to live anywhere but San Juan, clinging to their old ways, resisting white encroachment, and wreaking havoc on elements that eroded their way of life. Something had to be done, and the whites expected their government to do it.

As early as 1886, rumblings about Southern Ute removal and expulsion from Colorado to Utah began. By 1888, the Southern Ute Commission initiated steps to purchase all of San Juan County for a reservation. Its dialogue continued for seven years with all the drama of a first-rate political brouhaha.[1] The Ute Commission had the responsibility to report all improvements made by settlers in Bluff so that the government could reimburse them when relocated. Francis A. Hammond accepted the task of determining the extent of improvements on the land, their value, and how much the government should pay. This he did for both Mormon and non-Mormon settlers. Still, no one seemed thrilled with the prospect of moving. After insinuating mistrust for the government and outlining considerations it should take, Hammond wrote:

> I trust you will consider all these matters, and the great trouble and expense connected with the removal of our people from this section to God only knows

> where, to found new homes and give up our homes to the Indians. Some of the families who will have to move are not able to, unless they are paid for their claims, as they are about all they have of this world's goods—not even teams to move with.
>
> We have been here some nine years struggling hard to hold and redeem this country; standing guard as it were, on the outpost, to protect our more wealthy populous counties from the raids of Indians and renegade white men, white renegades being far the worst. We have had heavy and constant tax upon us of about three hundred Paiutes and renegade Indians from other tribes to feed and partially clothe since ever we located here; previous to our settling here life and property were not safe anywhere in this section, but owing to our pacific treatment of the Indians and our constant watch of the cattle and horse thieves, the country is now full of large cattle, sheep, and horse herds.[2]

True, the country was full of cattle, sheep, and horse herds, which were the primary contributing factors to growing Indian unrest. Hammond also provided a "snapshot" of developments in Comb and Butler washes, giving names and numbers for each individual claim. W. Joshua Stevens owned a ranch and improvements in Butler Wash, eighty rods of fence, ten acres broken land, and a dam, canal, and other improvements valued at $280. Francis B. Hammond, F. A.'s son, had a ranch with improvements in Comb Wash worth $178.50. Dutch, Day, and J. J. Davis, owners of the Elk Mountain Cattle Company, with John Reid as manager, owned their headquarters comprised of houses, corrals, and other improvements worth $600 at Rincon. The San Juan Co-operative Company held a branch store/house and blacksmith shop, one current wheel for hoisting water, and ten acres of broken land at Rincon assessed at $1,000 as well as a dairy ranch at the eastern base of Elk Mountain (Ridge), which had two cabins, 200 rods of fence, corrals, and other improvements worth $500. On Elk Ridge proper, the co-op owned a cattle ranch with house and corral, while F. A. Hammond had a ranch with a house, fenced corral, water ditch, and improved land valued at $178.50; his son, F. B., claimed a ranch with improvements worth $250; and W. J. Stevens had four cabins, three corrals, 135 rods of fence, and fifteen acres of broken land.[3] The only other reference to improvements near Comb Wash at this time comes from Albert R. Lyman, who refers to a hermit named "Posty" working for some cowboys. He grew juicy melons and vegetables on a small plot of land with a ditch at the mouth of Mule Creek where it flowed into upper Comb Wash. As for his name, there are two possibilities: He was both as deaf as a post and limped with a leg as stiff as one.[4]

From this snapshot, one can deduce a number of things. First, the expansion of ranches and farms from the community of Bluff had stretched miles from its point of origin. Not only had it spread, but the establishments were substantial, with cabins, gardens, fences, and specific territorial claims. Second, one can assume that each of these was located on a dependable source of water that sustained life during the summer months, when cowboys moved the cattle to higher elevations on Elk Ridge and farming required irrigation water. Even Posty's camp using the intermittent flow of Mule Creek probably relied on the more constant source of water from Arch Canyon during a dry season. A third consideration is the effect these satellite operations had in spreading livestock over a much larger distance. Rangeland was at a premium as thousands of cattle and sheep invaded the landscape. What had been prime hunting and gathering territory became a trampled desert and forest environment, with springs claimed by cabins, and a cowboy element that beheld game animals as competitors to livestock.

Francis F. Kane, who came to Bluff in 1891 to view the lands on behalf of the Indian Rights Association, recorded in his diary the severity of the situation. While visiting at Kigalia Springs on Elk Ridge, he wrote: "I looked for deer this morning east of Smeltzer and Sanford's cabin [at the springs], but did not even see a track. The only game, in fact, which we have seen on the proposed reservation have been some coyotes and a gray wolf. We have not seen any tracks or sign."[5] The end result and final point: the Utes, dependent on these wild animals, plants, and springs turned to those who took them away. Conflict intensified.

The Utes and Paiutes living near Bluff and Comb Ridge looked forward to having this land returned to them officially as their reservation. After six years of wrangling back and forth, with pressure from the people of Colorado to get rid of their unwanted charges, the Southern Utes, and with an opposite and equal reaction from the people of Utah to keep them where they were, the deal came off the table so that only the "renegades" already in San Juan remained. The low-grade fire in relations smoldered. Generally, the Mormons fared better in maintaining the peace, but each group had its incidents that occasionally flared into violence.

The best known of these occurred in February 1915, when a group of deputized cowboys from Colorado, eager for revenge after years of conflict with the Utes and Paiutes of San Juan, arrived in Bluff under the leadership of U.S. Marshal Aquila Nebeker.[6] He sought Tse-ne-gat, or Everett Hatch, son of Polk (Poke), a Weeminuche Ute and leader of a faction of people living around Montezuma Canyon. Tse-ne-gat, ten months earlier, reportedly killed a Mexican sheepherder, Juan Chacon, after a night of playing cards. It was time to bring him in. The Utes and Paiutes camped in Bluff had no idea that a seventy-five man posse approached. In the early light of dawn that February 21, the mounted white men attempted to encircle the tepees. A startled early riser gave whoops of warning to awaken the sleeping camp then opened fire. Initial volleys resulted in the death of two Indians and one white man and the wounding of another Ute. Warriors and their families fled to the nearby sandstone cliffs, holding off the advancing whites while providing covering fire for noncombatants seeking protection. Another band of Indians camped at Sand Island and estimated at forty men rode up the San Juan River into the rear of the white cordon. Posey, leader of this group, had heard the commotion and rallied to the attack. Caught in a vise between two forces, Nebeker and his men engaged in a brisk firefight before driving off Posey and allowing part of Polk's group to escape up Butler Wash and beyond while others remained for another day of fighting.[7] Two days after the initial attack, white scouts found the still-warm campfires of Posey's band near "Butler's

A few days following the attempted arrest of Tse-ne-gat in 1915, the posse, comprised primarily of Colorado cowboys under the direction of Marshal Aquila Nebeker, posed for this picture in Bluff.

Canyon" on the San Juan. This group of Indians, comprised of mostly noncombatants, fled across the river with their large flocks of sheep and goats.[8]

The struggle with Polk's band is an interesting study in hyperbole and conjecture, written by reporters in Bluff during the confrontation. Taking the opportunity to return to an Old West approach of yellow journalism, they milked it for their readership. Boldface type announced, "Indians Surround Marshall's Posse—Whites Taken by Surprise," "Indians Defiant," "Braves Make Night Hideous with Cries," "Five White Men Cut Off from Comrades," and "Trap Reds in Canyon."[9] An interesting sidelight to this event is the role assigned by the press to Butler Wash. A week after the initial fight, the newspapers reported, "The United States officers and posse here will probably adopt the plan of starving Old Polk and his band of outlaw Piutes, fortified in Butler Wash, into submission by surrounding the Indians and preventing their getting any more supplies and exhausting the small game in the vicinity of the Indians' camp."[10] The selection of Butler Wash for a defensive position is tactically questionable. As for removing any kind of game, there was no doubt: that had been accomplished long before.

A second group of "supposedly friendly Utes numbering 106," that were also camped in Butler Wash, moved toward Bluff to avoid association with those fighting. Navajo scouts from the Northern Navajo Agency in Shiprock escorted them. As the Indians conversed, the "friendlies" learned they were actually slated to only pass through Bluff on their way to the Southern Ute Reservation in Colorado. "They halted in their march and refused to come in. Leaders of the band declared rather than leave their ancestral hunting grounds they would resist the white authorities and join Old Polk and his bunch of renegades."[11] Further suggestion of their removal was quickly swept under the carpet.

While in Moab, the Ute participants involved in the 1915 fight had their picture taken. From left to right: Navajo interpreter, Robert Martin; Posey; his son, Anson Posey; Tse-ne-gat, or Everett Hatch, Polk's son; and Polk. Eventually all were acquitted by the courts.

As the "war" continued, Nebeker begrudgingly bestowed growing respect for his adversary by admitting "any attempt to 'rush' the Piutes in Butler Wash would result in the loss of many white men."[12] Under the headline "Cliff Dwellings Shelter Piutes," the press droned on about the Indians taking defensive positions in the Puebloan ruins high above Butler Wash.[13] "The straight rock walls of the ancient cliff dwellers make the Indians' position almost impregnable." Anticipated reinforcements for the Utes/Paiutes were purportedly on the way; starving the combatants seemed like the only option. Two days later, Polk had relocated his fighters "five miles further west" (north?) of his previous position in a narrow pass of Butler Wash, awaiting Nebeker's attack.[14]

It never materialized. In the evening of March 10, General Hugh L. Scott, chief of staff, arrived as a negotiator in the conflict to settle the uproar and bring in Tse-ne-gat peacefully. He learned that, by this time, the renegades were somewhere around Mexican Hat. With two other soldiers, trader John Wetherill, and four Navajo men, Scott went to Arthur H. Spencer's Trading Post and eventually coaxed the Indian leaders to surrender

Tse-ne-gat, Polk, Posey, and his son. By March 24, the general had his prisoners in Salt Lake City, where all but Tse-ne-gat were found innocent and released. Tse-ne-gat eventually went to Denver to stand trial and was later freed.[15] The Paiutes and Utes, like the flow of canyon water, resumed their life of ripples, lapping against the bank and passing over the rocks embedded in the stream.

For eight years, the impoverished Indians existed in an increasingly diminished world. Additional game laws, decreased access to the land, dependence on food from the Mormons, friction in relationships, and grinding poverty characterized their lives. By 1923, Posey, a Paiute who had married into the Ute band in Allen Canyon, had become the symbol of this mutual antagonism. Approximately sixty years old, he had been involved in much of the previous conflict, acquiring a reputation with many whites for his belligerence and thievery. He naturally became a focal point when in March 1923, Sheriff William Oliver arrested two Utes, Joe Bishop's Little Boy and Sanop's Boy, for robbing a sheep camp, killing a calf, and burning a bridge.

The two men stood trial, but during the noon recess, made a dramatic escape from Blanding with the sheriff in hot pursuit.[16] Posey assisted the fugitives in getting out of town and was cited as the arch villain who planned the whole event. Oliver failed to apprehend his charges, so he returned to Blanding to deputize a large body of men anxious to find a solution to the "Indian problem." The posse started by going to Westwater on the outskirts of Blanding, where they rounded up forty men, women, and children, first placing them in the basement of the elementary school and later in a 100-foot-square barbed wire stockade in the center of town. The rest of the Ute community that had not been captured began fleeing, first south to Murphy's Point five miles south of Blanding, thence west, most likely heading for Navajo Mountain, a traditional sanctuary during times of trouble. Comb Ridge moved center stage in the unfolding drama.

The exodus was not a well-planned retreat. As women and children moved away from Blanding with some of the men, others spread the word to outlying groups while some men served as rear guard. They watched to see if they were being followed, discovered they were, and fought a delaying action. Posey, among others, exchanged shots with members of the posse at Murphy's Point and at other places along the route. John D. Rogers had his horse shot out from under him while three men had a near miss with a bullet passing through the Model-T Ford they were riding in. The day concluded with most of the white men returning to Blanding while ten others remained close to the trail at Fred Lyman's cabin on the road eight miles south of Blanding.[17]

The next day, a posse of about fifty men renewed its efforts with increased determination based on the previous night's town meeting.[18] They planned to settle the "Indian problem" with no outside interference. By noon, the whites spied across Butler Wash the Indians' campfires at the head of what is now called Posey's Trail near the Highland Lady. The men dismounted, leaving their horses hidden and under guard in Butler Wash, spread out, and moved through the trees toward the camp. Dave Black and Bill Young reached the crest of Comb Ridge ahead of the others moving upslope. Below, gunshots rang out and warriors emerged from Butler Wash, taking fire at the enemy before retreating. Black, as leader of the group, ran downslope to better assess the situation, leaving Young at the top of the ridge. Posey emerged from the north and began firing, then used his horse as a shield and rode in the opposite direction, possibly heading for a trail further north, where today's old Highway 95 (which had not yet been built) dropped off Comb Ridge near the mouth of Arch Canyon.[19]

Meanwhile, Bill Young held his position on the crest. He spied Joe Bishop's Little Boy and Sanop's Boy riding toward his location, so he moved downslope trying to avoid detection. The Indians saw his movement and whipped their horses into a run to catch him. Realizing that he could not outdistance them, he moved behind a bushy juniper and waited. The two Utes rode on either side of the tree. Young saw the button of Joe Bishop's Little Boy's coat through the branches and fired. The Indian toppled off his horse and remained motionless while Young went around the other side of the tree to engage Sanop's Boy, who was in full retreat. Not wanting to kill needlessly, Young let him go, determined that the other Indian was dead, and rejoined his party. One testimony claimed that Young said, "There's one good Indian up there." Another person said he reported, "It was no fun to kill an injun." But probably the most realistic and sensitive account came from Alma Jones who remembered, "It wasn't long until he came down. He was upset. He said, 'I have killed a man.' He just kept saying that. That wasn't like Bill Young at all. He is one of the most calm and collected men that you ever saw. He was really upset."[20]

The men in Butler determined that at least one of the Indians, Jack Fly, had been released from Blanding for some reason. He was in their rear, sporadically firing at targets of opportunity. Fearing that all of the Ute prisoners were freed, the posse returned to town to determine exactly what happened. Fly had been turned loose to care for his livestock but chose to help those resisting. A second town meeting that night reaffirmed the whites' desire to either kill or capture the Indians not already incarcerated and end the issue. The next day, forty men from Blanding rendezvoused with twenty from Bluff then traveled up Comb Wash. Standing at the foot of Posey's Trail the united party spied the Utes on top of "The Island," a high mesa a half-mile wide. There were only two paths that traversed the mesa's easily defensible steep slopes. Splitting the force, the posse sent a handful of men to seal off the trail in the rear while the rest spread out and assaulted the heights. They encountered no resistance. There was only an abandoned camp, cooking fires still burning, and food in some frying pans. The Indians had "found a treacherous trail on the opposite side of the mesa, jumping their horses down four- and five-foot ledges, managing to scramble to safety just ahead of us."[21]

Night approached, the Utes held the next mesa to the west and Posey had exchanged shots with Black. The posse had no desire to wage war in the dark and so spent the night at Frank Karnell's Ranch at the mouth of Arch Canyon, sending volunteers to Blanding for food.[22] Sunrise saw the vigilantes riding toward where they had stopped the chase the previous day. The Utes abandoned their horses and livestock at the west end of the mesa top and disappeared through a crack in the rim into Dry Wash. The posse pursued. In the Utes'

Courtesy of San Juan County Historical Commission

Often portrayed as a rebellious malcontent, Posey, born at Navajo Mountain of Paiute ancestry, did what he could to slow the Indians' loss of land while making a statement against those who changed the Ute and Paiute way of life.

tracks and tied on trees, white pieces of cloth indicating a desire for peace fluttered in the canyon breeze. By evening, the whites had them surrounded within a three-mile radius of the head of Dry Wash. That night the Indians surrendered at the posse's campfire and prepared for their march down Dry Wash and into Comb, where trucks were to transport them to Blanding via Navajo Spring and Bluff.

That afternoon only one of the two requested vehicles arrived. Oliver squeezed the women and children and as many men as possible into the truck and started it rumbling on its way down Comb Wash. The eight remaining Utes became restless; the sheriff feared trouble. He ordered the rest of his posse members to get the prisoners moving.

> We lined the Indians up abreast in the bottom of Comb Wash, and a man with a gun got behind each Indian. The Sheriff on his horse rode out on one side of the wash, and I [John D. Rogers] on my mule rode out on the other side. We told the Indians that if Posey attacked or any trouble started, the posse men would immediately each kill an Indian without any questions. The sheriff and I were to fire shots if Indians were sighted or any trouble encountered. This would be the signal for the others to shoot the prisoners. If we had fired a shot for any reason at all, those eight Paiutes would have been killed.[23]

Fortunately, after two or three miles, the second truck arrived and took all but the men who remained with the horses to Bluff, where they spent the night.

Posey, the man whose name became synonymous with this fracas, was still at large. Last seen fighting around the large mesa to the west of Comb Wash, he never surrendered. During the month after the roundup when the Utes remained in an open stockade in the middle of Blanding, his signal fires appeared on Comb Ridge close to where he disappeared. Posey spent his last days in a small alcove near the mouth of Mule Canyon. Suddenly the signal fires stopped. His people, thinking that he was dead, guided Marshal Ray Ward to where he had been hiding—where he had been visited by Ute friends and had died of blood poisoning from a gunshot wound through the hip. The marshal secretly buried him, only to have him exhumed twice—once by some townspeople and once by the Ute Agent Edward E. McKean from Towaoc—to verify his death. The conclusion to over forty years of conflict between the Utes and Paiutes and the white man had played out on Comb Ridge.

The denouement to this drama ended in the same vicinity. The question of where to settle the Utes in 1923 was still unanswered. Before the Mormons released them from the stockade, the Indians had to accept individual allotments in the Cottonwood and Allen Canyon/Whiskers Draw drainages to the north of Comb Wash proper. Approximately 8,360 acres now belonged to the Ute/Paiute band, the land being broken into individual allotments to support farming and grazing.[24] For all purposes, the Utes and Paiutes were removed from the Butler Wash and Comb Ridge area near Bluff, being consigned farther north to their usual haunts of Allen and Hammond canyons and Cottonwood Wash. At this point, only the Navajos remained; they, too, were eventually removed.

Before leaving the Utes settled in Allen Canyon, a few points need to be emphasized. The most obvious is their deteriorating situation over the years; the loss of land to livestock interests as well as the restricting influence of farming and general settlement removed food from their mouths. Their entire way of life changed. Resentment festered and flared, attacks on livestock increased, and intimidation erupted into conflict. A second point is that those Paiutes and Utes living in southeastern Utah refused to come under the control of any agency, claiming their ancestral lands as the only place for them to live. There was no permanent, consistent authority to solve problems and issue commodities similar to those received by people living on a reservation. The Utes coerced local settlers to pay for their lunch ticket. Finally, they had little to offer the struggling white economy. While the Navajo had wool and blankets to trade, the baskets and beadwork of the Utes never filled a niche in local or regional economies. The result: a relatively peaceful people wrapped in conflict, reacting against their deteriorating situation, being characterized as aggressors. Consequently, much of what is known about them is derived from conflicts reported by those they fought.

The history of the Navajo people along Comb Ridge between 1890 and 1930 flowed through a different streambed. Often termed "progressive," they had ever-expanding herds of sheep and goats along with horticulture, giving them independence from a hunting-and-gathering lifestyle. Although they did hunt, their domesticated food supply stood between them and starvation. Wool, hides, and blankets opened a welcomed trade that fueled part of the Anglo economy. Along the San Juan River, trading posts opened their doors and flourished with customers anxious to incorporate new food, commercially manufactured clothing, and improved tools to benefit their life. Favorable exchange crossed both sides of the counter. In 1908, Captain E. A. Sturges visited with Frank Hyde, who had tracked the previous year's flow of customers in Bluff. Hyde proudly reported that over 950 Navajo adults had traded with him along with 65 Utes and Paiutes. Sturges, after talking with many of the local leaders, wrote, "All of the citizens of Bluff whom I have met were in accord in stating that the Navajo Indians were well-behaved, peaceable, and industrious, that only the Indians that have caused any trouble are the Utes. . . ."[25] Friendly relations appeared likely on both sides of the San Juan.

There was, however, one sticking point in this reciprocal friendship. It was the same thing that bothered the Utes but in a different way. Bluff, by the late 1880s and 1890s, was just as devoted to the livestock industry as the Navajo. Growing herds on both sides of the river sought greener pastures, which always seemed more abundant on the other bank, in the other canyon, or atop another mountain. Flocks and herds crossed at Sand Island and Comb/Chinle washes on their way to winter range and summer pasture. Neither the Navajo nor the Anglo accepted totally the San Juan River as a boundary, and so the quest for grass became a growing irritant with each side racing to be first to stake its claim. Reservation lands and the public domain became public points of contention.

Although the attempt to purchase Bluff and make it a home and subagency for the Utes failed in 1894, Navajo Agent Edwin H. Plummer saw this community as an ideal spot for the Navajo. Recognizing the need for education and the long distance between Bluff and facilities on the reservation, he sent Miss Anna C. Egan to Bluff to open a day school for Navajo children. She erected a tent on the site where a proposed building would stand, that is, as soon as the government allocated sufficient funds. She was to "commence work of preparing children for school and to be on hand to superintend the construction of the buildings, take charge of supplies as they arrive, etc."[26] Little came of this effort except to initiate a growing theme that Bluff should go to the Navajos.

Eight months later and with a new agent, Constant Williams, Bluff received another inspection. Williams painted a far less rosy picture. Three years of crop failure, denuded ranges, low prices for wool, and conflict over the public domain were pushing the Navajos to their limit. Something needed to be done to assist the roughly one thousand families trying to make a living in the general area.[27] The government did nothing. Years—some fruitful, others impoverished—followed, with only gentle suggestions about assisting the Navajos. Finally, in 1902, Kumen Jones, a Bluff settler and even-handed friend to the Indians, wrote to the Navajo agent saying his charges had reached starvation level. Agent George W. Hayzlett responded by sending a government farmer, Samuel Shoemaker, to Bluff to start work on Indian irrigation ditches. By mid-January, Shoemaker had performed a preliminary survey, identified 536 Indians in need, 115 of whom could and would work in digging ditches, and had received all kinds of tools for excavating. His survey of tentative land ended at Butler "Canyon." There was one problem; the ground was frozen solid. Nothing was done.[28] Nothing was done that spring either.

Change, however, did come that summer in the form of William T. Shelton. An avid advocate for the Navajo, he was also the founder and first superintendent of the Northern Navajo (San Juan) Agency in Shiprock, beginning in 1903. Unlike other agents who drifted in and out of office, he remained for thirteen years and made a difference. Facing numerous problems, Shelton extended his influence over a jurisdiction of three thousand miles that encompassed lands in New Mexico, Arizona, and Utah. To maintain order, he formed a Navajo police force and hired additional farmers to assist in economic development. In 1905, he employed former trader James M. Holley, living in Aneth, to mentor the Utah Navajo. Holley, like Shelton, had his hands full. Among other issues along the San Juan he reported that:

> The Mormons at Bluff have been hauling the Indians' fencing from around their corn patches and their house logs for wood and claiming their land which is government timber and also government land, the farthest up about twelve or thirteen miles this side of Bluff. [The names] of the men that have been engaged in hauling off their fencing [are] Frank Hyde, Indian Trader, Bluff, Utah; John Adams, ditto; Joe Barton, ditto; Lemuel Redd, ditto; and Mr. [Kumen] Jones, Indian trader, Bluff. [They] have been telling the Indians, so they say, to get back across the river as they are not wanted on the north side and the timber and land all belong to the Bluff people.[29]

In fairness to the accused, they viewed the reservation lands as belonging to the Navajo and the public domain as a place for white men's herds. Technically, the land was for all, until legislation dictated otherwise. Navajo encroachment not only deprived the white stockmen of pasturage, but occupied lands might actually become part of the reservation. On May 17, 1884, President Chester A. Arthur signed an executive order expanding the northern part of the reservation into Utah to the south side of the San Juan River, hoping to eliminate conflict over lands by providing official recognition of Navajo rights. Now, after some initial revisions due to survey problems, President Theodore Roosevelt signed Executive Order 324A on May 15, 1905. The lands encompassed in this order started at the mouth of Montezuma Creek, went east to the Colorado state line, south along the boundary, then down the San Juan River to Montezuma Creek.[30] The Navajos had again received more land for their burgeoning herds. The people in Bluff shifted in discomfort at the trend.

To preempt the loss of their land to reservation expansion and having to sell at a low price, "two gentlemen, representing the citizens of Bluff," approached Shelton in October 1906, and inquired into the possibility of his purchasing the town for a future Indian school.[31] The reason: "they claim they have been more or less embarrassed by being located among them [Indians], and so far from other white settlements."[32] The men pointed out the Navajos were crowding the residents of Bluff, preying upon their stock, and intimidating the settlers to the point that selling seemed like the wisest approach. Shelton had visited Bluff previously and noted the fine buildings, fruit-filled orchards, wide streets, excellent drinking water, and potential for the Navajo livestock industry. He had recently abandoned plans to build a boarding school in Aneth but recognized that the already established schools in Tuba City, Keams Canyon, and Fort Defiance in Arizona were each approximately 150 miles away. Situating a school in Bluff would improve the Indians financially as well as intellectually and morally. He awaited approval from the Commissioner of Indian Affairs.

Courtesy of San Juan County Historical Commission

Bluff, as it appeared in 1907, held the potential of becoming a Navajo boarding school. The price was right, the residents willing to sell, but the government saw too many challenges and let the issue die from inaction. The church and school on the left and the L. H. Redd home in the center show the town's prosperity.

Eight months later, Shelton veered from his course. Following a site reconnaissance in Bluff, he determined that building a school there looked less feasible. Even though he recognized many positive qualities, there were issues with crossing the river during high water, lack of wood and coal, limited land for irrigation, broken topography south of the river, and rough roads. The town could be purchased for $75,000 total—a reasonable price Shelton thought—but the plan just did not seem to work. He lamented, "No Indians in the country are so much in need of a school and its influence as the section adjacent to Bluff."[33] Still, nothing happened.

When discussing these events, the Navajos involved often appear as a faceless, nameless mass, their sole purpose bent on wresting control of the land from the beleaguered Mormons. There is another side to that story, best illustrated through the life of Jim Joe. No other Navajo in this region played a more central role with the residents of Bluff and in the history of Comb Ridge than this man. He was born before the Long Walk near the Bears Ears. His wife's mother, White Haired Woman (Asdzáán Bits'iiłgai), of the Táchii'nii (Red Running into the Water People) Clan and her grandmother Red Woman (Asdzáán Ch'ii) were born in the same area. His father, Mister Tall (Hastiin Nez), of the Ta'neeszahnii (Tangle People) Clan came from around Rock Point, Arizona, northwest of Round Rock.[34] Family members indicate that Jim Joe went to Fort Sumner while other relatives did not; he returned around 1868 and resumed living north of the San Juan River.

Special Collections, J. Willard Marriott Library, University of Utah

Jim Joe's main camp was located on the San Juan River near the mouth of Butler Wash. Behind his home is part of the old Mormon wagon road dugway. The road traversed a mesa above the floodplain, arrived at the Rincon, then either crossed the river, ascended Lime Ridge, or went up Comb Wash.

Little else is known about him until the arrival of the Mormons in 1880, when he commenced a life-long friendship. Kumen Jones remembers meeting him that first summer in Bluff, estimating Jim to be around twenty years old. He described him as "above the average of his people. I think he was raised by one of his uncles, who was a prominent leader among the Navajos of the northwestern part of the reservation, [a person who was] industrious, thrifty, careful with his means, hard worker, manly fellow."[35] Jim was much the same. He lived in a variety of camps along Butler Wash, Comb Wash, and on the San Juan River. Some of these sites had names such as "Sweet Water" [Navajo Spring] and "Cottonwoods in a Line" (T'iis'nt'ii), both on the west side of Comb Ridge. Near "the big point on Comb Ridge" called "Looking for Horses" (which may be either the Highland Lady or Mule Ear) and at three other sites on the east side of Comb, Jim built hogans. He is also reported to have been staying, at one point, in an abandoned cabin at Rincon. But his largest and most permanent camp was on the San Juan River near Butler Wash at Ledge Hewn Out.[36] A large garden spot there, watered by irrigation, yielded fine crops of corn and other vegetables. In 1904, his Bluff neighbors reported that he had grown ten to twelve tons of corn at this residence.[37]

From the beginning of relationships with the Mormons, Jim stood for honesty. A few anecdotal stories prove the point. Mamie Jones Adams recalled her father, Kumen Jones, telling of when he and a group of men were exploring San Juan for the first time. They were in their second "dry camp," and the travelers became increasingly concerned about getting feed and water for the horses. Jim Joe appeared alone, offered to take all of the mounts and care for them, and promised to have them back first thing in the morning. While the others balked, "father had an instant feeling of trust for this Indian and said, 'Let him take these horses; I know everything will be all right.'"[38] The next day, the horses arrived at camp in fine shape. Friendship between Kumen and Jim flourished to the end of their lives. Jim became one of the family, Mamie recalling, "Our folks used to say if there was preference going to be given to somebody it would be to Jim Joe."[39]

Christian L. Christensen, trader and translator, shared similar feelings. Jim was "as true a friend as the white settlers ever had."[40] Christensen went on to tell of how Jim lived at the mouth of Butler Wash where Richard Knight and Arnold Caster were selling stolen Mormon livestock to the Indians in April 1893.[41] They sold twelve cattle for one Indian mule, had already disposed of sixty-five beeves, received blankets and silver in trade, and were preparing to leave the area. Jim notified Sheriff Willard Butt, who arrested the outlaws and sent them to Provo, Utah, to stand trial. Christensen and his Navajo friend were co-witnesses at the trial in which the thieves received three years in jail. Jim also ventured out on the reservation to reclaim the cattle lost in these crooked transactions.

Albert R. Lyman tells of a similar incident. Five horse thieves running stolen stock from Colorado passed near Bluff on their way to the Navajo Reservation. Jim watched them cross the San Juan River and so when Sheriff Butt invited him and another Navajo to join the party, he readily accepted. Part of the sheriff's plan was to use the two Indians as advance scouts because they would not tip the outlaws off to the presence of the pursuing posse. The Navajos pinpointed the camp, helped formulate a plan for capture, then served as guides to emplace posse members entirely around the sleeping thieves. The startled outlaws awoke to a number of voices commanding them to surrender but were not anxious to be taken into custody. Futile attempts to escape the next night convinced them that laying down their guns was the only option. Manacled astride their horses, the thieves passed through Bluff on their way to jail, a silent testament to Jim Joe's effectiveness.[42]

Lyman tells of another time when Marshall Joe Bush pursued two train robbers, James Rumrall and Charles Curtis. Hoping to evade capture, the thieves crossed the river and moved into Navajo land. Again, Jim joined the posse, helped locate the men, climbed the high promontory they hid on, and made the arrest. When he reached the outlaws, who were afraid of the consequences of killing a Navajo on the reservation, Jim called below to the marshal, "Shootey? Killey?" Once he had them in manacles, Jim led the men downhill to the waiting Bush.[43] Lyman was convinced that because of this type of assistance Jim Joe and others provided, the Utah part of the reservation became a "wall instead of a gate" for those seeking refuge from the law.

Jim also understood some of his rights under the law. On April 24, 1905, tourist promoter A. H. Culmer visited his camp at Navajo Spring. Assessing him as "one of the brightest Indians in the country," Culmer mentioned how Jim was going to water his flock at the spring. The party of whites said that he could not do that, but Jim assured them he had a paper from Washington saying that he could. Exactly what this paper was is not clear—perhaps something derived from a number of surveys that had passed through the area recently. Whatever it was, Jim was secure enough to challenge white authority and promised to bring the document to Bluff the next day.[44]

It was not just the Mormons or travelers who depended on Jim. Shelton and other government officials found him helpfully supportive. The agent asked him on a number of occasions to assume responsibility as a policeman for his community. He preferred to be free and especially disliked the limelight. Regardless, Superintendent Shelton insisted that he would hold Jim responsible for the behavior of the Navajos in his neighborhood, "as he was about the only one the Indians would listen to."[45]

Western History Collection, Denver Public Library

Jim Joe, friend of the white settlers in the region, served as a spokesman for the Navajo people living around Bluff. He and his family established numerous camps along Comb and Butler washes, one of the most famous being at Navajo Spring.

In 1905, the agent visited two camps—one in Montezuma Creek belonging to Navajo Tom and the other Jim Joe's. There was not more than ninety acres cultivated in either one of the tracts. In Jim's case, eight families under his leadership lived at the Butler Wash site, but no doubt, there were many other relatives spread out in Butler and Comb washes. Rain had been a problem that year, causing the wheat crop to fail, but the corn thrived. The Navajos worked the lands in common with patches of vegetables scattered here and there. No one claimed permanent ownership since the sites had not been surveyed and appropriated to individuals.[46]

Two years later, trouble erupted along the San Juan in the Aneth area. A powerful medicine man named Ba'álílee had been a center of dissent for years against Shelton's progressive policy of change emanating from Shiprock.[47] In October 1907, Fifth Cavalry troops from Fort Wingate, New Mexico, in an early morning attack, killed two men and arrested Ba'álílee with nine other prisoners. Resentment reverberated along the river. To Jim Joe's credit, he gave his "Indians good advice and [tried] to keep them out of trouble."[48] He responded to Shelton's letter addressed to "Friend Jim" with a letter of his own, saying that the Navajos in his and the Oljato areas were peaceful and felt good about the action taken. "The Indians all have plenty of sheep and some of them plenty of cattle and there is lots of grass and corn so my people down here won't suffer any this winter. . . . I am going to donate some work now on the road this side of my farm; the Americans here are all doing it, so I will have a good road."[49] Even though one of the men killed in the Ba'álílee fight was from among

Courtesy of San Juan County Historical Commission

Friends to the end, Jim Joe and Kumen Jones spent their last years together, continuing a relationship built on mutual trust. Here, U. A. Nielson (white shirt) and his wife Beatrice (dark dress) watch Jim Joe repair a shoe while Kumen (dark shirt) looks on.

"Jim's Indians" and had been counseled not to go to Ba'álílee's to gamble, "he had no ear and went and got killed which is all right."[50]

A year later, Captain E. A. Sturges visited Bluff to ascertain the status of Navajos in that area. He reported that Jim Joe, living at the mouth of Butler Wash, had one hundred families under his control, although the officer thought this an overestimation.[51] Jim held positive sway over his band. And so life continued at peace with his people and his neighbors. Following the Ute conflict in 1923, the government sent A. W. Simmington to San Juan County to create individual allotments for the Indians being released in Blanding. As part of his assignment, he also registered land for a few Navajos, Jim being one of them. The following year, the allotment officially recognized ownership of where Jim had lived since his return from Fort Sumner in the late 1860s. He took title to five acres under cultivation, a corral, and two hogans near the mouth of Butler Wash.[52] His other campsites and those of his family members spread up and down Comb and Butler washes were ignored.

As late as 1942, Jim had visitors to his home on the San Juan River. Earl Richards stopped by his hogan, noting the old man was blind, crippled with bad knees and painful thighs, and barely able to hobble. "Me sick; me sick here," was the sum of his verbal communication. Richardson concluded his report by writing, "May this unsung friend of the whites soon find the happy hunting ground he well deserves."[53] Within a short time he did.

Jim Joe enjoyed a high profile along the San Juan. There were, however, a significant number of Navajo people who were not known to the white community who lived along Comb and Butler washes, grazed their livestock along Comb Ridge, and used its resources for various economic and cultural activities. John Holiday from Monument Valley was one of those who, as a youth, lived and herded sheep in this area. From him and others comes a personal glimpse of people, places, and lifestyles during the 1920s, before the whites expelled the Navajos in the 1930s. Even after they were forced south of the river onto reservation land, Navajos continued certain collecting and religious activities.

Harvesting wild plants to supplement agricultural efforts drew Navajos to Comb Ridge and its environs. Navajo Oshley, who grew up next to Comb, a little further south of the San Juan River, paints a memorable picture of how difficult life was in this environment during the very late 1800s and early 1900s. A "hand-to-mouth existence" was not just figurative speech. Oshley begins:

> It was not a beautiful life. We even got water from a long distance, a mile away, carrying it in pails by hand. . . . We ate rabbits, pack rats, and prairie dogs. They were hard to catch. When winter came we started hunting rabbits, which we killed with sticks and stones. Sometimes there was nothing to eat. . . . Sometimes it was hard to get a meal and so we stayed hungry throughout the day; life was not a pleasant time when I was growing up. . . . During the summer, things got better because we looked for plants like green yucca fruit to eat. There were wild onions and sumac berries. Sometimes these did not grow because they only flourish when it rains. When the water did not come, life was extra hard. . . . When it really rained in the fall, there would be piñon nuts the following year. Almost the whole family went to pick them. . . . There were other plants such as wolfberry and edible tubers that were dug up, green yucca fruit, and yucca stalks. . . . Leaves from the juniper tree were burned and the ashes added to water. Mother then filtered this through a brush, added it to corn, mixed it well, then took the *haza'aleeh* and dipped it into the mush. We thought that this tasted really great.[54]

Gladys Bitsinnie recalls going to a place on Comb to gather sumac berries. Pickers could fill three large canvas bags before having to move on. Once home, the women made the berries into mush. Weavers fashioned thin, split branches of the sumac into wedding baskets. Dried fruit from the broadleaf yucca tasted sweet like peaches, while prickly pear cactus fruits were eaten dried, cooked, or stewed. Rice grass had the stems burned off and its seeds were ground and baked into bread as was rush grass, or dropseed, which grew in abundance around Comb. Gladys offered that even though only a small amount may be gathered, "after this was ground, it comes out to be a good portion of flour. At that time it was more holy. If you ground only two ears of corn, there was much more. It seems like there is no holiness now." [55] Other people collected herbs for the Enemyway ceremony and different plants as various foods.[56]

Navajos gathered soil at Comb Ridge for three different purposes. There are deposits where they collected clay for making pottery and paints. Various types of clay, when mixed with ashes and different minerals, provided a variety of colors. They found white minerals in "a mine close to Comb Ridge." This soil served as a food extender and sweetener. John commented that sometimes clay appears in balls, which can be burned, ground, and used as food. White clay also whitened wool used in weaving. Soil and vegetation from where a mountain sheep landed was taken and placed on an infant so that when he or she fell, he would not be hurt, just as the mountain sheep did not get hurt. This protective soil was also applied to the "mud dancers" participating in an Enemyway celebration, to avoid injury.[57]

Prayers were another aspect of Comb Ridge, as travelers ascended and descended the often-treacherous trails. At either the bottom or top, those traversing the steep slopes and rocky trail might offer petitions for protection or prayers of thanksgiving.[58] Livestock met their death plummeting to the rocks below on more than one occasion. The same prayer practice is true of the San Juan River. Holiday recounts, "Everyone sprinkled corn pollen and said a prayer as they passed over, both coming and going. No one crossed without this sacred ritual and prayer because that was the only way to cross the river." Navajos performed similar prayers when crossing Comb Ridge because of its supernatural powers and as a type of defensive barrier.[59]

Daily life on Comb Ridge centered on livestock. Depending upon one's view, this lifestyle is either unremarkable—a day-to-day existence with few dramatic events—or provides a fascinating view of Navajo culture, making the entire landscape sing with stories. John Holiday shared some of his experiences in which Butler Wash, especially, held a series of mnemonic sites filled with stories of people and events long gone.[60]

John began by recalling some of the previous inhabitants, many of whom were related to Jim Joe. Abandoned hogan sites along Butler Wash and at the foot of Comb Ridge belonged to Jim's clan (Tá'chii'nii) members. One of Jim's children, named Red Spot on the Neck, and another, The One Who Has too Much Self Pride, lived in camps beside Comb. Other people, such as Hastiin Joe's son-in-law, Large Yucca Fruit (who danced in the Yé'ii Bicheii ceremony), and his maternal grandson, Tall Educated One (who attended school briefly); The Sheepherder (well known for producing rain); Mister Lives in the Shade (whose camp was in the shade of a mesa); Mister Green Grass under the Cottonwood Trees (referring to a homesite); and the Barren Woman (actually a man who had a ceremony that transformed his status into a woman) populated this area. Each was involved with seasonal migration, bringing his flocks to higher, greener, cooler pastures on Elk Ridge or Blue Mountain. Ada Benally, who lives in Bluff and is related through marriage to Red Spot on His Neck, recalls people saying, "Hastiin Joe has moved way up north again."[61]

John's herding practice also centered on seasonal change. He pastured the sheep on the west side of Comb Ridge in the summer and by fall moved them over to the east side. In the winter he drove them back to the Mexican Hat area then started the process again the next spring. Cool mountain breezes and shade in the summer gave way to places of less snow and cold in the winter. Back then, people changed ranges a lot. "The Diné would say, 'It's too cold here,' and pack up their belongings on their horses and move to another location, even though their children were small. Some of them built hogans to move into here and there for summer or winter camps." People mixed together and there were no fences. Nobody said, "That's my land." Instead they would say, "It rained over there. I will move my livestock out there to graze." Navajos moved to and from without conflict. They moved anywhere for greener pastures. Nowadays, land claims are fenced.

Mary Tsosie, when recalling the movements of Barren Woman, said that in the winter he and his family used to live on top of a mesa (unspecified). While this seems antithetical to the idea of staying low and out of the wind during the cold months, there obviously was a good reason for the effort. Family members hauled their belongings up a narrow crevice,

Courtesy of Kay Shumway

Corn Pollen, father of Tall Educated One, first built this hogan, which was later used by his son. Established near Long Fingers Canyon, this site was a popular gathering place for Navajos who came to race horses on an adjoining flat.

the width of a person's body. "That's why they used to call it Wind up One's Ass—it was so narrow that the wind blew up behind a person's back as they hauled up their stuff."[62] Once settled, Barren Woman performed all of his/her duties of grinding corn, carding and spinning wool, and cooking. Life maintained its cyclical round.

Near Long Fingers Canyon (named for a Puebloan pictograph), known to the Navajos as "Where the Cottonwoods Are Green," lie the remains of a camp belonging to Tall Educated One's family. His father, Corn Pollen, and his wife used to move there occasionally, but apparently, Tall Educated One remained for some time. The story is told that shortly after the Navajos returned from Fort Sumner, he attended school briefly at Fort Defiance. This was enough to give him a name. On the flat east of the Long Fingers camp is a "horse leg print," which is Navajo for "race track." People gathered from miles around for the races and other communal activities. They bet on whose horse would win, wagering bullets, pocket knives, money, saddle blankets, rope, hobble straps, and everything else imaginable. This became the prize for the winning group. Only one horse raced for each side, winner-take-all.

The Sheepherder, of the Water's Edge (Tábąąhá) Clan, also stayed here occasionally. He was a wanderer originally from Dennehotso, who offered his services of caring for other's livestock. John also saw him in the Mexican Hat area when he was a boy. John recalls living there with his maternal grandmother, who had many sheep to take care of. One very hot afternoon, Sheepherder came to their camp and received a meal. There was little vegetation; it had not rained for a long time, and the animals needed help. Grandmother asked him to sing and pray for rain, which he agreed to do. Sheepherder requested some white clay, and John led him to a point of land where he scooped some up, added water, and removed his clothes except for his loincloth. Next, he applied the moist white clay all over his body then began running. John, out of curiosity, discreetly followed on the other side of a parallel ridge until Sheepherder stopped. He sat down, sang and prayed, then took a square object and blew into it. A coyote howl followed. He did this several times and ran back to the summer shade in the camp, but not before John arrived. Once he returned, cleaned up, and got dressed, it was a short while before a hailstorm deluged the land with melting water several inches deep.[63]

The Navajos living and working along Comb Wash enjoyed friendships with some of the Mormon cowboys traveling in the same area. Big Cowboy (Akałii Tso), also known as Jacob Adams, was on good terms with some of the Navajos. Another, Ugly Cowboy (Akałii'chxǫ́í), was a rancher who spoke Navajo and was a kind, generous man. One late summer day, John and his family were in a canyon picking sumac berries when Ugly Cowboy passed by with a large herd of cattle. "'Give me a cow, Grandfather,' John said to him. He stopped his tan horse and sat there for a minute then said, 'You mean it? Are you going to butcher it right here?'" John assured him he would. "'That's how I like it,' he said. 'I like it when people ask me for the cow. I am not stingy with it. But if they steal the cow, then they get to me!' he said as he slammed his fist into his palm. 'It's good to ask first.'"

Ugly Cowboy turned to his herders and yelled for them to bring some cows over. He shot a fat one and told the Navajos to butcher it. After they had finished removing the entrails and cleaning the meat, Ugly Cowboy had them cut off a leg for him, which he in turn cut in half and stuffed in each side of a saddlebag hanging on a mule. "Enjoy yourselves while you feast on the cow," he said and off he went. To John, "He was a very kind man. His son was just the same. He also gave me a cow on another occasion."

It was good that there were these positive experiences between the two races. One gets the impression that they were becoming fewer and fewer as time passed. The 1930s witnessed dramatic changes in land use for both white men and Indians, as the Great Depression took its toll, the Taylor Grazing Act regulated the ranges, and the Navajo were forcibly removed from some areas and pushed onto the reservation, only to see their herds shrink because of livestock reduction. While the 1920s may not have been the golden era of the livestock industry in San Juan, the days of armed conflict were over, and the gentle stream of life managed the few ripples before it reached the approaching torrent of change.

6

Combing the Comb

Economic Developments, 1887–1930

You remember when Noah built the ark and it rained forty days and forty nights? San Juan got an inch and a quarter and we haven't had a hell of a lot since.

—Karl Barton, local rancher

When the Mormons came to the Salt Lake Valley in 1847, they arrived with a vision of the future based on the past. Having been driven from states and territories in the East, the Latter-day Saints sought isolation to establish the sprawling territory of Deseret, practice their own religious beliefs, follow a theocratic government, and remain self-sufficient, free from non-Mormon economic control. Within twenty years, outside forces changed much of that vision. The Utah War, the Civil War, shrinking of Deseret, establishment of Utah Territory, federal governance, the telegraph, the approaching transcontinental railroad, mining rushes in the western states, and Indian issues contributed to an unexpected thrust of economic development and flow of outsiders into Utah Territory.

A similar scenario, on a much smaller scale, played itself out in southeastern Utah during the last two decades of the nineteenth and first three decades of the twentieth century. Different forces were at work, but the results were the same—interaction with large non-Mormon groups competing for opportunities to make money. While there are many reasons given for Mormon settlement of this region—to relieve federal pressure on those practicing polygamy, the establishment of an outer cordon that secured Utah lands for Mormons, and as a place of settlement for new converts from the southern states—two paramount reasons are most often cited. Morgan Amasa Barton, son of Joseph F., stated succinctly the "vision" for early settlement in Bluff and beyond when he wrote, "they [Mormon settlers] were an established outpost, detracting marauding Indians from interior southern settlements of Utah Territory as well as a point of interception of bank robbers, horse thieves, cattle rustlers and jail breakers [etc.] . . . . These people were to be shock absorbers of premeditated plots of Caucasian outlaws and Indian renegades. . . ."[1]

Yet one could argue that the establishment of Bluff served as a magnet to attract just those elements—"Indians and outlaws" as well as non-Mormon entrepreneurs. Unanticipated change was afoot as events over the next forty years soon proved.

Mormons such as Francis A. Hammond encouraged part of the change by promoting the resources of San Juan through articles printed in the *Deseret News*. Touting the splendid winter and summer ranges, the prolific grass, and temperate climate, he drew outsiders as well as those of his faith to the Bluff area. However, long before he took pen in hand, cattlemen such as Harold and Edmund Carlisle of the Kansas and New Mexico Land and Cattle Company, I. W. Lacy of the L.C. outfit, and Charles H. Ogden of the Pittsburg Cattle Company took full advantage of rangelands north of Bluff. Ranchers from as far away as Texas also began eyeing the country. In the spring of 1888, John Crosby and a man named Calder herded two thousand Texas longhorns into the Comb Wash drainage and on Elk Ridge.[2] Since this was open range owned by the federal government, the company had as much legal right as did the citizens of Bluff, but the affront to the Mormons was obvious.

Albert R. Lyman provides an eyewitness description of the cattle as they headed through town and on to their pasture. No doubt, the settlers were as wide-eyed as the longhorns.

> This great bawling herd, a mile long, came straggling down the river through Bluff—yellow cattle, white, black, brindle; all of them starving and hollow from the long trail; all of them coyote like in form, little better in size. And horns! Such a river of horns as you might see in a nightmare—horns reaching out and up, out and up again in fantastic corkscrews. The children of Bluff laughed at it, but their parents looked on with alarm. The snaky little bulls, narrow and sunburned, could compete successfully for existence with goats on a rock. . . . This indestructible Texas stock would crowd the Bluff cattle against the rims, starve them to death, and predominate over them by their sheer native toughness.[3]

Dan Short, foreman of this outfit, had previously used the Horseshoe Nail brand on his stock.[4] Now the company assumed an ELKM brand that stretched from the neck to the tail of a calf, with a final identifying signature of a lopped-off right ear. There was no mistaking Bluff cattle for Texas longhorns, if such a concern ever existed. In Lyman's mind there never could have been. He wrote, "At two years old you might fancy you looked at them through the wrong end of a field glass, and at maturity they seemed to be a compromise between a joke and a nightmare. . . . Their backs had longitude without latitude, and they sloped off to nothing behind like the spinning end of an old style top."[5] Suitably adapted to the desert range of Comb Wash and the plateau country of Elk Ridge, these cattle created even stiffer competition for Ute, Navajo, and Mormon livestock.

As different as the Mormon cattle were to the longhorns, they were no more different than the people who herded them. To their credit, the owners "took no undue advantage" on using the ranges, but their hirelings were an assortment of the best and worst that the West had to offer.[6] The cowboys were by all accounts a rough and tumble crew that mixed about as well with the people of Bluff as oil did with water. Stories abound of Wild West incidents as drunken cowboys attempted attending Mormon dances, rode out of town

Courtesy of San Juan County Historical Commission

The caption for this photograph says, "The Perkins outfit," although individuals are not identified. The Perkinses, like the Bartons, Adamses, and a dozen other families, until recently made their livelihood on the ranges of southeastern Utah.

with pistols and rifles blazing, faced off with the stalwart unarmed settler, and mysteriously disappeared when law officers arrived in town. Perhaps for all of these reasons, and as a way of maintaining peace, the headquarters for the Elk Mountain Cattle Company became the cabins of the trading post at Rincon.

In addition to the troublemakers who came in with the cattle, an outlaw element that preyed upon herds troubled Bluff. Lyman tells of two such men who arrived near town in 1889. They invented a brand called the "M Pole" that consisted of the huge letter *M* with a bar running through it. The entire brand extended from a cow's ear to its tail. With all of its angles and flourishes, the brand was capable of covering every other brand except that of ELKM. Bluff cattle disappeared, Marshall Joe Bush and his deputies executed a warrant, and the search began. One night, L. H. Redd, Joe Hammond, and Kumen Jones camped at the head of Comb Wash. As the sun set, one of the leaders of the M Pole passed their camp on the way to the cabins at Rincon. Jones rode all night, awakened Bush and party in Bluff, and was present when the lawmen arrested the thief before sunrise the next day. The criminal spent eight months in jail but was never prosecuted because people refused to testify. Still, the message was strong enough that the M Pole gang left the country for good.[7]

By 1892, the original ELKM outfit prepared to sell its holdings to the San Juan Co-op. For twenty thousand dollars, the Bluff stockholders could now boast of a herd of five thousand cattle and adoption of the brand that had threatened them for years. The animals brought eleven dollars a head in Dolores, Colorado; those not captured and sold immediately became the project of Al Scorup and Franklin Adams, who delivered two thousand feral cattle from this herd to the Rincon/Barton Range for five dollars a head. Scorup and the Nielson brothers purchased them for twenty-five hundred dollars to build their holdings before sale.[8] The net effect was return of the ranges of Comb Wash and Elk Mountain (Ridge) to the Mormons, removal of the breed of longhorns from competition with Bluff cattle, and abandonment of the cabins at Rincon.[9]

The San Juan Co-op, however, resumed control of the old Barton Trading Post at Rincon around 1893 and hired Christian L. Christensen as its clerk. The road down Butler Wash was still open to wagon traffic, hauling wool, sheep pelts, cattle hides, and Navajo blankets to Bluff. Christensen one time floated two thousand pounds of flour and supplies to his establishment in a skiff sixteen feet long and eight feet wide, with a draft of eighteen inches. Sand waves beat against the heavily laden craft, causing him to grasp the sides and hold on for the ride. Once the boat landed at Rincon, it served as transport to ferry customers across the river.[10] The post remained open for several more years with Navajos as the primary customers, but a different clientele arrived with increasing frequency as Comb Ridge assumed a new dimension.

While the ranges bid farewell to the Texans and their longhorns and Christensen ordered stock, another facet of the mythic West appeared along the San Juan—the placer miner. December 1892 witnessed the first whisperings about gold. Within weeks, the hushed tones turned to a shrill shout that brought miners with gold pans in hand from every direction. Bluff burgeoned into the jumping-off point for claims scattered from the Four Corners to beyond the confluence of the San Juan and Colorado rivers. Most activity concentrated in the region around and below Mexican Hat, making Bluff vital in sustaining operations and Comb Ridge a visible landmark one should search for treasure. "Flour" gold, a fine particulate matter the size of silt grains of sand, flowed down from its sources in the San Juan Mountains in southwestern Colorado, the Carrizo Mountains in northeastern Arizona, and other ranges whose tributaries flowed into the San Juan.[11]

How many people actually worked the river will never be known. Near the height of the rush in January 1893, an estimated two to three thousand men, "with more arriving every day," mined their sites. Other figures vary from a low of seven hundred to a high of five thousand, with one person claiming that a thousand miners passed through Bluff on New Year's Day alone.[12] Many who arrived soon departed after having found little for their efforts. By March, most of the boomers had left the diggings to more determined individuals who could bring financial resources to bear. One disgruntled person testified

Courtesy of San Juan County Historical Commission

The 1890s gold rush brought people like Dell Raplee (center), his wife to his left, and his adopted son (foreground with lariat) to the San Juan River, where he established his home east of Mexican Hat Rock. After the enthusiasm for gold petered out, Raplee became involved in the oil industry.

that many of the articles he had read about the goldfields ended with the statement, "The San Juan is no country for a poor man." He went on to refute this: "It is the greatest place on earth for a poor man, and the longer he stays there the poorer will he become."[13]

Comb Ridge and Wash played two different roles in the initial mining onslaught. The most obvious is that the rock formation funneled all overland travelers from Bluff down Butler Wash and either across the San Juan River to Mexican Hat and beyond or around the corner and up Comb Wash then over Lime Ridge or the trail near Road Canyon to White Canyon and beyond.[14] On a map associated with a potential transfer of lands in 1893 to the Southern Utes, a trail is shown running from Bluff to the "Barton House," turning up "McComb Wash" with two springs in it (one of which is Navajo Spring, the other is possibly Arch Canyon).[15] The route then split with a branch going to Clay Hills, Halls Ferry, and beyond, while the other branch climbed to the Bears Ears only to diverge partway down Elk Mountain. One trail headed to Blue Mountain and the other to Dandy Crossing on the Colorado River near the Dirty Devil River. This entire network of roads evolved and shifted over time.

Courtesy of the Arizona Historical Society/Tucson, Cummings Collection, MS 200, Box 33, Folder 1

The crossing near Rincon, when the river was down, offered a solid bottom, negotiable banks, and a depth of water of two to three feet. Richard and Marietta Wetherill did not find the crossing easy but did find love and a marriage proposal. (Photo taken 1908.)

With all of the hustle and bustle of the growing economy, there also had to be time for romance. Marietta Wetherill tells of a trip she took with her future husband, Richard, most likely in the early 1890s, as they traveled to Monticello. Driving their wagon up Chinle Wash, the couple, in company with other wagons, arrived at Comb Wash near Barton's Trading Post. They camped for the night, watched the water level, and prepared to ford the river. The next morning, as the San Juan subsided, Richard urged his mules into the swift, deep water. He could not go straight across because of the strong current against the far bank, but he moved his swimming-walking-floating animals to the far shore only to realize they could not readily climb the muddy slope. Roping and "snubbing" a mule to some driftwood to give the team rest, he warned the other travelers on the far shore not to attempt crossing, then turned to Marietta, asking her if she was frightened. She responded, "I was scared to death." He inquired where she put her fear, then in the same breath asked her to marry him. An unsure response drew forth the promise that he would do everything he could to make her happy, to which she replied, "Well, then I will, I'll marry you."[16] The mules worked their way out of the water, and the engaged couple made their way to Barton's post. Perhaps this romance blossomed because of the initial soaking in the San Juan; the couple remained together until Richard's death in Chaco Canyon in 1910.

Placer mining on the San Juan River proliferated in the 1890s and early 1900s. More advanced machinery replaced the miner's pan and sluice box of the early years. In the distance are two other mining camps.

The placer mining operations were in full swing for three years before a road over Lime Ridge shortened the trip to Mexican Hat. Prior to this, many supplies came in by boat.[17] These routes were particularly crucial as miners realized that the stubborn riverbanks and bars refused to yield much wealth to just panning. Miners introduced rockers, sluice boxes, flumes, waterwheels, boats, and more permanent camps to wrest the gold by more sophisticated and focused means. Wagons pulled by oxen and men on horseback used the Butler trail to move increasingly ponderous loads as the rush gave way to a smaller and better-financed attempt at gold mining and, later, oil exploration.

Charles Spencer in 1893 freighted lumber to construct a wooden apparatus for placer efforts 75 miles below Bluff at Otto J. Zahn's camp near the mouth of Nakai Canyon. He took the road that went to Comb Wash, where he crossed the river, then made his own path as necessary.[18] Ernest Hyde, serving as foreman for one of the mining companies, followed the same trail to Moonlight Canyon, fording the river at Comb Wash. Even though he was no longer associated with the post at Rincon, he could not resist saying that "From Durango, Colorado, to the store at the mouth of Comb Wash, 150 miles, it took about fifteen days to make the round trip."[19] And Walter E. Mendenhall traveled from Lake City, Colorado, in June 1893, to begin his adventure. He hauled lumber from Bluff to the mouth of Comb Wash where he built a boat fifteen feet long by three and a half feet wide with a draft of eight inches, then loaded it with equipment and floated ten miles downstream to set up camp. From July 1893 to fall 1894, he extracted between four and five thousand dollars working the bars and banks of the river. He estimated that as many as 150 miners were on the river trying their luck at that time.[20]

Even with all the freighting, supplies were scarce. Some miners took to appropriating cattle grazing the Barton Range for their larders back in camp. Detecting this sort of mischief was difficult while proving it in court was equally hard. Richard Knight's previously mentioned run-in with Jim Joe was part of this operation. By rounding up stock that did not belong to him then selling the animals to miners and Indians alike, he profited from both sides. One of the meeting places for these transactions was the mouth of Comb Wash. Word leaked out about Knight's enterprise, and Sheriff Willard Butt intercepted him and his companion near the Bluff lime kiln in Butler Wash. The two men left town but this time with heavily armed guards, on their way to court.[21]

The second part that Comb played in the rush was to serve as a natural spot to seek wealth. Frank Hyde reported that the very first placer miners he saw on the river were panning at Rincon. With the floodplain established by the river and the entrance of a canyon that frequently washed down sediment from a large geographical area, the mouths of this and other canyons were natural places to look for gold. Low water during the winter months exposed bars and more of the banks, offering prime conditions for exploration.[22] Availability of supplies at the Barton Trading Post, ready access to Bluff, the flow of overland traffic from the goldfields, and the ability to use the river more easily than navigating in the restricted canyons below made Comb Wash a desirable site for mining.

Handy access for a miner meant that other, less desirable people could also be in reach. Take for instance Samuel Brooks, a man from Indiana, who came to southeastern Utah to earn his fortune. He went to the Comb Wash area and set up camp along one of the intermittent streams. Lady Luck bedded down with him; in a few days, he found uncharacteristically large nuggets on top of the ground in a dry gravel wash. Exuberant with his find, he took his samples to Bluff to buy supplies. The assay on the majority of his nuggets proved that he had struck fool's gold. However, after a second trip with another batch of minerals, he received positive proof of what he had come for—real gold.

When Brooks returned to his camp, he noticed that a pile of rejected fool's gold had been taken by two individuals wearing moccasins. Concerned for his welfare, he began carrying a weapon and keeping watch on the surrounding hills. In the meantime, Posey attempted to trade small golden rocks to a Bluff storekeeper, who recognized them as the same fool's gold that he had tested earlier.

Brooks continued to pick up nuggets, gathering more than one hundred pounds. Then one night, while preparing his meal, men ambushed him. He managed to get under cover and stop his bleeding wound. After some time, three Indians, weapons ready, approached the camp. Brooks shot one; the other two escaped unscathed, but his action earned him enough time to pack his stash and gear on two animals and set out for Bluff. There, the settlers cared for his infected wounds.

Brooks had had enough, and so with his gold he returned to Indiana. Before leaving, however, he described to friends the area of his discovery. He said that it was south of Bluff in Comb Wash, around Chinle and Walker creeks—"about four miles this side of that great rock that looks like a church; [from there] you turn into them saw-toothed ridges." Brooks drew a map that later proved to be difficult to follow; then he took his gold, went east, and bought a large farm where he spent the remainder of his days. John Nance heard of Brooks's story and decided to try his hand. Three weeks later, he returned to Bluff with the same type of gold nuggets that Brooks had found. Unfortunately, Nance went to Holbrook, Arizona, with his gold and was killed in a saloon brawl without ever telling anyone about the location of his strike.[23] Exactly how much credence can be given to such "lost mine" stories remains for the reader to determine.

Certainly for some miners, Comb Ridge proved to be synonymous with defeat. A. Koebler appeared in Durango long enough to have an article published in the newspapers heralding his return. In addition to noting that the roads around Bluff were terrible, he complained that many discouraged miners were retreating from the goldfields. He had "heard [that Comb Wash] was the center of an excitement. We went up the wash about twenty [actually three] miles to Navajo Spring and found nothing. They have since christened that point Turn Back Springs, because it is there that everyone camps returning."[24] Some miner took it upon himself to warn others by venting with graffiti on a sandstone boulder near the spring. "One hundred dollars reward for the damned fool who started the gold rush." His thought remains, but the writing disappeared during the construction of Highway 163 that replaced the old road.[25]

Gold mining operations continued on the San Juan River until 1920. The companies that worked the sand and gravel beds varied in size and sophistication, as did the machinery they hauled in to wrest a profit from the fickle river. Switching from mechanical crushing and sorting machines to those based on electrical and chemical reactions, the miners turned to the latest scientific gadgetry. The end result of the approximately twenty-five year experience of gold mining on the San Juan proved how uneconomical the whole thing was. Yet, long before the hope for gold was totally abandoned, a new goddess of wealth—oil—became the prime mover for anticipated prosperity. It proved almost as elusive as gold, creating different demands but fostering a mandate for breaching Comb Ridge.

Between the first rush for gold and the first gush of oil, entrepreneurs noticed the black slippery substance oozing from rock formations and casting a rainbow of colors into pools of water near Mexican Hat. Ten years before the gold rush, Ernest B. Hyde staked a claim on part of the oil-producing area but then let it lapse. Others such as Melvin Dempsey, A. L. Raplee, and Robert Mitchell became intimately familiar with the land and its wealth during the 1890s gold rush, subsequently preparing them for the oil boom.[26] Serious drilling for oil near Mexican Hat started around 1904 and declined in the 1920s, although there is still some production there today. Exploring and testing spread over a large geographical region that eventually encompassed the lands between Bluff and

Courtesy of San Juan County Historical Commission

Parked in front of the Bluff Co-op is machinery owned by the Chicago Exploration Company on its way to the San Juan oil fields. The long wagons, metal tires, and heavy loads presented a challenge for teamsters who had to move the equipment either down Butler Wash or, later, the Navajo Spring Trail.

Slickhorn Canyon many miles below Mexican Hat. With the exception of those located in the general vicinity of Mexican Hat, these wells proved to be either dry or uneconomical to develop. The home of E. L. Goodridge, a Colorado miner, was near the present-day town of Mexican Hat and became the freighting terminus and post office for the majority of businesses sprouting along the river.[27]

According to Frank Hyde, the first drill to bite into the earth for oil was in the mouth of Comb Wash and was under the supervision of Goodridge. No oil was found, but Hyde provides a general description of moving drilling equipment down Butler Wash. "The road from Bluff to Comb Wash was constructed by donated labor, so that they could get the drilling machinery down there. The drilling machinery was taken into Bluff with (six) horses to a wagon and eased down into the canyon with ropes or carried down."[28] This dry well gave way to the first substantially productive well drilled by Goodridge at the mouth of John's Canyon. Success set the wheels of development whirring. That year, 1907, Bluff "went wild with excitement."[29] A year later, news had spread sufficiently to encourage the initial influx of entrepreneurs ready to boost the town and its environs. Companies from Salt Lake City and Ogden, Utah; Colorado Springs and Denver, Colorado; Chicago, Illinois; Tucumcari, New Mexico; Oakland, California; Spokane, Washington; and Connecticut hauled drill rigs into the field over some of the most formidable terrain imaginable. The initial rigs brought in were relatively small and light—good for punching holes in the earth to locate pockets of oil close to the surface. Time quickly showed that larger drills that bore deeper were necessary to wrest the oil from lower levels. All of these initially came in wagons drawn by oxen down Butler Wash and up Comb Wash then over Lime Ridge.

Reasons for the 1908 euphoria made sense to local boosters. Claiming that this field was "favored over any other field ever discovered," the entrepreneurs explained that drilling in the canyons put the source closer to the surface, allowing shallow drilling. The quality of oil obtained from the wells had a high content of gasoline. This was particularly important in an environment where hauling wood to stoke the boilers that powered the steam engines was expensive and time consuming. Many of the rigs burned the oil coming out of their own hole, a form of self-cannibalism. The third reason was that in many oil fields, there were two strata conducive to storing oil, while here, there were six different "sands" that held possibilities.[30] Gold on the river, oil on the land, San Juan offered potential.

Geologist Herbert E. Gregory visited the field for three days in July 1909 and reported the developments. There were multiple routes to the town of Goodridge. Travelers using the Denver and Rio Grande Railroad passed through Dolores or Mancos, Colorado (either about 106 miles away); Farmington, New Mexico (110 miles); or Thompson thence Moab, Utah (158 miles). Those taking the Santa Fe Railroad went through Gallup, New Mexico (175 miles), or Holbrook, Arizona (160 miles), eventually crossing the newly constructed bridge at Mexican Hat.[31] Once an individual arrived, he would find twenty-five wells spread about the region with the most profitable ones generally in the Lime Creek basin. Of those wells, twenty reported striking oil to some degree, but Gregory did not endorse these ventures too enthusiastically. Even though he reported that "nearly 10,000 locations have been recorded at Monticello, the county seat of San Juan County," he closed his report by saying the evidence "indicates that there is little probability of finding gushers or wells of phenomenal yield. It seems reasonable to predict, however, that several wells will be found in this district from which oil may be pumped with profit."[32]

Gregory's well-informed prophecy proved accurate. Twice the Mexican Hat oil field showed promise and drew interest—during the 1908–1910 era and around 1917. In both instances, the need for transportation pushed itself to the forefront. Bluff became the jumping-off spot with dirt roads connecting to Colorado through McElmo Canyon or the Four Corners Road, while the rails at Thompson brought people through Monticello and newly established Blanding (known as Grayson from 1905 to 1914). All roads led to Bluff. Supplies to sustain operations in the field cost about the same as in Gallup or Cortez with the expense of freight ($7.50 from Dolores to Bluff and $1 for a hundred pounds from Bluff to Goodridge) tacked on.[33] Another surveyor of the field during the same period wrote, "I have rarely seen a community where the people were as uniformly courteous and hospitable to the stranger as here at Bluff. No one holds you up."[34] But once people and goods arrived in the small Mormon town, transportation became a much greater issue.

Bluff, from its inception, viewed roads as part of a package of economic development. Regardless of what "excited" prospects of financial gain, transportation was crucial. June 7, 1880, the day after the Mormons first arrived, Bluff and Montezuma precincts

Courtesy of San Juan County Historical Commission

Frank Hyde's Bluff City Oil Exchange here provides a local perspective of events occurring around Mexican Hat. The carefully staged picture with Frank (fifth from left), the ticker-tape and survey equipment alongside woven Navajo rugs, and Posey on the far right leaves the viewer with a composite picture of life and personalities in this "jumping off" place.

created a road district and appointed a road supervisor. A year later, the two districts separated, but they still cooperated, paying a $1.50 per day to those who worked on the roads, with a total allocation of $50. In 1882, funds paid for work on the road going from Bluff to Clay Hills. A year later, the road starting at Comb Wash and ending at the Colorado state line was rejected as a county road. Two years later, with the establishment of the Barton Trading Post, thirteen people, including Amasa Barton, presented a similar petition to "have the county roads extended from the Butler Wash to the Comb Wash." It was rejected although they did receive $150 for work on the road. And when the San Juan Co-op under the direction of L. H. Redd took over the post, there were constant attempts, right through 1892—some successful, some rejected—to have the road from Bluff to Rincon worked on.[35] Mother nature eventually ended the debate when she wiped out the land bridge between the two washes.

As early as 1893, Cass Hite, veteran miner and authority on activities along the San Juan and Colorado rivers, declared, "Rincon . . . is as far as a road can ever be taken

Courtesy of Kay Shumway

The Butler Wash Dugway, as it appears today, was a major thoroughfare for those participating in the gold rush and heading to the oil fields. Of them, U.S. Deputy Surveyor Elmer E. Miller wrote in 1909, that they should be some "of the most attractive for commercial investment of any in the United States." A small field is still in operation today.

down the river. . . ."[36] He was right, and by 1910 or 1911, even the connecting link of land between Butler Wash and Rincon had washed out. Prior to this, however, miners and entrepreneurs were already eying the old Navajo Spring Trail. The oil field spurred the impetus for change as early as 1908. Realizing that there was both a southern and northern route to ship in and out materials, businessmen in Bluff wished to corner the trade. In order to do so, a more direct route to the fields, one that could handle the large machinery hauled down Butler Wash, needed to be chiseled and dynamited out of the side of Comb Ridge. Miners and Bluffites alike envisioned the economic benefit not only for oilmen, miners, and city dwellers but also tourists. With this improvement, people could travel to Mexican Hat and the oil field to work and to Natural Bridges and the Colorado River to play. At first, only a sporadic party of sightseers ventured forth; eventually, there arose a swell.

Citizens from San Juan raised $2,000, and another $500–700 came from the county, with the additional benefit of a proposed bridge to be constructed at Mexican Hat.[37] Two

In 1917, W. H. Hopkins and Dolph Andrus were the first to traverse, in their Maxwell, the Navajo Spring Road with an auto. The travail they encountered is captured in these photos, giving a sense of early conditions on today's Highway 163.

weeks later, the road committee reported that a new route going down Navajo Spring Trail would only cost fifteen hundred dollars, the funds for which had already "been raised by subscription in a few days," the work begun.[38] Years later, Albert R. Lyman, with his usual tongue-in-cheek prose, described what he called a "wagon road" down the tortuous Navajo Trail and into Comb Wash, "at least it was called a road, and will perhaps continue by that name though it becomes impassible to the most acrobatic burro that ever carried a pack."[39] While the intentions were good, the road was fit for only the most limited traffic.

On September 8, 1910, additional improvements to support the oil field arrived in Bluff. The town now boasted its first telephone system, linking it to Blanding, Monticello, and Cortez. The biggest complaint from those who installed and maintained this service was that people kept cutting the line to use it for tying loads onto their horses or wagons. In one instance, over one thousand feet of wire went to someone's use, forcing the county to hire "watchers" to prevent this from reoccurring.[40]

By 1917, tourism joined the Mexican Hat oil field to spur improvements. On May 8, Dr. W. H. Hopkins from Salt Lake City and Dolph Andrus from Bluff credited themselves with driving the first automobile down the Navajo Spring Trail. The Maxwell car, "with lots of repairs to take along," set about to prove that autos could travel from Bluff to many of the scenic wonders of Utah and arrive at St. George safely. The idea began incubating six months before, but weather and issues connected with World War I slowed the birthing process. Now Hopkins and Andrus were ready. Dolph volunteered his car for the adventure, earning the epithet of being a "Christopher Columbus and a North Pole discoverer all in one." (There is nothing like hometown boosterism.)

The people of Blanding and Bluff caught the vision, raising two hundred dollars to cover expenses. After naming all of the donating luminaries from the two towns, the newspaper outlined the plan. Besides blazing the trail over relatively uncharted territory, the feat could be advertised throughout the United States to automobilists, Rotary clubs, and tour groups to get them to do the same thing. The outcome: establish a recognized road that promoters could use to go to the federal government to demand funds. Stanley Henrichs, chief of the U.S. Land Office in Salt Lake and backer of the scheme, offered, "If you get a road, I can go to the U.S. Government and claim it as it goes mostly through government land. We can secure an appropriation to improve it. I can get money easily to improve a road, but I have never been able to get a cent to make a new road."[41] For insurance, Ed Doyle and William Reed accompanied the Maxwell to Kayenta to see that it made it through the sands of Monument Valley.

Four months later, the local papers carried a brief report of the successful 420-mile journey. As promised, a detailed log of the roads, distances, landmarks, crossings, supply and water stations, guides, and places of interest spread across the pages, each one of which was stamped with the phrase, "Fix the roads; the tourists are waiting."[42] The "Monumental Highway" from Bluff to St. George could now be part of the exodus for those going to California for the winter, a draw for Americans to keep their dollars at home, a lure to attract Europeans with their money, and an impetus for the government to improve the road system—especially that on the Navajo Reservation. Bluff, as a pass-through on this future highway, could feature side trips to local attractions such as Mexican Hat and the oil field, Natural Bridges, Monument Valley, and Ancestral Puebloan ruins. Future generations would pay tribute to Hopkins and Andrus, "these daring and enterprising pathfinders," for their establishing a highway that would "bring within reach of all nature lovers the scenic wonders" of southeastern Utah. While Hopkins and Andrus have been largely forgotten, the result that they sought has become a reality.

Before the Monumental Highway log was in the hands of the people of San Juan County, officials from the Denver and Rio Grande Railroad were already in Bluff, inquiring as to when the road would open. Claiming "there would have been five thousand people who would have made the trip this year," the three railroad men said there was an incessant demand for information from people who wanted to go to Natural Bridges and travel the highway. The editor of the *San Juan Blade* took the opportunity to point out that, "Owing to the fact that no work had been done on either of the routes mentioned, it was necessary to inform them that at the present it would be impossible for auto parties to make the trip through here, but that we hoped to have both roads opened for travel next spring."[43] The remainder of the article was an indictment against county and state for not taking road development seriously. Economic growth in this part of rural Utah could not move forward until issues of accessibility were resolved. The fear that tourists would brand San Juan for the "rough places for which this county will be famed" could only be allayed if there were a "get-together movement" to fix the roads. "Next spring" saw little movement from either the county or state.

The oil field continued to pump slight profits but pursued significant road development. Investors stood in the wings waiting for the big find. Poor roads deterred them from wanting to sink money into a venture handicapped by dangerous and difficult transportation. Comb Ridge and Butler Wash were the two worst offenders along this road that required immediate attention. One person wrote, "After a trip over such roads as exist between this point [Blanding] and the Mexican Hat, about the only thing that anyone would be interested in would be a bed."[44] Two months later, three executives from Utah, Colorado, and New York passed through Bluff in their Franklin automobile on their way to the oil field. Doubtless they traversed the trail down Comb Ridge, but no further mention was made as to their sleeping needs.[45]

As 1917 came to a close, A. L. Raplee—still living in Mexican Hat, drilling wells with money from local investors and promoting the oil field—became exasperated. Official reports from financial backers still cited the "inaccessibility to the field owing to the conditions of the roads west of Bluff" as a major deterrent to future development.[46] Tired of waiting for the sluggish county or state to start road improvements, he set his own crew of men to work on the road through Butler and Comb. The newspaper called for a "veritable boulevard" to be created or else face the consequence of oil-field traffic and economic development coming in from the south bypassing Bluff. A week later, Raplee

Courtesy of San Juan County Historical Commission

Transporting equipment, such as this Mexican Hat cable-tool drilling rig, highlighted the necessity of road improvement. Not until economic need was tied to local development would a suitable system of transportation be obtained. The conquests of Comb Wash, Comb Ridge, and Butler Wash were three of the biggest challenges in San Juan County.

reported that work on the road was progressing slowly, with the "Comb Hill now in pretty fair condition."[47] In a few days, the work crew would move over to Lime Ridge and start a new road, ending the use of the old one coming from Rincon. County Commissioner Al Scorup from Bluff mentioned in the article that he remained powerless to assist in this project because the other two commissioners were interested only in developing the northern part of the county. Partisan politics over economic enterprise took its toll.

Five years later, local boosters expressed the same fear of losing business to the south. This time, however, Blanding, Monticello, and Moab joined forces to request a fifteen thousand-dollar state appropriation from their legislative representatives for the Bluff–Mexican Hat road. "Hundreds of thousands of dollars" were to be spent on the oil field that spring and failure to smooth the road would jeopardize local involvement with traffic that could pass either through Utah or Arizona and New Mexico. Arizona was already furnishing tractors, graders, and Fresno scrapers to smooth the road between Flagstaff and Mexican Hat, while Arizona citizens donated money for construction efforts. If Utah did not move forward, Arizona would win the race in joining oil field to railroad. On the positive side, Arizona's effort, then only nine miles short of reaching its goal, also made a reality of the Monumental Highway as an interstate auto road open for tourists. Comb Ridge was still the fly in the ointment when it came to route development. San Juan County Road Manager Heber Frost, however, was "making giant strides with his work at Butler Wash [with] the shaling of Navajo Hill now well under way."[48] Thanks to the prompting of outside interests, the long-awaited road over Comb Ridge was becoming a reality.

Travelers over the road during the years of construction left memorable impressions of their encounters. Some came as pilgrims to the wilderness with the exuberance of youth to buoy them. Physical exertion was all part of the adventure. For example, Robert Aird, in July 1923, walked from Mexican Hat to Comb Wash. After a hefty hike, he seemed no worse for wear. "When we ate lunch at Navajo Spring, we were encouraged by the thought that we would then be entering new country to us. The appearance of clouds that shielded us from the sun was also encouraging, but even so it was a hot and dusty hike of some twenty-five miles for the day. John's [Newell—a traveling companion] diary records, 'Long walk to Bluff. Very tired and peevish.' Although I do not recall the peevishness, he was probably right, for all the psychological and physical conditions were present to make it so."[49]

For others it was a combination of adventure and aesthetic experience. The artist H. L. A. Culmer, on his way to Natural Bridges in April 1905, recalled his euphoria.

> I never enjoyed myself better than today [April 12]. It was cloudy and threatening but did not rain until 4 p.m. A local photographer named [Charles] Goodman—a very skilful man—took the cavalcade on our departure and again as we splashed through the swollen waters of Cottonwood Creek. The first adventure was six miles further in crossing Butler Wash. I took photos of the party coming down the trail then stopped to renew my films. By the time I came to the wash, the others were all across, but my handsome horse (misnamed Dobbin), dashed down into the quicksand and rushing torrent and up the impossible rocks with a speed that took my breath away. I had an audience that was scarcely over the excitement of crossing and I guess they concluded that I was no tenderfoot the way Dobbin carried me through. The next adventure was two miles later crossing Navajo Pass. This is over Comb Ridge into Comb Wash. This ridge is about 500 feet high and runs north and south thirty miles with only this place to cross it, and it is one of the dizziest things on earth—narrow, steep, and rocky. But at the foot is Navajo Spring, a cold, clear, sweet, and never failing supply that is famous for its excellence. Here we took lunch. Then up Comb Wash, fording a fierce stream a number of times, then up rocky steeps to the cedar mesas above. We were at a high altitude and the view in every direction was superb; rocky canyons, breaks and cliffs, the Blues to the northeast, the Elks to the northwest where we were heading, and swooping swirling thunderclouds everywhere. Then the rain overtook us and every rock and cliff glistened in the rainshine. Among the sand and cedars, is a land where the sheep have never browsed, for none have been permitted to pass Navajo Trail. Grass and flowers and an abundance of sweet water are found at this season.[50]

Culmer was obviously wrong about the Navajo, not to mention the Bartons and Bluff Co-op, not grazing sheep past Navajo Trail but the exuberance with which he embraced the San Juan country is evident.

Navajo Oshley, a long-time resident of the area, was born in Dennehotso, Arizona, and raised between there and Bluff, in spots all along Comb Ridge. As a Navajo stockman who moved herds to Bluff from the Monument Valley/Mexican Hat region, he encountered Comb Ridge as a barrier to travel on a number of occasions. A composite view of these efforts traces the evolutionary character of the trail. His earliest recollection tells of a "terribly rough road" going over the top. "We got the horse over the ridge, but the sheep were a real problem. It took us a long time to get them safely over this rock formation."[51]

The Navajo Spring Road seen from this angle gives a new meaning to corduroy and washboard. A section of this old road is visible from today's paved highway as one enters the blasted part of Comb Ridge near the top.

Water was always a concern when herding livestock, and so Navajo Spring was a common resting spot. One time Oshley, with an aunt and her husband, moved a flock of sheep to Valley of the Gods where they drank the alkali water of Lime Creek. Oshley tells how, "My aunt wanted to eat because the next water was a long ways, but her husband said he was not hungry and assured her that they would not starve before they got there. We got on top of the hill, and there was Comb Ridge with two trails before us. They asked me which road we would take, but I let them choose. My aunt wanted to know where the water was, and I told her it was ahead of us, so she said we would take the shorter road into Bluff City. We got to the water which was good, because it was not salty or bitter and flowed from the mountain. After we ate, we saddled the horses and went over Comb Ridge."[52] The two roads he refers to should not be confused with today's route. Highway 163, built in the 1970s, rests to the north of the two older roads. The road furthest south was the earliest one used to connect the Rincon route to Lime Ridge then on to Mexican Hat. In 1917, when the road over Comb Ridge was under improvement, the work crew built a second road with the same destination that went to "Perkins Twist," a now unidentified location; that road lay between the earliest and latest routes.[53]

In later years, Oshley drove sheep to Bluff for a trader named Ray Hunt, owner of the Mexican Hat Trading Post. Oshley herded the flock to Navajo Spring where the animals grazed in the wash while he camped for the night. Comb created a barrier for the sheep, which would "lie against the rock walls so they would not try to run off." In the meantime, Hunt drove his car to Bluff. Oshley recalls, "The road to Bluff City was in poor condition in those days. I do not know how many times the trader in Mexican Hat went to Bluff to get supplies in his old vehicle, but I do know that it kept stopping on him." To remedy this, Hunt improvised. He described his vehicle as a "stripped down Ford with a box on the back." Comb Ridge was so steep and difficult to traverse that he had a bicycle pump installed in the fuel system so that, as he drove, an assistant could hand-pump enough gas to the engine to propel the car up the grade.[54]

A final example of travelers encountering Comb Ridge comes from Will Evans, owner of the Shiprock Trading Company, and John Stewart MacClary, author and Evans' friend.[55] In November 1930, the two set out on a vacation exploration of the "wild country west of Shiprock." Their car, serviced and heavily laden with everything from food to cameras and from camping gear to typewriter, made good time until two flat tires turned them back to Cortez for repairs. Then they were off to Blanding and, the next day, to Natural Bridges. The men were well pleased with their tour thus far, returned to Blanding, restocked, then headed to Bluff. MacClary paints a graphic picture of the town and Comb Ridge in 1930.

> Bluff is a ghost city. A big flood of the San Juan in 1911 wrecked most of the ranches and homes and the residents migrated to Blanding and Monticello. Block after block of deserted homes, many of them quite pretentious, met our gaze. We filled the tank with gas—it would only take a fraction over a gallon—and started west. At a large wash [Cottonwood] just west of town, a grading crew of two men was at work with shovels and team filling a hole in the sandy bank. We had to wait for them to fill a little more before we could pass. Then I hit the bank with all the speed I could muster, only to mire down in the sand. I tried it three or four times with no success. Then Will unloaded and he and the two men pushed and gave me sufficient traction to allow the car to pull free.
>
> There were miles upon miles of blow sand and sagebrush, with the river always in sight to the south and the ruddy hills on both sides. The sun sank ever lower and interfered with my driving a great deal. We crossed Comb Ridge, a high wall of sandstone whose outline looked like a large comb—if one's imagination were strong enough—and up which the road was very steep and also very narrow.
>
> That road, though, was a boulevard compared to the one which led down the opposite side, the west side. This was so steep I had to put the car in low gear and let it go under compression. At the foot of the hill I took a picture which I hope will show the steepness.
>
> A rough, steep, exceedingly narrow wash was the course of the road from here on. The angles were sharp, the sun growing lower by inches and feet and yards. Finally after half an hour of this, my nerves began to blow up. I wanted to get out of the car and scream and yell and 'cuss'. I had strength enough only to collapse over the steering wheel and explain the trouble to Will. He took the wheel and we went ahead, entering the field of the real monument country.[56]

While MacClary lost patience during his encounter at Comb and was unaware of what a struggle it had been to get the route even to that point in construction, it would still be years before substantial change improved the road to the highway it is today. In the meantime, small incremental changes were all that could be expected until uranium—a later form of economic development—appeared on the scene.

E. C. LaRue photo, #827, U.S. Geological Survey

Control of the San Juan River has been a continuing theme for those who settled along it. The Bluff dam site, a mile downstream from the mouth of Chinle Wash, was first proposed in 1916. In addition to harnessing the flow of water, it would have generated hydroelectric power but was never developed.

Before that occurred, men were eyeing the San Juan–Comb Ridge connection for another source of power—hydroelectric. But this was secondary to the main effort of building a dam for flood control and water storage. A site slightly below the Comb Ridge–Chinle juncture became the chosen location for what was going to be the Bluff Dam. Of primary concern was the slowing of the occasionally rampaging San Juan with its destructive carving away of river bottoms and dumping of huge amounts of silt downstream into the Colorado River. On September 5, 1909, heavy continuous rains engorged the river, moving its sluggish flow of 1,500 cubic feet per second to a roaring 40,000 cubic feet within forty-eight hours. Again, between September 25 and October 6, 1911, the highest flood ever recorded on the lower San Juan ripped out the channel bed and the river overflowed its banks, taking out the new bridges at Shiprock and Mexican Hat, both built in 1909. Engineers estimated that the discharge during this storm was 150,000 cubic feet per second.[57] Either one of these floods could have been the culprit that wiped out the connecting land link with the road that went from Butler Wash to the Rincon if it had not already been washed away by previous torrents.

Something had to be done. Raymond M. Priest, in October 1914, was part of a survey team under N. P. Conway of the Bureau of Reclamation, who investigated a series of potential dam sites along the entire stretch of the San Juan River running through Colorado, New Mexico, and Utah. The confluence of Comb and Chinle washes was important since building a dam below them would control two major sources of runoff. For four or five weeks, Priest examined the river bottom as well as the surrounding cliffs to locate such a spot. A mile below Chinle Wash offered a place with a wide floodplain that choked down

Comb Wash presented different challenges than the Navajo Spring dugway. Spring floods and heavy rainstorms deepened the banks of the wash, created a mire that bogged vehicles, and swept away unsuspecting travelers.

to high rock walls and a rock bottom that went entirely across the riverbed. To contain a massive water flow, a dam estimated at 214 feet in height was necessary. The structure would create a storage capacity of over 1.5 million acre-feet. Unfortunately, this would also back up the water twenty to twenty-five miles above Bluff, drowning the town that had tried to tame it.[58] But by containing the silt that would have entered the Colorado, this future reservoir would prolong the life of other projected dams at Boulder and Glen Canyon. The water lapping over the rooftops of Bluff could also be used for agriculture and hydroelectric power.[59]

Nothing was done; ten years later the issue returned, so engineers cited the previous report.[60] Nothing happened. The Colorado River Bed Case in 1930–31 determined that the San Juan River below Chinle Wash was non-navigable and so again in 1960 the United States brought suit against Utah and obtained control of the rest of the river between Four Corners and Chinle Wash. As for the dam, there were rumblings in the 1940s and 1950s, but control of the San Juan shifted to Navajo Dam, New Mexico, completed in 1962, ending the debate.[61]

Looking at this forty-year period of history, it appears that a lot of things fizzled. The longhorns were gone, gold proved too difficult to wrench from the river, oil flowed slowly at best and was not terribly abundant, no one moved a single rock on behalf of the Bluff Dam, and economic prosperity was still a will-o'-the-wisp. Was anything gained? Certainly. This was a wonderfully colorful period in the history of San Juan with Bluff, the river, and Comb Ridge playing significant parts in the drama that waltzed across the landscape; pioneering the system of roads and communications set the stage for greater works in the future. The nascent tourist industry laid its foundation for one of the most prominent economic enterprises the region now sponsors. And the initial intent of providing a stable community at a time and place where Wild West ways could have, and in some cases did, run roughshod over whites and Indians alike was achieved. The whole civilizing, city-building process did not turn out as anticipated and, as mentioned earlier, in some ways became a magnet for the lawless elements it was supposed to temper. From it, however, came an experience that tried those who came, often improving them as people. On this point, Comb Ridge will have to sit in judgment.

7

Interpreting the Comb

Indians, Travelers, and Archaeologists

It is said that the [Ancestral Puebloans] learned every way of the Holy Beings, who felt it was not good, so they discussed the matter. They performed a wind ceremony that caused rocks to fly about which killed the Anaasází. Some were living in the rocks and fire blew into their dwelling and killed them off. It is said.

—Ada Black, Navajo[1]

Judging from the large number of loopholes in these ruins [site in box canyon between Butler and Comb washes], the structure was evidently intended as a fortification. In one room alone we counted twenty-five loopholes. From these the defenders could send their deadly arrows in every direction, up or down the canyon.

—Warren K. Moorehead, 1904[2]

The Ancestral Puebloan abandonment of the Comb Ridge area left lonely ruins in a picturesque yet desolate landscape. Their sudden departure and the material evidence left behind opened a door to various interpretations. As noted in the chapter on creation, there are two differing views of who these prehistoric Indians were. One is derived from religious values, the other from science and archaeology. Where these Puebloan people came from, what they did, and why they disappeared call forth explanations dependent on the framework from which the questions are asked. What results is a fascinating study of values and worldviews that provide answers and lessons for today.

The Utes and Paiutes were very aware of the ruins that dotted their hunting territories, but they avoided them. Referring to Ancestral Puebloans as Mokwič, which has been anglicized into Moki, the Utes connect these prehistoric people to the Hopi. According to one Northern Ute, "The [Moki] went back down south a long time ago when they found there were a lot of other Indians coming in."[3] Edward Dutchie, Sr., born at Sand Island close to Butler Wash, and his wife, Patty, offered their understanding of Ute traditions concerning the Moki.[4] When asked what the Utes say about them, Edward promptly replied, "They don't say anything. They are scared of them." Henry McCabe, a cowboy who spent much of his time on the range in southwestern Colorado and southeastern Utah at the turn of the twentieth century, agrees. He tells of how the Utes did not like talking about the Moki and would not enter a site "beyond the point where the water from the overhanging cliff fell."[5]

The Puebloan people are often associated with conflict. Lola Mike believes that there are sites around Comb Ridge that have strong spiritual energy, but there are also places where something bad has happened—"that was in Comb Wash;"[6] exactly what and where she did not say. Pioneer photographer William Henry Jackson, however, received specific information as he rode through McElmo Canyon in 1874. On one hand he wrote that the Utes he encountered "have no knowledge whatever of their [the cliff dwellings'] former occupants. Not even traditions," just that the sites were "Moquis" dwellings. But with the next breath, Jackson pointed to "Fortified Rock" (today known as Battle Rock) and said, "There our guide informed us, these [Moki] aborigines made their last stand before being dispossessed and driven out of the country by the northern bands, the American Aztecs [other prehistoric (not actually Aztec) Indians]. Moqui tradition has it that here 10,000 warriors were engaged upon either side, that 2,000 were slain, that blood ran in rivers on the rocks, staining them with unalterable dye. From here they went to their present habitations in New Mexico."[7]

McCabe shares a similar story, this time set on the Dolores River. Unlike many other streams in the vicinity, this one has spirits living in it. The Utes would not eat fish they caught in its waters but would trade them to other people because the spirit of the Mokis was in the fish. This idea may be connected with a site two miles below the town of Dolores where "the Ute Indians and the Mokies had their battle," and where farmers often surfaced human remains.[8]

Going into a cliff dwelling ruin holds different challenges. Once one enters beyond the drip line, he or she is in the Mokis' "home." In order to avoid angering the spirits of the prior occupants, one offers a prayer and "talks to the person." The spirits are very aware of what goes on in their home, so if something is needed or an object taken, an offering is left behind so that the spirit will not follow the person home.[9] Patty Dutchie, who was raised in the Mesa Verde area, tells of how her mother and grandmother said, "they have seen the last of the Mokis up there. Not just one or two or three, but a family. . . . Others were wiped out by some kind of sickness, that's what they say. Those who were left were so lonely they had to move away from there."[10] Edward chimed in that the Utes did not "mess" around with bones or pottery because "it is still alive. . . . It is still alive yet. . . . They say you can still hear them move around in the museums where the remains are. They make noise like they are moving around. You might hear something if you sit in there all night." The old people used to know the prayers said before entering a site, but this generation of grandmothers and grandfathers knows little about it.

Ute people lived and traveled in a land filled with Ancestral Puebloan ruins. Much of the traditional knowledge of how to treat sites and remains has since been lost.

One of Edward's daughters brought home a Moki pot full of seeds. Prayers made it safe. The only thing that can be picked up and brought home without concern is a surface-find arrowhead, but even this should be prayed over with an offering to determine its original purpose.[11] If it was for killing people, then the power must be appeased and can then be used for protection against ghosts and evil. When hung above the head at night, the point keeps bad dreams away. Ghosts and spirits, in general, are abroad at night and must be avoided. The elders used to teach, "'They'll take you' when you are a little kid. You'll be lost. They have a BIG basket water jug they will take you in and carry you on their back to that place. That's what they used to tell us. . . . Now it seems like the ghosts are already here with us. The kids wander around and everything. They do unusual things like breaking windows or take things away. The kids are with the ghosts."[12]

Failure to keep a Moki object in "a precious way—a religious way" may result in disorientation, accident, or loss. Prayers ascend to the "Great Spirit" (Sinawav) because he was the one who taught them how to make the pottery and their homes. Patty said, "The Mokis were more intelligent than we are. We Indians have wandered all over and never put up that kind of house. We never made jugs that we could cook in." But Edward felt more kinship. As he talked about the burial of Ute bodies in Moki caves, he offered a number of explanations as to why it was acceptable. The first was pragmatic. In the winter, if a death occurred, alcoves offered sheltered soil that was soft for digging. So, "Some Utes are buried there too, just like Mokis." By leaving the Puebloan bones undisturbed, they will not come back looking for the person. Ute and Moki bones are compatible—"everything is the same. They're the same color. . . . If you buried a white man in there, I don't know about that. White men were brought up differently from the beginning of time."[13]

The Navajos have a more complex, fuller set of teachings about Puebloan sites, which has been discussed in detail elsewhere.[14] While Navajo teachings are not tied to specific locations in the Comb Ridge area (with one exception), a general system of beliefs is in force for all of the sites in the vicinity. Confirmation of this comes from Navajo elders. The only specific site that apparently ties into Navajo traditional knowledge is the Butler Wash Indian Ruin. John Holiday felt "that is where some of the songs come from," but provided no further explanation.[15] Puebloan peoples existed with the Navajo in the worlds beneath this one. Following the emergence, each group went their separate way, in some versions coming in conflict with the Navajo while in other stories intermarrying, giving rise to certain clans. In either case, the Ancestral Puebloans were a gifted people with the ability to control wind and lightning, to fly, to destroy things through supernatural means, and to live an impressive lifestyle. Their blessing was also their curse. They abused their power, failed to recognize the role of the Holy Beings in their creativity, and profaned that which was sacred. Consequently, the gods destroyed them in a variety of ways—wind that sucked the oxygen from their lungs, wind that whirled small rocks in the air that battered them, fire that burned their homes, and drowning. The powers they received had been turned against them. Whatever the means, they perished, leaving behind their homes and implements as mnemonic devices on the land, reminding the Navajo to follow the path provided by the Holy Beings. To ignore it is death.

Navajos practice much of what the Utes believe concerning the Moki. Spirits of the dead fill ruins. Marietta Wetherill, wife of Richard, lived in Chaco Canyon for years as her husband excavated ruins. She noticed that Navajos did not live in the canyon by the sites, and when she asked why was told, "The evil spirits make you sick, that the air was bad around the ruins," while at another time she learned that "it was crowded with the souls of too many dead people there."[16] Some of these Puebloans may be ancestors of the Navajo, since the oldest Navajo clan was said to derive from a place called Tsénííjíkini, translated as The Honey Combed Rock People or the Cliff Dwellers People Clan. This is believed

Navajos believe that desert varnish, black and red iron-manganese streaks on the rock, was caused by fires that burned the ruins. The Holy Beings were angry about the people's pride and so destroyed them.

to be the oldest clan, derived from a couple made of corn coming from a cliff dwelling north of the San Juan River "perhaps on the Mancos or McElmo [River]."[17] When this and another clan disappear at the end of the world, so will the People.[18]

For other Navajos, these Puebloans are thought of as the enemy, and so a bone or piece of hair may be used in the Enemyway (Anaa'jí) to aggressively remove the influence of a malevolent spirit from a sick person. Objects also held negative powers. Fred Yazzie recalls, "People were afraid of them because the Anaasází were thought of as the enemy. Before picking up a piece of pottery, you would cry first. Then you could pick it up. When you picked up an arrowhead, you inhaled from it four times, then it belongs to you and you are no longer afraid of it. But you were not supposed to handle their bones."[19] Archaeologist T. Mitchell Prudden capitalized on this fear during his investigation of ruins in Navajo country. He cached his provisions and gear under a canvas tarpaulin then placed an Ancestral Puebloan jawbone, "which he carried along for this purpose," on top of the heap. He may have been gone for days, and the supply point visited, "but I never lost an article thus guarded."[20]

Courtesy of Kay Shumway

This Puebloan petroglyph etched in Long Fingers Canyon gave the name to this site. Navajos teach that putting one's hands in painted or etched prints invites the spirit of the person who created it to have an influence over you.

Puebloan sites held other dangers. The ubiquitous pictograph of a hand—either painted on or sprayed around—contains part of the artist's essence. When one places his or her hand in the print, they invite the person who created it to have influence over them. There is no way of knowing what the artist was thinking or feeling when the picture appeared on the wall. Whatever it was can be extended to others who become haunted. Others use these same pictographs for witchcraft. Joe Manygoats believes that "a person who knows witchcraft will draw you amongst other pictographs on the wall, using similar weapon symbols pointed toward the figure to kill it. . . . There is another thing called 'níziin' [witchery] used to kill animals and enemies. . . . It is forbidden and dangerous to use; our ancestors used it long ago. I believe the Anaasází once used it too because they drew something portraying this act on the walls (an arrow sticking through the heart of an animal)."[21] Mary Blueyes thinks that Navajos now involved in witchcraft still do this. "It is said that a person would put another person on the rock where the sun shines the hardest for witchcraft purposes."[22]

Pictographs hold other powers. Ada Black tells of how the Puebloans learned the way of the wind with all of its potency. They placed patterns of the wind on their pottery, in their homes, and near their sites. They also learned to fly. Pictograph panels are designs of "electricity, the wind, and the arrowheads which were in the designs and the stone ax—things that were used for protection. . . . Some have rainbows . . . and also lightning which probably have to do with flying."[23] John Holiday, on the other hand, tells of a cave where the Holy Beings sat and planned during the creation. The drawings were part of the plans written on the wall as on a blackboard. "All types of sacred ceremonies, songs, prayers, and sandpaintings were once written in a cave deep, deep, in a cave near Lake Powell. . . . This is what the Holy Beings placed there for us."[24] John visited this cave three times with other medicine men and government officials during land surveys for the Navajo Claims Commission.

Sites are also associated with cliff dweller water. Navajos believe that at most sites the inhabitants took water from the sacred mountains, mixed it with pollen, clay, and other materials, then put it in a jar on the east side of the pueblo, where it can be found today. Described by contemporary Navajos as pottery painted with frogs, tadpoles, plants, or a design that has "openings," it still has power to bring moisture to the site and the region. The gods do not allow these bowls to be found unless the person is a medicine man who understands their importance and holiness.[25]

Like the Utes, Navajos generally avoid these ruins because they are places of the dead. By visiting one, the dead spirit will take hold of the trespasser and drag the living person's spirit to the "ghost place." The specter will haunt you. "This is real to people who believe in these things."[26] Sites and spirits are also connected to cancer, "the sore that does not heal"; it is a Puebloan disease. "When the wind blew, sand covered the dead and their skin dried to their bones. They died of starvation. So when a person goes among their ruins, this disease gets on them. That is how it kills."[27]

John Holiday, when looking at a Puebloan road in Comb Wash and then being told of a herradura shrine high on the ridge, summarized much of what has been discussed by saying, "Only places like that, situated high and in hidden places were for witchcrafting activities for skinwalkers [evil Navajos who use supernatural powers to harm others]. They say that is the kind of trail and rocks and rock formations they have. . . . It was said that K'aa Yélii had such a witchcraft dwelling around here somewhere long ago. And they said that the trail leading to the skinwalker's dwelling was made of stepping stones which they used."[28] John then asked if the shrine on Comb Ridge had a hole at its bottom with a round rock lid that could serve as a door. Winston Hurst told him that it had not been excavated. To John, it sounded like a witchcraft dwelling. If so, gold, turquoise birds, and silver concho belts would be found there. "They say that K'aa Yélii hid away some silver/gold somewhere on Comb Ridge, but nobody knows where. People have hunted for it, but found nothing. . . . There are other witchcraft dwellings on Comb Ridge too, but people won't say where. It is a real secret."[29]

John also linked witchcraft to petroglyphs and pictographs. Hurst asked about a Puebloan rock panel in Butler Wash that had figures carefully defaced (dismembered) in a way that resembled certain ceremonial activities. This occurred probably 100 to 200 years

Courtesy of Winston Hurst

Defaced petroglyphs suggest the influence of Navajo witchcraft and protection from it. Two forms of deformation are pictured here—on the left, total obliteration occurred to heal people by removing an offensive drawing. On the right, selective working against vulnerable joints and body parts is a technique used in witchcraft.

ago. John responded that it was likely done to curse someone by killing him, removing his health, or losing his wealth. The marks cut across the base of the arms, legs, and neck. When asked what it did, John emphatically replied, "Look at me. I could have had that done to me. I can't walk well. . . . It causes a person to be crippled or a quadriplegic or be totally paralyzed and shaky. That is how those types of witchcraft affect you. . . . Witches probably think Anaasází art work is more powerful and effective [than more contemporary rock art]."[30]

A final note on Navajo witchcraft: When Lola Mike, a Ute elder, was asked why the Utes moved away from Comb Ridge, abdicating it to Navajo occupation, she responded that Navajo witchcraft is much stronger and that it was used to remove the Utes from this area.[31] This was the first time she mentioned the subject but she offered no other specifics. Still, the idea is not an anomaly in either culture. For both groups, Puebloan remains—in whatever form—hold power that they treat with respect. Only those knowledgeable in its use can avoid the problems that arise in both the physical and spiritual world.

Given Navajo and Ute teachings about Ancestral Puebloans, it is not surprising that they left dwellings and artifacts alone. For roughly four hundred to five hundred years, the ruins lay dormant, deteriorating in the weather of southeastern Utah. Enter the Euro-American. By the late 1600s and early 1700s, the Spanish, established in New Mexico, made occasional entradas into the Four Corners area. Juan Maria Antonio Rivera (1765), and Fray Francisco Atanasio Dominguez and Fray Silvestre Velez de Escalante (1776) led official expeditions into southeastern Utah. These, along with punitive raids against Indians, small mining expeditions in the mountains, slave raiding parties, and the creation of the Spanish Trail to California were the limited activities of both the Spaniards and Mexicans up to 1848.[32] Comb Ridge sat undisturbed.

American trappers seeking beaver skins along the San Juan River during the 1830s and 1840s left little documentary evidence of their presence, though some of them must have come in contact with Comb Ridge and the canyons and washes surrounding it. Captain John N. Macomb of the Corps of Topographical Engineers led an expedition through the corner of southeastern Utah, passing over the Great Sage Plain then north to Canyonlands and beyond. While his narrative does not mention Comb Ridge, and his map does not show it, he undoubtedly saw it and is sometimes given credit for naming it. The title of the rock formation was definitely in use before the main body of Mormons arrived in the area in 1880. Macomb was also one of the first Anglo-Americans to comment on the ruins left by the Puebloans. Calling a deserted site in Colorado by the Ute name Surouaro (translated as desolation), Macomb described this pueblo and surrounding villages as being built of "stone, hammer-dressed . . . showing great age."[33] Pot shards, metates, irrigation ditches, cisterns, and other artifacts abounded. What Macomb could not understand was how so many people—which he estimated as "a population of many thousands"—could have existed in such a seemingly sparse environment. The abandonment was easier to explain—it must have been the Navajos and Utes, those "warlike and aggressive tribes." Macomb would not be the last to wonder and conclude with thoughts along these lines.

In 1875 and again in 1876, Ferdinand V. Hayden sent a U.S. Geologic and Geographic Survey team through southeastern Utah to explore and map the region. After two years, members of the survey parties had traveled throughout the La Sals and parts of Blue Mountain; passed down McElmo, Recapture, and Montezuma canyons; journeyed down the San Juan River as far as Chinle and Comb washes; and named features including Mount Peale, Mount Tukuhnikivatz (both in the La Sals), and Casa del Eco.[34] Separate groups went to different areas, and fortunately, William H. Jackson, the group photographer and a journal keeper, visited Comb Ridge. His travels took him from Hovenweep and McElmo Canyon to the San Juan River.

The party noted abundant ruins all along the riverbanks, but across the river from where Bluff City arose five years later, sat a site of particular interest. The party crossed and ascended the steep slope to a circular alcove that held a large block of Pueblo II dwellings. The men took measurements with exactness and interpreted their findings with imagination. There was a workshop, a weaving area, "window-like apertures" for communicating between rooms, three-inch peep-holes in the outer walls that looked down the slope at an angle, and a kitchen for one of the houses. Handprints and corn cobs were embedded in the dried adobe, arrowheads left lying on the ground, while the alcove itself "echoed and re-echoed every word uttered with marvelous distinctness," giving rise to the name of "Casa del Eco" or House of Echoes.[35] However, the site had "been ransacked time after time by wandering bands of Utes and Navajos, who would search with keen eyes for any articles of use." Thus, "the whole appearance of the place and its surroundings indicates that the family or little community who inhabited it was in good circumstances and the lords of the surrounding country. . . . These old people, whom even the imagination can hardly clothe with reality, must have felt a sense of security that even the incursions of their barbarian foes could hardly have disturbed."[36] Ah, the peaceful cliff dwellers.

By the time Jackson reached the vicinity of Comb Wash, which he called Epsom Creek, and Chinle Wash, or "Rio De Chelly," he appeared determined to reserve detailed description of sites only for the dramatic. There were just too many. But he was not too tired for Comb Ridge and Wash. After noting that it and Chinle Wash were dry, with the exception of "shallow pools of very red muddy water," he turned to the rock. "Upon every side—except where the broad valley of Epsom Creek opened northwardly, with the deep blue summits of the Sierra Abajo (Blue Mountain) appearing in the vista—steep rugged bluffs of bare red rock rose up, weathering occasionally into sharp needle-like pinnacles, discernible for long distances in any direction. The San Juan emerged from a considerable canyon at the head of this little valley but to sink into a still greater one below."[37] Jackson's party took Limestone Canyon through Lime Ridge then proceeded out of the area, exploring more wonders as they made their way to the Hopi Mesas.

In August, the party returned, camped, then traveled up Epsom (Comb) Creek. Trapped by extreme heat—125 degrees in the sun, 100 degrees in the shade, with the San Juan registering at 88 degrees—the group cherished water.[38] Jackson wrote, "The Epsom water, as we call it, has anything but a cheerful effect upon us."[39] Still, exploration must go on and so Jackson and two companions tramped up the side canyon of Fish Creek. They visited ruins galore that were, "all small, most mainly little cubby holes from three to five feet in diameter, some smaller" with "generally a large living room in the vicinity." Returning to camp, they prepared for the next day's journey, which took them up Comb Wash. When the group reached a place where three towers stood, "quite a batch of Ute, who first made themselves known from away up on the bluff by loud shouts," descended to talk with the party. Three of the Indians accompanied the explorers to Arch Canyon and then over Comb Ridge to Cottonwood Creek to camp for the night. After feeding their new companions supper, the explorers settled down for the evening, only to have the Utes stampede their stock and "raise a rumpus generally." The event soon ended, with the livestock retrieved.[40] Jackson continued his travels to Blue Mountain and eventually joined forces with the main party, ending the survey of 1875.

Mormon entrance into the area is discussed in chapter 4. Suffice it to say that, once they arrived, they formed their own understanding of the Ancestral Puebloans. Life in Bluff

Field Museum of Natural History, Green Collection, Neg. #63333

Bluff residents excavated Ancestral Puebloan ruins either as hired hands or for their own personal gain. Shovels and horse-drawn scrapers required little finesse; little documentary evidence was recorded during the 1890s when this photo was taken in Cottonwood Wash.

was a struggle. Those settlers who remained lived a hand-to-mouth existence as they fought the ravages of the San Juan, endured fluctuations in weather, witnessed thefts of crops and mutilation of cattle, struggled to purchase goods and equipment in a capitalist system, and obeyed the counsel of their leaders. Most did not have time to be philosophical or record thoughts about who these early inhabitants were. Some, such as Charles B. Lang and Bob Allan, worked for non-Mormon groups, such as the Wetherills, excavating ruins in Butler Wash. Freighting, guiding, cooking, digging—whatever was needed—put bread on the table for these men. Some Mormons, such as Platte D. Lyman and Benjamin Perkins, did their own digging to obtain artifacts for sale, visited sites for community picnics or socials, and decorated their homes with pottery or other artifacts. Few wrote much about the Indian people who preceded them.

There was one, however, who spent much of his life writing the history of San Juan and was not afraid to dabble in the prehistory too. Albert R. Lyman became the spokesperson for the local LDS interpretation of who these Puebloan people were and what their life was like. His views are very much in keeping with other Mormon writers in the Four Corners area at this time.[41] There were two sources for his understanding. The first was the Book of Mormon, a scriptural account of a number of different groups of people who arrived in the Americas from the Middle East and whose story stretches between 600 BC and AD 421. As a religious history, its theme centers around the importance of keeping God's commandments; the problems that accompany pride, worldly wealth, and forgetting God; the struggle between two peoples—the Nephites (generally those who followed God's commandments but who were finally destroyed for ignoring them) and the Lamanites (a savage, warlike people who regressed from civilized ways and preyed upon the Nephites); and the visit of Jesus Christ to this continent. The book is foundational to LDS belief.

The second source that informed Lyman's writing was observation. He lived in Bluff during his early years, was a teenager when his father, the Wetherills, and others excavated sites in Butler Wash; traveled through much of the county as a cowboy; was the first settler in Blanding; built homes near ruins; remembered many of the artifacts brought in by others; and ultimately established a small museum in Blanding. From this tangible world, he melded the two—scripture and ruins—together into an understanding of who these people were. He published these ideas as either "factual" accounts (with interpretations) in the *San Juan Blade* newspaper or in a fictional narrative, *The Trails of the Ancients*.[42] While mention of the Book of Mormon and its people is missing from the text of both, there is no doubt that Lyman allowed them center stage in his thinking.

In his fictional *Trails of the Ancients* he takes Book of Mormon themes and employs them in a Puebloan setting. There are "long suffering people" plagued by a warlike, savage, blood-thirsty enemies (Piedes, a name for Paiutes, or Utes); a seer and "seeress" who gaze into the future to warn and direct the people; a dominant leader whose "sturdy," peaceful people have dwellings in Cottonwood, Comb, and Butler washes; challenges with prosperity leading to pride; and judges who divide food and treasure left in "the castle." The struggle culminates with the "the Peaceful Ones" being pushed out of "Cottonwood Gulch and its branches to the valleys and the forks of the Butler, to the cavernous box canyons west of Comb Wash and to the echoing depths of Grand Gulch with its maze of precipitous tributaries," thence to the south where the pueblo people live today. The Peaceful Ones are the Hopis, people of Isleta, and other contemporary Pueblo tribes.

Lyman, at the end of his novella, does not want to leave doubt as to why he interpreted things as he did. Even though classified as fiction, he appended fifty-two endnotes that cite Puebloan artifacts, ruins, and remains he refers to in the book. For example, in 1893, the Wetherills unearthed in Grand Gulch a Puebloan man who had been cut in two then stitched back together with human hair. The same thing happens in Lyman's story. While some may scoff at this type of writing, Lyman bequeathed a treasure trove of information about sites and artifacts that have since disappeared from the area.

He also appended his personal experiences in visiting the Hopi and other contemporary Pueblo groups. Crucial to this experience that welds the Book of Mormon to these prehistoric people is the diary of apostle, and later LDS Church president, Wilford Woodruff, who visited Isleta in 1879. Lyman wrote:

Courtesy of San Juan County Historical Commission

Albert R. Lyman roamed about southeastern Utah, observing Ancestral Puebloan sites and artifacts. From this experience came an appreciation for these people and a desire to preserve their lifeways in a local museum.

> Wilford Woodruff calls attention to the proof that they [Nephites] preserved their identity to a certain degree. In his journal, which he wrote in Isleta in the winter of 1879, he declares that the Isletas are Nephites, that the surrounding Pueblo tribes, fifteen or more of them, and the Zuni tribe, and the Hopis on farther to the west, are Nephites.
>
> As a last resort to save their lives, they surrendered to the enemy, and they had to conform to certain requirements in order to be tolerated. Yet they were not Lamanites, the blood of many Nephite generations ran in their veins. They drew together and tried to preserve what they could of the virtues of their fathers. . . . But they were persecuted, and robbed, and slain. They fled to the cliffs, to the deserts, and to the undesirable corners of the earth, hunting a place where they could live and worship in peace.[44]

Given this interpretive framework, one finds parallels between the book and newspaper articles in the *San Juan Blade* and *San Juan Record*, as Lyman wended his way through archaeological discoveries. Focusing on those found in the Comb Ridge area, he made a number of references to the Bluff Great House, one of two "castles," the other being Edge of the Cedars in Blanding. The Bluff Great House was described as "a castle that crowned the hill" with "a deep worn roadway [that] led up to it from the river bottom to the southeast and ran over the hill to the mouth of Cottonwood northwest. This much traveled highway ran by the very doors of the kiva where it is probable a priest administered some rite or pronounced some service or ceremony for the passerby."[44]

The Bluff and Blanding Great Houses were two of "among hundreds, of among thousands" of their kind spread throughout the San Juan region. Lyman envisioned it all as a unified, defended empire. There was an old "fort" at Dandy Crossing on the Colorado River, while "dim scars around the passes thru the great Comb Reef" provided additional testimony that "these Indians had a knowledge of how rims and gulches can be made a mighty security from all pursuit. What a splendid system of safety barriers. . . . the yawning gorge of the San Juan River on the south, the almost impassable chasm of the Colorado on the northwest, and the Comb Reef on the east."[45] Within this defensive triangle were other redoubts, providing for the people an impregnable fortress that "entrenched them from all comers."

Topography was not enough to save the "hill dwellers" and "cliff dwellers" from destruction. Lyman found plenty of evidence of the struggle. Casa del Eco was built to hide the homes from "the searching eyes of their enemies," while in a Butler Wash midden there were the remains of a small baby. The body had been tossed onto the heap without any kind of wrapping then had hot ashes thrown on it, charring part of the skull. Another alcove in Butler Wash held bodies of men strewn around its entrance. They appeared to

Lyman to have "taken refuge there from their pursuers and had died defending their retreat. In the bleached backbone of one of them was embedded the flint point of an arrow."[46] With plenty of other sites reaffirming chaos and death, Lyman assumed an invasion and expulsion of the Peaceful Ones to the south. He recognized that the dwellings and artifacts left behind were only a hint of what had transpired. At one point, he tells of returning to one of his former homes the exact location of which he had been unable to identify. Then, comparing it to the Bluff Great House and road he mused, "Vandals have broken some of its upper walls, and the winds have filled the old kiva again with sand, but the ancient generation is still calling after a lapse of nine hundred years, calling as positively from their silent dwellings as this generation will be calling nine hundred years in the future."[47]

Courtesy of Kay Shumway

Lyman's "cliff dwellers" left behind ruins unique to each facet of landscape. This ruin in the North Fork of Whiskers Draw speaks of a community of people who capitalized on building homes in alcoves or "cliffs."

In the non-Mormon community, the 1890s saw an explosion of interest in excavating, collecting, and displaying Ancestral Puebloan material culture. There is now an excellent corpus of material derived from scholars and hobbyists, who have studied this era of exploitation in southeastern Utah to explain what happened.[48] The *terra incognita* that it had once been now sprang to national attention. Infatuation with Native American antiquities and a rising market for ancient relics bolstered a feeling of nostalgia and respect by those living in the East, while those in the West were still wrestling with displaced Indian cultures, the process of which raised some tough questions. The Chicago World's Fair in 1893 spurred the growing desire to know more about ancient cultures while juxtaposing them to the latest and greatest successes in American society. Archaeology was making its mark as a new and still uncertain academic discipline, with methods that were unclear and no laws to protect antiquity. Specimen collecting was its primary goal.

While these philosophical interests were building in the East a more mundane interest enticed people in the West—economic exploitation. Just as the San Juan gold rush brought outsiders to the river's banks, another kind of rush occurred throughout western San Juan County—some of the most frenzied excavation of the archaeological record in the history of the United States. Miners, cowboys, settlers, even government surveyors turned to the ruins for salable artifacts, responding to a booming market in antiquities. The first of these "cultural prospectors" to leave any record was Charles McLoyd, a Colorado miner who dug in southeastern Utah's canyons for three winters (1890–93). His collections ended up being spread from coast to coast in four major urban museums. Grand Gulch was his primary area of discovery; he, with various partners from Durango's Graham family, hauled from there wagon loads of exquisitely preserved baskets, blankets, sandals, tanned hides, wooden tools, pottery, and other materials. He also started to distinguish between "Cave Dwellers" (later called Basketmakers) and "Cliff Dwellers" (Puebloan) cultures—a thought which two years later would be "discovered" and developed by the Wetherills.

McLoyd hired local Mormons to guide and pack for him, so it is not surprising that a group from Bluff embraced the entrepreneurial spirit and did some excavating on their own. Platte D. Lyman, Hanson Bayles, Benjamin Perkins, Hyrum Perkins, and Kumen Jones, stimulated by a call from Utah Territory for artifacts to show in the Chicago World's Fair exhibit, formed a partnership and began digging. No doubt, some of their finds came from Butler Wash, given its close proximity to Bluff, but they left little documentation of their efforts. At least one mummy and its associated burial goods are identified as coming from Allen Canyon. Nicknamed the "King of Blue Mountain," this large, fleshy, fully extended individual, wrapped in fabric and feather blanket, became a hit attraction at the world's fair the following summer.[49] Other artifacts made their way into the possession of T. Mitchell Prudden, a medical doctor and part-time archaeologist. Some he dug from Butler Wash in 1900; others, also from Butler, he purchased from Platte Lyman.

One of the largest discoveries of Puebloan human remains came in the winter of 1893–94 by the Hyde Exploring Expedition. Led by Richard Wetherill and assisted by his brothers John and Al, the group of eight men was financially backed by B. Talbot Hyde and his brother Fred, two young men from New York whose family had acquired its fortune in making soap. Enticed by the artifacts they had already seen, the brothers wanted more. In November 1893, the *Mancos Times* announced that the Hyde Exploring Expedition would be leaving for their "winter tour . . . to visit and explore the Cliff Dwellings of the Grand Canyon of the Colorado and also the ruins in the interior of Arizona" and was expected to be gone four months.[50] On January 5, 1894, the readership received an update that, "The Wetherill boys are unearthing some rare specimens of Aztec history along the borders of southern Utah."[51]

While the Aztec claim is amusing, the "unearthing" part was real business. Harry French, the last surviving member of the expedition recalled in 1947:

> We camped in Butler Wash, Utah, the last week of December 1893, and a day or two in January, 1894. We took out quite a collection from this place, but I do not remember how many mummies. We found very well preserved pottery, skulls, arrowheads, baby boards, feather cloth, spearheads, small beads, and an unusual amount of turkey feathers.[52]

The expedition excavated in more than thirty locations in Cottonwood Wash, Butler Wash, Whiskers Draw, Grand Gulch, and Chinle Wash, bringing to light more than 1,200 objects.[53] Known sites that fell under the shovel include Whiskers Draw, Fishmouth Cave in Butler, Poncho House in Chinle Wash, and Green Mask and Red Elk caves in Grand Gulch, among others. Cave 7 in Whiskers was the site of the over ninety Basketmaker skeletons, as previously discussed. Success like this spurred others on.

Courtesy of San Juan County Historical Commission

In December 1893, members of the Hyde Exploring Expedition excavated Cave 7 in Whiskers Draw. Standing farthest to the right is John Wetherill, to his right is Bluff resident Robert Allan, and next to him is Al Wetherill.

Charles Lang, who hailed from Pittsburgh but was lured west by the promise of adventure and aspirations of a career in landscape photography, arrived in Bluff at least as early as 1888.[54] Between 1894 and 1899, a group of young men, led by Lang, formed a partnership to exploit the ruins. One collection pulled 385 artifacts out of Hammond and Allen canyons, and Cottonwood and Butler washes. Another collection came from the canyons west of Bluff, but there is no record of its contents; a fourth expedition shoveled 409 artifacts out of unidentified locations in Comb, Chinle Wash, and the canyons east of Bluff. They sold all of the collections, mostly to rich patrons who donated them to major museums, where they remain largely intact.

A critical part of business is marketing, and both the Wetherills and Lang were not cautious about advertising their wares. While a local paper carried a snippet on Lang "finding many rare and wonderfully preserved articles" then described "a feather and fur robe, as perfect as when woven," this report paled next to the one published in the *Washington*

Post.[55] Under the title of "Rich Finds in Utah," the article explores at great length an excavation in Allen Canyon. Located in loose sand five feet below the surface, there sat a man, six foot three inches tall, entombed in a woven yucca basket with a smaller basket tray on his head and shoulders. "The body, which is in a wonderful state of preservation, has the brown, parchment-like look to be expected, and is that of a man, apparently about fifty years of age. The dried flesh and skin, which clings tightly to the bones, and the size of the latter, show that in life the man, evidently a chief or personage of some consequence, was one whom, we would have called a big handsome fellow." The article goes on to describe buried objects, funerary practices, and other bodies found in the vicinity, then closes with a testimonial saying that the objects discovered are "equal to anything ever found as the product of Aztec, Eskimo, Zuni, or Moki."[56] Lang left Bluff in 1902, but there were other collectors to follow in his pot holes.

By 1900, a large portion of the archaeological record, particularly that in the major dry alcoves, was destroyed or left incomplete and randomized. Several expeditions, a score of small collecting parties, and a host of individuals had excavated in hundreds of sheltered caves and open ruins. Diggers removed tens of thousands of artifacts and sold them with minimal-to-no archaeological documentation, many ending up in large, urban museums across the country. In response to Prudden and other preservation-oriented activists, the government passed the Antiquities Act outlawing unauthorized artifact digging on federally administered lands in 1906; its effect was more symbolic than substantial. Not until 1979 did the government pass a stronger law in response to a frenzy of artifact looting in the 1970s that may have surpassed even that in the 1890s.

Not all of the visitors to San Juan interested in Ancestral Puebloans were collectors. In 1892, the Illustrated American Exploring Expedition, comprised of a group of young adventurers from Ohio, traveled from Durango, Colorado, to their first Puebloan site in Aztec, New Mexico. Archaeologist Warren K. Moorehead directed the eleven-man team whose ambition was mapping "the exact location of every dwelling, tower wall, pueblo, or modern reservation village" along the San Juan River and its tributaries from the Animas to the Colorado River.[57] Talk about ambitious—this was mission impossible. They did, however submit an interesting series of reports back to their sponsor, the *Illustrated American Magazine*, which published them in a series of articles between April 2 and August 27 of that year. The party traveled overland along the San Juan River to Bluff, then up Butler Wash, across to Whiskers Draw, and into Allen Canyon, describing and mapping as they went.

Sites named and inscribed by the expedition include Cold Spring Cave (because of a pool of clear water in the back of the alcove—a pleasant source of relief from the May heat); the Eagle's Nest (because of the "dizzy heights" and climbing needed to enter the ruin); Monarch Cave (because of the commanding view and the portholes cut in the front of the ruin's wall, giving it a fortress appearance); and Giant's Cave (because of its huge size). The latter has since been renamed Fishmouth Cave because of the oval shape of the alcove entrance). Considering that McLoyd had not worked the Comb region and

The Illustrated American Exploring Expedition visited the Eagle Nest Ruin in 1892. Still well preserved, this site has remained that way because it is difficult to access.

neither the Lyman partnership nor the Wetherills had begun their work, the Illustrated American Expedition must have visited fairly pristine sites. Sticking to their objective of mapping, the group did little digging. They did provide a site map of Monarch Cave, the first archaeological documentation in the area since Jackson's Fish Creek photographs and sketch map of a ruin on Comb Ridge in 1875. By May 21, the expedition had completed its loop, re-entered Bluff, and had begun arrangements for the return trip.

Another person who explored the region around this same time, who was equally bent on classifying things in the area west of Bluff, was botanist Alice Eastwood. A native of Canada, she grew up in Denver where she taught high school. During the summers, she collected plants all over Colorado, eventually meeting Al Wetherill, with whom she made two trips into southeastern Utah. The first trip in 1892 took her down Montezuma Creek to the San Juan River and thence up McElmo Canyon back to the Wetherill Ranch. The second journey she made in 1895 at the age of thirty-five. This one brought her back through McElmo, along the San Juan River to Bluff, down Butler Wash, up part of Comb Wash, and across the Barton Range to "Willow Creek," which is known today as John's Canyon.

Eastwood's 1895 account is important for two reasons and delightful for a third. Of primary importance, she was the first botanist in the Four Corners area to leave a record of the flora encountered at the turn of the century. Her reports in professional journals to her later employer—the California Academy of Sciences—and her associates in the Sierra Club, speak of an avid botanist who collected "475 specimens, representing 162 species and varieties, of which 19 are completely new and almost all were rare."[58] These published accounts are thick with scientific terminology.

> That night we rode through Butler Canyon in the dusk and camped after dark on the banks of the San Juan just above where the gorge begins. A dense thicket of *Cleome integrifolia* [bee plant], more than six feet high had to be pulled up to make a camping place. The odor of the *Cleome* and the *Datura meteloides* [datura or jimsonweed] which also grew in the same spot, made the atmosphere almost unendurable. On the return we camped at Butler Spring and some interesting plants were found in the canyon below and on the wash above. *Quercus Gambellii* and *Quercus undulate* [two types of oak] both grew in the canyon, the latter easily distinguishable by its blue-green foliage. *Rosa Fendleri* [rose] was abundant. These shrubs were apparently confined to that canyon.[59]

Another reason that her efforts are appreciated is that she left writings filled with observations of the land she passed through. Both she and Al Wetherill provided excellent descriptions of who they visited and what they saw. For instance, Alice writes about arriving in Bluff when the local men were repairing the then useless irrigation ditch because the river had shifted its course; comments on the two stores, the supplies from which could have been loaded into one wagon; and, when departing town, recounts meeting "the last human beings, some half-starved Navajos, just coming in."[60] Wetherill, on the other hand, describes the trail down Butler Wash and along the river. "The road down was largely corduroy, made from poles and logs where the ledge was not wide enough for wagons. I suppose the Mormons made the road when they came into the San Juan Basin years ago."[61]

A third aspect of Eastwood's writing that makes it enjoyable is that she provides a woman's perspective in a man's world. With the exception of some Hole-in-the-Rock accounts, the female view was usually absent from writing on the region. As a feminist, Alice, at times, challenged social conventions of the day but was still careful. Often touring only with male company, she remained sensitive to what was acceptable. Her memoirs hint at the conflict. One time when riding with Al Wetherill through Montezuma Valley, Colorado, they stopped at a ranch overnight. The house was unbearably hot and she much preferred sleeping outside on the ground, but "we were too near civilization to disregard convention. My reputation meant nothing to these people, but Al's did."

During the 1895 trip, she had the unpleasant task of riding a stubborn mule on a new army saddle that after the first ten miles was pure pain. Between the equipment and animal, Alice opined, "It was a very hard trip because the mule that I rode lived up to the reputation of those animals and I was strongly tempted to use the only language that mules are supposed to understand, but 'confound you' was the strongest swear words I used. I was saddle sore all the time and whenever I dismounted it was torture, for my underwear which would stick to the sore spots would be pulled off and it was like being skinned. However, it did not deter me from dismounting whenever I saw a plant new to me."[62] Whatever the pain, Alice left a lasting legacy through her botanical studies, identifying some plants that lived only in the Comb Ridge area and providing a historic snapshot of the land at the turn of the century.

Courtesy of the BLM, Anasazi Heritage Center, Wetherill Archives

Avid botanist and adventurer, Alice Eastwood collected "475 specimens, representing 162 species and varieties, of which 19 are completely new and almost all rare" from the eco-niches around Comb Ridge and Butler Wash.

The beginning of the 1900s witnessed the start of archaeology as a serious, but unpolished and unsophisticated, profession. Well-intentioned, poorly equipped, and unburdened by careful documentation, a string of "professional" archaeologists, many of them sponsored by academic institutions, invaded the canyon lands to investigate the Ancestral Puebloans. Comb and Butler washes provided field experience for many. T. Mitchell Prudden, guided by Charley Lang, passed through Butler and Comb washes recording observations of the Comb Wash and Arch Canyon Great Houses. He described these and other smaller sites as "dug," referring to the middens. Prudden cites Lang as having done some of the excavating north of Arch Canyon, while a man named "Gaines," elsewhere described by Richard Wetherill as a government surveyor, reportedly dug sites in the vicinity of the Comb Wash Great House.[63] Prudden's notes also preserve the only known record of the old historic name of the "Highland Lady" for the pinnacle on Comb Ridge opposite the Comb Wash Great House.[64]

Prudden was an active observer who synthesized what he viewed and humanized his subject, the "Cliff-dweller." For instance, he found a red clay pipe or "cloud blower" as contemporary Puebloan peoples call them, and he fantasized that the user could have laid in the shade, free from concerns and puffed idly to ease his difficult life. The extensive use and abundance of yucca, "was one of the things which he [cliff dwellers] had to thank his gods for, hour by hour." And when the question arose as to why there were "numerous small irregular wads of fine strips of corn husks" in the rubbish heaps—he turned to contemporary ethnographic comparison. The Hopi provided the answer. "Here I saw them pick out of a bowl of thick brown stuff, which they said was sweet, and which

Special Collections, J. Willard Marriott Library, University of Utah

Byron Cummings, pictured outside the Oljato Trading Post owned by John Wetherill, explored and excavated sites in much of San Juan County. He spent time in Butler Wash, but most of his effort concentrated in northern Arizona.

certainly was sticky, similar wads of fiber, and thrusting them into their mouths, begin vigorous mastication. Then I realized that the husk wads of the rubbish heaps had probably been, while in their pristine state, the prehistoric avatars of the chewing-gum."[65] Prudden was intellectually connected to his work, but he also brought a sense of compassion to those "Cliff-dwellers" who had struggled in a harsh environment.

Quick on Prudden's heels came Byron Cummings, who, in 1907, arrived in San Juan to discover the Puebloans for himself. Working with Professor Edgar L. Hewett of the Smithsonian Institution, Professor Cummings and student Neil Judd from the University of Utah began an interest that brought them back to southeastern Utah for many years to come. Billed in the newspapers as "The Explorers," this party of seven men approached their task from an academic perspective. Cummings, "an authority on ancient languages and ethnology," partnered with Judd, the "sketcher and draftsman," as well as others assigned as surveyors and two reporters. The newly legislated Antiquities Act (1906) was buttressed by a Utah bill introduced by San Juan County's Representative Hott, "against the destruction or removal of anything pertaining to cliff dweller ruins, requiring the consent of the governor of the state to even explore the ruins. This consent has been secured by Prof. Cummings, and he goes on his mission of education with high hopes of bringing to light secrets of a prehistoric race, which for centuries have remained hidden in the ruins of the cliff dwellers."[66] Theoretically gone were the days of public exploitation of sites for personal gain. Education now characterized the pursuit of the prehistoric Indian.

Kumen Jones met the group in Monticello, provided them with horses, then took them to Bluff where they secured Randolph Benally as their Navajo guide. The objective for this first year was to survey and map the lands surrounding the newly created Natural Bridges Monument in "Fry's Cabin country." They did have time to map Comb, Cottonwood, and Recapture washes "in order to fix the relative position of the Natural Bridges to them." It was expected that "The Department of the Interior will be asked to recommend to the President the setting aside of the country surrounding the Natural Bridges as a national monument. In this way three points of general interest will be kept from falling into the hands of private parties and their educational value preserved for future generations."[67] It is interesting to note that the government recognized Comb and the other areas as national treasures of the prehistoric past.

Cummings had little time for excavating during this first year—just a small site at the mouth of Cottonwood Wash—but he did obtain, either from digging or as a donation from Jones, sixteen fine pieces of pottery, a feather blanket, and the mummified foot of a child found in a midden.[68] He and Hewett also had the good sense to record conversations with local people who had been involved with the ruins for years. Hewett's field diary recreates one of these discussions with Jones, noting that he had done a lot of digging in Butler Canyon:

> He reports no difference in house building between this and other canyons. He reports no mummified bodies, skeletons found in refuse heaps just outside of walls and back of houses in the cave. Bodies sometimes in sitting position but usually on back, sometimes on side. No beads, turquoise, or shells. The large coiled jars seem to have been used for cooking purposes almost exclusively. Found no red ware. Much black and white. Some cotton cloth and cord, much yucca cord. Many sandals of yucca. No leather sandals and little leather work of any kind. No leather strings tying, always with yucca or willow. In bone nothing but awls. No bone whistles. . . . He reports no real cemeteries and no cist burials.[69]

This kind of information added to a growing body of knowledge being preserved to better understand the Ancestral Puebloans. One wonders what could have been learned if earlier collectors had been approached for contextual, specific observations.

Cummings visited Bluff repeatedly during his long archaeological career, first as a professor at the University of Utah prior to 1915, then from his post with the Arizona State Museum after that. His records are not noteworthy for their detail, but he left two sets of notes that make specific mention of Butler Wash. His most important documentation occurred in the summer of 1908 when he, along with Judd and another student, excavated a kiva at Cold Spring Cave in Butler. The party was waiting for an unusually swollen San Juan River to subside and let them cross to their planned explorations in Oljato. Fording the river delayed them long enough for Cummings, in order to fill in the time, to capture somewhat greater detail than was his custom. Although there was little non-architectural information, this was the first excavation in the immediate Comb Wash area to be conducted under the auspices of a bona fide archaeological permit issued to Hewett of the School of American Research in Santa Fe. It was also the last authorized and documented excavation to take place in Butler or Comb washes for more than six decades.[70]

Like many other archaeologists of the day, Cummings wrestled with the problem of identifying the descendants of these people. By 1911, he had determined that the Hopis and Navajos held the claim. He felt the customs and practices, based on the prehistoric Indians' material remains, were similar. Corn, buried in jars, "was in as fine a condition of preservation as the day it was placed in the jar."[71] Even more potent evidence came in the medicine bags that he excavated from ruins. These religious objects, "which medicine men claim to have power to heal the afflicted are practically the same as those of the ancient inhabitants of the cliff houses."[72] Ethnographic comparison seemed to hold answers.

Between 1925 and 1929, Dr. Andrew A. Kerr of the University of Utah amassed a sizable collection of artifacts. In August of that first year, he traveled to Bluff to obtain the Frank Hyde Collection of Indian relics. Valued at $3,500, the assemblage of materials was "probably the best assortment of ancient Indian relics in Utah with the exception of the state museum exhibit. . . . The Hyde relics have long been recognized as one of the best private collections in the country."[73] Kerr also purchased artifacts from Arah E. Shumway and other Blanding residents who dug in ruins throughout central San Juan County at his request. Documentation of what they found, where they found it, and other contextual information is sorely lacking.

Many other professional and "hobby" archaeologists who followed Kerr would not do much better in documenting site information. A short summary identifies some of these groups. In 1929, gentleman explorer Charles A. Bernheimer, a wealthy New Yorker, paid for John Wetherill and archaeologist Earl H. Morris to accompany him in an exploration of western San Juan County. En route, they excavated in middens of two Comb Wash sites near Arch Canyon, but left only minimal documentation. Deric Nusbaum conducted a reconnaissance for Gila Pueblo in Arizona during 1941. He recorded fifteen sites in Butler Wash, took dendrochronology samples, and completed then filed short site reports on all of those visited. His record became permanent. The Carnegie Institution for Science in Washington, D.C., between 1945 and 1947, sponsored archaeologists David W. Rial and J. Leroy Kay in three annual expeditions. They, too, did some work in Butler, but it was poorly documented and of little value. There were other groups in the 1950s that passed through the area, but it was a fairly quiet archaeological scene until the pot-hunting days of the mid-1960s, when the canyons reopened to the ring of a shovel.

In summarizing the roughly one hundred years of interpreting the Ancestral Puebloans and their domain, one finds two underlying currents of thought. The early Navajo, Ute, and Mormon views emphasized a religious-philosophical basis that harkened back to the beginning of time and holy scriptures. The remnants of early Puebloans were part of a divine plan that taught lessons and provided a guide for proper behavior. Failure to follow the teachings of the Holy Beings led to destruction; inappropriate involvement in their sites led to sickness and death. On the other side of the ledger was a non-religious worldview that saw the sites as economic resources. As a ladder out of poverty, the Puebloans provided a marketable entity to be mined just as actively as the gold believed to be along the banks of the San Juan. As with any non-renewable resource, there was a limit, an end to the supply. From this early perspective arose a more enlightened belief that there was also educational value to be found in the lives of these prehistoric Indians. Not until the late 1980s through the voice of Native America, would most non-Indians recognize the spiritual side and the insensitive results of physically exploiting this Puebloan heritage. There was still one step necessary before taking that final step.

8

The Comb at Mid-Twentieth Century

Rigid or a Wash?

Do you remember the old dirt 95?
How about the Dugway at Comb?
To get anywhere it took hours to drive,
a dusty road to home.

—A. Dan Shumway, "The Mines on Old Highway 95"[1]

Comb Ridge sat as silent witness to the increasing pressure placed on the lands about it. By the early 1920s, much of the old way of life was disappearing. In San Juan County, automobiles began stylishly pushing the horse and wagon into yesteryear. Graveled roads, public education, Prohibition, expanding tourism, and economic speculation arrived in muted forms that beckoned rural inhabitants to join mainstream America. Prosperity spawned progress, and although there were post–World War I dips in the economy, the general desire for wealth appeared achievable. Around Comb Ridge, this meant intensifying a pattern established forty years before—consolidating control of the one thing that everyone knew the land could produce: food and water for livestock. Eliminating competition was one of the rungs on the ladder to success.

The biggest contender arrived from across the river and out of the canyons in the form of Navajo flocks of sheep. The eternal search for green pastures and the mushrooming herds of livestock created both internal and external pressure on resources held by each group. Anglos also drove their livestock on parts of the reservation, making no one exempt from perceived trespass. Herders constantly looked for new opportunities, whether they drove their herds north or south or beckoned them to public domain or reservation lands. Both groups eventually sought a hardening of the lines—some kind of determination to justify their presence on the land and grant legal rights to resources. Where there was no decision, stockmen cast their own vote through action.

This old corral at the mouth of Arch Canyon is on what used to be the Perkins Ranch. Hyrum E. Perkins, a member of the "Council of Nine," was a prominent stockman who had a vested interest in the Comb Ridge range.

Herbert Redshaw, government farmer in Aneth, penned an anxious letter to Shiprock Agent Evan W. Estep in 1921. As more settlers took lands on the north side of the San Juan, livestock owners scrambled to get whatever range remained. They pushed their herds across the river and onto Indian lands. Redshaw, who was having a "strenuous time of keep[ing] them [whites] off the Reservation" advised the Indians to herd the intruding livestock back over.[2] This advice drew threats from the cowboys who would "kill their dogs and them." Redshaw bemoaned the fact that without some type of law enforcement, every move attempted appeared as a wind-filled bluff. "For years we have held our own because of the fair attitude of the old timers, but the new and younger elements have decided to defy us and unless the government backs me up in my work, there will be serious trouble."[3]

Estep agreed and added his comment in a letter to the commissioner of Indian affairs. Noting that previous relations with earlier stockmen, "all of [whom] are members of the Mormon Church," had been considerate and peaceful, he now felt that "apparently the younger Mormons are not of the same caliber as their fathers."[4] Similar events were occurring on the eastern side of the Navajo Reservation, where white livestock associations with congressional support were lobbying the government to either remove the Indians or grant white ranchers access to reservation lands for grazing. Estep also pointed out that the larceny of Indian cattle had been a profitable business for a number of years and some whites were rumored to have become wealthy from it.

Comb Wash, leading to Chinle Wash, was one of the paths of ingress to the reservation. Land south of the river and west of the 110th Meridian, roughly a north–south line passing through Mexican Hat, became increasingly tantalizing for grazing and oil exploration. Known as the Paiute Strip, this piece of real estate seesawed back and forth from Indian control to public domain, at one time pasturing over five hundred cows belonging to white men.[5] Domination of rangelands north of the river came by using and filing on the limited sources of water. What Anglo stockmen considered their winter and early-spring range became summer range for the Navajos. Once the white men's sheep or cattle began their pilgrimage to summer ranges within the national forest, the Indians brought their herds across the river on the public domain and grazed them there until the cowboys returned. The result: badly trampled and denuded lands subject to erosion.

Both groups realized the extent of the damage and the necessity of improving the situation and decreasing conflict. Shiprock Superintendent B. P. Six attended a meeting with the Indians and local stockmen on March 9, 1930, in Blanding and meetings on March 12 and 13 in Montezuma Creek. The two sides reached a verbal agreement that divided the range with a boundary between Montezuma and Recapture creeks so that the Anglos would be "assured that the Indians would not use their winter range during the summer time and so that the Indians might be assured that the white stockmen would not come on their range at any time during the year."[6] Both parties, keying on natural terrain features, understood the boundary line and agreed to abide by it. This gave the Indians approximately seventy-five thousand acres in the public domain and placed the Comb Ridge area under the control of white residents. By reaching this agreement, the cattlemen were also willing to concede control of the lands in the Paiute Strip to the Indians as an addition to the reservation.[7]

The same day the Navajos and cattlemen agreed, Governor George H. Dern published a letter in the Moab newspaper attacking and "vigorously oppos[ing] the efforts of Congressman Don B. Colton." There were six reasons: (1) The Navajos did not need the land; they already had enough. (2) The Paiute Strip was an emergency winter range for the white stockmen. If the Indians wanted to use it they could, but making the transfer official just stirred up trouble. (3) If oil was discovered in that area, it would be a loss to the state. (4) Tourism through this dramatic landscape would be greatly hindered and obtaining support for building roads on the reservation more difficult. (5) Navajo sheep were covered with scabs, and they would infect the whites' livestock. (6) "A state is never benefited in any respect by having a portion of its area set aside as an Indian reservation. On the contrary, a state is injured by having such an area withdrawn from development and hence as a possible source of tax revenue, to say nothing of the disadvantages of losing control in other respects."[8]

The gentlemen's agreement did not last long. A second series of meetings in Blanding on September 18 and 19 brought Superintendents Six and C. L. Walker of the Western Navajo Agency in Tuba City, with Navajo Chairman Deshna Cłah Cheschillige from Window Rock, together with six of the large cattle owners and Congressman Colton. On the 18th, they traveled to Monument Valley—"forty miles over the roughest kinds of roads"—before returning to Bluff where some of the residents resurrected the theme of selling the town for use as a hospital and boarding school.[9] Again, the Paiute Strip went back on the table to be added to the reservation as long as the Indians in Montezuma Creek and Allen Canyon were permanently confined. "Bluff and the grounds adjacent to it" could be used for that purpose as things coalesced around a future school. "There are approximately 500 acres of excellent land that could be irrigated from the river. . . . The entire village of Bluff consists of but ten or twelve houses worth considering, but these are of stone structure and worth from about $1,500 to $10,000 each. The citizens desire to give up the place because of lack of grazing facilities and because there are not enough people left to maintain a satisfactory public school."[10]

The meeting proved inconclusive. Although the Ute and Navajo agents participated in the "splendid feeling of cooperation and good will" and with others "stressed the necessity of a give and take spirit and of a hasty and friendly settlement," the deal did not close.[11] Cattleman Charlie Redd showed his ignorance of historical fact when he wrote in a letter, "The Navajos north of the river have no 'land of our fathers' ground to stand on since they all slopped over on the north side of the river off the reservation in comparatively recent years."[12] A second meeting netted the plan the cattlemen desired to cinch the deal. It included the loss of all Indian allotments in an area lying between the San Juan River on the south, Blanding to the north, Butler Wash on the west, and the Colorado state line on the east. In addition, no new Indian applications for land could be made. Redd specified other territory to be either available or unavailable to the Navajos north of the river then broached the topic of Bluff becoming an Indian school. If that were to happen then "range lands will be canceled bounded by Recapture Creek on the east, the high bluff rim on the north, the white Comb Ridge on the west, and the San Juan River on the south."[13]

For two more years, the question remained in limbo—not for lack of interest, since the cattlemen wanted a conclusive boundary and settlement. So did the government, worried about not only friction over range but the new allotments being made primarily by Navajos on public land north of the river. Finally, on July 15, 1932, a decisive meeting in Blanding ended the issue. A wide array of luminaries with varied views graced the meeting. Those in attendance included Utah Governor George H. Dern, who came opposed to the loss of state land but had an open mind; Commissioner of Indian Affairs Charles J. Rhoads from Washington, D.C.; J. M. Stewart, section chief of the Land Division, also from Washington; M. K. Sniffen from the Indian Rights Association, Philadelphia; Navajo and Ute Superintendents Walker, McCray, and Peacore; C. E. Faris, superintendent of the Santa Fe Indian School; and Maxwell Yazzie, councilman from the Navajo

Prominent families involved in the livestock industry in southeastern Utah fought for ranges north of the San Juan River. Constant vigilance on range conditions and use included controlling livestock drives.

Nation. Local representation coalesced into the "Council of Nine" comprised of Chairman George Adams, Charles Redd, Karl Barton, Marion Hunt, B. D. Black, Al Scorup, Walter C. Lyman, Arthur Hurst, and H. E. Perkins. The point of discussion: "the [Don B.] Colton Bill that argued for addition of the Paiute Strip and 46,000 acres of land north of Aneth to be added to the Navajo Reservation."[14]

Saturday morning over one hundred citizens attended the mass meeting in the LDS church to hear various positions. After an opening prayer, Commissioner Rhoads began by stating the BIA wanted to "keep the Indians together and that they did not want to grant allotments of land all over the county as they would be forced to do unless the strip could be secured for their use. . . . Under the law the Indian department must grant Indians who made application for them any unappropriated Federal lands in the county and that while the department was not in favor of such allotments, it was helpless to refuse to grant them if asked for."[15] If the Colton Bill was agreed to, then further Indian allotments in San Juan County would be prohibited.

Adams and Redd spoke for the cattlemen in favor of relinquishing the Paiute Strip. Lands north of Aneth were not as easily turned loose. J. M. Stewart produced a map showing that all but four thousand of the forty-six thousand acres of land had been filed on for allotment and that the lands south of the river were pretty well occupied already. Utah was not going to lose much and, in fact, would gain by having further allotments denied. Maxwell Yazzie said the Navajos were waiting for the official word to occupy and then,

"They would be as thick as flies on the Strip." If they failed to respect the boundaries of the agreement, they would be punished. "His statements were well received and made a very good impression on his listeners."[16]

That afternoon, a smaller meeting of the principals convened on the porch of the Ute Dormitory in Blanding. The Paiute Strip was a foregone conclusion; the land north of Aneth was the sticking point. Several times the cattlemen and constituents left the porch and stood under a large tree by the street discussing what seemed to be an impasse. Finally, when it appeared that all the discussions and effort for the past two years were about to evaporate, Rhoads offered that in fairness to the Indians, if the agreement was not signed, he would approve all of the allotments filed on their behalf for this land. Deal done. The Council of Nine appointed Charles Redd and B. D. Black to finalize aspects of the Colton Bill and move it on to Congress in the form of HR 11735, passed on March 1, 1933.[17] Stewart, in summarizing the meeting, felt that "the discussions were exceedingly friendly on the part of the committee, even though spirited, and that the people in and around Blanding are very kindly disposed toward the Indians generally."[18] Thus ended "the largest land deal ever made in the state, as it involves approximately 500,000 acres of land lying south of the San Juan River that run[s] to the Arizona line. Also in the deal is about 46,000 acres in the east corner of the state north of the present Indian reservation."[19]

The major points in the bill, besides designating the boundaries of the additions to the reservation, had a significant impact for Navajos living along Comb Ridge. The second of nine items specified that there would be no further allotments or Indian homesteads outside of the lands now a part of the Navajo Reservation. Other items included the National Park Service being responsible for developing scenic tracts of land, state agencies controlling the hunt for game animals beyond reservation boundaries, Indian allotments north of the river being fenced, and Indians driving livestock across non-Indian land following standard rules established by white law.[20] Based on what would ensue, it is important to emphasize that the Navajo Nation desired this transaction. Tribal Chairman Deshna Clah Cheschillige wrote a strong letter in December offering to bring a delegation to Washington to insure its passage. Communicating on behalf of the Navajo and Paiute people living in the Strip, he urged Rhoads to "insist" that Congress pass the bill to "protect" the Navajo and their stock.[21] By doing this, forty-three pending applications for allotment, undoubtedly some of which would have been in the Comb Ridge area, were now cancelled, because the San Juan River was the northern limit of Navajo land.[22]

A year later, the vise tightened again on the free range for Navajo herds grazing in Butler and Comb. In 1934, the government placed controls on land use by Anglo stockmen through the Taylor Grazing Act. Science now dictated the carrying capacity of the public domain used by cattle, sheep, goats, and horses. The amount of feed was measured by animal unit month (AUM): the forage necessary to feed one cow, one horse, or five sheep for one month on a specific piece of ground. Grazing districts subdivided the ranges and parceled them out in one-to-ten-year leases. The Grazing Service, later combined with the

Courtesy of Kay Shumway

Abandoned Navajo hogans dot the lands along Comb and Butler Wash. This hogan, owned by Jim Joe, was built in the 1930s and abandoned around 1952 when most Navajos living on the north side of the river were driven onto reservation lands by the BLM and local stockmen.

General Land Office to become the Bureau of Land Management (BLM), determined the capacity of a specific range, assigning permits and collecting fees from ranchers. In 1936, the Navajo Tribe adopted a similar system of livestock control and range management, bringing both sides of the San Juan into conformity.[23] At the same time that Congress was passing the Colton Bill, a federal program of livestock reduction implemented by the Soil Conservation Service removed excess animals on the Navajo Reservation. In one of the two darkest periods in tribal history, the program, in many cases, reduced flocks of sheep, goats, horses, and cattle by one-half. Economically, socially, and culturally this devastated the Navajos, forcing them off the reservation and into the wage economy for survival.[24] The days of the Old West and the open range were over.

On the Comb and Butler ranges cowboys pushed the Indians south across the river. Oral testimony is not clear on the dates of removal, since there were actually two different times—one in the 1930s and again in the early 1950s. Speaking of the earlier effort, John Holiday recalled, "They all moved back across the river a few at a time, except for a few who remained around here. If it weren't for John Collier [the commissioner of the BIA blamed for livestock reduction], our people would have still been living here. For those who refused to go back across the river, they're still on this side of the river."[25] Most of those who were not driven across remained in the Montezuma Creek area. The only Navajo who remained with everyone's blessing was Jim Joe, who held onto his allotment near the mouth of Butler Wash. In 1953, his daughter, Jim Joe's Girl, was living on the farm when four men told her to leave. They gave her seven days to vacate the camp. So with her daughter and five children she moved south of the river, but she eventually returned.[26] Mary Jim, one of Jim Joe's granddaughters, now holds title to this site and filed on additional land on the mesa above in 1986.[27]

Vincent Jones tells of a confrontation in Butler Wash (probably in the 1950s) with a Navajo man herding sheep. He had told him twice before "in a nice way" that he could no longer use the land and needed to remove his sheep, but the Navajo did not respond. The third time raised a response.

> Well, there he was right in the same place, sheep and all, and so I beat the hell out of him. He took the sheep and went across the San Juan River that day, and he didn't come back. That was all there was to it; I never had any more Indian trouble down there. . . . [He had] maybe a hundred head. It was just a little old bunch of goats mostly. They went down there so fast that they didn't even stop to open the gates. That man went under that fence down there just like the sheep did.[28]

Warrior Woman (Desbaa) encountered similar attitudes in the 1930s when "Mormon settlers" forced her to move away from the Comb Ridge–Bears Ears area to Montezuma Creek. They then burned her hogan for "firewood."[29]

Similar events occurred in both the 1930s and 1950s. Navajo families for one reason or another had either returned or never left the area following the 1933 agreement. After the initial removal in 1933, there is little mention of Navajo people living north of the San Juan River until 1952–53. Before this time, a difficult winter created drought conditions in the Four Corners area. Some Navajos herded flocks across the river and joined small groups of Indians already living there. Many of the newly arrived Navajos returned to the reservation, but their initial presence drew attention to those already trespassing—enough so that the stockmen and the BLM took their concerns to the Utah Supreme Court in 1952. The court ruled that the Navajos were in violation; local stockmen and BLM employees implemented their plan. Anthropologist Beth King in 1996 interviewed Navajo people involved with this second relocation.[30] Her work is the only substantial publication concerning Navajo eyewitness accounts. What follows is a taste of what happened from their perspective.

The roundup started when the watermelons had "put forth their vines." Most of the people cited lived in Butler or Comb washes and tributary canyons. K. M., who lived along Comb Ridge, told of friendly relations with the ranchers saying, "We lived well with the people in Bluff. . . . They would hold on to wandering livestock and feed the stock while it was under their care." Another person mentioned how the cowboys visited the Navajo camps and hired young boys for work. "For many months before the people were forced off the land, the ranchers had been coming by every once in a while, riding horses among the people and talking to them. Then one day, all of a sudden, they came down and told the people to move today."

The BLM had posted notices on sagebrush and dead trees, warning that they would impound Navajo livestock. Few Navajos could read. Once the relocation started, officials handcuffed or restrained Navajos while others herded the livestock onto trucks for transportation. Hogans and summer shades went up in smoke, some Indians claiming they heard of cattle being driven through the camps and gardens, others saying people were tied and whipped, while others reported livestock being killed. Whether hearsay or not, these reports reflect the fear prevalent at the time. A. N. recalls, "I was in my late teens. I remember the water being high. I was on my toes and it came up at my mouth. We lost many of our animals. I moved the horses across the river first. The cowboys started to harass my mother so I went back to help her. They were whipping our animals to get them to move across the river."

Some families had relatives and friends who could take them in on the south side of the river. Others were not so fortunate. M. S., who had lived in both Butler and Comb washes, had to leave her herds on a sand dune by the river and flee across. She lost all her livestock. Neighbors took her to Shiprock, but she eventually returned home, yet not before both her mother and father had passed away. "I felt so discouraged. Everyone kept it a secret. It was like a curse. No one wanted to talk about it so we kept it a secret. I never talked about it because I had to worry about the kids." Some of the people returned long enough to see what they could salvage, but quickly went back to the south side of the river.

According to King, a group of Navajos filed a complaint against the BLM and received $100,000 for lost livestock. While attending the trial in Salt Lake City, they camped in a field behind their lawyer's house. In court, BLM rangers did not provide convincing testimony about being aware of problems in legality of how they handled the situation. The judge is reported to have said, "It's nonsense, pure nonsense, and I don't want to hear any more about it."[31] He ordered a further investigation but little came of it. While legally, the Navajos had agreed in 1933 to remain on the south side of the river and a formal decision had been rendered on behalf of the ranchers and BLM, this event is not one of the more glorious moments in the history of Comb Ridge.

With the Utes in Allen Canyon and the Navajos south of the river, the range on both sides of Comb Ridge was available for Anglo livestock. Owners of federal grazing permits passed them down to family members, who in turn bought and sold their rights at different times. Broad brushstrokes paint a picture of intense use and varied ownership. For instance, what had historically been called the Barton Range extended over Lime Ridge to Mexican Hat. The newly formed Unit 12 included all of the Barton Range and Comb Wash; Unit 8 encompassed lands north of 12, including Cedar Mesa and Slickhorn

Canyon. In 1943, a BLM grazing map shows the Comb Wash area owned by the Perkins brothers, sons of George Perkins, the previous owner of the Comb Wash Cattle Company. This included Arch Canyon and the Perkins Ranch where efforts concentrated solely on cattle. In 1955, Earl Perkins, the oldest of George's sons, sold these use rights to the Ute Mountain Ute Tribe, who passed the lands to the Allen Canyon Ute Cooperative Livestock Association in 1960; they control it today.[32] This sale included the entrance to Arch Canyon, a site of contention, discussed later.

On the east side of Comb in the Butler Wash area, Unit 11, there were a number of permits, most of which were for sheep. Starting at the San Juan River and moving north, William R. Young and brothers held the lands between Comb Ridge and Cottonwood Wash up to Black Mesa; north of there, L. K. Jones controlled the lands encompassing Butler Wash and Black Mesa; to the north lay Karl Barton's sheep allotment. The point to draw from this detail is that before their expulsion, Navajo sheep were directly competing with Anglos for sheep range. Until the 1933 agreement was enforced then re-enforced, Anglo stockmen were at a disadvantage since Paiute Strip lands were denied to them.

A few vignettes suggest what life was like for both cattlemen and sheep ranchers between 1940 and 1970. Ray Perkins, one of the sons in the Comb Wash Cattle Company, provides a good example of the transition between the old-time cowboy of the open range and the mechanized one, dependent on motorized transportation of livestock, who has to follow BLM grazing rules. Regardless of its place in history, the land still generated stories. Grass and desert shrubs were always the issue. Even as a boy (born in 1915), Ray could see the range was badly overgrazed due to lack of regulation. "If somebody wanted to go into the cow business, he'd turn a cow out on the range and took his chances that she'd live and multiply. He'd start branding calves and catching mavericks until pretty soon he had a herd."[33] In the same breath, he tells of grazing two thousand cattle on South Elk Ridge. By the time the AUMs had been calculated for the now-enforced permit procedure, the number dropped to four hundred. Ray and his brothers sold their shares in the permits to Earl and sent their herd to Colorado. Earl eventually sold out too.

Ray offers the same understanding held by other cattlemen of his time concerning the desert lands and grazing cattle around Comb. The entire issue revolved around rain, not how many cows were pastured on the land.

> Old timers just figured if it rained, the [cows] would have feed; and if it didn't, they wouldn't. They didn't think that the number of cattle they ran had much effect either way. . . . You can take this desert range and if it doesn't rain, even if you haven't got a cow on it, it's not going to look too much different than if you've got a lot of them on it. Then you can get a lot of rain on it, and it will really bloom and produce.
>
> * * * *
>
> Grasses that will grow on the desert are gramma grasses and desert grasses. Desert shrubs are greasewoods, chamisa [rabbitbrush], saltbush, black brush

> and these sorts of shrubs. . . . When you have a lot of feed on the desert they [livestock] will get fat, maybe just as fat as they will on the mountain. But most generally, you don't have that kind of moisture and growth on the desert.[34]

In the same breath, Ray mused that the range was overgrazed. "They [the cattlemen] were running more cattle than the range could really take care of."[35]

Competition for pasture became a target for elimination. Comb Wash had a bunch of donkeys running wild, eating twice the grass that a cow did, and they multiplied quickly. Cowboys viewed these animals as direct competition and so whenever possible tried to rope and kill them. Ray and a group of five men attempted to ambush a herd of the critters one time—Ray was the only one that actually got one. He commented that the donkeys ran only in the Comb Wash area. "A good horse could catch one pretty easily on solid footing like in the bottom of the wash. Out on both sides of Comb Wash there are a lot of little arroyos, gopher holes, rat holes, slick rock, and everything. It was hard to catch a burro in that kind of country."[36] There were also many wild horses. The BLM and Forest Service eliminated both.

The coyote was a different kind of competitor. At one point, the Perkins outfit ran both cattle and sheep in the Comb Wash drainage. Coyotes were a "real menace" when it came to sheep and a lesser threat to calves. On the east side of Comb from Butler Wash to Black Mesa, starting around 1925, the entire area turned to sheep production. Here, coyotes became a huge determining factor in the success of the range industry. Karl Barton (grandson of the previously mentioned Karl Barton) remembers moving his father Clyde's sheep to his summer range on Blue Mountain in 1959 and losing 230 sheep while there, before returning them to the Butler Wash–Black Mesa range. This was a final straw in an ongoing battle against coyotes that had raged for years. When coupled with the scarcity of good herders, there was enough of a challenge that Clyde shifted his sheep business, which he had been in since the early 1930s, to cattle. The 1960s and 1970s saw the cattle industry replace most, if not all, the sheep.[37]

As Vint Jones, another herder who in the winter ran three thousand sheep in Butler put it, "The coyotes were getting their share, the government was getting its share, and the coyotes were getting my share. . . . The BLM was threatening on one end [Butler] the Forest Service was raising hell on the other end [Blue Mountain] and the coyotes had me in the middle."[38] With a loss of four hundred to five hundred animals a summer, he also left the sheep business. Government trappers and poison helped reduce the threat, but it was not enough.

For both sheep and cattle, Butler Wash was an excellent range. Naturally occurring water was plentiful, and when combined with reservoirs that caught runoff and wells drilled on Black Mesa and elsewhere, livestock prospered. Karl Barton (the younger) felt the best fence in the area, and he put in a number of them, was "Comb Reef—never had to pound a staple or stretch a wire."[39] Milder temperatures, shelter from storms, accessibility of roads either on horseback or in pickup trucks, sufficient forage, and availability of herders made Butler attractive. Concerning this last point, Karl remembers two Navajo brothers, Ashley and Ernest Atene from Monument Valley, who for years worked for and befriended his family. The Bartons also hired Hispanic men from New Mexico. Melvin Adams, another rancher, recalls having thirty or forty Navajos come up from the reservation during shearing time to help collect wool. At their best, one of these men could shear fifty head a day.[40]

Clyde Barton pointed out just how important the land in Butler Wash could be during difficult times. In 1972, a period when modern conveniences like trucks for shipping cattle and baled feed were available, things went to pot. Winter came early that year, just as it had in 1948, but this time hung on for six months. Heavy snows and cold temperatures pushed the cattle into a survival situation. Trucks with bales of hay could not get in to them, so horses became the sole means of transportation. Usually, when the cattle sensed a storm, they naturally drifted into Butler. Not this time. Some of them had worked their way onto an exposed point of land and could not get out. Clyde and his sons, Karl and David, rode horses following tracks to locate the animals. Then the first storm hit. The horses soon tired from bucking the snow so the ranchers returned the next day after a second storm had rolled in. Mud under the snow, slippery footing all around, and a circuitous route to the cattle made conditions worse.

> There was too much snow to bring them back so we got them off the point onto a side hill and finally worked them down into the bottom of Butler Canyon. . . . We could only get to our cattle by horseback for quite a spell. After we got them off into the canyon we still couldn't get our blocks to them for two weeks. We would push them around different places under those rims where they could get fresh browse. On the top of the point even the tall sagebrush was covered with snow. . . . But the brush was tall enough; they could get something to eat. So we didn't have much loss. However, I saw twenty head of our neighbor's in just a little ways that were dead.[41]

When spring arrived, it was time to move the cattle onto Blue Mountain. By 1968, with increased motorized traffic on the roads, the Bartons shifted from driving the herd on horseback to hauling them in trucks. Eight cows fit in the two-ton Ford while the calves rode in a pickup. With a herd of 180 cows at "eight cows a whack," it took four days and a lot of trips to relocate the stock. The horses got to ride too. Corrals in Butler served as collecting points for branding and castrating calves, before putting them back on the range. Each corral had its own stories. Karl stood in one he and his dad had built not too far from the Highland Lady. A calf bolted under the gate with Clyde taking after it and Karl not far behind. His horse hit a series of prairie dog holes, toppled over onto Karl, and then righted itself. He remounted and joined his dad who had a calf in tow. Dad: "What the hell is the matter with you?" Karl: "This horse just went over the top of me." "Where's your glasses?" Karl did not even know they were missing. Father and son went back and found them on the ground, then dad inquired, "You hurt?" Karl blurted out, "Well, I'm hurt, but I'm going to be alright. I don't have a serious injury." He closed by saying, "We branded nearly eighty cattle that day. The next day I could hardly move."[42] Cowboying, in any age, can be a tough business.

Courtesy of San Juan County Historical Commission

Sheep and cattle grazed much of the Comb Ridge area and its environs. Clyde Barton and his flock, pictured here, ranged on Black Mesa near Butler, which had continuously served as part of the winter range for Bluff livestock owners.

Improving existing trails and roads was another part of the cowboy experience. In 1930, George Perkins widened the Posey Trail from its existing one- to two-foot span to three –to four feet, using dynamite and shovel. Piling rocks and dirt on the outside edge of the trail and emplacing log braces to shore the sides, the circuitous path moved from an Ancestral Puebloan footpath to a Navajo and Ute trail capable of handling livestock at a slow rate to an even wider but still dangerous herding trail. It was important for moving animals from the top of Comb Ridge to the bottom of Comb Wash. Anyone who has hiked the trail is not surprised by the statement, "Numerous ungulate bones, probably horse, were observed along the trail."[43]

An equally death-defying spot along Comb Ridge was the road west of Bluff. Comb, with its sand, mud, and 22 percent slope, made for an either tortuously slow or precipitously fast experience. Even with improvements, the trail was hazardous. Ray Perkins and Bill Oliver were descending the west slope one day when Ray asked if Bill was not going to dismount, which drew the reply, "No. Where I can go my horses can go."[44] Floyd Nielson, who ran cattle on part of the old Barton Range, would not necessarily agree. When asked if wagons and cars could go over it, he said "yes" but went on to tell of the time he and Corey Perkins were halfway down when the tongue of their wagon broke, the horses' harnesses released, and the real ride began. Remaining in the wagon, the two men tried to use the brake to no avail. "We couldn't do anything but sit there and let our hair raise." Raise it did until the runaway wagon careened into Comb Wash below, where the broken tongue embedded five to six feet into the embankment. With understatement, Nielson recalled, "Of course that stopped everything and everything piled up."[45]

The tourist industry, discussed in the next chapter, also placed new demands on an economy working its way out of the Depression, through the developments of World War II, and into the uranium boom years of the 1950s and 1960s. States in the Four

The Navajo Spring road as it appeared in 1947 before major road construction changed the land. On the floor of Comb Wash in the upper right of the photo lies Navajo Spring, near one of Jim Joe's camps (not pictured). Blasting and excavation for the road would eventually bury the spring.

Corners region sought a unified string of highways to unite the Navajo Reservation and many scenic wonders like Natural Bridges and Monument Valley. An integral part of the growing trade on roads across the reservation was part of the infrastructure known to truckers as the "Billy Goat Highway." Comb Ridge, as a small link in this extensive road system, remained high on everyone's list of areas-most-needed-to-improve.[46] In January 1934, Utah, Arizona, and Colorado held a meeting in Flagstaff, Arizona, that resulted in a petition to Harold Ickes, secretary of the Department of the Interior. The letter requested road construction from Tuba City to Kayenta to Bluff and beyond to link the Grand Canyon, Navajo National Park, and Mesa Verde. A month later, the *San Juan Record* optimistically reported that the wheels of progress were moving on this "main line." The paper editorialized, "Every man with red blood and ambition knows that a good start towards opening up our Natural Bridges means that the job will not be long delayed. Utah is obliged to at least make a special effort to make them accessible. Our country calls for the highway. . . . [which would] insure more visitors, more business, and added life and optimism."[47] Local, state, and federal governments would play an active part, but there needed to be another impetus.

Some new necessity had to arise to infuse significant funding into the long-standing issue of roads. Only an economic interest large enough to throw its weight into the national arena could spur this kind of development. Uranium, in various forms, provided the answer. Compare two newspaper clips from the *San Juan Record*, twenty years apart. In 1932, before carnotite and other forms of uranium had become highly desirable, the county offered $15 for work on the Comb Wash road with the understanding that "the cowboys will also put up $15 for the same road." In 1952, "$120,000 is to be spent on a six mile stretch on Butler Wash, Comb Hill, and Snake Canyon [part of Lime Ridge]," requiring "160 working days and 47,000 tons of gravel."[48] A company from Ogden performed the labor. While there were obvious differences in time and value, there was also a shift in attitude and responsibility.

The history of uranium mining is a long and fascinating tale, too long to be outlined here, that links a local economy to strong national trends.[49] While many people staked and claimed the land in Comb and Butler washes, little if any ever came out of Comb because

Small uranium mines called "dog holes" sprang up around San Juan County in the 1950s. The Hangover Mine (Cottonwood Wash) was a similar neighbor to the Lonesome Mine in Butler. DeVar Shumway (pushing wheelbarrow) and Burdette Shumway are hauling ore from the Hangover in 1943.

the rock formations were not uranium-bearing. Butler, on the other hand, showed an exposed Morrison layer that offered nine outcrops of ore deposits, most of which were small when compared to finds in neighboring Cottonwood Canyon to the east.[50] The earliest interest in uranium came in the form of carnotite, used for making different ceramic colors and in processing high-grade steel. Howard Balsley, a purchaser from Moab, contracted with the Vitro Corporation of Pittsburgh, Pennsylvania, and later the Vanadium Corporation of America (VCA), to buy and ship uranium to the East.[51] Immediately, the product emerging from Butler Wash entered into the national economy.

Lee and Harris Shumway, two of four brothers from a staunch mining family, discovered in 1932 the biggest and best deposit ever mined in Butler. Walking in the canyon one day, the two spied the distinctive yellow remnants of two high-grade fossil trees of carnotite, an oxidized form of uranium. They filed a claim, as they and their brothers had with many other sites, then divided their holdings spread over a large geographical turf. Lee and Harris traded the Cottonwood and Comb area to their brothers, Seth and Arah, in exchange for the Montezuma Creek region to the east. With pick and shovel, the two new owners of the "Lonesome Mine" blazed a quarter-mile truck path off the primitive "Old Salt Road" that traversed the length of the canyon.[52]

The two carnotite trees were ripe for the picking. There was little overburden (dirt and rock) to remove, only a little blasting once underground ("never had to use a light"), and the grade of ore—22 percent—was extremely high, hence the term for this type of operation: "high-grading." Lee Shumway described the site as two trees, three to four feet in diameter, seventy feet long, that were close to the surface then eventually went underground.[53] Pickings became extremely rich when working the stump or butt of the tree, where the leached minerals become concentrated or "butted up." In some instances, a stump with its roots can produce up to 100 tons of high-grade ore or "host rock."[54] The miners simply shoveled what Lee described as "flour dyed yellow" into seamless sacks and carted them off in their old Dodge pickup truck.

Kenny, son of Seth Shumway, remembers seeing these sacks of uranium from the Lonesome stored in a shed behind his house. When dad had a load, he heaved eighteen to twenty bags, about a ton, in the Dodge, put his son in the cab, and off they went to Moab and Howard Balsley. Most miners' accounts about Balsley indicate he gave a very fair price, encouraged the small "dog hole" miners as much as he did larger outfits, and as Kenny put it, "he was a heck of a fine old guy."[55] A one-hundred-pound sack of uranium with 5 percent ore brought around five dollars, high-grade ore at 22 percent considerably more.[56]

The history of the Lonesome Mine is typical of many in the area. While specifics like dates and names of ownership, tonnage of ore mined, and money earned are difficult to obtain, an oral history about each mine exists within the family that worked it. Over the years, the Lonesome picked up two other names—the Golden Butte and V-8—from other miners. The diggings produced for its first owners in the late 1930s and early 1940s. Seth Shumway then sold it to "eleven people out of Colorado," who mined it for some time then sold it to Glen A. Shumway, Seth's son, returning it to the family. Glen later deeded the mine to Kelly, his son, who with his brother, Corey, and his uncle, Tim Perkins, worked it for the last time between 1978 and 1980. By then, the price of ore dropped and the uranium industry petered out on the Colorado Plateau. Eugene Shumway, an active uranium miner in Butler during the late 1950s and early 1960s, estimated that miners throughout its history scooped four thousand tons of ore from these diggings.[57]

Even at the end of the uranium era, the Lonesome (then V-8) produced high-grade ore. Kelly was mining below the "trees" into the east side of Butler with excavating machines and a buggy to haul the ore above ground. Contracted trucks hauled the uranium to buying stations, which then shipped it to processing plants like Energy Fuels, founded in 1976 near Blanding. There was at least one good yellow carnotite tree, eight to twelve feet long, back in the mine. Generally, veins of ore were two and a half feet in diameter, six feet long, yielding 11 percent vanadium and 9 percent uranium. This was the "highest grade of vanadium ever purchased by Plateau Resources," a buying station located at Shirttail Corner, four miles south of Blanding. Other than being flooded out by a gully-washing rainstorm or two, the mine was relatively easy to operate because of the more temperate weather found in this lower elevation. As for a living, Kelly estimated that he made $30,000 a month before expenses.[58]

Eight miles south of Lonesome is the Sunshine Mine, and two to three miles below that is the CC or Sandy. The latter, mined by Burdette and Merwin Shumway, produced a little ore from some trees but was not very significant. The Sunshine, another separate trend of ore, on the other hand, yielded about two thousand tons of uranium. Eugene Shumway mined it in the late 1950s and early 1960s, characterizing it as a "fun" mine because of the lack of danger and the fact that the BLM left the miners alone to do their job without burying them in regulations. Winter travel on steep, slippery roads was difficult and working with diesel loader or shuttle car inside the mine at close quarters tested skills. This did not stop him from saying that today, if he were going to stake claims, he would put them on Ridge One (a formation that lies between Butler and Cottonwood washes), the V-8, and Sunshine. These mines are where family members have made a living for generations.[59]

It was also uranium mining, from the 1930s to 1970s, that spurred the development of roads across Butler and Comb washes and Comb Ridge like nothing ever had before. When one listens to tales told by drivers who maneuvered heavy ore trucks up and down those inclines, one can understand why. Men and modern equipment have transformed the steep, narrow road into a beautiful, curvaceous highway. At the beginning of the uranium era, the road was narrow with a 25 percent grade, rougher than a cob, with no bridges or culverts in either Comb or Butler washes. Each part of the traverse had its challenges.

Working as a driver for one of the mines, Lynn Lyman recalled, "I came into town once to get a load of supplies and I was driving back out and the boss was with me. There had been a big flood in Comb Wash and we got stuck in quicksand. I couldn't make it across and before I could dig out, another flood came. The water just came right up over the hood of the truck and almost buried it. If I had been alone and I had to explain what happened, I don't know whether I could have made my boss believe it or not."[60] As for steepness, Lynn remembers a man who hauled gasoline from an oil refinery in Mexican Hat. He had a specially built platform constructed at the bottom of the ridge where he left a number of barrels of gas before his ascent. After driving to the top of the hill, he unloaded, returned to the platform, retrieved the barrels left behind, drove to the summit, then reloaded the rest.

Donald Bayles applied the same principle one day when hauling a 7.5-ton load. Exclaiming, "Mercy, what a job," he told of two six-inch "jumps" on the incline that gave truckers a problem. When he encountered the first one, he had his wife, Ora, hop out and block the rear wheels so that he could rev the engine and make it over. The second jump was not as accommodating. He removed four chunks of ore, weighing ten pounds apiece, and chugged over the bump. "Now this might be a story that is hard to believe, but that's what it was. Of course we went back and picked up the ore and put it back on once we made it up on top."[61] After that, Donald hauled a little smaller load.

"The roads in San Juan County were something to behold, but not necessarily to enjoy, and in almost every turn and curve there is a story that would blister the ears or curl hair."[62] A series of those turns was in Snake Canyon that fed into Comb Wash from the Valley of the Gods to the west. Today's highway that runs up its middle, hides what that place used to be like. True to its name, the road—one vehicle wide—snaked back and forth with curves that were only two truck lengths long and difficult to maneuver. Vehicle encounters, whether loaded or not, tested gentlemanly virtues in which the lighter truck had to back up until out of the canyon. This, coupled with the ascent of Comb Ridge, littered with snapped axles and twisted drivelines, brought a person to prayer. If a truck broke down, repairs generally took place on the slope, as other vehicles backed up, waiting their turn on the single-lane road.[63]

By the 1950s and the surge in uranium mining for the defense industry, road construction became paramount. The earliest long-distance east–west road emanating from Blanding (State Route 95) traversed Big Canyon, Brushy Basin, and Cottonwood Wash, ran onto Milk Ranch Point and across Elk Ridge, and then dropped down to Natural Bridges. While this facilitated horseback and later vehicular tourist traffic to Natural Bridges National Monument (created in 1908), it was insufficient for what the mining industry demanded. The 1950s ushered in the first of two road-building booms that opened up the western part of southeastern Utah.

Courtesy of San Juan County Historical Commission

Large dump trucks like this were part of the excavation and building project that created Highway 95, going all the way to the Colorado River and the future Lake Powell. Until completion of the road, getting the equipment to the two crews working above and below Comb Ridge was a challenge.

In January 1951, D. H. Whittenburg, chairman of the Utah State Road Commission, unveiled a far-reaching plan to improve the highways of San Juan County. Six different projects amounting to $1,648,000 were available for two hundred miles of "San Juan mine roads" (with a casual nod to the tourist industry). Ninety percent of the funds were federal, testifying to the government's interest in uranium.[64] Everything from start to finish, survey to gravel, was included in the package. First on the list was to change the existing route U 95 that went north of the Bears Ears to Natural Bridges, to a new U 95 at a lower elevation, by two thousand feet, south of the Bear Ears. By doing this, the road bypassed terrain that was "very difficult, hazardous, and expensive to maintain for all season travel." The new "low type all year route," for a cost of $250,000, would descend Comb Ridge on what had previously been an old Indian foot trail near the mouth of Arch Canyon and the Perkins Ranch. Improvements on the much-maligned six-mile stretch of Butler-Comb Ridge-Comb Wash road outside of Bluff would also take a giant step forward. A new two-way bridge would replace an old one-way suspension bridge with a maximum capacity of 7.5 tons.

The Atomic Energy Commission worked through the Utah State Road Commission to get construction underway. Paying for state equipment and personnel, the feds poured money into the project on the "low road" or "Highway to Hite" (U 95). James Hurst of the state road commission flew down from Green River in his plane to help survey part of the route between Comb Wash and Natural Bridges. The Whiting and Haymond Construction Company from Springville, Utah, hired James Wardle as foreman for the task.[65] In order to obtain a grade of no more than 14 percent, forty men set to work with an estimated eighty tons of dynamite to blast out the necessary switchbacks.[66] Crews started above and below the two hundred feet of vertical slickrock in view of the Perkins Ranch, where one of the groups stayed. The men on top had a fifty-foot cleft in the rock before hitting the face. The second crew below blasted and bulldozed the talus slope along a surveyed line where the two groups would meet.[67] Even getting the equipment to the crew below was a challenge. For instance, Ken Bailey had to maneuver a compressor from Blanding "over Elk Mountain, through the Bears Ears, then across a road just brushed out with a Cat to the bottom of Comb, a major undertaking in itself."[68]

The greatest challenge, however, was the rock face. Both crews labored on it simultaneously; besides the obvious danger of working on a cliff, the rock was difficult to crack. The crews worked for months, trying to blast vertical shafts of rock that would break off, but it was hard to "muck out." After a specialist advised them to try horizontal drilling and blasting, the pace accelerated.[69] The winter of 1952–53 witnessed the last of the drilling and shooting when the two crews met, then graded the road. After that adventure, the push west went rapidly.

Courtesy of San Juan County Historical Commission

What is now called Old Highway 95, which descended Comb to the Perkins Ranch near Arch Canyon, was anything but a superhighway. The road had to be constantly patrolled for washouts, mudslides, falling rock, and general repair. Wet seasons were the hardest.

All of this was not without its dangers. Lester Hansen, working on the lower crew, looked up one day to see little pebbles the size of a match head cascading down the side of the cliff. One of the workers yelled, "There's a slide coming," and everyone fled pell-mell for some kind of cover. Lester got down behind a Cat; Randy "Keyhole" Johnson said that he ran off the cliff, looked at the space three hundred feet below and "treaded air back on to" land. A second slide followed with a roar so loud that Lester thought, "Well that's just going to push that Cat right off from that cliff."[70] Although the bulldozer held its ground, a big boulder rolled on top of it while another rock squashed a truck nearby. Fortunately, no one was hurt. Lester fixed the Cat just fine, by drilling a two-foot hole in the boulder, placing a fifth of a stick of powder with cap in it, and cracking the rock so it rolled off both sides. "We used that [bulldozer] for years afterwards, didn't hurt it."

A similar slide occurred farther south at the construction site on Highway U 47 (today's U 163) at Comb Ridge near Bluff. This happened in January 1953, when two cars with six passengers were making their way to Mexican Hat. Partway down Comb Ridge, they saw rocks lying in the road ahead. LaVar Wilkerson got out to inspect then realized he was in an avalanche zone. The slope was too steep for the cars to simply back up. Wilkerson called for his wife to get out, which she attempted, only to get her foot caught in the running board. Trapped with rocks pelting the car, she lay there until a stone hit the auto, relieved the pressure on her foot, and freed her. A rock weighing three tons now hit the other car and "slid over it," followed by a larger boulder weighing one hundred tons. His cars in flames, Wilkerson, fearing an explosion, tossed handfuls of dirt onto the burning engine. Construction crews, above and below the slide, made their way to the stranded motorists. Eventually the other car limped its way back to Blanding with injured people; twenty minutes after the car left, the one-hundred-ton rock slid onto the road where the vehicle had been.[71]

Like the work on U 95, U 47 progressed. Among their accomplishments, workers relocated the road onto smoother terrain, widened it for two-way traffic, placed a bridge over Butler Wash, created a much gentler grade, bypassed the tortuous route in Snake Canyon, and graveled the surface with crushed rock.[72] On the down side, the well-known stopping place of Navajo Spring or "Sweet Water Coming Out" was no more. The blasting and bulldozing tumbled boulders and debris into the canyon below, covering a favorite resting place and historic site. Today, a small part of the corduroy road remains at the top of Comb Ridge while a sign commemorates the now-buried spring at the cliff's foot.

Road improvements through Comb were gratifying. The Atomic Energy Commission was pleased with the amount of road built for the money expended. Its relation with Utah's highway engineers blossomed into mutual respect. Governor J. Bracken Lee had taken an active part in negotiations and planning for the project, and this point helped his reelection to a second term. The tourist industry rode on the coattails of uranium mining and gas exploration, benefiting from the large area opened by three million dollars' worth of new and improved roads. By 1956, contracts to have these highways oiled were placed in the hands of different private companies. In 1964, Highway 47 received additional alignment in Comb Wash, a new bridge eased the flow of traffic, and two ten-foot-diameter corrugated pipes replaced the Bailey Bridge in Butler Wash.[73] Southeastern Utah now had the infrastructure in place to support the boom in extracted resources.[74]

Highway 95 over Comb still presented problems. Sharp switchbacks, sections of dirt that sloughed from the side, tumbling rocks, slick roadways when wet, and constant maintenance encouraged the next generation of road builders to take a second look. Rather than trying to mend the 1950s road, a new link promised better results. The task formed into three phases. In June 1971, a new two-lane alignment blasted and carved its way through the 750-foot ridge to Comb Wash below; a year later, a crew paved the road over Comb Ridge all the way to Cottonwood Wash. The final phase, in November 1972, paved the section of road from Comb Wash to Utah Highway 261, which passes over Cedar Mesa and the Moki Dugway, then connects with the Goosenecks outside of Mexican Hat. The cost: over five million dollars.[75]

Comb Ridge did not accept its conquest without exacting tribute. On July 17, 1975, Lynn Palmer, a state highway foreman who had worked on San Juan County roads for

Courtesy of San Juan County Historical Commission

Even people hauling uranium ore had their share of stories. Slick roads, heavy loads, continuously used equipment, and long distances confronted the miners, many of whom could not draw on the resources of large companies.

years, went to Butler Wash following a torrential rainstorm that washed out a thirty-inch piece of pipe. Lynn arrived at the site and set to work with pick and shovel, attempting to salvage the pipe before using heavy equipment to emplace it. Without warning, thirty to forty tons of earth collapsed from the seventeen-foot-high embankment, burying the foreman and killing him instantly. He would have retired in less than a year.[76] The county lost a good man that day.

Hugh Kirkham, Utah Department of Transportation (UDOT) project engineer, viewed the improvements on Highway 95 as one more addition to "the backbone for the overall network of roads that will serve Utah's red rock country."[77] Although the bypass from the old U 95 to today's highway was only two miles away, it cost $1,167,994, adding to the already $13 million spent on roads since World War II. By the end of the construction that finished U 95, its spurs, and other projects spread over the last fifteen years throughout the

Courtesy of Kay Shumway

The old Highway 95, as it appears today, is still trafficable. The most difficult part is near the top, where the sandstone of Comb Ridge presents the biggest challenge.

county, the total rose to $20 million.[78] Some of these figures are questionable, depending on how one counts the dollars, but there is no mistaking the intent. Compare the statement cited earlier in the chapter about the county providing fifteen dollars and the cowboys matching the amount, to the role of state and federal agencies at this point. The picture is totally different.

What was achieved by the many years spent in improving and linking roads? Beyond the obvious support for the extractive industries, whose pace slowed and in some cases stopped in the 1980s, there were continuing forms of development. By 1976, paved highways tied the Golden Circle network of tourist sites throughout the Four Corners region. Not only was Natural Bridges, the oldest national monument in Utah, now readily accessible, but so were Canyonlands National Park, Lake Powell, Hovenweep, Monument Valley, Zion and Bryce in southwestern Utah, and Mesa Verde and Chaco Canyon in neighboring states. In September of that year, Governor Calvin L. Rampton proclaimed U-95 as the Bicentennial Highway on future maps and road signs. Others talked of U-95 as the "backbone of the Golden Circle."[79] It did not take long, however, for people to forget the sacrifice it took to pioneer the initial road over the "backbone of the earth."

9

The Comb and I

Contemporary Issues and the "Me-ification" of a Rock

The story of the discovery of Procession Panel—or the rediscovery, for surely certain Anglos must have blundered across the site in the earlier decades—is a fascinating one. By the late 1980s, day hikers had begun to throng this section of Comb. . . . It's like in just a two-or-three week period, somebody had thrown a switch. And within a year, there was a beaten path up to the Procession Panel.

—from David Roberts, *Sandstone Spine*[1]

The last quarter of the twentieth and first glimmer of the twenty-first centuries heralded unprecedented change in the canyons and washes surrounding Comb Ridge. It was not the rock that changed but the people. Never before had comfort, ease, and personal agenda been so prevalent. The 1960s, '70s, and '80s insured that. These years introduced the hippie movement, accompanied by a drug culture, individual expression, anti-materialistic views in an increasingly materialistic society, idealization of a natural lifestyle, concern for the environment, and the acceptance of diversity. As sponsor of this individual expression stood the court system that recognized everyone's right to enter into a lawsuit. By the 1980s, America had become an extremely litigious society, bent on protecting group and individual rights no matter how plausible or implausible those rights may be. Society had reached the "me-ification" of the individual, where personal demands often outweighed "group" welfare.

Accompanying this loss of cohesion was the glorification of the individual and individual accomplishment. Introspective prose, the personal experience, wrested lessons for life from the natural surroundings, reflecting the writer's reality. Nature or "natural" writing, which has often been popular in growingly mechanistic societies, gave birth to contemplation of man's relationship to the environment. Old pros like Wallace Stegner and Joseph Wood Krutch were dragged out to stand beside the new crowd of Edward Abbey, Terry Tempest Williams, Ellen Meloy, Ann Zwinger, and Craig Childs—all of whom wrote about personal experiences in southeastern Utah. Life plus environment equals soul-searching, San Juan-style.

So it was not surprising that adventure writer David Roberts selected Comb Ridge for his personal exposition. Based on an eighteen-day experience with two other backpackers, Roberts crafted a book, *Sandstone Spine*, about his hike on Comb Ridge. The trip started in Kayenta and ended near Whiskers Draw with stops along the way to examine ruins, visit historic sites, explore side canyons, and seek water. The dust jacket's subtitle, "Seeking the Anasazi on the First Traverse of the Comb Ridge," appeals to the American ideal of being "first" along with the categories of biggest, best, longest, shortest, etc. Add to this, "They set off on one of the *last* geographic challenges left in North America: to hike the rugged Comb Ridge in one continuous push" and one sees immediately qualities that characterize contemporary society. For Roberts, to hike this "mini-mountain . . . is to run a gauntlet of up-and-down severities, with a sheer precipice lurking on the west, a fiendishly convoluted maze of bedrock slabs and narrow gullies on the east—always at a sideways, ankle-wrenching pitch. There is not a single mile of established trail in the Comb's hundred mile reach. The challenge would prove to be a stern one for the three friends."[2]

A number of elements are embedded in this personal account that reflect cultural trends of our times. Most obvious is that we view Comb Ridge as a physical challenge. In keeping with an age when marathons, triathalons, and Iron Man contests have peaked in popularity, the challenge here is to hike the ridge. Roberts often reminds the reader of his age (sixty-one at the time) and the physical exertion it took to accomplish the feat. The "hook" in the story to keep readers going is not in his use of secondary sources that scrutinize snippets of prehistory, history, and Navajo culture, but rather what it took to walk the rock.

A second element is personal relations. Roberts's very candid exposé of group dynamics between him and his two partners is in the best tradition of television "reality" shows like *Survivor*, *The Apprentice*, *Big Brother*, and *The Bachelor*, all of which put interpersonal relations under a microscope as people swim through a cauldron of conflict. Comb Ridge is also a testing ground for social fabric. Another point is that the author reflects on some of the better-known historic events but misses the overall point that this challenge was part of someone's daily way of life in the past, without all of the gear and high tech solutions to basic problems. What may be a feat in today's world was probably not worth mentioning in theirs—another sign of the luxury and ease that surrounds us, even on our eighteen-day walks. Personal experience reigns supreme in the twenty-first century.

This concluding chapter focuses on three topics that have threaded their way through previous chapters. The first is economic development in the form of cattle grazing, the only real enterprise now underway on these public lands. Oil and mineral exploration has come and gone and may return, but at present it lies dormant and will face stiff opposition if it awakes. The next is the exploitation and protection of Ancestral Puebloan sites; the former peaked in the 1960s, '70s, and '80s but still occurs today. The third and final topic is the current dispute over how the land should be used and preserved. Arch Canyon has become a particularly volatile scene for confrontation, but it is not the only place in the

Comb Ridge area turned arena. The issues say more about contemporary society and its values than they ever will about the landscape.

On October 27, 1955, the Ute Mountain Ute Tribe bought the only private land in Comb Wash along with the grazing permits to surrounding public lands from Earl H. Perkins and his wife, Tamar. At the same time, the Allen Canyon Ute Cooperative Livestock Association, comprised of people from the White Mesa Ute reservation, purchased the accompanying cattle.[3] What had been the Perkins Ranch that sat astride the entry to Arch Canyon was, ironically, in the hands of the Utes whose ancestors had fought against the advent of the cattle industry seventy years before and whose family members had been marched at gunpoint down Comb Wash thirty years previous. The 1,534-acre parcel of land had a water source that was constant—either running or pooled—throughout the year. There was also good bottomland and shelter for the livestock, making it an excellent winter range. Surrounding areas provided additional grazing; soon the Utes were in business.

Dependent on mutual cooperation, the Allen Canyon Livestock Association and the Ute Mountain Ute Tribe sat down with the Bureau of Land Management (BLM), Soil Conservation Service, and the Bureau of Indian Affairs (BIA) to draft a use plan. Scientific land management for the cattle industry, as first introduced in the Taylor Grazing Act, had reached new levels of sophistication. By 1968, when the group convened, there were high expectations, made tangible by the growing environmentalist movement. The ranch now sprawled over 115,000 acres—65,000 belonging to the BLM, 41,000 to the Forest Service, 7,000 to the state, and 1,500 to the tribe.[4]

The Utes held grazing privileges for 527 cattle (3,951 AUMs) based on the concept of winter-summer range rotation. By controlling the base property and the permit, tribal members ran their own cattle under the Allen Canyon Livestock Association with its BIA advisors. The problem was that 67 percent of the range was classified as in either poor or bad condition with only 2 percent in good condition.[5] Severe erosion, caused by overgrazing, was taking its toll. To prevent losing the grasses beyond recovery, the land, much of which was not in Comb Wash, was divided into six pastures with a limited time allotted in each one. Indian ricegrass was the key species on native ranges. Upper Comb-Arch Canyon Pasture served as the gathering and drift way to and from the forest and other surrounding locations. The BLM and the livestock company shared joint responsibility to make the plan work.

But the best laid plans of mice and men oft go astray. A snapshot from 1976–1977 illustrates the problem: the cattle had not read the plan. The BLM files tell of grazing trespass after grazing trespass: March 8, 180 cows; December 15, 9 cows; February 21, 44; March 16, 21; March 24, 7; April 14, 10; April 26, 18; April 27, 24; July 2, 4; August 31, 10; and November 9, 52. Charges based on AUMs followed.[6] Threats to entirely remove grazing privileges were also made. The livestock company changed range managers, worked hard to stay apace with the cattle, and rotated the herd to its different pastures while the BLM tried to be good neighbors yet uphold the schedule. The cattle, however, did what they do best and acted like cattle.

Environmental groups were not amused. Increased tourism and growing activism came into direct conflict with stockmen grazing cattle in highly traveled areas, especially Comb Wash with its five tributaries of Arch, Mule, Fish Creek, Owl, and Road canyons. By 1989, enough manure had been splattered in the wrong places that a lawsuit followed.[7] Much in keeping with the spirit of the times, groups outside of southeastern Utah rose to protect the land that they loved against others who loved it too but used it in a different way. Neither group reached a middle ground—the cowboys hoping the environmentalists would choke on their hamburger, the environmentalists hoping the cowboys would be trampled before all the cows reached the slaughterhouse. The BLM, however, became the target for bad management charges because of a "poor" environmental impact statement.

Familiar players drew the line in the sand. Arrayed on one side were the National Wildlife Federation, Southern Utah Wilderness Alliance (SUWA), and Joseph M. Feller. Feller, a professor of environmental law at Arizona State University, was a particularly interesting individual since he was one of the founding champions of public rights, allowing individuals to become part of the fray. On the other side of the stream stood the BLM, American and Utah Farm Bureau Federations, Public Lands Council, National Cattlemen's Association, American Sheep Industry Association, and the Ute Mountain Ute Tribe. Comb Ridge and its tributaries lay bare before the contestants who sought answers to questions being asked on a national level. Is it economic development over the environment or vice versa? Similar questions are still being asked.

The charges against the BLM and its respondents were many and varied but can be categorized into three main groups: The BLM was not a wise steward because of a poor assessment of the land's potential in its environmental impact statement (EIS), the land was badly abused and needed a plan for recovery, and the cultural (Ancestral Puebloan) and recreational resources were being destroyed. Experts from various disciplines testified on both sides as to what they saw happening. Add to this mix the volatile fact that since 1979, the five canyons had been proposed as Wilderness Study Areas (WSA) and the complexity grows. A few examples illustrate the type of give and take found in discussion surrounding these lands.

The appellants started with Hugh A. Harper, an expert who had worked for the Idaho Fish and Game. He testified that the EIS did not identify native vegetative communities, did not describe the deteriorated range conditions or the causes for the deterioration, failed to ameliorate the already identified (1968) poor range conditions, had no analysis of a proposed watering system for the cattle, and failed to provide information about the suitability of the five tributary canyons for grazing livestock. The rotation plan did not and would not work. Cattle created paths, beat down trails, congregated around water points, broke down stream banks, fouled the water, destroyed native vegetation making room for undesirable "pioneer" weeds, and generally accelerated soil erosion.

Jim Hook, Bluff motel owner and backpack guide, was next. He was particularly concerned with Fish Creek and Road canyons, two of the five tributaries, representing part of the 150 miles of canyon in the study. He had recently brought six- and seven-person

San Juan County Commission

Rephotography (same spot and angle) depict changes in the landscape. These pictures taken in 1916 (with riders) and 1998 a half-mile southwest of Navajo Spring, show the addition of saltbush and shadscale, but also the increase of curlygrass, Indian ricegrass, globemallow, and other types of groundcover.

groups with his pack llamas for an outdoor experience. Describing "each canyon [as] a different neighborhood of a great ancient city," he felt they held "secrets of Indian ruins and artifacts."[8] Unfortunately, the cattle were destroying the city. In April 1991, on a trip in Road Canyon, he ran into some of the culprits—a herd of 50 to 60 hoofed locusts on the rampage. The benches along the streams were thick with cow pies, badly trampled, and overgrazed. The water was full of manure, not to mention a dead cow. "On the last day, the tour group was caught in a heavy windstorm, which picked up large quantities of dirt and dust that had been churned up by the cattle. The group sought shelter in the only remaining nearby grove of cottonwood trees. Under the cottonwood trees, the manure was so thick that the travelers had to use a shovel to clear a campsite."[9] No one was happy that day.

Dr. Bob Ohmart was an expert on environmental impacts in riparian areas. Decreased vegetation along stream banks caused the water flow to broaden and increase in velocity, harmed the watershed, disrupted wildlife, lowered the water table, and altered the type and amount of vegetation in the five canyons. John Ritchey spoke of the loss of recreational value and how everything from scenery to rock climbing was negatively impacted. Archaeologists Winston Hurst and Michael Berry spoke to the issue of site preservation. They pointed out that cows find shelter from the elements in alcoves and standing walls of towers, cliff dwellings, and room blocks. The animals knock over the walls, defecate in the ruins, trample subsurface artifacts, churn the soil, and remove vegetation, which speeds erosion. Something had to be done to stop all of this.

The BLM did not agree. What they saw on the ground did not jive with much of the expert testimony of the other side. The allotment was not in a deteriorated condition, utilization did not necessarily equate to overgrazing, the general charges sounded serious but did not stand up to specific scrutiny, and the BLM did not have the responsibility to insure the success of private outfitters. They hired their own experts, one of whom—Dr. Catherine Vandemoer—visited allotted lands in February 1992 and arrived at very different conclusions.[10]

Briefly, she analyzed "stream channel cutting, movement and redistribution of sediment . . . cliff retreat and weathering patterns" as affected by "a complex interaction of factors, including geology, soils, slope, aspect, drainage area, channel width, depth and desert fluvial events. . . . The impact of cattle grazing on these factors has not been significant enough to account for the current form, shape and evolution of the sub-watersheds of Comb Wash."[11] The dendritic drainage pattern that characterized the area is based on the geology, water flow, and materials moved by the water. Sudden flows of water such as in summer thundershowers can produce rivers, causing flash floods that scour the canyons and carry huge bed load deposits of boulders, rocks, and sediment long distances until the velocity and volume of water subsides and drops its load. The water that falls on the slickrock benches runs quickly off the slopes and into the canyons magnifying its effect through channeling. For example, two inches of rain falling on the Arch Canyon watershed can produce a flow of 600 cubic feet per second that courses down Comb Wash and into the San Juan River.[12]

In response to the query about different types of plants invading the area, she pointed out that it is often the type of soils available not the presence of cows, that determines what grows where. Shales, mudstones, and clays produce soils with high salt content leading to the "greasewood bottoms" that characterize the southern portion of Comb Wash. High evaporation rates in this area leave behind salts that become concentrated in the soil and either encourage or deny certain types of plant growth. Cattle grazing also did not impact the stream channel's down-cutting. "The large-scale down-cutting of Comb Wash which left terrace as much as 20 feet above the current valley floor, occurred more than 100 years ago and is thought to be representative of large scale regional down-cutting of all major streams in the southwestern United States."[13] Rain intensity, drought conditions, and distribution were all part of this earlier canyon erosion.

Gregory Collection, Special Collections, J. Williard Mariott Library, University of Utah

San Juan County Commission

Fish Creek in 1927 (with horses) and again in 1998 show a contemporary narrowing of the floodplain and an expanding riparian plant community. Cottonwoods, bulrushes, cattails, and tamarisk are some of the plants now found along the streambed.

The debate between the two entities dragged on into 1993 when the court reached a settlement. There would be no cattle grazing in the five tributary canyons. The BLM agreed that given the topography and the high rate of recreational visitation, it would not pursue the avenue left open to them of developing an EIS for each canyon so that they could be used for grazing. Given the recreation value, cattle were not compatible in this environment. Congress has chosen not to move on the WSA issue and so the BLM currently ministers these lands under an Interim Management Policy used for all areas with this designation.[14] As for Comb Wash, roughly the northern two-thirds is still open for Ute cattle while the lower segment—with a northern boundary of Highway 163 and a southern boundary of the San Juan River—is what remains of the old Perkins range and is in the hands of Darin Goodall. Butler Wash grazing allotments are also divided between Lynn Patterson in the south and Keith Ivins in the north.[15] A 2008 ten-year draft management plan for Comb Wash is under review and promises to take into consideration "the archaeological sites, wildlife habitat, scenery, recreational opportunities, and extensive riparian vegetation contained within its boundaries."[16] Control of the cows through range rotation remains at the heart of the plan.

Courtesy of Kay Shumway

Arch Canyon Great House, at the mouth of the canyon, is heavily visited by tourists. Much of the ruin has not been excavated, but the surface structure has been stabilized.

Another issue that dominated the San Juan landscape in the last half of the twentieth century was archaeological vandalism, known locally by the euphemisms of "pot-hunting" or "Moki poaching." As early as 1931, Albert R. Lyman prophetically announced what would happen in the future by gazing at the past. He started by recounting where large collections of Puebloan artifacts from the county were then located—Deseret Museum (Salt Lake City); University of Utah (Salt Lake City); museums in Denver, Chicago, and New York; and Berlin, Germany. He then mused that if everything that had been removed was returned, it would still not get close to the amount of what was left. He opined on "the many fine buildings that had been sadly disfigured, treasure chambers that [had] been rifled, [and the] interesting old landmarks brushed away."[17] Someday, the public would view those who did this as "savages."

There was, however, hope. Lyman felt that these sites could be restored to tell a stunning story of who lived here before the despoilers. A museum should be reared in the midst of this ancient civilization to house their artifacts. "These restored wonders would give the hazy past a sharp punch of reality. The great nations of farmers would seem to come back from their remote uncertainty with splendid proof that their lives were not in vain but that the nucleus of their hard experience is a worthwhile message to us."[18] In December 1978, the Edge of the Cedars Museum State Park opened the doors of this $600,000 facility. Fifteen years and $1.6 million later, the museum had increased its space by one-third with the addition of a repository for artifacts coming from San Juan County, as well as laboratory and storage space.[19] Groups started returning collections—Energy Fuels Nuclear Company deposited artifacts unearthed while clearing their site south of Blanding, Brigham Young University donated its collection from Recapture Wash, the BLM encouraged individuals and groups to give back what had been taken, and the University of Denver returned its collection taken from Butler Wash.[20] Prophecy was fulfilled.

Problem: the "savages," as Lyman characterized them, were still out there. The 1960s witnessed a growing number of diggers who turned to the ruins for economic gain. Some rationalized that it was part of a continuing family heritage, a right and a rite, that came with birth in San Juan County. Others felt that outsiders, in the name of education or cultural preservation, had come in and done what they wanted, so the locals were no worse than the professionals. Some looked at the economic opportunities, where objects brought high prices in a black market for the wealthy. And some just enjoyed the spirit of discovery masked by the comforting belief that an object was simply there and might as well be put to use on their bookshelf or coffee table. For whatever reason, the citizens of Blanding held the reputation for being at the center of the problem.

Effectively policing the broken country of San Juan was impossible. Nobody will ever know how many Puebloan sites exist in the 2.6 million acres of land managed by the BLM Field Office in Monticello, but one estimate offered a low total at ten thousand, without defining what constituted a site. Intensely settled areas, such as in Grand Gulch, may have twenty-five to thirty-five sites per square mile.[21] As early as 1965, the BLM announced "weekend 'Moki Digger' patrols" to ferret out violators of the 1906 Antiquities Act. If apprehended, the guilty party could face ninety days in jail and a $500 fine.[22] Benefits from a sale far outweighed the penalty. Just a small mug sold for between $250 and $450. Many other artifacts could demand three or four times the price.[23] Whether coming illegally from public land or from private land, which was legal, relics were good business.

The BLM was poorly funded, undermanned, and logistically strapped to wage a war against such a mobile enemy. In 1980, there were six rangers to cover the vast territory, and only one of them had the power to arrest a culprit caught in the act. Instead of trying to control the entire piece of terrain, they selected a 400,000-acre region rich in sites and made it their priority. Grand Gulch, Comb Wash, and Butler Wash were a primary focus. Foot, vehicular, horseback, and helicopter patrols at unscheduled and unpredictable times became part of the tactics. Rangers seeded more likely sites with sensing devices. In 1979, the federal government strengthened the Antiquities Act by passing the Archaeological Resource Protection Act (ARPA), making it a felony to buy and sell illegally obtained artifacts and offering cash awards for testimony against individuals involved in the illegal trade. Fines could now go as high as $250,000 with up to two years in jail. New statutes provided law enforcement training for land managers with arresting authority and side arms for protection. Lynell Schalk was one of the first females to undergo this training as she worked in and out of the county during the 1970s and 1980s.

Even with increased manpower, aircraft, and more authority, the job was still not easy. Schalk recalls in the mid-seventies going on helicopter flights that took her over Comb Ridge. During this same era, Hill Air Force Base sent F-111 jets through the same area for low-level nap-of-the-earth flight training. The little BLM helicopters cautiously nosed their way over Comb Wash in fear that the "fast boys" might suddenly appear and either hit their aircraft or engulf it in extreme turbulence. In spring of 1976, a helicopter engaged in archaeological site protection overflight in the lower Butler Wash area crashed because of weather, seriously injuring the pilot, breaking the back of one ranger and the hand of another. The man with the injured hand walked out to Bluff to get the town's Emergency Medical Technicians (EMTs) to respond.[24]

Incident reports on file in the Monticello BLM office give a sense of the frequency and type of infractions the rangers encountered. Those mentioned here occurred either in Comb or Butler washes during the late seventies or early eighties. What also becomes apparent is the variety of people involved. For example, a university professor with his family from Denver was "digging for ants" and unearthed a mano, potsherds, and chert flakes in a site; a local Blanding couple out arrowhead hunting requested information about the helicopter patrols and said they enjoyed cleaning up Basketmaker sites after someone else had dug them; four children (ages nine to fourteen in one group) and a man with two older teenage girls (a second but related group) were apprehended carrying shovels and bags of potsherds while digging in Comb Wash; sections of fence were torn down and the register box pulled out of the ground at an Arch Canyon Indian ruin; sites and surrounding terrain came under assault by off-road vehicles creating multiple trails; interpretive signs were shot, uprooted, and discarded; and kivas and dwellings were extensively excavated with bones left on the surface and contemporary trash (in one campsite twenty-five pounds) left about.[25] Multiply this over the entire region and it becomes apparent why there was concern.

In 1979, following passage of the ARPA that took effect on October 31, there seemed to be no abatement in the digging. During the summer and fall, six raids occurred on a single site called Turkey Pen Ruins in Grand Gulch, with a seventh one in November. BLM Rangers arrived at the scene, caught and talked to one dirt be-spattered individual and eventually located a second participant in Blanding following a traffic stop by an alerted sheriff. The rangers visited the site and reported: "There were 20-some holes one to three feet deep, and two large, gaping holes about 14 to 18 feet in diameter and five to six feet deep; they were new holes. There was a roof beam from a kiva which was, I think, dated in the 1200s, which was burnt in half. There appeared to be two walls that were pushed over. There were all types of artifacts scattered around the site, such as parts of baskets, tools, manos, turkey feather blankets, what appeared to be some type of rope, desert bighorn sheep hides—this was scattered about the surface."[26] Eventually arraigned, one man

Copyright by Andrew Gulliford

Three types of destruction—vandalism, looting, and love—take their toll on prehistoric and historic sites. The vandalism at Wolf Man Panel is the most mindless, where target practice irreparably damaged this Basketmaker rock art.

turned evidence against the other, who was found guilty of destroying government property but innocent of violating the new act. He was, however, the first person ever convicted of a felony for digging in federal Indian ruins.

Butler Wash came under scrutiny that same month. Two different men, intent on digging, failed to detect a BLM ranger watching them through field glasses until his radio sounded. The sheriff made the arrests, the men pled guilty to a misdemeanor under the act, and were the first convicted under the new law. All four men in these two cases spent time on probation and paid fines ranging from $200 to $750.[27] They were only four of the estimated fifteen individuals receiving big dollars for large sales in the black market.

Not everyone was guilty. In the same BLM files is a report submitted in March 1980 with an addendum attached in August 2007. The ranger's statement told of finding a black Ford pickup truck, with license plates removed, parked off the road at the Cold Spring site. She spied two people in front of the alcove, one of whom appeared to be digging. The ranger parked her vehicle behind the truck, waited for the two men to return, and questioned them about who they were and what they were doing. One of them identified himself as Winston Hurst, mentioning that he had worked for the BLM before and was then a graduate student in archaeology. Despite his flippant reply of what he was doing there—"Oh just digging a few holes and knocking down a few walls"—the two struck up

Looting for artifacts and profit scrambles the archaeological record while removing objects and information from context. This Puebloan site shows pothunters' pits and gives a sense of destruction encountered at these sites in the 1960s to the 1980s.

a friendly conversation before being released. A couple of additional stops by the sheriff and deputy sheriff on the Butler Wash Road released Hurst from the gauntlet, and he was gone. The ranger went to the Cold Spring site and found signs of fresh digging but could not locate a shovel. That is what the official report said.

Twenty-seven years later, Hurst blanched when he read the statement in the BLM files. Under the attached, "What really happened," the story gets better. He recalls being on break from graduate school and his pot-hunting nephew inviting him to look at sites. This was one of a number of volatile discussions, part of which had even entered San Juan newspapers, that pitted the preservationist mentality of the professional archaeologist against the cherished freedom of locals to do what they wanted with Puebloan sites. As they visited various locations, the diatribe on each side unfolded, "he challenging various poorly understood tenets of archaeology and sharing derisive tales about BLM rangers and archaeologists, I [Winston] pompously and humorlessly responding with my little lectures."[28] The nephew all but admitted that he had been actively digging, then pulled out from behind the seat a box of artifacts that included part of an atlatl. "This scared the hell out of me, because I knew that just being associated with that stuff was enough to trash my career in archaeology before I even got out of school."[29]

The two arrived at the Cold Spring site and hiked in. A freshly dug hole a meter wide gave Winston another opportunity to give a lecture to his unreceptive nephew before returning to their vehicle that was now boxed in. The BLM markings on the side of the second truck alerted both to future possibilities.

> As we approached [my nephew's] truck, we could see the BLM markings on the truck, and [nephew] started getting his fight up, ready to go to fisticuffs with any BLMer. He was hot-headed and ready to kick some ass, and I was scared by the possibility that his box of artifacts was about to cost me my career. We must have looked pretty "hinky," in ranger-speak, he argumentative, I nervous. By the time we got to the trucks, I had convinced him to leave the talking to me, and he withdrew to his truck while I chatted with the ranger. . . . I tried to be clever, chatty, and disarming, in my incompetent and blundering way. . . .[30]

A release by the ranger and two law enforcement stops later, with the nephew red and fuming and ready for a fight, Hurst escaped the situation, having "sweat bullets the whole time." A BLM friend later told Hurst that he had already been condemned by members of the BLM staff as guilty until proven innocent. What had started out as an attempt to convert an errant pothunter relative to the gospel of archaeology had almost turned into the death knell of one of its most ardent disciples.

The 1980s saw no lessening in the severity of the assault on the Puebloans. Characterized as a "feeding frenzy," pothunters at Hovenweep used bulldozers to expose artifacts, pushed over or cratered walls at other sites to find their treasure, and left human remains scattered on the surface—enraging Native American communities near and far.[31] Equally devastating was the loss of information, the jumbling of layers of prehistory, and the total lack of respect for the dead. Governor Scott Matheson called for "quick action" before all sites were totally vandalized. But in the five years prior to 1984, there had not been a single arrest in southeastern Utah. New tactics were offered as part of the solution: local range riders who could patrol the sites, map and inventory losses to determine threatened areas, grant amnesty for those with artifacts to come forward and have contextual information documented, and encourage private investors to help with excavation then give them the option of purchasing the object after a study had been completed.[32]

There needed to be a find, a catch, a conviction of someone in the center of the illegal trade to serve as a warning. The break came on November 14, 1984, when U.S. attorney general for Utah, Brent Ward, announced that twenty-seven-year-old Earl K. Shumway from Blanding was to be arraigned on four counts of violating ARPA. Shumway could face up to ten years in prison and a twenty-thousand dollar fine.[33] To Ward, it was the "opening salvo in the war on pot hunters and artifact dealers in the black market for antiquities." The evidence—thirty rare baskets approximately one thousand years old, taken from a site in Allen Canyon. Only half were eventually recovered. Shumway plea-bargained himself into a position that resulted in no punishment in exchange for identifying other poachers and the location of artifacts taken from federal lands.

Courtesy of San Juan County Historical Commission

On the outskirts of Blanding is the Westwater Five Kiva Ruin, photographed around the start of the twentieth century and again in 2005.

A year prior to this, Governor Matheson had formed a Task Force for Archaeological Site Preservation comprised of professional preservationists and local people charged with fostering goodwill and solving problems on a decentralized level. Perceptions about federal and law enforcement roles were changing, archaeologists appeared to be human, and antagonism decreased between groups. A new governor, Norm Bangerter, was not overly concerned, so he dissolved the task force. This, coupled with others who felt kicking doors and brandishing warrants was a greater deterrent, changed the goals. When Earl Shumway provided names—many of who were people he held grudges against—twenty-five BLM and Forest Service agents moved in. "The Raid," as it is known locally, commenced on May 8, 1986. The target: seven homes of individuals purported to have illegal artifacts. By the end of the day, 325 objects from various towns in Utah and Colorado were in federal custody with charges being prepared.

Reaction was instantaneous, the hyperbole volatile. Some examples: the agents were "a Gestapo-type group of Nazis inspired by BLM and Forest Rangers"; the Blanding

Courtesy of Winston Hurst

While there has been both vandalism and looting, this site has also had a constant stream of visitors. Many of these people love the ruin, and though well meaning, they unintentionally damage it.

mayor called for "withdrawal from the Union of the United States," promising that the "South [ern Utah] shall rise again"; another group called for outlawing the BLM.[34] This made for entertaining reading, but on a more serious note, federal agencies had an almost impossible task of distinguishing between what artifacts had come from private and federal lands. Any kind of goodwill and enlightened education concerning site preservation disappeared down the drain. Middle ground between the factions evaporated; local government opposed any other government agency's interference; and the pothunters, self-styled as Robin Hood (who gave to themselves—the poor), gained a boost in the war for local support. Hurst, a member of the Site Preservation Task Force, summarized the effect of the raid:

> We had made good strides with hearts and minds at that point, but the raid set us back decades, and we're [archaeologists and federal officials] still trying to regain people's trust. The sad denouement is that Earl walked, not a single

> conviction came from it, and everyone who could afford the legal fees necessary to challenge it got some or all of their stuff back. The rest of the artifacts came to repose at Edge of the Cedars, giving the diggers fodder for their oft-made claim that the museum was in cahoots with the government to take away people's collections in order to fill its shelves. Earl had given them information that he knew would not lead to convictions, but would make life miserable for a long list of people against whom he held grudges. In the end, it was a masterful coup.[35]

Reverberations from the raid are still felt today.

On a more positive note, the times were changing. Following the raid, illegal excavation went underground, no pun intended. The mid-1980s saw an overall decrease in activity, and that which was going on became much more subtle. For the hobbyist, it became apparent that penalties were attached. Professional looters realized that serious penalties could be hung around their necks if caught. The land agencies were assuming a much tougher stance, backed by their own ability to enforce the law. Finally, one elusive Robin Hood eventually served time. Convicted in December 1995 of digging in prehistoric sites and desecrating graves in Canyonlands National Park and near Allen Canyon, Earl Shumway received a seventy-eight month sentence, later reduced to sixty-three months imprisonment. This was the stiffest penalty yet given under ARPA. Hopi Will Numkena, then director of the Utah Division of Indian Affairs, reminded the public that burial sites were sacred and to defile them was to interrupt the journey of the dead in the afterlife. "It is important for the generations of pothunters to understand that the violation of American Indian gravesites needs to cease."[36] It has not, but it has certainly decreased since the high mark of the 1980s.

Legitimate excavations have also continued. The Bluff Great House attracted new attention in 1995 when the Southwest Heritage Foundation, University of Colorado, and Abajo Archaeology (Bluff) teamed together to determine the extent of Chaco's influence on its inhabitants. The earliest construction was definitely linked to what was occurring at the same time in New Mexico, suggesting the possibility of its being an outlier or outpost, while pottery fragments showed "stylistic emulation" by the people in Bluff for the arts of their southern neighbors.[37] Testing of the site continued for three years before funding ran out.

Around this same time, Northern Arizona University entered Butler Wash to assess the condition of selected Archaic and Basketmaker sites in rock alcoves after a century of uncontrolled looting. Boomerang Shelter yielded a complex stratigraphy—five layers—of Basketmaker cists. In one part of the site, an Archaic sandal saw the light of day for the first time in eight thousand years. The fear that pothunters had totally scrambled the archaeological record beyond recognition was put to rest. The sand in the alcove was so difficult to work in because of its fluid nature, that it discouraged pothunters from going down to the lower depths, preserving some of the layers. The University of Colorado also sampled elements of the Comb Wash Great House, discussed previously, for Chacoan influences. Three years of excavation, 2002 to 2004, determined that Mesa

Verde prevailed as the dominant force.[38] Beginning in 2005, planning for the Comb Ridge Survey Project started, with site evaluation and mapping continuing through 2009.

Ancestral Puebloan sites and artifacts continue to fascinate the public today. Remains are still subject to theft, dwellings open to destruction by well-intentioned but misinformed people, rock art targeted by vandals, and skeletal remains available for desecration. With the advent of the Native American Graves Protection and Repatriation Act (NAGPRA) in 1990, the Indian voice became stronger in its demand to treat ancestral remains with respect. This law affected not only the illegal acquisition of skeletal remains and artifacts but also those legally held by federal and state entities. The bill placed the entire white community on notice that the old days of collecting and exploiting Native American culture had ended.

Courtesy of Kay Shumway

One of the sites for which Arch Canyon is named. The peaceful tranquility captured in the photo belies the underlying debate of who has access, to what extent, and what type of conveyance visitors should take to view such sights.

A third point of conflict surrounding Comb Ridge and its environs is the land itself. While cattle can be controlled and scientifically maneuvered to meet ecological needs and pothunters can be chased, incarcerated, and anathematized, how land is to be used elicits everyone's opinion. Individual ideas find strongest expression when joined to others of a like mind, creating organizations with positions leading to financial support that ends in lawsuits and zealotry. Butler Wash and Comb Wash, especially Arch Canyon, have become key battlegrounds for protagonists and antagonists in the debate of over a dozen entities. Major local, regional, and national organizations have entered the fray: the Southern Utah Wilderness Alliance (SUWA), Wilderness Society, Sierra Club, Great Old Broads for Wilderness (GOB), and the Navajo Utah Commission have linked arms on one side while San Juan Public Entry and Access Rights (SPEAR), San Juan County Commission, Blanding City Council, White Mesa Utes, and the BLM oppose them to varying degrees on the other side. Each group appeals to a certain clientele, has its own agenda, and may be only temporarily aligned on certain issues. Shifts in position occur with each different concern.

The heavy fireworks started in 1990. Arch Canyon, with its scenic canyon walls, running stream, archaeological sites, and potential for inclusion as a WSA became a prime target for local confrontation with wilderness groups. Locally, the Utes held partial control of access, large family gatherings enjoyed the cottonwood groves and water, off-road vehicles (ORVs) provided a means of traveling the canyon, and the BLM had overall supervisory responsibility. This agency had also been involved in a long-standing dispute with the county over dozens of historic roads that came under county, not federal, regulation. Revised Statute (RS) 2477 recognized the county's right-of-way and control of these previously existing roads, one of which happened to ascend Arch Canyon. The recognition did not come easily. Aerial photographs and affidavits from Ute Indians, cowboys, miners, and others testified that it had been used for over forty years and was pre-existing before contemporary issues arose. The county and the BLM agreed that the road was a public highway, making it open to "the free passage of all use."[39]

That played right into the hands of the wilderness groups. The previous year had seen wranglings between them and the BLM, who had not been enforcing what was perceived as appropriate standards of stewardship, especially when it came to the 1989 Jeep Jamboree held in Arch Canyon. Now, three weeks before official recognition of the right-of-way, Michael F. Heyrend, a Utah attorney and member of SUWA, "happened" to be preparing for a three-day hike in Arch Canyon when the 1990 jamboree arrived. He warned the occupants in the first few vehicles that the road was closed and then started jotting down license plate numbers as the lead jeeps splashed through the stream and ground their way up the canyon. A White Mesa Ute policeman asked Heyrend if he had a permit to be on Ute land. The lawyer countered that he was not on Ute land, to which the policeman replied that he had to cross it to get on federal land, and so received a citation.[40] The 5,000 SUWA, 500,000 Sierra Club, and 350,000 Wilderness Society members now had a cause célèbre.[41]

The environmental groups took a well-tried course of action—the legal appeal process—to deny immediate vehicular use of Arch Canyon. Their concerns centered around impact on wildlife, trail damage, and proper control of use. The canyon was home to mule deer, bighorn sheep, bobcat, mountain lion, coyote, and ringtail cat; reptile and amphibian species; six fish species, including the bluehead sucker (a state sensitive species); and many types of birds, possibly including the federally listed Mexican spotted owl, the southwestern willow flycatcher, and the American peregrine falcon. Damage to Puebloan sites and the scenery were other concerns. The primary focus, however, was the trail system that stretched eight miles up the canyon to the Forest Service boundary. During the course of the trip, travelers crisscrossed the stream fifty-nine times, muddying the water, tearing at the banks, and ripping away vegetation.[42] Multiply this by the seventy vehicles allowed in the Jeep Jamboree permit, and one can see the impact. A final concern was that with recognition of the road as a legitimate thoroughfare, the possibility of ever having the land set aside as wilderness area grew smaller.

The appeal process inexorably took its course, both sides determined that educating the public and garnering its support was crucial. The preponderance of those favoring SUWA's position were from outside of the county and called on assistance from large environmental groups, like the Sierra Club, for support. People from Colorado make up one of the most frequent and largest groups of visitors to southeastern Utah. Indeed, during the 1990s, as interest and sympathy grew for ruins, the appearance of the distinctive white and green license plate on parked vehicles in the canyons of Utah led to locals quipping that it was the "greening" of San Juan County. So it is not surprising that Colorado provided a vocal and active contingent of people ready to save the land. Take the Great Old Broads for Wilderness as an example.

In Durango, Colorado, sits a two-story house converted into office space. A doormat warns, "Dull women have immaculate houses." On the landing's wall before the staircase reposes an oversized lavender bra, large enough to make a grown man faint. Upstairs are the offices where monitoring of sites across the nation occurs—50 to 60 percent of which concerns Utah. The database contains thirty thousand records, nine thousand of which are in San Juan County—two thousand of which spread across Comb and Butler washes and seven hundred of which are in Arch Canyon.[43] The map on the computer displays a large concentration of data, representing a mass of separate incident reports, sightings, and monitored information collected through observation and electronic means, then recorded and passed on for analysis.

Formed in 1989 in commemoration of the twenty-fifth anniversary of the Wilderness Act, Great Old Broads' mission is "to provide necessary information to improve recreation management on public lands in the United States. BHLP (Broads Healthy Lands Project) has a cooperative mission, because only by working together can we find constructive solutions to reducing the negative impacts of recreation on public lands."[44] Affiliated with the Sierra Club but very much allied with SUWA and the Wilderness Society, GOB emphasizes three major concerns: grazing, oil and gas exploration, and ORV activity. All three enter into the Comb Ridge area, but the ORV issue has garnered the most passion.

Claiming "there are particular advantages to being old and gray" and "endeavoring to use a sense of humor and well-aged grace," the Broads outline their position on ORVs as preventing new roads in wilderness areas, keeping motorized use to designated trails, following the practice of "closed unless posted open," and holding public agencies accountable for proper management. An example of this occurred in 2005 in two canyons outside of Kanab, Utah. Overuse and abuse of Trail and Hog canyons created an opportunity for training sessions of local people and government managers of the lands, which in turn resulted in a service project to restore damaged land and forced an emergency closure of most of the two canyons to future abuse. A similar project took place in Buckhorn Wash in the San Rafael Swell in 2002, where closure of impacted sites and reseeding gave a facelift to the landscape.[45]

SPEAR is a different group, on the other end of the spectrum, whose mission is to keep public lands open and used and promoted for ORV trail use. Formed in 1999, the organization today has a membership of about 320 enthusiasts, the majority of whom are from San Juan County, but it also draws people from as far away as Missouri.[46] Between 2002 and 2006, registration of ORVs in San Juan County increased by 252 percent.[47] Originally known as SULU (Southeastern Utah Land Users), the group stands in direct opposition to SUWA (jokingly called "sewer" or "sue-er"). Like Broads, SPEAR has contributed many man-hours of service by emplacing cattle guards (Indian Creek) and small bridges (Kane Creek), widening (Arch Canyon) and marking (Hole-in-the-Rock) trails, providing trail guides (in Blanding and Monticello visitor centers), and sponsoring tours. The San

Permitted by law and backed by the BLM, four-wheeling tours in Arch Canyon have become a popular recreation for ORV advocates. Local businesses offer tours while Blanding and Monticello sponsor an annual ORV jamboree.

Juan Heritage Festival ATV Ride is a good example. An advertisement for it announced, "Bring your own ATV . . . Groups will be limited to 20 riders each with two guides per group. Groups will leave every five minutes; rides will run about 5 hours."[48]

The underlying advocacy position is that the land should be kept open for multiple-use—not locked away in some environmental dream of wilderness where only the young and healthy have access for recreation. Local people should prosper and not be subject to controls set by elitist organizations of "granolas" or "tree huggers" as found in groups like SUWA. Since 92 percent of San Juan County is public land of some type—Indian reservation, BLM, National Park Service, Forest Service, etc.—there has already been enough external control. Surprisingly, SPEAR and the BLM have had a compatible relationship in working on joint projects, since multiple use is a shared vision. Necessity makes strange bedfellows when considering past grumblings about the federal government.

The theme of their argument weighs heavily in the arena of personal rights, emphasizing the *R* in SPEAR. Appealing to the depressed economic situation in the county, the "my forefathers" heritage issue, and the deleterious effects of "outsiders," the organization opposes any inroads by SUWA. Heated rhetoric pushes for recognition of the "little man's" rights: "They [environmental groups] have moved into OUR county and have brought with them their strange ideas on how OUR public lands should be managed. . . . SUWA and their gang need to stand down and allow the residents of San Juan

County, their elected officials, and the federal agencies in charge of public lands to do what they do best—manage OUR public lands."[49] How this conflict has played across the lands of southeastern Utah is an interesting study in multifaceted group dynamics.

Heated debate over Arch Canyon and the surrounding area reached a crescendo in 2007. In the waning months of the previous year, archaeologist Jerry D. Spangler submitted his "Site Condition and Vandalism Assessment of Archaeological Sites, Lower and Middle Arch Canyon, San Juan County, Utah," which was quickly followed by SUWA's "Petition to Preserve Arch Canyon's Natural and Cultural Heritage."[50] Both reports called for a greatly restricted use of the canyon, spoke of site and habitat degradation, and placed pressure on the BLM to be a wiser steward, which included keeping vehicles out of the canyon.

In March, the San Juan County commissioners were at odds with each other. One, Kenneth Maryboy, was also a member of the Navajo Utah Commission who had sided with SUWA in trying to close the canyon. Another commissioner, Lynn Stevens, who held the position of state public lands policy coordinator, had been heavily involved in the previous Jeep Jamboree in Arch Canyon and in the fight for the county to maintain its rural road system (RS 2477). Accusations flew from both sides, making headline news and polarizing factions into various camps.[51]

Simultaneously, other issues surfaced. Sandra Meyers, BLM manager, responded to recent complaints that fall storms had increased the likelihood of damage to stream and cultural resources in Arch Canyon if the traffic flow continued unabated. BLM resource specialists visited the area and found no such threat, helping Meyers to deduce that the alarm was just one more attempt to close the canyon.[52] At the other end of Comb Wash, another voice sounded. Efforts to make an ORV trail around Comb Ridge and near the original pioneer (1880) trail up San Juan Hill created concern with Bluff citizens and historic preservationists. In February 2005, a BLM investigative report found "21 points of damage . . . a large boulder with historic chisel marks moved using a rock bar to pry the rock from the trail . . . several locations where rock had been split and crushed using a sledge hammer . . . and that the trail as an archaeological resource had been significantly damaged."[53] Add to this the ORV trail that followed part of the old pioneer road stretching from Comb Wash up Lime Ridge and preservationists became more concerned. The county cleared this trail with their Trail Cat, thus involving local government, the BLM, local citizenry on both sides of the issue, and environmental groups.[54] One of the major concerns was the loss of historic site information—on both San Juan Hill and Lime Ridge. Once a trail is bulldozed, has rocks removed, and is subjected to heavy ORV use, subtle archaeological information is lost. It also removes the historic significance from the trail and makes it a thoroughfare. Site mitigation becomes impossible.

The fight for the hearts and minds of residents goes on. Math enters in. One Bluff resident took out her calculator, multiplying potential figures from the draft "Jeep Use of Arch Canyon and the Hotel Rock Area." Noting the number of events and vehicles allowed, as well as the days, people, and times across the Arch Canyon stream when spread over a five year period, she arrived at a grand total of 210,000 times vehicles would cross the

The future of Comb Ridge lies in the hands of government agencies and the public. The practice of land ethics, environmental stewardship, multiple use, and planning will decide what subsequent generations will enjoy.

creek, not to mention all of the daily traffic not included in these figures.[55] For SPEAR, Mark Twain's adage, "There are lies, damn lies, and statistics," holds true. SPEAR members reached a different conclusion. The problem was that the BLM was buying into these lies and caving in. One person wrote that he visited the BLM office in Monticello and "it took only a few minutes to figure out [the chief administrator] is in total fear of SUWA. Talk about terrorism. You do not have to go to Iraq or Afghanistan to find it. . . . The continued filing of lawsuits and threats of lawsuits are rapidly turning the BLM and the Forest Service into puppets of these organizations."[56]

By January 2008, the BLM offered a new Management Resource Plan, addressing critical areas in San Juan County. There were five options for people to evaluate. Choices ranged from maintaining the status quo to a highly pro-environmentalist agenda. If one believes the newspapers, many people could not find anything they liked. Two headlines summarize the situation: "Green activists say BLM plan will turn landscape into industrial zone" and "Blanding Council says BLM not able to draft impartial land use rules."[57] Nestled at the foot of the controversy was Arch Canyon, the poster child for both sides of the conflict. Both sides well meaning. Both sides demanding individual rights through group expression. Both sides turning to litigation for answers—neither side willing to budge an inch.

Above it all sits Comb Ridge, its canyons and washes, mute witnesses to centuries of conflict. Each era brought its own concerns: the Puebloans trying to wrest a living from the land and control inter- and intra-societal conflict, the Navajos' and Utes' relations during the Fearing Time, the Mormons facing the Texas cattle companies and outlaw elements, the settling of Native Americans on reservations, the boom and bust economy of the early twentieth century, and the age of me-ification and litigation have all been a part of the rock's prehistory and history. What has happened in the past will never be repeated, given the changes in society and technology, but what lies ahead can also be similar. The direction and extent of change may shift and accelerate, but Comb Ridge will remain a constant, its unique visual and topographical features giving a distinct quality to the landscape of southeastern Utah and northeastern Arizona. Much has been said and much more will be said about this rock and its people.

Notes

Introduction: Comb Ridge

1. Craig Childs, *House of Rain: Tracking a Vanished Civilization Across the American Southwest* (New York: Little, Brown, 2006): 202, 204.
2. Winston Hurst, "This Landscape Remembers" (draft), March 1996, manuscript in possession of author, 1.
3. Ibid., 1–2.
4. Winston Hurst, Catherine Cameron, William Davis, Steve Lekson, and Jonathan Till, "Comb Ridge Survey Project, Initial Proposal" (draft), September 21, 2004, manuscript in possession of author.
5. Joseph A. Amato, *Rethinking Home: A Case for Writing Local History* (Berkeley: University of California Press, 2002): 191.
6. William A. Haviland, *Anthropology*, 9th ed. (New York: Harcourt College Publishers, 1974, 2000): 29.
7. Bette L. Stanton, *Where God Put the West: Movie Making in the Desert* (Moab, UT: Canyonlands Natural History Association, 1994): 1.

One: Creating the Comb

1. Joseph Wood Krutch, *The Desert Year* (New York: Penguin, 1952): 251–52.
2. Ibid., 250, 252–53.
3. See Donald L. Baars, *The Colorado Plateau: A Geologic History* (Albuquerque: University of New Mexico Press, 1983); Donald L. Baars, *Navajo Country: A Geology and Natural History of the Four Corners Region* (Albuquerque: University of New Mexico Press, 1995); F. A. Barnes, *Canyon Country Geology* (Salt Lake City, UT: Wasatch Publishers, 1978); and Halka Chronic, *Roadside Geology of Utah* (Missoula, MT: Mountain Press Publishing, 1990).
4. Barnes, *Canyon Country Geology*, 89, 100–101.
5. Winston Hurst, Comb Ridge Project Report, in progress.
6. Ibid.
7. There are numerous versions of the Navajo creation story. Four of the more complete versions are Washington Matthews, *Navaho Legends* (Salt Lake City: University of Utah Press, 1897, 1994); Father Berard Haile, *The Upward Moving and Emergence Way: The Gishin Biyé Version* (Lincoln: University of Nebraska Press, 1981); Aileen O'Bryan, *Navaho Indian Myths* (New York: Dover, 1956, 1993); and Paul G. Zolbrod, *Diné bahane': The Navajo Creation Story* (Albuquerque: University of New Mexico Press, 1984).
8. Haile, *Upward Moving*, 119–20.
9. Matthews, *Navaho Legends*, 76.
10. Haile, *Upward Moving*, 121.
11. Ibid., 121–22
12. Matthews, *Navaho Legends*, 219, fn. 44. In addition to this version, Ada Black from Monument Valley also talks of this cutting or plowing which created major rivers like the San Juan and Colorado in the four directions. See Ada Black, interview with Robert S. McPherson and Marilyn Holiday, December 16, 1991, in possession of author.
13. Terms like *medicine man*, *Anasazi* (or *Anaasází*), and *Navajo* have been in use for decades but are now being replaced by more politically acceptable terms like *native healer*, *Ancestral Puebloan*, and *Diné* due to the etymology of the word or the lack of precision through inference. Still, as I listen to Navajo people in southeastern Utah speak, the older terms are the ones they use. Right or wrong, I have opted

to use some of these older terms because they reflect general use in this region and are more readily recognized by the general public. The term *Ancestral Puebloan*, however, is widely accepted in the anthropological community and so I use it in this text.

14. John Holiday is a primary source of Navajo history and culture in southeastern Utah. He tells of local formations and how they fit into the general knowledge of the Blessingway ceremony narrative, the basis for his understanding and practice. In his autobiography, he recounts part of this process. Here I have taken directly from his life story the teaching he shares about the creation. This can be found in John Holiday and Robert S. McPherson, *A Navajo Legacy: The Life and Teachings of John Holiday* (Norman: University of Oklahoma Press, 2005): 256–57. Additional information has been included from a later interview to give a more complete picture. This interview occurred on April 15, 2005, translated by Marilyn Holiday, and is in the possession of the author.
15. Suzie Yazzie, interview with Robert S. McPherson and Marilyn Holiday, November 10, 2000, in possession of author.
16. Martha Nez, interview with Robert S. McPherson and Baxter Benally, August 2, 1988, in possession of author.
17. Jim Dandy, conversation with Robert S. McPherson, September 10, 2007.
18. Don E. Smith, Ph.D., geologist specializing in the Four Corners region, conversation with author on August 21, 2007. Before taking this observation too far, one need recognize that Monument Valley is on the west side of Comb Ridge. Smith points out that it is an exception to where remains of dinosaurs are found today.
19. Ada Benally, interview with Robert S. McPherson and Baxter Benally, May 17, 2007, in possession of author.
20. John Holiday, interview, April 15, 2005; Ada Benally, interview, May 17, 2007; Mary Jim, interview with Robert S. McPherson and Baxter Benally, June 7, 1988; Billy Yellow, interview with Robert S. McPherson and Evelyn Yellow, November 6, 1987; Tallis Holiday, interview with Robert S. McPherson and Jessie Holiday, November 3, 1987; Fred Yazzie, interview with Robert S. McPherson and Marilyn Holiday, November 1, 1985, all in possession of author.
21. John Holiday, interview with Robert S. McPherson and Baxter Benally, December 10, 2004, and interview, April 15, 2005, in possession of author.
22. John Holiday, interview, April 15, 2005. This story is far more complex than presented here. The relevance to Comb Ridge is the purpose for its inclusion.
23. Leland C. Wyman, *Blessingway* (Tucson: University of Arizona Press, 1970, 1975): 388–93.
24. Edward Dutchie, Sr., interview with Robert S. McPherson, May 7, 1996, in possession of author.
25. Stanley W. Bronson, *The Ute Spiritual Cross of the San Juan Mission* (Blanding, UT, Self-published, 1999): 6.
26. The terms "myth" and "mythological" often ignite a firestorm of protest, being associated with fabrication and "just-so" stories. Nothing could be further from the truth, as used here. Myths are sacred and true; as anthropologist Victor Turner noted, they are "the powerhouses of culture." These narratives make sense of a world that is otherwise chaotic. They provide the religious believer with a reason for being and a guide through the many struggles of life that is accomplished with the assistance of the gods.
27. Stella Eyetoo, interview with Robert S. McPherson and Aldean Ketchum, November 16, 2005, in possession of author.
28. Billy Mike, interview with Robert S. McPherson and Aldean Ketchum, October 13, 1993; Edward Dutchie, Sr., interview with Robert S. McPherson, May 7, 1996, in possession of author.
29. Lola Mike, interview with Robert S. McPherson and Aldean Ketchum, November 16, 2005; Stella Eyetoo, interview, November 16, 2005.
30. Stella Eyetoo, interview, November 16, 2005.
31. Keith H. Basso, *Wisdom Sits in Places, Landscape and Language among the Western Apache* (Albuquerque: University of New Mexico Press, 1996).
32. David E. Miller, *Hole-in-the-Rock: An Epic in the Colonization of the Great American West* (Salt Lake City: University of Utah Press, 1959): 208–13. George Hobbs, Mormon explorer, records that by 1880 the formation was generally known as Comb Ridge. Exactly who named it and when is still open to discussion.
33. Albert R. Lyman to Maurice L. Howe, March 4, 1937 (located in "Place Names" file, Utah State Historical Society Library, Salt Lake City). There is another possible explanation of how Comb Ridge received its name. In 1859, Captain J. N. Macomb of the U.S. Army Corps of Topographical Engineers left Santa Fe, New Mexico, on a survey. He passed within a few miles and in sight of Comb Ridge and so may have been responsible for naming it, although an exact origin of the name is undocumented. On the map generated by this expedition, published in 1860, Comb Ridge was not named.

34. Stella Eyetoo, interview, November 16, 2005.
35. Ibid.
36. Stella Eyetoo, interview with Aldean Ketchum and Robert S. McPherson, December 21, 1994; Lola Mike, interview, November 16, 2005; Chester Cantsee, interview with Robert S. McPherson and Aldean Ketchum, September 6, 1994, in possession of author.
37. John Holiday, interviews, December 10, 2004, and April 15, 2005.
38. See John Holiday's experience with his grandmother in Holiday and McPherson, *A Navajo Legacy*, 71–80.
39. This could have been one of a number of his workers. Most likely, it was either Bert Davis or Bullet Hardy. Both of these men traveled about, purchasing sheep. See Samuel Moon, *Tall Sheep: Harry Goulding, Monument Valley Trader* (Norman: University of Oklahoma Press, 1992): 66–67.
40. Holiday and McPherson, *A Navajo Legacy*, 83.
41. Billy Yellow, interview with Robert S. McPherson and Evelyn Yellow, November 6, 1987, in possession of author.
42. Klara Kelly, personal communication with author, August 31, 2007.
43. There is some dispute over specific geographical sites and even if "Nagashi" is a Navajo word. Technically, the name "Mountain Sheep's Trail" would be translated Tsétah Dibé Bitiin. See Laurance D. Linford, *Navajo Places: History, Legend, and Landscape* (Salt Lake City: University of Utah Press, 2000): 288. The fact that John Holiday was using the term indicates its acceptance regardless of its derivation.
44. Lisa W. Huckell and Mollie S. Toll, "Wild Plant Use in the North American Southwest," in *People and Plants in Ancient Western North America*, ed. Paul E. Minnis (Washington, DC: Smithsonian Institution, 2004): 55.
45. William W. Dunmire and Gail D. Tierney, *Wild Plants of the Pueblo Province, Exploring Ancient and Enduring Uses* (Santa Fe: Museum of New Mexico Press, 1995): 156.
46. Ibid., 175, 182–83, 171–72, 179.
47. Ibid., 190, 124–26, 119, 106–7.
48. Winston Hurst, archaeologist, conversation with author, January 28, 2008.
49. Dunmire and Tierney, *Wild Plants of the Pueblo Province*, 33.
50. Ibid., 115.
51. Hurst conversation, January 28, 2008.
52. Steven D. Emslie, "Cultural and Climatic Implications in Anasazi Faunal Exploitation: A Review and Perspectives," in *Proceedings of the Anasazi Symposium, 1981*, ed. Jack E. Smith (Mesa Verde National Park, CO: Mesa Verde Museum Association, 1981): 119–23.
53. See Alan D. Reed, "Ute Cultural Chronology" in *An Archaeology of the Eastern Ute: A Symposium*, ed. Paul R. Nickens, Colorado Council of Professional Archaeology Occasional Paper Number 1 (Denver 1988): 80–82, for a discussion of Ute entrance into the Four Corners region.
54. Anne M. Smith, *Ethnography of the Northern Utes*, Papers in Anthropology Number 17 (Albuquerque: University of New Mexico Press, 1974): 46–53.
55. Edward Dutchie, Sr., interview, May 7, 1996; Smith, *Ethnography of the Northern Utes*, 269–70.
56. Smith, *Ethnography of the Northern Utes*, 50.
57. See Vernon O. Mayes and Barbara Bayless Lacy, *Nanise' A Navajo Herbal: One Hundred Plants from the Navajo Reservation* (Tsaile, AZ: Navajo Community College Press, 1989).
58. John Holiday, interview, April 15, 2005.

Two: Discovering the Comb

1. From Matilda Coxe Stevenson, *The Sia*, Eleventh Annual Report of the Bureau of American Ethnology (Washington, DC: Smithsonian Institution, 1904), as cited in Kathryn Gabriel, *Roads to Center Place: A Cultural Atlas of Chaco Canyon and the Anasazi* (Boulder, CO: Johnson Books, 1991): 168.
2. Information for this chapter, unless otherwise cited, came from interviews with Winston Hurst, field director for the Comb Ridge Heritage Initiative Project (2005–2010). The Bureau of Land Management funded this multi-year effort in partnership through the University of Colorado at Boulder, with Cathy Cameron as principal investigator. The synthesis that follows includes some new information and insight gained from intense efforts during the project to document the prehistory and historical archaeology of the Comb Ridge area. Any error of content or interpretation of proper source citation is the sole responsibility of the author.
3. William E. Davis, "The First Americans in San Juan County," *Blue Mountain Shadows* 13 (Summer 1994): 4–6.
4. Ibid.

5. Archaeologists still debate as to whether there was a new influx of people or just an evolutionary shift from big game hunters to the Archaic lifeways. Currently, there is not enough proof from the physical record to definitively answer the question.
6. Phil R. Geib and Dale Davidson, "Anasazi Origins: A Perspective from Preliminary Work at Old Man Cave," *Kiva* 60, no. 2 (Winter 1994): 191–202.
7. Phil R. Geib, "Sandal Types and Archaic Prehistory on the Colorado Plateau," *American Antiquity* 65, no. 3 (2000): 509–24.
8. Winston B. Hurst and Christy G. Turner II, "Rediscovering the 'Great Discovery': Wetherill's First Cave 7 and Its Record of Basketmaker Violence," in Victoria M. Atkins, ed., *Anasazi Basketmaker: Papers from the 1990 Wetherill-Grand Gulch Symposium*, Cultural Resource Series Number 24 (Salt Lake City, UT: Bureau of Land Management, 1993): 143–91.
9. Ibid., 145–46.
10. Ibid., 168.
11. Ibid., 166.
12. Polly Schaafsma, *Indian Rock Art of the Southwest* (Santa Fe, NM: School of American Research Press, 1980): 109–19.
13. Sarah M. Nelson, *Investigation of Cholla Knoll* (Denver, CO: Department of Anthropology, University of Denver, 1978).
14. Winston Hurst, Ba Bellorado, Hugh Robinson, Tucker Robinson, and Catherine M. Cameron, "Raise High the Roofbeams: Evidence for Multi-story Roomblock Architecture in the Western Mesa Verde Region," poster presentation, Society for American Archaeology Annual Meeting, Vancouver, British Columbia, 2007.
15. Winston Hurst and Jonathan Till, "A Brief Survey of Great Houses and Related Features in Southeastern Utah," in *Chaco and Post-Chaco in the Northern San Juan Region: Excavations at the Bluff Great House* (in press), ed. Catherine M. Cameron (Tucson: University of Arizona Press, 2008).
16. Owen Severance, "Prehistoric Roads in Southeastern Utah," in *La Frontera: Papers in Honor of Patrick H. Beckett* 25, Meliha S. Duran and David T. Kirkpatrick, eds. (Albuquerque: Archaeological Society of New Mexico, 1999): 185–96; Jonathan D. Till, "Chacoan Road and Road-associated Sites in the Lower San Juan Region: Assessing the Role of Chacoan Influences in the Northwestern Periphery" (master's thesis, Anthropology Department, University of Colorado at Boulder, 2001); Jonathan D. Till and Winston Hurst, "Trail of the Ancients: A Network of Ancient Roads and Great Houses in Southeastern Utah," paper presentation, 67th Annual Meeting of the Society for American Archaeology, Denver, CO, 2002.
17. Kendrick Frazier, *People of Chaco: A Canyon and Its Culture* (New York: W. W. Norton, 1986): 108.
18. Albert R. Lyman, interview with Charles S. Peterson, "Southeastern Utah Experiences," February 4, 1970, Southeastern Utah Oral History Project, transcript, Edge of the Cedars State Park, Blanding, UT.
19. Winston Hurst, Owen Severance, and Dale Davidson, "Uncle Albert's Ancient Roads: Anasazi Formal Trails in Southeastern Utah," *Blue Mountain Shadows* 12 (Summer 1993): 2–9.
20. Hurst and Till, "Brief Survey of Great Houses."
21. Ibid.; Winston Hurst, "Archaeological Investigations in the Pueblo II-III Comb Wash Community, San Juan County, Utah, 2002–2004," in preparation, technical report submitted to Catherine M. Cameron, principal investigator, Bluff/Comb Wash Project, University of Colorado at Boulder.
22. F. Nials, J. Stein, and J. Roney, *Chacoan Roads in the Southern Periphery: Results of Phase II of the BLM Chaco Roads Project*, Cultural Resource Series Number 1 (U.S. Department of the Interior, Bureau of Land Management, Albuquerque District, NM, 1987).
23. Frank Waters, *Book of the Hopi* (New York: Ballantine Books, 1963): 51–52.
24. Severance, "Prehistoric Roads."
25. The archaeological community still struggles with a concise definition of a tower, because there are many exceptions. For the lay reader it is defined as a "typically free-standing, one room footprint, usually circular but may be square, that is separate from a room block and usually more than one story tall."
26. R. Gwinn Vivian, "Chacoan Roads: Morphology," *Kiva* 62 (1997a): 7–34; R. Gwinn Vivian, "Chacoan Roads: Function," *Kiva* 63 (1997b): 35–68; Hurst and Till, "Brief Survey of Great Houses."
27. H. M. Wormington, *Prehistoric Indians of the Southwest*, Popular Series Number 7 (Denver, CO: Denver Museum of Natural History, 1947, 1978): 76.
28. Ekkehart Malotki, *Hopi Tales of Destruction* (Lincoln: University of Nebraska Press, 2002).
29. James A. Goss, "Culture-Historical Inference from Utaztekan Linguistic Evidence," paper presentation, Plenary Symposium on Utaztekan Prehistory of the Society for American Archaeology and the Great Basin Anthropological Conference, May 1966, 11, 27.

30. For further information about Ute/Paiute entrance into the San Juan region, see Robert S. McPherson, *A History of San Juan County: In the Palm of Time* (Salt Lake City: Utah State Historical Society, 1995): 49–56.
31. See J. Lee Correll, "Navajo Frontiers and Troublous Times in Monument Valley," *Utah Historical Quarterly* 39 (Spring 1971): 145–61.

Three: Inside and Outside the Comb

1. John Holiday, interview with Robert S. McPherson and Baxter Benally, November 9, 2001, in possession of author.
2. The teachings in this chapter are a result of interviews with John Holiday conducted on December 10, 2004, and April 15, 2005, and are in possession of the author. Unless otherwise noted, this is the primary source of information.
3. For additional information concerning Navajo teachings about southeastern Utah, see Robert S. McPherson, *Sacred Land, Sacred View: Navajo Perceptions of the Four Corners Region* (Provo, UT: Brigham Young University, 1992).
4. Gladys A. Reichard, *Navaho Religion: A Study of Symbolism* (Princeton, NJ: Princeton University Press, 1950): 384; McPherson, *Sacred Land, Sacred View*, 29–30; Aileen O'Bryan, *Navaho Indian Myths* (New York: Dover, 1993): 171; Berard Haile, *The Upward Moving and Emergence Way: The Gishin Biye' Version* (Lincoln: University of Nebraska Press, 1981): 170.
5. Karl Luckert, *The Navajo Hunter Tradition* (Tucson: University of Arizona Press, 1975): 152–53, 212, 173; W. W. Hill, *The Agricultural and Hunting Methods of the Navaho Indians* (New Haven: Yale University Press, 1938): 113–17.
6. Donald Sandner, *Navaho Symbols of Healing* (New York: Harcourt, Brace, Jovanovich, 1979): 177–80; Maureen Trudelle Schwarz, *Navajo Lifeways: Contemporary Issues, Ancient Knowledge* (Norman: University of Oklahoma Press, 2001): 129.
7. Reichard, *Navaho Religion*, 12.
8. Ernest Bulow, *Navajo Taboos* (Gallup, NM: Southwestern Books, 1982): 19–21; Schwarz, *Navajo Lifeways*, 127.
9. Howard M. Bahr, ed., *The Navajo as Seen by the Franciscans, 1898–1921: A Sourcebook* (Lanham, MD: Scarecrow Press, 2004): 566.
10. Schwarz, *Navajo Lifeways*, 111–33.
11. Haile, *Upward Moving*, 136.
12. Franciscan Fathers, *An Ethnologic Dictionary of the Navaho Language* (Saint Michaels, AZ: Saint Michaels Press, 1910, 1968): 415, 176.
13. Slim Benally, interview with Robert S. McPherson and Baxter Benally, July 8, 1988; Stanley Holiday, interview with Robert S. McPherson and Frances Holiday, November 9, 2006; Martha Nez, interview with Robert S. McPherson and Baxter Benally, August 10, 1988, all in possession of author.
14. Stanley Holiday, interview, November 9, 2006.
15. Ibid.
16. Reichard, *Navaho Religion*, 467 (cited from Beadway Chant by Washington Matthews); Paul G. Zolbrod, *Diné bahane': The Navajo Creation Story* (Albuquerque: University of New Mexico Press, 1984): 231.
17. Martha Nez, interview, August 10, 1988.
18. Slim Benally, interview, July 8, 1988; John Holiday, interviews, December 10, 2004, and April 15, 2005.
19. John Holiday, interviews, December 10, 2004, and April 15, 2005; Stanley Holiday, interview, November 9, 2006.
20. Martha Nez, interview, August 10, 1988; Slim Benally, interview, July 8, 1988; Charlie Blueyes, interview with Robert S. McPherson and Baxter Benally, June 7, 1988; Billy Yellow, interview with Robert S. McPherson and Evelyn Yellow, November 6, 1987; Tallis Holiday, interview with Robert S. McPherson and Jessie Holiday, November 3, 1987, all in possession of author.
21. Ada Black, interview with Robert S. McPherson and Marilyn Holiday, October 11, 1991; Joe Manygoats, interview with Robert S. McPherson and Marilyn Holiday, December 18, 1991; John Holiday, interviews, December 10, 2004, and April 15, 2005, all in possession of author.
22. Joe Manygoats, interview, December 18, 1991.
23. Leland C. Wyman, *Blessingway* (Tucson: University of Arizona Press, 1970, 1975): 25, 110.
24. For further information concerning this event and the use of "shake offs," see Holiday and McPherson, *A Navajo Legacy*, 90–92, 352–54.
25. Slim Benally, interview, July 8, 1988.

26. Suzie Yazzie, interview, November 10, 2000, in possession of author.
27. Franc J. Newcomb and Gladys A. Reichard, *Sandpaintings of the Navajo Shooting Chant* (New York: Dover, 1975): 33.
28. Reichard, *Navaho Religion*, 10 (also 485).
29. Buck Navajo, interview with Robert S. McPherson and Marilyn Holiday, December 16, 1991, in possession of author.
30. Billy Yellow, interview, November 6, 1987; Mary Blueyes, interview with Robert S. McPherson and Baxter Benally, July 25, 1988, in possession of author.
31. Zolbrod, *Diné bahane'*, 220.
32. Joe Manygoats, interview, December 18, 2001.
33. Ada Black, interview, October 11, 1991; Reichard, *Navaho Religion*, 556, 512.
34. Tallis Holiday, interview, November 3, 1987.
35. Fred Yazzie, interview, November 1, 1985.
36. Ibid.
37. S. P. Jones, interview with Robert S. McPherson and Sam Goodman, December 20, 1985, in possession of author.
38. Reichard, *Navaho Religion*, 497–99, 64–66; Ada Black interview, October 11, 1991.
39. Ada Black, interview, October 11, 1991
40. James Kale McNeley, *Holy Wind in Navajo Philosophy* (Tucson: University of Arizona Press, 1982).
41. Stanley Holiday, interview, November 9, 2006.
42. Tonalea or Red Lake is approximately fifty miles from Kayenta and the end of Comb Ridge. Previously, John identified a spot on Black Mesa. What appears as conflicting information is resolved in understanding traditional teachings about communicating with the Holy Beings. Every person and being has on its head invisible feathers that are both a means of sacred identification and of communicating spiritually; these are often depicted in sandpaintings. The feathers that protrude from and are part of the head of Comb Ridge are located in Tonalea.
43. During John's discussion of this event, he uses the term "Nakai" or "Mexican," insisting that they were here before the Ancestral Puebloans and that the pottery shards and ruins left around the land actually belonged to them. This is a very different point of view since most Navajos recognize the remains as belonging to the Anaasází.
44. Haile, *Upward Moving*, 84.
45. Joe Manygoats, interview, December 18, 1991; Ada Black, interview,October 11, 1991.
46. Gilmore Graymountain, interview with Robert S. McPherson and Marilyn Holiday, April 7, 1992, in possession of author.
47. Ada Black, interview,October 11, 1991.
48. Ibid.
49. Joe Manygoats, interview, December 18, 1991; Sally Manygoats, interview with Robert S. McPherson and Marilyn Holiday, April 8, 1992, in possession of author.
50. Hasteen Klah and Mary C. Wheelwright, *Wind Chant and Feather Chant*, Bulletin 4 (Santa Fe, NM: Museum of Navajo Ceremonial Art, 1946): 1–3.
51. Franciscan Fathers, *An Ethnologic Dictionary*, 174.
52. Reichard, *Navaho Religion*, 384–85.
53. Hasteen Klah and Mary C. Wheelwright, *Navajo Creation Myth: The Story of the Emergence* (Santa Fe, NM: Museum of Navajo Ceremonial Art, 1942): 118; see also O'Bryan, *Navaho Indian Myths*, 170.
54. Pliny E. Goddard, *Navajo Texts* (New York: American Museum of Natural History, 1933): 177.
55. Ada Black, interview,October 11, 1991.
56. Tallis Holiday, interview, November 3, 1987.
57. Mary Blueyes, interview, July 25, 1988.
58. Leland C. Wyman, *The Mountainway of the Navajo* (Tucson: University of Arizona Press, 1975): 182–83; DJ interview with Robert S. McPherson. DJ was very traditional and wished to remain anonymous.
59. Published versions of this story are found in Haile, *Upward Moving*, 207–16; O'Bryan, *Navaho Indian Myths*, 40–48; Washington Matthews, *Navaho Legends* (Salt Lake City: University of Utah Press, 1897, 1994): 92–103; Zolbrod, *Diné bahane'*, 152–68; Sandner, *Navaho Symbols*, 175–76. For a chart comparing different versions of this story, see Leland C. Wyman, *The Red Antway of the Navajo* (Santa Fe: Museum of Navajo Ceremonial Art, 1973): 99–101. Unpublished full or partial accounts given by local people include Slim Benally, interview, July 8, 1988; Martha Nez, interview, August 10, 1988; Charlie Blueyes, interview, June 7, 1988; Mary Blueyes, interview, July 25, 1988; and Oscar Sloan, interview with Robert S. McPherson and Marilyn Holiday, December 18, 1993, in possession of author.

60. Haile, *Upward Moving*, 215; Wyman, *Red Antway*, 101; Charlie Blueyes, interview, June 7, 1988; Slim Benally, interview, July 8, 1988.
61. Oscar Sloan, interview, December 18, 1993.
62. Ada Black, interview,October 11, 1991.
63. Wyman, *Blessingway*, 562–63.
64. Wyman, *Mountainway*, 117.
65. Florence Begay, interview with Nelson Begay and Robert S. McPherson, April 29, 1988, in possession of author.
66. Tallis Holiday, interview, November 3, 1987.
67. Wyman, *Red Antway*, 20; Wyman, *Mountainway*, 106–107.
68. Ada Black, interview,October 11, 1991.
69. Florence Begay, interview, April 29, 1988; Slim Benally interview, July 8, 1988.
70. See Clyde Kluckhohn, *Navaho Witchcraft* (Boston, MA: Beacon, 1944, 1970); Margaret K. Brady, *Some Kind of Power: Navajo Children's Skinwalker Narratives* (Salt Lake City: University of Utah Press, 1984); William Morgan, Sr., *Human-Wolves among the Navaho* (New Haven, CT: Yale University Press): 1–43; Jerrold E. Levy, Raymond Neutra, and Dennis Parker, *Hand Trembling, Frenzy Witchcraft, and Moth Madness: A Study of Navajo Seizure Disorders* (Tucson: University of Arizona Press, 1987).
71. Mary Blueyes, interview, July 25, 1988.
72. Slim Benally, interview, July 8, 1988; Mamie Howard, interview with Robert S. McPherson and Baxter Benally, August 2, 1988, in possession of author; Charlie Blueyes, interview, June 7, 1988.
73. See McPherson, *Sacred Land, Sacred View*, 77–127. I have quoted liberally from this book as it pertains to Comb Ridge.
74. Matthews, *Navaho Legends*, 211; Charlie Blueyes, interview, June 7, 1988; Florence Begay, interview, April 29, 1988; Ada Black, interview,October 11, 1991; Fred Yazzie, interview, ; Joe Manygoats, interview, December 18, 1991; Editha L. Watson, essay presentation, March 17, 1968, Doris Duke Oral History Project #796, Special Collections, J. Willard Marriott Library, University of Utah, Salt Lake City, 22.
75. Florence Begay, interview, April 29, 1988.
76. Tallis Holiday, interview, November 3, 1987. See also Charlie Blueyes, interview, June 7, 1988.
77. Florence Begay, interview, April 29, 1988.
78. Sally Manygoats, interview, April 8, 1992.
79. For a discussion of the concept of sacred versus profane space and how it is delimited and handled, see Mircea Eliade, *The Sacred and the Profane: The Nature of Religion* (New York: Harcourt, Brace, and World, 1959).
80. Ada Black, interview, October 11, 1991.
81. Ibid. Other people who have mentioned that Comb Ridge is a boundary include Charlie Blueyes, Stanley Holiday, John Holiday, and Florence Begay.
82. Stanley Holiday, interview, November 9, 2006.
83. Joe Manygoats, interview, December 18, 1991.

Four: Navajos, Utes, and Mormons

1. See L. R. Bailey, *The Long Walk: A History of the Navajo Wars, 1846–68* (Pasadena, CA: Westernlore Publications, 1978); Peter Iverson, *Diné: A History of the Navajos* (Albuquerque: University of New Mexico Press, 2002); Broderick H. Johnson, ed., *Navajo Stories of the Long Walk Period* (Tsaile, AZ: Navajo Community College Press, 1973); and Gerald Thompson, *The Army and the Navajo: The Bosque Redondo Reservation Experiment, 1863–1868* (Tucson: University of Arizona Press, 1982).
2. U.S. Congress, Indian Hostilities in New Mexico, 36th Cong., 1st sess., House Executive Document 69, 1860, 29.
3. See Louisa Wade Wetherill and Harvey Leake, ed., *Wolfkiller: Wisdom from a Nineteenth Century Navajo Shepherd* (Salt Lake City, UT: Gibbs Smith, 2007).
4. Old Man Bob, testimony, January 27, 1961, Doris Duke #734. All Doris Duke materials cited are in Special Collections, J. Willard Marriott Library, University of Utah, Salt Lake City.
5. Old Ruins (Kit'siili), testimony, January 18, 1961, Doris Duke #704.
6. Eddie Nakai, testimony, January 21, 1961, Doris Duke #23.
7. Ibid.
8. Garrick and Roberta Bailey, *A History of the Navajos: The Reservation Years* (Santa Fe, NM: School of American Research, 1986): 19; James L. Collins, "New Mexico Superintendency," August 30, 1857, *Report of the Commissioner of Indian Affairs* (Washington, DC: GPO, 1857): 273. Collins estimates

12,000 members of the Navajo Tribe. Others suggest as many as 20,000, but this seems too high, although no one will ever know. For an interesting discussion of tabulating how many did not go to Fort Sumner, see Marilyn R. Wagner, "Navajo Settlement Patterns, 1846–1870: A Geographical History" (master's thesis, University of Utah, December 1978, 122–66).

9. Mary Bitisili (Old Lady Sweetwater), testimony, January 19, 1961, Doris Duke #710.
10. For a discussion of friendly relations with the local Utes and Paiutes living in the Bears Ears area, see testimonies of Billy Holiday, July 21 1961, Doris Duke #668; George Martin, Sr., March 22, 1961, Doris Duke #913; Cecil Parrish, January 6, 1961, Doris Duke #667; Paul Goodman, January 6, 1961, Doris Duke #689; Pat Shortfinger, January 11, 1961, Doris Duke #694; Anderson Cantsee (Ute), January 28, 1961, Doris Duke #739.
11. White Sheep, testimonies, March 15, 1953, and January 6, 1961, Doris Duke #687A and 687B.
12. Goodman, testimony, January 6, 1961.
13. Testimonies of Mexican Woman (Asdzaan Nakai), January 23, 1961, Doris Duke #731; Hastiin Claw, January 7, 1961, Doris Duke #672; Hastiin Nez Begay, January 18, 1961, Doris Duke #706; Hetty Nepah, January 7, 1961, Doris Duke #671; Tom Stash, July 17, 1968, Doris Duke #386; Hastiin Toh Tłizhini Bitsi, January 28, 1961, no Doris Duke number.
14. Goodman, testimony, January 6, 1961.
15. Robert S. McPherson, *The Northern Navajo Frontier, 1860–1900* (Logan: Utah State University Press, 2001): 9; Charles Kelly, "Chief Hoskaninni," *Utah Historical Quarterly* 21 (July 1953): 219–26.
16. Parrish, testimony, January 6, 1961.
17. White Sheep, testimonies, March 15, 1953, and January 6, 1961.
18. Eddie Nakai, testimony, January 21, 1961.
19. Warrior Woman (Desbaa'), testimony, January 18, 1961, Doris Duke #703.
20. Ibid.
21. Ibid.; Sally Draper Bailey, testimony, January 29, 1961, Doris Duke #740. Sally does not tell the person's name but describes him as "my mother's mother's father . . . who was born near the Bears Ears."
22. Anderson Cantsee, testimony, January 28, 1961.
23. Jim Mike, testimony, January 29, 1961, Doris Duke # 916.
24. Mary Jelly, testimony, January 21, 1961, Doris Duke #722.
25. Billy Holiday, testimony, July 21, 1961.
26. W. W. Hill, "Navaho Trading and Trading Ritual: A Study of Cultural Dynamics," *Southwestern Journal of Anthropology* 4 (Fall 1948): 377, 380.
27. Mabel Dry, testimony, July 25, 1967, Doris Duke #110.
28. George Martin, Sr., testimony, March 22, 1961.
29. Paul Jones, testimony, January 19, 1961, Doris Duke #712.
30. Maggie Holgate, interview with Gary Shumway, June 13, 1968, Doris Duke #956.
31. Major Albert Pfeiffer to A. K. Graves, December 10, 1866, Record Group 75, Letters Received by Office of Indian Affairs, New Mexico Superintendency, 1866, National Archives, Washington, D. C.
32. For a detailed account of the exploring party's experience as well as the Hole-in-the-Rock Expedition, see David E. Miller, *Hole-in-the-Rock, An Epic in the Colonization of the Great American West* (Salt Lake City: University of Utah Press, 1959); Ron F. McDonald, *Fort Montezuma, An Account of the First Mormon Settlers in San Juan County, Utah* (2003; rev., Blanding, UT: Self-published 2006).
33. Albert R. Lyman to Maurice L. Howe, March 4, 1937, "Place Names" in General Subject File, Utah State Historical Society Library, Salt Lake City.
34. Miller, *Hole-in-the-Rock*, 88–92. Miller's footnote accompanying this quote is instructive. "This is at Navajo Hill where the present highway from Bluff to Mexican Hat cuts through Comb Ridge. Remnants of the old Indian trail were still visible during the summer of 1957 on the south side of the draw. The modern highway has been cut on the north side, leaving the old trail undestroyed. Navajo Hill is some five miles north of the San Juan River. Contrary to some printed accounts, wagons of the Hole-in-the-Rock expedition were not taken up Navajo Hill" (98).
35. Ibid., 89.
36. James H. Knipmeyer, *Butch Cassidy Was Here: Historic Inscriptions of the Colorado Plateau* (Salt Lake City: University of Utah Press, 2002): 70.
37. George Hobbs account, "San Juan Stake History," unpublished manuscript, Special Collections, Harold B. Lee Library, Provo, UT, 48–49.
38. Ibid., 58.
39. Ibid., 60.

40. Platte D. Lyman, "Journal of Platte DeAlton Lyman," unpublished manuscript, Utah State Historical Society, Salt Lake City, 11.
41. Knipmeyer, *Butch Cassidy*, 80.
42. Hobbs, "San Juan Stake History," 71.
43. Ibid., 72.
44. McDonald, *Fort Montezuma*, 50 (A).
45. Albert R. Lyman, "History of San Juan County, 1879–1917," unpublished manuscript, Special Collections, Harold B. Lee Library, Provo, UT, 12.
46. White Sheep, testimonies, March 15, 1953, and January 6, 1961.
47. Hetty Nepah, testimony, January 7, 1961.
48. Warrior Woman, testimony, January 18, 1961.
49. Albert R. Lyman, testimony, July 30, 1968, Doris Duke #395.
50. For a history of the San Juan River and the battle to control it, see James M. Aton and Robert S. McPherson, *River Flowing from the Sunrise: An Environmental History of the Lower San Juan* (Logan: Utah State University Press, 2000).
51. Albert R. Lyman, "History of San Juan," 20.
52. Daniel K. Muhlstein, "The Rise and Fall of the Cattle Companies in San Juan, 1880–1900," unpublished manuscript, Utah State Historical Society, Salt Lake City, n.d., 31
53. Albert R. Lyman, "History of San Juan," 22, 31.
54. Albert R. Lyman to Howe, March 4, 1937.
55. Albert R. Lyman, "History of San Juan," 35–36.
56. Ibid., 44.
57. The Colorado River Bed Case Hearings were held in 1929–1930 to determine if the San Juan River was navigable in 1896 when Utah achieved statehood. Dozens of sworn testimonies were given by people familiar with the river and activities dependent upon it. Frank and Ernest Hyde were just two of many who testified about the crossing at Rincon and their activities at the post. Unfortunately, roughly thirty years had elapsed, and so dates and some other specifics were somewhat confused. Ron McDonald, local historian, has recreated through diaries and journals many aspects of the Hyde family's life at Rincon. See McDonald, *Fort Montezuma*.
58. Jens Nielson, testimony, September 12, 1929, 1177; Louisa Wetherill, testimony, n.d., 691–92; John Wetherill, testimony, October, 1930, 477, 673, 1333; A. S. Woods, testimony, October 1930, 1098, Colorado River Bed Case (hereafter cited as CRB Case) microfilm, Utah State Historical Society, Salt Lake City.
59. Frank H. Hyde, testimony, October, 1930, 1208; Ernest B. Hyde, October, 1930, 700–707, CRB Case.
60. Platte D. Lyman, "Journal," 307.
61. Albert R. Lyman, "History of San Juan," 38.
62. Frank H. Hyde, testimony, October, 1930,1209. Francis M. Lyman visited the post at Rincon on May 12, 1885, noting that William had moved up river (other accounts suggesting Peak City in the Aneth area) and opened up a new business. Francis Lyman, *Deseret News*, May 12, 1885, cited in "San Juan Stake History," n.p.
63. McDonald, *Fort Montezuma*, 59. McDonald has also done a lot of on-the-ground detective work in determining tentative locations of different structures associated with the trading post at Rincon.
64. Frank H. Hyde, testimony, October, 1930, 164.
65. Ibid., 171.
66. Ibid., 161.
67. Evelyn Hyde Dunn, "History of the Family of Ernest Bertrand Hyde and Alice Gertrude Mortensen," unpublished manuscript, in possession of family, May 1978, Logan, UT, 26, 38.
68. Francis A. Hammond to Colonel P. T. Swaine, June 23, 1887, Record Group 94, Records of the War Department, Department of New Mexico, National Archives, Washington, DC; Albert R. Lyman, "History of San Juan," 51–52.
69. Ibid.
70. Ibid.; Kumen Jones, "Writing of Kumen Jones" (unpublished manuscript, Special Collections, Harold B. Lee Library, Provo, UT, 206–7.
71. Muhlstein, "Rise and Fall of Cattle Companies," 3–4.
72. The following account is taken from two Albert R. Lyman sources: "History of San Juan," 46–48; Albert R. Lyman interview with Gary Guymon, "Bill Ball and the Horse Thieves," *Blue Mountain Shadows* 29 (Winter 2003–04): 61–62.
73. Albert R. Lyman, "History of San Juan," 47.
74. Ibid., 75.

75. Platte D. Lyman, "Journal," 51.
76. Albert R. Lyman, "History of San Juan," 36.
77. Francis A. Hammond, "Journal" Number 2, January 19, 1886, Special Collections, Harold B. Lee Library, Provo, UT.
78. Ibid., March 10, 1886.
79. Ibid., February 11, 1887.
80. Ibid., February 28, 1887.
81. John Taylor to F. A. Hammond, January 5, 1887, Special Collections, Harold B. Lee Library, Provo, UT.
82. Wilford Woodruff to F. A. Hammond, October 3, 1887, Special Collections, Harold B. Lee Library, Provo, UT.
83. W. J. Forham, *Deseret News*, October 12, 1887, cited in "San Juan Stake History," unpublished manuscript, Special Collections, Harold B. Lee Library, Provo, UT.
84. Ibid., November 28, 1887.
85. Ibid., March 14, 1887; January 23, 1888; January 24, 1888.
86. Ibid., April 24, 1888; April 26, 1888.

Five: Who Owns the Comb

1. For a brief summary of the issues surrounding the Utes and Paiutes in San Juan at this time, see Robert S. McPherson, *A History of San Juan County: In the Palm of Time* (Salt Lake City: Utah State Historical Society, 1995): 145–69.
2. *Ute Indian Commission*, 50th Cong., 2d sess., Senate Executive Document 67, Washington, DC, January 11, 1889, 79.
3. Ibid., 81–84.
4. Albert R. Lyman, "History of San Juan County, 1879–1917," unpublished manuscript, Special Collections, Harold B. Lee Library, Provo, UT, 84.
5. Francis Fisher Kane, "Diary," unpublished manuscript, Indian Rights Association Papers, 1868–1968, in possession of author, 92.
6. See Forbes Parkhill, *The Last of the Indian Wars* (New York: Crowell-Collier Press, 1961).
7. "Indians Surround Marshal's Posse," *Salt Lake Herald Republican* (hereafter cited as *SLHR*), February 22, 1915, 1, 11.
8. "Posse Plans to Attack in Force Today," *SLHR*, February 24, 1915, 1.
9. Ibid.; "Lose Five in Battle at Bluff," *SLHR*, February 23, 1915, 1.
10. "Nebeker Now Plans Siege of Outlaws," *SLHR*, March 1, 1915, 1.
11. "Friendly Utes May Join Polk," *SLHR*, March 3, 1915, 1.
12. "Nebeker Now Plans Siege," *SLHR*, 1.
13. "Cliff Dwellings Shelter Piutes," *SLHR*, March 3, 1915, 5.
14. "Reds Entrench in Narrow Pass," *SLHR*, March 5, 1915, 1.
15. "Modesty of Scott Reflected in His Report on Capture of Piute Outlaws," *Cincinnati Enquirer*, April 11, 1915, 1.
16. See "Paiute Posey and the Last White Uprising," *Utah Historical Quarterly* 53 (Summer 1985): 248–67.
17. The following account is from John D. Rogers, "Piute Posey and the Last Indian Uprising," Appendix to John Rogers, interview with Michael T. Hurst, April 29, 1972, CRC-J6, Charles Redd Center for Western Studies, Special Collections, Harold B. Lee Library, Provo, UT. There are dozens of interviews of people with their own version of what happened in this fight, but Rogers's is the most complete. He was an active participant throughout the incident and has had additional interviews for clarification of detail. He was involved in all that occurred in the Comb Ridge area.
18. Rogers, "Piute Posey," 22.
19. The conventional wisdom from many involved in the fight was that Posey took the old Indian trail through where Highway 95 would be built. Another possibility is that he went farther north to another, easier and more manageable trail into Comb Wash from Whiskers Draw since he had just been wounded in the hip by Dave Black.
20. Ibid., 34; Fern Oliver Shelley, "The Life Story of William Edward Oliver, 1858–1935," in possession of James W. Oliver, Jr., Mapleton, Utah; Alma Uriah Jones, interview with Gary Shumway, August 4–7, 1981, LDS Polygamy Oral History, CRC-K157, Charles Redd Center for Western Studies, Special Collections, Harold B. Lee Library, Provo, UT, 68–69
21. Ibid., 35.

22. Frank H. Karnell was born around 1871, came from Pueblo, Colorado, in 1904 as part of the placer mining effort, and eventually worked at the ranch that is shown on maps today as (George) Perkins Ranch. During the 1920s, it was known as Karnell's ranch. However, Ray Perkins, son of George, wrote, "We had a ranch at the head of Comb Wash and had an old German, Frank Karnell, on the ranch," indicating that ownership at the time of the Posey conflict was in the hands of the Perkinses.
23. Karnell served as a justice of the peace in Bluff and in 1929, testified in the Colorado River Bed Trial. The following are two brief anecdotes. In early June 1907, John Wetherill tried to engage two Navajo men, who ran the "Bluff ferry," to haul his purchase of flour across the river so that he could load it into his wagon and bring it to his post in Arizona. The boatmen demanded six dollars instead of the usual three, and so John turned to Frank Karnell, "a strong limbed youth who had faced shot and shell with Roosevelt in the charge up San Juan Hill—then what was the San Juan River to him. He tackled the job and in three hours safely transferred Wetherill's load of flour and other supplies to the other shore and got his three dollars and the Navajos got nothing." ("Bluff City News," *Montezuma Journal*, June 6, 1907, 2.)
24. Hilda Perkins, a young girl at this time, remembered, "He used to come in a buggy down Comb Wash. He worked for George Perkins and lived at a ranch out here in Comb. He'd come down to Bluff on Sundays in this little old buggy with an old fashioned cover over it and with just one pony pulling it. He'd come down every Sunday to church." Hilda Perkins, interview with Pat Whitaker, July 9, 1972, O.H. 1176, Southeastern Utah Oral History Project, 28.
25. Ibid., 37.
26. Charles S. Peterson, *Look to the Mountains: Southeastern Utah and the La Sal National Forest* (Provo, UT: Brigham Young University Press, 1975): 155–56.
27. Captain E. A. Sturges to Adjutant, Black Mountain Expeditionary Forces, August 12, 1908, Record Group 98, Records of the War Department, U.S. Army Command, Department of Colorado, 2.
28. Edwin H. Plummer to Commissioner of Indian Affairs, March 13, 1894, cited in David M. Brugge, "Navajo Use and Occupation of Lands North of the San Juan River in Present-day Utah to 1935" (hereafter cited as NUOL), unpublished manuscript in possession of author, 60. This document is comprised of original source material gathered by J. Lee Correll and others as part of the Navajo Land Claims material. Brugge collected, copied, and compiled large numbers of these documents to support Navajo claims of residency in the San Juan area.
29. Constant Williams to Commissioner of Indian Affairs, December 11, 1894, NUOL, 64–65.
30. Hayzlett to Commissioner of Indian Affairs, January 16, 1903, NUOL, 102–4; Harriett M. Peabody to Commissioner of Indian Affairs, July 8, 1904, NUOL, 111–13.
31. James M. Holley to William T. Shelton, February 20, 1905, NUOL, 119.
32. "Navaho Reservation, Utah—Cancellation of Lands Set Apart in Utah," Executive Order 324A, cited in Charles J. Kappler, *Indian Affairs: Laws and Treaties*, Vol. 3 (Washington, DC: GPO, 1971): 690.
33. William T. Shelton to Commissioner of Indian Affairs, October 26, 1906, J. Lee Correll Collection Navajo Nation Archives, Window Rock, AZ (hereafter cited as JLC Collection).
34. Ibid.
35. William T. Shelton to Commissioner of Indian Affairs, June 10, 1907, JLC Collection.
36. Statement of Jim Joe's Girl (aka Bunzibah), March 20, 1953, JLC Collection.
37. Kumen Jones, "Writings of Kumen Jones," family self-published manuscript, Kay Jones family, Blanding, UT, 30.
38. Statement of Jim Joe's Girl; John Holiday, interview with Robert S. McPherson, April 15, 2005, in possession of author.
39. "Bluff City Notes," *Grand Valley Times*, September 23, 1904, 1.
40. Mamie Adams, interview with Terry Kirker, July 12, 1975, O.H. 1322, Southeastern Utah Oral History Project, 3.
41. Ibid., 4.
42. Christian L. Christensen, "Some Early Indian History," *The Times-Independent*, April 25, 1935, 3.
43. "Minutes of County Commission of San Juan County from April 26, 1880–March 5, 1900," Special Collections, Library, College of Eastern Utah—San Juan Campus, Blanding, UT, 144.
44. Albert R. Lyman, *Indians and Outlaws, Settling of the San Juan Frontier* (Salt Lake City, UT: Bookcraft, 1962): 121–24.
45. Ibid., 125. According to the commissioner's notes, this event occurred in August 1889. See "Minutes of County Commission," 94.
46. Charlie R. Steen, "The Natural Bridges of White Canyon: A Diary of H. L. A. Culmer, 1905," *Utah Historical Quarterly* 40 (Winter 1972): 84.
47. Kumen Jones, "Writings," 31.

48. Shelton to Commissioner of Indian Affairs, July 25, 1905, NUOL, 124.
49. See Robert S. McPherson, "'Too Much Noise in that Bunch across the River': Ba'álílee and the 1907 Aneth Brawl," *Utah Historical Quarterly* 78 (Winter 2009): 26–51.
50. Shelton to Jim Joe, November 7, 1907, JLC Collection.
51. Jim Joe to Shelton, November 20, 1907, JLC Collection.
52. Ibid.
53. E. A. Sturges to Adjutant, Black Mountain Expeditionary Forces, August 12, 1908, RG 393, Continental Commands, Department of Colorado, National Archives, Washington, DC.
54. Indian Allotment Papers, Jim Joe, cited in NUOL, 175–76.
55. Earl Richards, "Bluff," *San Juan Record*, January 15, 1942, 5.
56. Robert S. McPherson, ed., *The Journey of Navajo Oshley: An Autobiography and Life History* (Logan: Utah State University Press, 2000): 33–34.
57. Gladys Bitsinnie, interview with Robert S. McPherson, March 26, 1993, in possession of author.
58. Mary Blueyes, interview, July 25, 1988; John Holiday, interview, April 15, 2005; Mary Jim, interview, June 7, 1988; Buck Navajo, interview, December 16, 1991, all in possession of author.
59. John Holiday, interview, April 15, 2005; Ada Black, interview October 11, 1991, in possession of author.
60. Mary Jim, interview, June 7, 1988; John Holiday, interview, April 15, 2005.
61. Holiday and McPherson, *A Navajo Legacy*, 162.
62. Unless otherwise noted, the remainder of this chapter is derived from an interview with John Holiday on April 15, 2005, in possession of author.
63. Ada Benally, interview with Robert S. McPherson, May 17, 2007, in possession of author.
64. Mary Tsosie, interview with Robert S. McPherson, January 30, 1991, in possession of author.
65. This story, with slight variations, can also be found in Holiday and McPherson, *A Navajo Legacy*, 85–86.

Six: Combing the Comb

1. Morgan Amasa Barton, cited in David E. Miller, *Hole-in-the-Rock, An Epic in the Colonization of the Great American West* (Salt Lake City: University of Utah Press, 1959, 1966): 8–9.
2. Forest Service records indicate the two owners as "Calder and Crosby with Dan Short as foreman," found in "Elk Mountain," General File, National Forest Service Records, Monticello Records Division, Monticello, UT, while Albert R. Lyman wrote "John Crosby and a man named Reed managed the outfit," found in "History of San Juan County, 1879–1917," unpublished manuscript, Special Collections, Harold B. Lee Library, Provo, UT, 56.
3. Albert R. Lyman, "The Fort on the Firing Line," *The Improvement Era* 52, no. 12 (December 1949): 820.
4. Forest Service Records, "Elk Outfit."
5. Lyman, "History of San Juan," 56.
6. Ibid.
7. Ibid., 62.
8. Forest Service Records, "Elk Outfit." The record does not specify which of the Nielson brothers this account refers to but all three—Jens, Joseph, and Francis—were involved in the livestock industry.
9. Lyman, "History of San Juan," 73.
10. Christen L. Christensen, testimony, October 1930, Colorado River Bed Case Hearings (hereafter cited as CRB Case) microfilm, Utah State Historical Society, Salt Lake City, 1154–56.
11. See Robert S. McPherson and Richard Kitchen, "Much Ado about Nothing: The San Juan River Gold Rush, 1892–93," *Utah Historical Quarterly* 67, no. 1 (Winter 1999): 68–87; James M. Aton and Robert S. McPherson, *River Flowing from the Sunrise: An Environmental History of the Lower San Juan* (Logan: Utah State University Press, 2000): 113–20.
12. *Mancos Times*, February 9, 1894, 4; Bryant L. Jensen, "An Historical Study of Bluff City, Utah, from 1878 to 1906," master's thesis, Brigham Young University,1966, 77–78.
13. "Howard's Letter from Salina," *Salt Lake Tribune*, January 30, 1893, 3.
14. John Wetherill, testimony, October 1930, CRB Case, vol. 1, 469, 673.
15. Map, "Part of Proposed Southern Ute Indian Reservation in Utah," copyrighted by Emil B. Fischer, 1893, Wetherill-Grand Gulch Archives, Edge of the Cedars Museum, Blanding, Utah.
16. Kathryn Gabriel, ed., *Marietta Wetherill: Life with the Navajos in Chaco Canyon* (Albuquerque: University of New Mexico Press, 1992): 52–55.
17. A. L. Raplee, testimony, October 1930, CRB Case, vol. 1, 127.
18. Charles Spencer, testimony, October 1930, CRB Case, vol. 1, 194.
19. Ernest Hyde, testimony, October 1930, CRB Case, vol. 1, 489.

20. Walter E. Mendenhall, testimony, October 1930, CRB Case, vol. 2, 890, 899.
21. Lyman, "History of San Juan," 79.
22. Frank H. Hyde, testimony, October 1930, CRB Case, vol. 2, 1215; A. S. Woods, testimony, October 1930, CRB Case, vol. 2, 1098; Bert Loper, testimony, October 1930, CRB Case, vol. 1, 623.
23. Anonymous, "A Report of Gold in Comb Wash," typed manuscript in possession of author.
24. "A. Koebler Returns," *Durango Herald*, January 11, 1893, 1. Note: If Koebler's estimate of twenty miles is correct, then he traveled to Arch Canyon, the only continuously flowing source of water in Comb Wash. Navajo Spring, however, is the more likely spot because it was famous for its good water and place to rest. Most likely, those returning from upper Comb Wash would have labeled it Turn Back Spring. Footnote 23 supports this possibility
25. James H. Knipmeyer, *Butch Cassidy Was Here: Historic Inscriptions of the Colorado Plateau* (Salt Lake City: University of Utah Press, 2002): 95.
26. Charles Goodman, "History of the Oil Fields in San Juan County," *Salt Lake Mining Review*, April 15, 1910, 17–18; for more information concerning some of the personalities associated with the gold rush and oil industry in the Mexican Hat area, see Doris Valle, *Looking Back around the Hat: A History of Mexican Hat* (Mexican Hat, UT: Author, 1986).
27. Herbert E. Gregory, "The San Juan Oil Field, San Juan County, Utah," in *Contributions to Economic Geology, 1909*, part 2, Bulletin no. 431 (Washington, DC: GPO, 1911): 11, 21–23.
28. Frank H. Hyde, testimony, October, 1930, 166.
29. Goodman, "History of the Oil Fields," 18.
30. "Tells of Bluff Oil Fields," *Grand Valley Times,* November 20, 1908, 1, 3.
31. Gregory, "San Juan Oil Field," 11.
32. Ibid., 21–24.
33. Ibid., 13.
34. James R. Martin, "The Oil Fields of San Juan County," *Montezuma Journal*, December 9, 1910, 1.
35. "Minutes of County Commission of San Juan County, From April 26, 1880–March 5, 1900," unpublished manuscript, Special Collections, Library, College of Eastern Utah–San Juan Campus, Blanding, UT, 11, 18, 29, 128.
36. Cass Hite, "No Place for Poor Men," *Cortez Herald*, January 10, 1893, 3.
37. "Grayson Doings," *Grand Valley Times*, April 10, 1908, 1.
38. "Bluff City Items," *Montezuma Journal*, April 30, 1908, 2.
39. Lyman, "History of San Juan," 105.
40. "Bluff City is Prosperous," *Montezuma Journal*, September 8, 1910, 1.
41. "Trail Blazers leave Bluff on long Auto Trip to St. George," *Grand Valley Times*, May 8, 1917, 1.
42. "Monumental Route Located," *San Juan Blade*, September 7, 1917, 1.
43. "R. R. Officials Visit Bluff," *San Juan Blade*, August 31, 1917, 1.
44. "Bluff Oil Field again Looms Up," *San Juan Blade*, September 14, 1917, 1.
45. "Prominent Party goes to Bluff Oil Fields," *San Juan Blade*, November 30, 1917, 1.
46. "To Open Roads to Oil Fields," *San Juan Blade*, December 21, 1917, 1.
47. No Title, *San Juan Blade*, December 28, 1917, 5.
48. "Seek Funds for Road to Bluff Oil Fields," *Times-Independent*, February 15, 1923, 8; "Oil Interests Building Roads in San Juan Field," *Times-Independent*, May 31, 1923, 5.
49. Gary Topping, ed., "An Adventure for Adventure's Sake Recounted by Robert B. Aird," *Utah Historical Quarterly* 62, no. 3 (Summer 1994): 285.
50. Charlie R. Steen, "The Natural Bridges of White Canyon: A Diary of H. L. A. Culmer, 1905," *Utah Historical Quarterly* 40, no. 1 (Winter 1972): 71.
51. Robert S. McPherson, ed., *The Journey of Navajo Oshley: An Autobiography and Life History* (Logan: Utah State University Press, 2000): 70.
52. Ibid., 91–92.
53. No Title, *San Juan Blade*, December 28, 1917, 5.
54. McPherson, *Oshley*, 105–7; Ray Hunt interview, August 22, 1995, notes in possession of author.
55. For information about Evans and his life in the Four Corners region, see Will Evans with Susan E. Woods and Robert S. McPherson, eds., *Along Navajo Trails: Recollections of a Trader* (Logan: Utah State University Press, 2005).
56. Will Evans and John Stewart MacClary, "Trip into the Desert—1930," unpublished manuscript in possession of author.
57. E. C. La Rue, *Colorado River and Its Utilization* (Washington, DC: Department of the Interior, GPO, 1916): 213.

58. Ibid., 123; Raymond M. Priest, testimony, October 1930, CRB Case, vol. 1, 531–32.
59. Charles A. Bissell, testimony, October 1930, CRB Case, vol. 2, 1039.
60. E. C. La Rue, *Water Power and Flood Control of Colorado River below Green River, Utah*, Water-Supply Paper 556 (Washington, DC: GPO, 1925): 18–19.
61. For further discussion of the San Juan River and its role in dam construction, see Aton and McPherson, *River Flowing from the Sunrise*, 129–40

Seven: Interpreting the Comb

1. Ada Black, interview with Robert S. McPherson and Marilyn Holiday, October 11, 1991, in possession of author.
2. Warren King Moorehead, "The Field Diary of an Archaeological Collector," manuscript in Moorehead Collection, Ohio Historical Society, Columbus, 67.
3. Anne M. Smith, *Ethnography of the Northern Utes* (Santa Fe: Museum of New Mexico Press, 1974): 16.
4. Edward Dutchie, Sr., and Patty Dutchie, interview with Robert S. McPherson, May 13, 1996, in possession of author.
5. Henry McCabe, *Cowboys, Indians, and Homesteaders* (Salt Lake City, UT: Deseret Press, 1975): 183.
6. Lola Mike, interview with Robert S. McPherson, November 16, 2005, in possession of author.
7. William H. Jackson, *William H. Jackson Frontier Photographer Diaries, 1866–1874* (Glendale, CA: Arthur H. Clark, 1959): 316–19.
8. McCabe, *Cowboys, Indians, and Homesteaders*, 6.
9. Ibid.
10. Patty Dutchie, interview, May 13, 1996.
11. Stella Eyetoo, interview with Robert S. McPherson, December 21, 1994, in possession of author.
12. Patty Dutchie, interview, May 13, 1996.
13. Edward Dutchie, Sr., interview, May 13, 1996.
14. See Robert S. McPherson, *Sacred Land, Sacred View: Navajo Perceptions of the Four Corners Region* (Provo, UT: Brigham Young University, 1992): 77–127.
15. John Holiday, interview with Robert S. McPherson, December 10, 2004, in possession of author.
16. Kathryn Gabriel, ed. *Marietta Wetherill: Life with the Navajos in Chaco Canyon* (Albuquerque: University of New Mexico Press, 1992): 105, 22.
17. Frederick W. Hodge, "The Early Navajo and Apache," *American Anthropologist* 8 (July 1895): 223.
18. Father Berard Haile, O.F.M., *The Upward Moving and Emergence Way: The Gishin Biyé Version* (Lincoln: University of Nebraska Press, 1981): 171.
19. Fred Yazzie, interview with Robert S. McPherson, November 5, 1987, in possession of author.
20. T. Mitchell Prudden, *On the Great American Plateau* (New York: G. P. Putnam's Sons, 1906): 172.
21. Joe Manygoats, interview with Robert S. McPherson, December 18, 1991, in possession of author.
22. Mary Blueyes, interview with Robert S. McPherson, July 25, 1988, in possession of author.
23. Ada Black, interview, October 11, 1991.
24. John Holiday, interview, December 10, 2004.
25. Franciscan Fathers, *An Ethnologic Dictionary of the Navaho Language* (Saint Michaels, AZ: Saint Michaels Press, 1910): 400–401; Slim Benally, interview with Robert S. McPherson, July 8, 1988; Florence Begay interview, with Robert S. McPherson, April 29, 1988, all in possession of author.
26. Fred Yazzie, interview, November 5, 1987.
27. Rose Begay, interview with Bertha Parrish, June 17, 1987, in possession of author.
28. John Holiday, interview with Robert S. McPherson, April 15, 2005, in possession of author.
29. Ibid.
30. Ibid.
31. Lola Mike, interview, November 16, 2005.
32. For a brief overview of this era, see Robert S. McPherson, *A History of San Juan County: In the Palm of Time* (Salt Lake City: Utah State Historical Society, 1995): 73–83.
33. Captain J. N. Macomb, *Report of the Exploring Expedition From Santa Fe, New Mexico to the Junction of the Grand and Green Rivers of the Great Colorado of the West in 1859* (Washington, DC: GPO, 1876): 88–89.
34. Ferdinand V. Hayden, *Ninth Annual Report of the United States Geological and Geographic Survey* (Washington, DC: GPO, 1876).
35. William H. Jackson, "A Notice of the Ancient Ruins in Arizona and Utah Lying about the Rio San Juan," *United States Geological Survey*, Bulletin 1 (Washington, DC: GPO, 1876): 32–33.

36. Ibid., 33.
37. Ibid., 34.
38. William H. Jackson and Howard R. Driggs, *The Pioneer Photographer* (New York: World Book Company, 1929): 249.
39. William H. Jackson, "Diary—June 22, 1875 thru October 6, 1875," August 22, 1875, microfilm, Colorado Historical Society, Denver.
40. Ibid., August 23, 1875.
41. See Will Evans, *Along Navajo Trails: Recollections of a Trader* (Logan: Utah State University Press, 2005): 2–35; John Fahey and Robert S. McPherson, "Seeing is Believing: The Odyssey of the Pectol Shields," *Utah Historical Quarterly* 76, no. 4 (Fall 2008): 357–76.
42. Albert R. Lyman, *The Trails of the Ancients* (Blanding, UT: Trails of the Ancients Association, 1972).
43. Ibid., 61.
44. Albert R. Lyman, "San Juan in the Years 1130–1140 AD," *San Juan Record*, July 16, 1931, 5.
45. Albert R. Lyman , "San Juan, The Walls of Ancient Empire," *San Juan Record*, June 4, 1931, 5.
46. Albert R. Lyman, "Aborigines of San Juan," *San Juan Blade*, January 18 and 25, 1918, 1; Albert R. Lyman, "Aborigines of San Juan," *San Juan Blade*, December 14, 1917, 1.
47. Albert R. Lyman, "Old Settler," *San Juan Record*, May 8, 1947, 1.
48. For an excellent study in determining who was in the canyons of southeastern Utah digging in Ancestral Puebloan sites, then shipping collections off to museums or private individuals, see Fred M. Blackburn and Ray A. Williamson, *Cowboys and Cave Dwellers: Basketmaker Archaeology in Utah's Grand Gulch* (Santa Fe, NM: School of American Research Press, 1997). The best summary of what went on in the Comb Ridge area during this time is in Winston Hurst, "Colonizing the Dead: Early Archaeology in Western San Juan County," *Blue Mountain Shadows* 17 (Summer 1996): 2–13. In discussing this era, I have borrowed heavily from this source with permission of the author. Unless otherwise noted, information has come directly from it.
49. E. A. McDaniels, *Utah at the World's Columbian Exposition* (Salt Lake City, UT: Salt Lake Lithograph, 1894).
50. *Mancos Times*, November 24, 1893, 1.
51. *Mancos Times*, January 5, 1894, 4.
52. Harry French, cited in Blackburn and Williamson, *Cowboys and Cave Dwellers*, 104.
53. Anonymous (but probably Richard Wetherill), "Original Field Catalogue of the First Wetherill Collection, 1893–95," American Museum of Natural History Archives, New York.
54. See Fred Blackburn and Winston Hurst, "Charley Lang: Pioneer Photographer, Musician, and Archaeologist," *Blue Mountain Shadows* 14 (Winter 1994): 5–13.
55. *Mancos Times*, March 16, 1894, 4.
56. Eugene Traughber, "Rich Finds in Utah," *Washington Post*, July 15, 1894.
57. "In Search of a Lost Race," *The Illustrated American*, April 2, 1892, 305.
58. Alice Eastwood, "Report on a Collection of Plants from San Juan County in Southeastern Utah," *California Academy of Sciences Proceedings* 6 (August 1896): 279
59. Ibid., 276.
60. Ibid., 274–75.
61. Maurine S. Fletcher, ed., *The Wetherills of Mesa Verde: Autobiography of Benjamin Alfred Wetherill* (Lincoln: University of Nebraska Press, 1977, 1987): 206.
62. Alice Eastwood, "Memoirs," Alice Eastwood Archive, California Academy of Sciences, San Francisco.
63. Richard Wetherill, "The Expedition of 1896 and 1897," n.d., typescript on file, American Museum of Natural History, New York, 56.
64. T. Mitchell Prudden, "Field Notes of Reconnaissance of San Juan Watershed, 1900," n.d., unpublished manuscript and typescript on file, Peabody Museum of Natural History Archives, Yale University, New Haven, Connecticut, 2.
65. Prudden, *On the Great American Plateau*, 123, 124, 128.
66. "The Explorers," *Grand Valley Times*, June 21, 1907, 1.
67. "Explorers Return," *Grand Valley Times*, August 2, 1907, 1.
68. Ibid.
69. Edgar L. Hewett, "Field Notes E. L. Hewett, 1906–1909," n.d. (prepared by A. H. Schroeder in 1967), unpublished typescript on file at Natural Bridges National Monument, Utah, 56–57.
70. Todd W. Bostwick, *Byron Cummings: Dean of Southwest Archaeology* (Tucson: University of Arizona Press, 2006): 42.
71. "Descendants of Cliff-Dwellers," *Grand Valley Times*, September 8, 1911, 1.

72. Ibid.
73. "Large Collection of Indian Relics Secured," *Grand Valley Times*, August 25, 1925, 1.

Eight: The Comb at Mid-Twentieth Century

1. A. Daniel Shumway, "The Mines on Old Highway 95," *Blue Mountain Shadows* 16 (Winter 1995): 79.
2. Herbert Redshaw to Evan W. Estep, January 29, 1921, cited in David M. Brugge, "Navajo Use and Occupation of Lands North of the San Juan River in Present-day Utah to 1935" (hereafter cited as NUOL), unpublished manuscript in possession of author, 168.
3. Ibid., 169.
4. Estep to Commissioner of Indian Affairs, February 9, 1921, NUOL, 170.
5. For a brief history of the Paiute Strip, see Robert S. McPherson, *A History of San Juan County: In the Palm of Time* (Salt Lake City: Utah State Historical Society, 1995): 134–35.
6. B. P. Six to Commissioner of Indian Affairs, March 20, 1930, J. Lee Correll Collection (hereafter cited as JLC Collection), Navajo Archives, Window Rock, AZ.
7. C. L. Walker to Commissioner of Indian Affairs, March 21, 1930, JLC Collection.
8. "Dern Opposes Giving Land to Navajos," *Times-Independent*, March 13, 1930, 1.
9. Walker to Commissioner of Indian Affairs, September 22, 1930, NUOL, 184.
10. Ibid., 187.
11. "Blanding Department," *San Juan Record*, September 28, 1930, 8.
12. Charles Redd to Don B. Colton, October 13, 1930, NUOL, 189.
13. Redd to Colton, November 17, 1930, JLC Collection.
14. J. M. Stewart to Assistant Commissioner of Indian Affairs, July 19, 1932, JLC Collection; "'Piute Strip' Controversy Settled at Last," *San Juan Record*, July 21, 1932, 1, 5.
15. "Piute Strip Controversy," 1.
16. Ibid.
17. U.S. Congress, *Permanently Set Aside Lands in Utah . . . Navajo Indian Reservation*, report no. 1883, 72d Cong., 2d sess., January 19, 1933, 1–4; Senate, *Addition to Navajo Indian Reservation in Utah*, report no. 1199, 72d Cong., 2d sess., February 10, 1933, 1–4.
18. Stewart to Assistant Commissioner, July 19, 1932, JLC Collection.
19. "Piute Strip Controversy," 1.
20. "Memorandum of Agreement Made Between Council of Nine Representing the Citizens of Blanding, Utah, and the Commissioner of Indian Affairs, Regarding the Piute Strip," July 15, 1932, JLC Collection.
21. Deshna Clah Cheschillige to Charles J. Rhoads, December 11, 1932, JLC Collection.
22. "The Official Addition of Indian Land," *San Juan Record*, May 25, 1933, 4.
23. James Muhn and Hanson R. Stuart, *Opportunity and Challenge: The Story of BLM* (Washington, DC: Department of the Interior, Bureau of Land Management, 1988): 35–41.
24. See Robert S. McPherson, "History Repeats Itself: Navajo Livestock Reduction in Southeastern Utah, 1933–1946," in *Navajo Land, Navajo Culture: The Utah Experience in the Twentieth Century* (Norman: University of Oklahoma Press, 2001): 102–20.
25. John Holiday, interview with Robert S. McPherson, April 15, 2005, in possession of author.
26. "Statement of Jim Joe's Girl" taken by Richard Van Valkenburgh, March 20, 1953, JLC Collection.
27. Mary Jim and Mary Hernandez, entitled through an amended land patent originally issued to Jim Joe, case file U59684, filed under patent number 43–86–0025 on September 9, 1986, Bureau of Land Management, Salt Lake City, UT.
28. Vincent L. Jones, interview with James D. Redd, September 3, 1971, O.H. 1090, Southeastern Utah Oral History Project, Utah State Historical Society, Salt Lake City, 12–13.
29. Warrior Woman (Desbaa'), testimony, January 18, 1961, Doris Duke #703, Special Collections, J Willard Marriott Library, University of Utah, Salt Lake City.
30. Beth E. King, "The Utah Navajos Relocation in the 1950s," *Life Along the San Juan River*, Bluff Legacy Project, July 1996, 1–4. Quotes from this article are given by six Navajo people who are identified only by their initials to maintain anonymity. Their words will be used but only occasional distinction is drawn as to who is speaking.
31. Ibid., 4.
32. Earl Hanson Perkins, case file 047986, Land Patent Number 1092585, Bureau of Land Management, Salt Lake City, Utah; Earl H. and Tamar Y. Perkins, warranty deed no. 4886 to Ute Mountain Ute Tribe, October 27, 1955, San Juan County, UT.

33. Ray Perkins, interview with James D. Redd, September 13, 1971, O.H. 1083, Southeastern Utah Oral History Project, Utah State Historical Society, Salt Lake City, 8.
34. Ibid., 14–15.
35. Ibid., 5.
36. Ibid.
37. Karl Barton, interview with Winston Hurst and Robert S. McPherson, December 29, 2006, in possession of author, 1, 6–7, 25–27.
38. Vincent L. Jones, interview, September 3, 1971, 3, 7–8.
39. Karl Barton, interview, December 29, 2006, 13.
40. Melvin Adams, interview with James D. Redd, September 21, 1971, O.H. 1098, Southeastern Utah Oral History Project, Utah State Historical Society, Salt Lake City, 12.
41. Clyde M. Barton, interview with John Bluth, July 26, 1973, CRC-B14, Southeastern Utah Oral History Project, Charles Redd Center, Brigham Young University, Provo, UT, 22–23, 9.
42. Karl Barton, interview, December 29, 2006, 13–14, 21, 29–30.
43. Comb Ridge Field Site Report, completed by David M. Brugge, January 10, 1959, Navajo Land Claims Files, Navajo Nation, Window Rock, AZ.
44. Ray Perkins, interview notes, January 14, 1985, in possession of author.
45. Floyd and Clara Nielson, interview with Gary Shumway and Kim Stewart, July 14, 1971, O.H. 699, Southeastern Utah Oral History Project, Utah State Historical Society, Salt Lake City, 7.
46. Preston "Pep" Redd, *From Horseback to Cadillac, I'm Still a Cowboy* (Tempe, AZ: Tavas Cash Press, 1988): 83.
47. "Tri-state Road Meeting at Flagstaff Secures Gov't. Aid," *San Juan Record*, January 18, 1934, 1; "Past Year Has Been Unequaled in the Building of Highways," *San Juan Record*, March 15, 1934, 1.
48. "Co. Commissioners Appropriate Funds for Road Projects," *San Juan Record*, September 8, 1932, 1; "Road Contract Let to Ogden Firm," *San Juan Record*, August 14, 1952, 1.
49. For an excellent summary of the uranium industry and its impact on San Juan County, see the entire issue but especially Darroll P. Young, "Economic Impact of the Uranium Industry in San Juan County," *Blue Mountain Shadows* 16 (Winter 1995): 3–40; also *Blue Mountain Shadows* 25–27 (Winter 2001, Winter 2001–2002, and Summer 2002), all of which emphasize the Cottonwood Wash area, adjacent to Butler Wash.
50. A. Daniel Shumway, telephone conversation with author, March 6, 2008.
51. Gary Lee Shumway, "The Development of the Uranium Industry in San Juan County," master's thesis, July 3, 1964, Brigham Young University, Provo, UT, 39–40.
52. Ibid., 41; Dan Shumway, telephone conversation with author, March 7, 2008; DeVar Shumway, telephone conversation with author, March 8, 2008.
53. Dan Shumway, telephone conversation, March 7, 2008.
54. DeVar Shumway, telephone conversation, March 8, 2008.
55. Kenny Shumway, telephone conversation with author, March 8, 2008.
56. Gary Shumway, "The Development of the Uranium Industry," 40.
57. Eugene Shumway, telephone conversation with author, March 7, 2008.
58. Kelly Shumway, telephone conversation with author, March 6, 2008.
59. Eugene Shumway, telephone conversation, March 7, 2008.
60. Lynn and Hazel Lyman, interview with Sandy McFadden and Kim Stewart, July 6, 1971, Southeastern Utah Oral History Project, cited by San Juan County Road Project, 4, 6.
61. LaVerne Tate, "Mining and Trucking," *Blue Mountain Shadows* 27 (Summer 2002): 72.
62. Helen Shumway, "Trucking Ore: Adventures on San Juan County Roads," *Blue Mountain Shadows* 27 (Summer 2002): 81.
63. Ibid.
64. "Road Program for San Juan County Reviewed in Letter by Whittenburg," *San Juan Record*, January 22, 1951, 1; "Three Quarter Million Dollars to be Spent on San Juan Mine Roads," *San Juan Record*, March 8, 1951, 1.
65. Deniane Kartchner, "Two Men on the Road," *Blue Mountain Shadows* 12 (Summer 1993): 55.
66. "We'll Take the Scenic Road," *San Juan Record*, April 30, 1953, 3.
67. Jay M. Haymond, "San Juan County Roads: Arteries to Natural Resources and Survival," in Allan Kent Powell, ed., *San Juan County, Utah: People, Resources, and History* (Salt Lake City: Utah State Historical Society, 1983): 235–36.
68. Ibid., Kenneth R. Bailey, "Roads and Resources of San Juan County," 259.
69. Lester Hansen, interview with Jay M. Haymond, August 17, 1972, O.H. 00, 470, Southeastern Utah Oral History Project, Utah State Historical Society, Salt Lake City, 2.

70. Ibid., 3.
71. "Six Persons Narrowly Escape Death in Rock Slide at Comb Hill Friday," *San Juan Record*, January 9, 1953, 3.
72. Julian D. Sears, *Geology of Comb Ridge and Vicinity North of San Juan River, San Juan County, Utah*, Geological Survey Bulletin 1021–E (Washington, DC: GPO, 1956): 174–77.
73. Haymond, "San Juan County Roads," 237.
74. "We'll Take the Scenic Road," 3; "San Juan County, Governor Lee, and $3,000,000.00 Worth of Roads," *San Juan Record*, August 30, 1956, 2; ""Winter Stops Oil on Bluff-Hat Road," *San Juan Record*, September 13, 1956, 1.
75. "Dedicate U-95 Section," *San Juan Record*, October 31, 1974, 1; Kulani Fisher, "Utah State Highway 95," *Blue Mountain Shadows* 12 (Summer 1993): 75.
76. Kartchner, "Two Men on the Road," 57; Jack Palmer, "On the Road with Dad," *Blue Mountain Shadows* 35 (Winter 2006): 98.
77. Fisher, "Utah State Highway 95," 74.
78. "Progress on U-95!," *San Juan Record*, May 20, 1971, 1; "U-95 Critical to San Juan Growth," *San Juan Record*, August 12, 1971, 1; "It's Official: $1.3 million for U-95," *San Juan Record*, November 4, 1971, 1; "Highway 95 Dedication set for September 17–18," *San Juan Record*, September 2, 1976, 1.
79. "Highway 95 Dedication," 1; "U-95 is Well-Dedicated, and Welcome," *San Juan Record*, September 7, 1974, 2.

Nine: The Comb and I

1. David Roberts, *Sandstone Spine: Seeking the Anasazi on the First Traverse of Comb Ridge* (Seattle, WA: The Mountaineers, 2006): 141.
2. Ibid., dust jacket.
3. Transfer Deed, October 27, 1955 and March 29, 1960, Comb Wash Files, Bureau of Land Management Field Office, Monticello, UT (hereafter cited as CWF).
4. "Ute Mountain Tribe (Perkins Ranch) Plan," June 13, 1968, CWF, 2.
5. Ibid., 3.
6. "Comb Wash Trespass," n.d., CWF.
7. The following information concerning this court case is taken from "National Wildlife Federation, Southern Utah Wilderness Alliance, and Joseph M. Feller (Appellants), verses Bureau of Land Management (Respondents) American Farm Bureau Federation, Utah Farm Bureau Federation, Public Lands Council, National Cattlemen's Association, American Sheep Industry Association, and Ute Mountain Ute Indian Tribe," number UT-06–91–01, Office of Hearings and Appeals, United States Department of the Interior, CWF.
8. Ibid., 21.
9. Ibid., 33.
10. Catherine Vandemoer, "Outline of Matters Upon which Dr. Catherine Vandemoer Will Testify—Comb Wash Grazing Allotment," CWF.
11. Ibid., 1.
12. Ibid., 3.
13. Ibid., 5.
14. Nick Sandberg (associate field manager BLM), telephone conversation with Robert S. McPherson, April 11, 2008.
15. Grazing Allotment Map (unofficial), 2008, received from Paul Curtis, BLM Field Office, Monticello, UT.
16. "Ten Year Grazing Permit Issuance—Comb Wash Allotment," UT-090–05–12, on file in BLM Monticello Field Office, Monticello, UT, 1.
17. "San Juan, A Source for Museums," *San Juan Record*, July 30, 1931, 5.
18. Ibid.
19. "Rampton Signs Museum Bill," *San Juan Record*, February 14, 1974, 1; "Edge of Cedars Plans Advance," *San Juan Record*, September 18, 1975, 1; "Edge of Cedars Dedication Set," *San Juan Record*, October 26, 1978, 2.
20. "Edge of the Cedars Museum, Anasazi Artifacts Are Returning to Utah Research Facility," *Farmington Daily Times*, January 25, 1987, B-1.
21. "Threatened Legacy—Most Anasazi Sites Spoiled," part 3, *Deseret News*, n.d., 1980, A-1.
22. "BLM Announces weekend 'Moki Digger' Patrol Effort," *San Juan Record*, May 27, 1965, 1.
23. "Threatened Legacy—Private Lands' Relics for Sale," part 2, *Deseret News*, n.d., 1980, A-1.

24. Lynell Schalk, interview with Robert S. McPherson, March 14, 2008, notes in possession of author.
25. "Incident Reports," BLM Moab District Office, 1977–1982, on file in BLM Field Office, Monticello, UT.
26. "Threatened Legacy—Rangers Catch Vandals but Can't Arrest Them," part 5, *Deseret News*, n.d., 1980, A-1.
27. Ibid., A-2.
28. "Incident Report," BLM Moab District Office, March 2, 1980, on file in BLM Field Office, Monticello, UT.
29. Ibid.
30. Ibid.
31. "Artifact Looters Systematically Rape Indian Ruins in Southeastern Utah," *Salt Lake Tribune*, October 28, 1984, B-1.
32. "Matheson Calling for 'Quick' Action to Halt Vandalism of Indian Ruins," *Salt Lake Tribune*, November 2, 1984, B-1; "Range Riders Might be Used to Protect Ruins," *Deseret News*, November 18, 1984, B-1.
33. "Blanding Man Charged with Illegal Dealings of Artifacts," *Deseret News*, November 19, 1984.
34. Mark Shafer, "U.S., Utah 'Moki Diggers' Wage Archaeological War; Town Described as Center of Artifact-Smuggling Ring," *Arizona Republic*, July 27, 1986, A-9.
35. Winston Hurst to Robert S. McPherson, e-mail, April 14, 2008, in possession of author.
36. "Man Who 'Stole Time' Sentenced; Third Generation Grave Robber," *The Indian Trader*, January 1995, 5; "Judge Cuts Sentence for Raider of Ancient Indian Gravesites," *The Indian Trader*, July 1997, 10.
37. "Testing to Begin this Month at Bluff's Great House Site," *Canyon Echo*, October/November 1995, 13; "Excavations Continue on Bluff Great House," *San Juan Record*, June 11, 1997, 4.
38. Winston Hurst, conversation with Robert S. McPherson, April 13, 2008.
39. "Administrative Determination," April 30, 1990, on file in CWF.
40. "Affidavit of Michael F. Heyrend," 2800–UTU-66100, May 22, 1990, CWF.
41. Heyrend et al. to Gene Nodine, BLM district manager, February 23, 1990, CWF.
42. "Arch Canyon as ORV Park," Southern Utah Wilderness Alliance newsletter (Summer 1999): 17–18.
43. Logan Morley, interview with Robert S. McPherson, March 13, 2008, notes in possession of author.
44. "Travel Corridor Monitoring Volunteer Guide—Broads Healthy Lands Project," April 6, 2007, 1.
45. "Broads Position on Off-Road Vehicle Activity," http://greatoldbroads.org/ohvposition.htm.
46. Brent Johansen, telephone conversation with Robert S. McPherson, April 15, 2008.
47. "Petition to Preserve Arch Canyon's Natural and Cultural Heritage," submitted by Southern Utah Wilderness Alliance, Navajo Utah Commission, Great Old Broads for Wilderness, Far Out Expeditions, Wild Rivers Expeditions, and Calf Canyon Bed and Breakfast, December 2006, CWF.
48. "San Juan Heritage Festival ATV Ride," SPEAR newsletter, Spring 2007, http//spear4all.com.
49. Ibid., "San Juan County is a Special Place," 2.
50. "Petition to Preserve Arch Canyon;" Jerry D. Spangler, "Site Condition and Vandalism Assessment of Archaeological Sites, Lower and Middle Arch Canyon, San Juan County, Utah," November 10, 2006, CWF.
51. "Stevens under fire from Navajo Utah Commission," *Blue Mountain Panorama*, March 21, 2007, 1.
52. Ibid., "Your View—Arch Canyon," 2.
53. BLM report cited in "Letters to the Editor—A Response to the Response," *San Juan Record*, April 4, 2007, 7.
54. "Your View—San Juan Hill Trail," *Blue Mountain Panorama*, March 21, 2007, 2.
55. "Letters to the Editor—Utter Lack of Regard," *San Juan Record*, April 4, 2007, 6.
56. "Letters to the Editor—Wake Up San Juan County," *San Juan Record*, July 11, 2007, 6
57. "Green activists say BLM plan will turn landscape into industrial zone," *Blue Mountain Panorama*, February 6, 2008, 1; "Blanding Council says BLM not able to draft impartial land use rules," *Blue Mountain Panorama*, January 30, 2008, 1.

Bibliography

Manuscripts

Anonymous. "Original Field Catalogue of the First Wetherill Collection, 1893–95." American Museum of Natural History, New York.

Brugge, David M. "Navajo Use and Occupation of Lands North of the San Juan River in Present-day Utah to 1935." Unpublished manuscript in possession of author.

———. Comb Ridge Field Site Report, January 10, 1959. Navajo Land Claims Files, Navajo Nation Museum, Window Rock, Arizona.

Correll, J. Lee. J. Lee Correll Collection. Navajo Nation Archives, Window Rock, Arizona.

Dunn, Evelyn Hyde. "History of the Family of Ernest Bertrand Hyde and Alice Gertrude Mortensen," unpublished manuscript, May 1978. In possession of family, Logan, Utah.

Eastwood, Alice. "Memoirs." Alice Eastwood Archive, California Academy of Sciences, San Francisco.

Goss, James A. "Culture-Historical Inference from Utaztekan Linguistic Evidence." Paper presented at Plenary Symposium on Utaztekan Prehistory of the Society for American Archaeology and the Great Basin Anthropological Conference, 1966.

Hammond, Francis. "Journal." L. Tom Perry Special Collections, Harold B. Lee Library, Brigham Young University, Provo, Utah.

Hewett, Edgar L. "Field Notes E. L. Hewett, 1906–1909." Natural Bridges National Monument, Utah.

Hobbs, George. Account in "San Juan Stake History." L. Tom Perry Special Collections, Harold B. Lee Library, Brigham Young University, Provo, Utah.

Hurst, Winston. "Archaeological Investigations in the Pueblo II-III Comb Wash Community, San Juan County, Utah 2002–2004," (in preparation) technical report submitted to Dr. Catherine M. Cameron, principal investigator, Bluff/Comb Wash Project, University of Colorado at Boulder, in possession of author.

———, Ba Bellorado, Hugh Robinson, Tucker Robinson, and Catherine M. Cameron. "Raise High the Roofbeams: Evidence for Multi-story Roomblock Architecture in the Western Mesa Verde Region," Poster presentation. American Archaeology Annual Meeting, 2007.

———. Comb Ridge Project Report (in progress). In possession of author.

———, Catherine Cameron, William Davis, Steve Leckson, and Jonathan Till. "Comb Ridge Survey Project, Initial Proposal" (draft), September 21, 2004. In possession of author.

———. "This Landscape Remembers" (draft), March 1996. In possession of author.

Jackson, William H. "Diary—June 22, 1875 thru October 6, 1875." Microfilm. Colorado Historical Society, Denver, Colorado.

Jensen, Bryant L. "An Historical Study of Bluff City, Utah from 1878 to 1906." Master's thesis, Brigham Young University, 1966.

Jones, Kumen. "The Writing of Kumen Jones." L. Tom Perry Special Collections, Harold B. Lee Library, Brigham Young University, Provo, Utah.

Kane, Francis Fisher. "Diary, 1891." Indian Rights Association Papers, 1868–1968 (Reel 8–microfilm). Historical Society of Pennsylvania, Philadelphia.

Lyman, Albert R. "History of San Juan County, 1879–1917." L. Tom Perry Special Collections, Harold B. Lee Library, Brigham Young University, Provo, Utah.

——— to Maurice L. Howe, March 4, 1937. In "Place Names" file, Utah State Historical Society, Salt Lake City.

Lyman, Platte D. "Journal of Platte DeAlton Lyman." Utah State Historical Society, Salt Lake City.

Minutes of County Commission of San Juan County from April 26, 1880–March 5, 1900. College of Eastern Utah–San Juan Campus Library, Blanding, Utah.

Moorhead, Warren King. "The Field Diary of an Archaeological Collector." Moorhead Collection, Ohio Historical Society, Columbus.

Muhlstein, Daniel K. "The Rise and Fall of the Cattle Companies in San Juan, 1880–1900," n.d., Utah State Historical Society, Salt Lake City.

Prudden, T. Mitchell. "Field Notes of Reconnaissance of San Juan Watershed." Peabody Museum of Natural History Archives, Yale University, New Haven, Connecticut.

Shelley, Fern Oliver. "The Life Story of William Edward Oliver, 1858–1935." In possession of James W. Oliver, Mapleton, Utah.

Shumway, Gary Lee. "The Development of the Uranium Industry in San Juan County." Master's thesis, Brigham Young University, 1964.

Till, Jonathan. "Chacoan Road and Road-associated Sites in the Lower San Juan Region: Assessing the Role of Chacoan Influences in the Northwestern Periphery." Master's thesis, University of Colorado at Boulder, 2001.

Wagner, Marilyn R. "Navajo Settlement Patterns, 1846–1870: A Geographical History." Master's thesis, University of Utah, 1978.

Watson, Editha L. Essay presented March 17, 1968, Doris Duke Oral History Project #796. Special Collections, J. Willard Marriott Library, University of Utah, Salt Lake City.

Wetherill, Richard. "The Expedition of 1896 and 1897." Typescript on file, American Museum of Natural History, New York.

Interviews

Adams, Mamie. Interview by Terry Kirker, July 12, 1975, O.H. 1322. Southeastern Utah Oral History Project, College of Eastern Utah—San Juan Campus Library, Blanding, Utah.

Adams, Melvin. Interview by James D. Redd, September 21, 1971. O.H. 1098, Southeastern Utah Oral History Project, Utah State Historical Society, Salt Lake City, Utah.

Bailey, Sally Draper. Testimony given January 29, 1961. Doris Duke #740, Special Collections, J. Willard Marriott Library, University of Utah, Salt Lake City.

Barton, Clyde M. Interview by John Bluth, July 26, 1973, CRC-B14. Southeastern Utah Oral History Project, Charles Redd Center for Western Studies, Brigham Young University, Provo, Utah.

Barton, Karl. Interview by Winston Hurst and Robert S. McPherson, December 9, 2006.

Begay, Florence. Interview by Nelson Begay and Robert S. McPherson, April 29, 1988.

Begay, Rose. Interview by Bertha Parrish, June 17, 1987.

Benally, Ada. Interview by Baxter Benally and Robert S. McPherson, May 17, 2007.

Benally, Slim. Interview by Baxter Benally and Robert S. McPherson, July 8, 1988.

Bitsili, Mary (Old Lady Sweetwater). Testimony given January 19, 1961. Doris Duke #710, Special Collections, J. Willard Marriott Library, University of Utah, Salt Lake City.

Bitsinnie, Gladys. Interview by Baxter Benally and Robert S. McPherson, March 26, 1993.

Black, Ada. Interviews by Marilyn Holiday and Robert S. McPherson, October 11, 1991; December 16, 1991.

Blueyes, Charlie. Interview by Baxter Benally and Robert S. McPherson, June 7, 1988.

Blueyes, Mary. Interview by Baxter Benally and Robert S. McPherson, July 25, 1988.

Cantsee, Anderson. Testimony given January 28, 1961. Doris Duke #739, Special Collections, J. Willard Marriott Library, University of Utah, Salt Lake City.

Cantsee, Chester. Interview by Aldean Ketchum and Robert S. McPherson, September 6, 1994.

Dandy, Jim. Conversation with Robert S. McPherson, September 10, 2007.

Dry, Mabel. Testimony given July 25, 1967. Doris Duke #110, Special Collections, J. Willard Marriott Library, University of Utah, Salt Lake City.

Dutchie, Edward, Sr., and Patty Dutchie. Interviews by Robert S. McPherson, May 7, 1996; May 13, 1996.

Eyetoo, Stella. Interviews by Aldean Ketchum and Robert S. McPherson, December 21, 1994; November 16, 2005.

Goodman, Paul. Testimony given January 6, 1961. Doris Duke #689, Special Collections, J. Willard Marriott Library, University of Utah, Salt Lake City.

Graymountain, Gilmore. Interview by Marilyn Holiday and Robert S. McPherson, April 7, 1992.

Hansen, Lester. Interview by Jay Haymond, August 17, 1972. O.H. 00470, Southeastern Utah Oral History Project, Utah State Historical Society, Salt Lake City.

Hastiin Claw. Testimony given January 7, 1961. Doris Duke #672, Special Collections, J. Willard Marriott Library, University of Utah, Salt Lake City.

Hastiin Nez Begay. Testimony given January 18, 1961. Doris Duke #706, Special Collections, J. Willard Marriott Library, University of Utah, Salt Lake City.
Hastiin Toh Tłizhini Bitsi. Testimony given January 28, 1961. No Doris Duke number given, Special Collections, J. Willard Marriott Library, University of Utah, Salt Lake City.
Holgate, Maggie. Testimony given June 13, 1968. Doris Duke #956, Special Collections, J. Willard Marriott Library, University of Utah, Salt Lake City.
Holiday, Billy. Testimony given July 21, 1961. Doris Duke #668, Special Collections, J. Willard Marriott Library, University of Utah, Salt Lake City.
Holiday, John. Interview by Marilyn Holiday and Robert S. McPherson, April 15, 2005.
———. Interviews by Baxter Benally and Robert S. McPherson, November 9, 2001; December 10, 2004.
Holiday, Stanley. Interview by Frances Holiday and Robert S. McPherson, November 9, 2006.
Holiday, Tallis. Interview by Jessie Holiday and Robert S. McPherson, November 3, 1987.
Howard, Mamie. Interview by Baxter Benally and Robert S. McPherson, August 2, 1988.
Hunt, Ray. Interview by Robert S. McPherson, August 22, 1995.
Jelly, Mary. Testimony given January 21, 1961. Doris Duke #722, Special Collections, J. Willard Marriott Library, University of Utah, Salt Lake City.
Jim, Mary. Interview by Baxter Benally and Robert S. McPherson, June 7, 1988.
Kelly, Klara. Personal communication with Robert S. McPherson, August 31, 2007.
Johansen, Brent. Telephone conversation with Robert S. McPherson, April 15, 2008.
Jones, Alma. Interview by Gary Shumway, CRC-K157. LDS Polygamy Oral History, Charles Redd Center for Western Studies, Brigham Young University, Provo, Utah.
Jones, Paul. Testimony given January 19, 1961. Doris Duke #712, Special Collections, J. Willard Marriott Library, University of Utah, Salt Lake City.
Jones, S. P. Interview by Sam Goodman and Robert S. McPherson, December 20, 1985.
Jones, Vincent. Interview by James D. Redd, September 3, 1971. O.H. 1090, Southeastern Utah Oral History Project, Utah State Historical Society, Salt Lake City.
Lyman, Albert R. Interview by Charles S. Peterson, February 4, 1970. O.H. 1256, Southeastern Utah Oral History Project, on file in Edge of the Cedars Museum, Blanding, Utah.
———. Testimony given July 30, 1968. Doris Duke #395, Special Collections, J. Willard Marriott Library, University of Utah, Salt Lake City.
Lyman, Lynn. and Hazel Lyman. Interview by Sandy McFadden and Kim Stewart, July 16, 1971. O.H. 788a, Southeastern Utah Oral History Project, Utah State Historical Society, Salt Lake City.
Manygoats, Joe. Interview by Marilyn Holiday and Robert S. McPherson, December 18, 1991.
Manygoats, Sally. Interview by Marilyn Holiday and Robert S. McPherson, April 8, 1992.
Martin, George, Sr. Testimony given March 22, 1961. Doris Duke #913, Special Collections, J. Willard Marriott Library, University of Utah, Salt Lake City.
Mexican Woman. Testimony given January 23, 1961. Doris Duke #731, Special Collections, J. Willard Marriott Library, University of Utah, Salt Lake City.
Mike, Billy. Interview by Aldean Ketchum and Robert S. McPherson, October 13, 1993.
Mike, Jim. Testimony given January 29, 1961. Doris Duke #916, Special Collections, J. Willard Marriott Library, University of Utah, Salt Lake City.
Mike, Lola. Interview by Aldean Ketchum and Robert S. McPherson, November 16, 2005.
Morley, Logan. Interview by Robert S. McPherson, March 13, 2008.
Nakai, Eddie. Testimony given January 21, 1961. Doris Duke #23, Special Collections, J. Willard Marriott Library, University of Utah, Salt Lake City.
Navajo, Buck. Interview by Marilyn Holiday and Robert S. McPherson, December 16, 1991.
Nielson, Floyd, and Clara Nielson. Interview by Gary Shumway and Kim Stewart, July 14, 1971. O.H. 699, Southeastern Utah Oral History Project, Utah State Historical Society, Salt Lake City, Utah.
Nepah, Hetty. Testimony given January 7, 1961. Doris Duke #671, Special Collections, J. Willard Marriott Library, University of Utah, Salt Lake City.
Nez, Martha. Interview by Baxter Benally and Robert S. McPherson, August 2, 1988; August 10, 1988.
Old Man Bob. Testimony given January 27, 1961. Doris Duke #734, Special Collections, J. Willard Marriott Library, University of Utah, Salt Lake City.
Old Ruins (Kit'siili). Testimony given January 18, 1961. Doris Duke #704, Special Collections, J. Willard Marriott Library, University of Utah, Salt Lake City.
Parrish, Cecil. Testimony given January 6, 1961. Doris Duke #667, Special Collections, J. Willard Marriott Library, University of Utah, Salt Lake City.

Perkins, Hilda. Interview by Pat Whitaker, July 9, 1972. O.H. 1176, Southeastern Utah Oral History Project, College of Eastern Utah–San Juan Campus Library, Blanding, Utah.

Perkins, Ray. Interview by James D. Redd, September 13, 1971. O.H. 1083, Southeastern Utah Oral History Project, Utah State Historical Society, Salt Lake City.

———. Interview notes, January 14, 1985, in possession of author.

Rogers, John D. Interview by Michael T. Hurst, April 29, 1927. CRC-J6, Charles Redd Center for Western Studies, Brigham Young University, Provo, Utah.

Sandberg, Nick. Telephone conversation with Robert S. McPherson, April 11, 2008.

Schalk, Lynell. Interview by Robert S. McPherson, March 14, 2008.

Shortfinger, Pat. Testimony given January 11, 1961. Doris Duke #694, Special Collections, J. Willard Marriott Library, University of Utah, Salt Lake City.

Shumway, A. Daniel. Telephone conversation with Robert S. McPherson, March 6, 2008.

Shumway, DeVar. Telephone conversation with Robert S. McPherson, March 8, 2008.

Shumway, Eugene. Telephone conversation with Robert S. McPherson, March 7, 2008.

Shumway, Kelly. Telephone conversation with Robert S. McPherson, March 6, 2008.

Shumway, Kenny. Telephone conversation with Robert S. McPherson, March 8, 2008.

Sloan, Oscar. Interview by Marilyn Holiday and Robert S. McPherson, December 18, 1993.

Smith, Don E. Conversation with Robert S. McPherson, August 21, 2007.

Stash, Tom. Testimony given July 17, 1968. Doris Duke #386, Special Collections, J. Willard Marriott Library, University of Utah, Salt Lake City.

Tsosie, Mary. Interview by Baxter Benally and Robert S. McPherson, January 30, 1991.

Warrior Woman. Testimony given January 18, 1961. Doris Duke #703, Special Collections, J. Willard Marriott Library, University of Utah, Salt Lake City.

White Sheep. Testimony given March 15, 1953 and January 6, 1961. Doris Duke #687 A & B, Special Collections, J. Willard Marriott Library, University of Utah, Salt Lake City.

Yazzie, Fred. Interviews by Marilyn Holiday and Robert S. McPherson, November 1, 1985; November 5, 1987.

Yazzie, Susie. Interview by Marilyn Holiday and Robert S. McPherson, November 10, 2000.

Yellow, Billy. Interview by Evelyn Yellow and Robert S. McPherson, November 6, 1987.

Government Documents

Bureau of Land Management. Comb Wash Files. Bureau of Land Management Field Office, Monticello, Utah.

Continental Commands. Black Mountain Expeditionary Forces. Record Group 393, Department of Colorado, National Archives, Washington, DC, 1908.

———. Black Mountain Expeditionary Forces. Record Group 98, U.S. Army Command, Department of Colorado, 1908.

Gregory, Herbert E. "The San Juan Oil Fields in San Juan County, Utah." *Contributions to Economic Geology, 1909.* Bulletin 431. Washington, DC, 1911.

Hayden, Ferdinand V. *Ninth Annual Report of the United States Geological and Geographic Survey.* Washington, DC: GPO, 1876.

Jackson, William H. "A Notice of the Ancient Ruins in Arizona and Utah Lying about the Rio San Juan." *United States Geological Survey.* Bulletin 1. Washington, DC: GPO, 1876.

Kappler, Charles J. *Indian Affairs: Laws and Treaties*, Vol. 3. Washington, DC: GPO, 1971.

La Rue, E. C. *Colorado River and Its Utilization.* U.S. Geological Survey Water Supply Paper 395. Washington, DC: GPO, 1916.

———. *Water Power and Flood Control of Colorado River below Green River, Utah.* U.S. Geological Water Supply Paper 556. Washington, DC: GPO, 1925.

Letters Received by Office of Indian Affairs. New Mexico Superintendency. Record Group 75, National Archives, Washington, DC, 1886.

Macomb, J. N. *Report of the Exploring Expedition from Santa Fe, New Mexico to the Junction of the Grand and Green Rivers of the Great Colorado of the West in 1859.* Washington, DC: GPO, 1876.

Muhn, James, and Hanson R. Stewart. *Opportunity and Challenge: The Story of BLM.* Washington, DC: Department of the Interior, Bureau of Land Management, 1988.

National Forest Service Records. General File. Monticello Records Division, Monticello Utah.

Nials, F., J. Stein, and J. Roney. *Chacoan Roads in the Southern Periphery: Results of Phase II of the BLM Chaco Roads Project.* Cultural Resource Series Number 1. U.S. Department of the Interior, Bureau of Land Management, Albuquerque District, NM, 1987.

Records of the War Department. Department of New Mexico, 1887. Record Group 94, National Archives, Washington, DC.

Report of the Commissioner of Indian Affairs. Washington, DC: GPO, 1857.

Sears, Julian D. *Geology of Comb Ridge and Vicinity North of San Juan River, San Juan County, Utah,* Geological Bulletin 1021–E. Washington, DC: GPO, 1956.

U. S. Congress. *Indian Hostilities in New Mexico.* 36th Cong., 1st sess. House Executive Document 69. Washington, DC: GPO, 1860.

U. S. Congress. *Permanently Set Aside Lands in Utah . . . Navajo Indian Reservation.* 72d Cong., 2d sess. Report No. 1883. Washington DC: GPO, January 19, 1933.

U. S. Congress. *Ute Indian Commission.* 50th Cong., 2d sess. Senate Executive Document 67. Washington, DC: GPO, January 11, 1889.

U. S. Congress. *Addition to Navajo Indian Reservation in Utah.* 72d Cong., 2d sess. Report No. 1199. Washington, DC: GPO, February 10, 1933.

United States v. Utah (1931), Colorado River Bed Case. Utah State Historical Society, Salt Lake City.

Bissell, Charles A., testimony, October 1930.
Christensen, Christen L., testimony, October 1930.
Hyde, Frank, testimony, October 1930.
Hyde, Ernest, testimony, October 1930.
Loper, Bert, testimony, October 1930.
Mendenhall, Walter E., testimony, October 1930.
Nielson, Jens, September 1929.
Priest, Raymond M., testimony, October 1930.
Raplee, A. L., testimony, October 1930.
Spencer, Charles, testimony, October 1930.
Wetherill, John, testimony, October 1930.
Wetherill, Louise, n.d.
Woods, A. S., testimony, October 1930.

Books and Articles

Amato, Joseph A. *Rethinking Home: A Case for Writing Local History.* Berkeley: University of California Press, 2002.

Anonymous. "In Search of a Lost Race." *The Illustrated American,* April 2, 1892 to August 27, 1892.

———. "Arch Canyon as ORV Park." *Southern Utah Wilderness Alliance Newsletter* (Summer 1999): 17–18.

Aton, James, and Robert S. McPherson. *River Flowing from the Sunrise: An Environmental History of the Lower San Juan.* Logan: Utah State University Press, 2000.

Baars, Donald L. *The Colorado Plateau: A Geologic History.* Albuquerque: University of New Mexico Press, 1983.

———. *Navajo Country: A Geology and Natural History of the Four Corners Region.* Albuquerque: University of New Mexico Press, 1995.

Bahr, Howard M., ed. *The Navajo as Seen by the Franciscans, 1898–1921: A Sourcebook.* Lanham, MD: Scarecrow Press, 2004.

Bailey, Garrick, and Roberta Bailey. *A History of the Navajos: The Reservation Years.* Santa Fe, NM: School of American Research, 1986.

Bailey, Kenneth R. "Roads and Resources of San Juan County." In *San Juan County, Utah: People, Resources, and History,* edited by Allan Kent Powell. Salt Lake City: Utah State Historical Society, 1983.

Bailey, L. R. *The Long Walk: A History of the Navajo Wars, 1846–68.* Pasadena, CA: Westernlore Publications, 1978.

Barnes, F. A. *Canyon Country Geology.* Salt Lake City, UT: Wasatch Publishers, 1978.

Basso, Keith H. *Wisdom Sits in Places: Landscape and Language among the Western Apache.* Albuquerque: University of New Mexico Press, 1996.

Blackburn, Fred, and Ray A. Williamson. *Cowboys and Cave Dwellers: Basketmaker Archaeology in Utah's Grand Gulch.* Santa Fe, NM: School of American Research Press, 1997.

Blackburn, Fred, and Winston Hurst. "Charley Lang: Pioneer Photographer, Musician, and Archaeologist." *Blue Mountain Shadows* 14 (Winter 1994): 5–13.

Bostwick, Todd W. *Byron Cummings: Dean of Southwest Archaeology.* Tucson: University of Arizona Press, 2006.

Brady, Margaret K. *Some Kind of Power: Navajo Children's Skinwalker Narratives.* Salt Lake City: University of Utah Press, 1984.

Bronson, Stanley W. *The Ute Spiritual Cross of the San Juan Mission*. Blanding, UT: Self-published, 1999.

Bulow, Ernest. *Navajo Taboos.* Gallup, NM: Southwestern Books, 1982.

Childs, Craig. *House of Rain: Tracking Vanished Civilization across the American Southwest.* New York: Little, Brown, 2006.

Chronic, Halka. *Roadside Geology of Utah.* Missoula, MT: Mountain Press Publishing, 1990.

Correll, J. Lee. "Navajo Frontiers and Troublous Times in Monument Valley." *Utah Historical Quarterly* 39 (Spring 1971): 145–61.

Davis, William E. "The First Americans in San Juan County." *Blue Mountain Shadows* 13 (Summer 1994): 4–6.

Dunmire, William W., and Gail D. Tierney. *Wild Plants of the Pueblo Province: Exploring Ancient and Enduring Uses.* Santa Fe: Museum of New Mexico Press, 1995.

Eastwood, Alice. "Report on a Collection of Plants from San Juan County in Southeastern Utah." *California Academy of Sciences Proceedings* 6 (August 1896): 271–329.

Eliade, Mircea. *The Sacred and the Profane: The Nature of Religion.* New York: Harcourt, Brace, and World, 1959.

Emslie, Steven D. "Cultural and Climatic Implications in Anasazi Faunal Exploitation: A Review and Perspectives." In *Proceedings of the Anasazi Symposium, 1981,* edited by Jack E. Smith. Mesa Verde National Park, CO: Mesa Verde Museum Association, 1981.

Evans, Will. *Along Navajo Trails: Recollections of a Trader,* edited by Susan Woods and Robert S. McPherson. Logan: Utah State University Press, 2000.

———, and Stewart MacClary. "Trip into the Desert—1930." Unpublished manuscript in possession of author.

Fahey, John, and Robert S. McPherson. "Seeing is Believing: The Odyssey of the Pectol Shields." *Utah Historical Quarterly* 77 (Fall 2008): 357–76.

Fisher, Kulani. "Utah State Highway 95." *Blue Mountain Shadows* 12 (Summer 1993): 74–76.

Fletcher, Maurine S., ed. *The Wetherills of Mesa Verde: Autobiography of Benjamin Alfred Wetherill.* Lincoln: University of Nebraska Press, 1977, 1987.

Franciscan Fathers. *An Ethnologic Dictionary of the Navaho Language.* Saint Michaels, AZ: Saint Michaels Press, 1910, 1968.

Frazier, Kendrick. *People of Chaco: A Canyon and Its Culture*. New York: W. W. Norton, 1986.

Gabriel, Kathryn. *Roads to Center Place: A Cultural Atlas of Chaco Canyon and the Anasazi.* Boulder, CO: Johnson Books, 1991.

———, ed. *Marietta Wetherill: Life with the Navajos in Chaco Canyon.* Albuquerque: University of New Mexico Press, 1992.

Geib, Phil R. "Sandal Types and Archaic Prehistory on the Colorado Plateau." *American Antiquity* 65 (2000).

———, and Dale Davidson. "Anasazi Origins: A Perspective from Preliminary Work at Old Man Cave." *Kiva* 60 (Winter 1994): 191–202.

Goddard, Pliny E. *Navajo Texts.* New York: American Museum of Natural History, 1933.

Goodman, Charles. "History of the Oil Fields in San Juan County." *Salt Lake Mining Review* 12 (April 15, 1910): 17–20.

Great Old Broads for Wilderness. "Broads Position on Off-Road Vehicle Activity." http://greatoldbroads.org.

———. "Travel Corridor Monitoring Volunteer Guide—Broads Healthy Lands Project," April 6, 2007.

Guymon, Gary. "Bill Ball and the Horse Thieves." *Blue Mountain Shadows* 29 (Winter 2003): 61–62.

Haile, Berard. *The Upward Moving and Emergence Way: The Gishin Biyé Version.* Lincoln: University of Nebraska Press, 1981.

Haviland, William A. *Anthropology*. 9th ed. New York: Harcourt College Publishers, 2000.

Haymond, Jay. "San Juan County Roads: Arteries to Natural Resources and Survival." In *San Juan County, Utah: People, Resources, and History,* edited by Allan Kent Powell. Salt Lake City: Utah State Historical Society, 1983.

Hill, W. W. *The Agricultural and Hunting Methods of the Navaho Indians*. New Haven, CT: Yale University Press, 1938.

———. "Navaho Trading and Trading Ritual: A Study of Cultural Dynamics." *Southwestern Journal of Anthropology* 4 (Fall 1948): 371–96.

Hodge, Frederick W. "The Early Navajo and Apache." *American Anthropologist* 8 (July 1895): 223–40.

Holiday, John, and Robert S. McPherson. *A Navajo Legacy: The Life and Teachings of John Holiday*. Norman: University of Oklahoma Press, 2005.

Huckell, Lisa W., and Mollie S. Toll, "Wild Plant Use in North American Southwest." In *People and Plants in Ancient Western North America,* edited by Paul E. Minnis. Washington, DC: Smithsonian Institution, 2004.

Hurst, Winston B. "Colonizing the Dead: Early Archaeology in Western San Juan County." *Blue Mountain Shadows* 17 (Summer 1996): 2–13.

———, and Jonathan Till. "A Brief Survey of Great Houses and Related Features in Southeastern Utah." In *Chaco and Post-Chaco in the Northern San Juan Region: Excavations at the Bluff Great House* (in press), edited by Catherine M. Cameron. Tucson: University of Arizona Press, 2008.

———, and Christy Turner II. "Rediscovering the "Great Discovery:' Wetherill's First Cave 7 and Its Record of Basketmaker Violence." In *Anasazi Basketmaker: Papers from the 1990 Wetherill-Grand Gulch Symposium,* edited by Victoria M. Atkins. Cultural Resource Series 24. Salt Lake City, UT: Bureau of Land Management, 1993.

———, Owen Severance, and Dale Davidson. "Uncle Albert's Ancient Roads: Anasazi Formal Trails in Southeastern Utah." *Blue Mountain Shadows* 12 (Summer 1993): 2–9.

Iverson, Peter. *Diné: A History of the Navajos.* Albuquerque: University of New Mexico Press, 2002.

Jackson, William H. *William H. Jackson Frontier Photographer Diaries, 1866–1874.* Glendale, CA: Arthur H. Clark, 1959.

———, and Howard R. Driggs. *The Pioneer Photographer.* New York: World Book, 1929.

Johnson, Broderick H. *Navajo Stories of the Long Walk Period.* Tsaile, AZ: Navajo Community College Press, 1973.

Kartchner, Deniane. "Two Men on the Road." *Blue Mountain Shadows* 12 (Summer 1993): 51–58.

Kelly, Charles. "Chief Hoskaninni." *Utah Historical Quarterly* 21 (July 1953): 219–26.

King, Beth E. "The Utah Navajos Relocation in the 1950s." *Life along the San Juan River.* Bluff, UT: Bluff Legacy Project, July 1996.

Klah, Hasteen, and Mary C. Wheelwright. *Navajo Creation Myth: The Story of the Emergence.* Santa Fe, NM: Museum of Navajo Ceremonial Art, 1942.

———, *Wind Chant and Feather Chant.* Bulletin 4. Santa Fe, NM: Museum of Navajo Ceremonial Art, 1946.

Kluckhohn, Clyde. *Navaho Witchcraft.* Boston, MA: Beacon, 1944, 1970.

Knipmeyer, James H. *Butch Cassidy Was Here: Historic Inscriptions of the Colorado Plateau.* Salt Lake City: University of Utah Press, 2002.

Krutch, Joseph Wood. *The Desert Year.* New York: Penguin Books, 1952.

Levy, Jerrold E., Raymond Neutra, and Dennis Parker. *Hand Trembling, Frenzy Witchcraft, and Moth Madness: A Study of Navajo Seizure Disorders.* Tucson: University of Arizona Press, 1987.

Linford, Laurance D. *Navajo Places: History, Legend, and Landscape.* Salt Lake City: University of Utah Press, 2000.

Luckert, Karl. *The Navajo Hunter Tradition.* Tucson: University of Arizona Press, 1975.

Lyman, Albert R. "The Fort on the Firing Line." *The Improvement Era* 52, no. 12 (December 1949): 796–98.

———. *Indians and Outlaws: Settling of the San Juan Frontier.* Salt Lake City, UT: Bookcraft, 1962.

———. *The Trail of the Ancients.* Blanding, UT: Trails of the Ancients, 1972.

Malotki, Ekkehart. *Hopi Tales of Destruction.* Lincoln: University of Nebraska Press, 2002.

Matthews, Washington. *Navaho Legends.* Salt Lake City: University of Utah Press, 1897, 1994.

Mayes, Vernon O., and Barbara Bayless Lacy. *Nanise' A Navajo Herbal: One Hundred Plants from the Navajo Reservation.* Tsaile, AZ: Navajo Community College Press, 1989.

McCabe, Henry. *Cowboys, Indians, and Homesteaders.* Salt Lake City, UT: Deseret Press, 1975.

McDaniels, E. A. *Utah at the World's Columbian Exposition.* Salt Lake City, UT: Salt Lake Lithograph, 1894.

McDonald, Ronald F. *Fort Montezuma: An Account of the First Mormon Settlers in San Juan County, Utah.* Blanding, UT: Self-published, revised 2006.

McNeley, James Kale. *Holy Wind in Navajo Philosophy.* Tucson: University of Arizona Press, 1982.

McPherson, Robert S. *A History of San Juan County: In the Palm of Time.* Salt Lake City: Utah State Historical Society, 1995.

———. *The Journey of Navajo Oshley: An Autobiography and Life History.* Logan: Utah State University Press, 2000.

———. "Much Ado about Nothing: The San Juan River Gold Rush, 1892–93." *Utah Historical Quarterly* 67 (Winter 1999): 68–87.

———. *Navajo Land, Navajo Culture: The Utah Experience in the Twentieth Century.* Norman: University of Oklahoma Press, 2001.

———. *The Northern Navajo Frontier, 1860–1900.* Logan: Utah State University Press, 2001.

———. "Paiute Posey and the Last White Uprising." *Utah Historical Quarterly* 53 (Summer 1985): 248–67.

———. *Sacred Land, Sacred View: Navajo Perceptions of the Four Corners Region.* Provo, UT: Brigham Young University, 1992.

———. "'Too Much Noise in that Bunch across the River:' Ba'álílee and the 1907 Aneth Brawl." *Utah Historical Quarterly* 78 (Winter 2009).

Miller, David E. *Hole-in-the-Rock: An Epic in the Colonization of the Great American West.* Salt Lake City: University of Utah Press, 1959.

Moon, Samuel. *Tall Sheep: Harry Goulding, Monument Valley Trader.* Norman: University of Oklahoma Press, 1992.

Morgan, William Sr. *Human-Wolves among the Navaho.* New Haven, CT: Yale University Press, 1936.

Nelson, Sarah M. *Investigation of Cholla Knoll.* Denver, CO: University of Denver, 1978.

Newcomb, Franc J. and Gladys A. Reichard. *Sandpaintings of the Navajo Shooting Chant.* New York: Dover, 1975.

O'Bryan, Aileen. *Navaho Indian Myths*. New York: Dover Publications, 1956, 1993.

Palmer, Jack. "On the Road with Dad." *Blue Mountain Shadows* 35 (Winter 2006): 94–98.

Parkhill, Forbes. *The Last of the Indian Wars.* New York: Crowell-Collier Press, 1961.

Peterson, Charles S. *Look to the Mountains: Southeastern Utah and the La Sal National Forest.* Provo, UT: Brigham Young University Press, 1975.

Prudden, T. Mitchell. *On the Great American Plateau.* New York: G. P. Putnam's Sons, 1906.

Redd, Preston "Pep." *From Horseback to Cadillac, I'm Still a Cowboy*. Tempe, AZ: Tavas Cash Press, 1988.

Reed, Alan D. "Ute Cultural Chronology." In *An Archaeology of the Eastern Ute: A Symposium*, edited by Paul R. Nickens. Occasional Paper Number 1. Denver: Colorado Council of Archaeology, 1988.

Reichard, Gladys A. *Navaho Religion: A Study of Symbolism.* Princeton, NJ: Princeton University Press, 1950.

Roberts, David. *Sandstone Spine: Seeking the Anasazi on the First Traverse of Comb Ridge*. Seattle, WA: The Mountaineers, 2006.

Sandner, Donald. *Navaho Symbols of Healing*. New York: Harcourt, Brace, Jovanovich, 1979.

Schaafsma, Polly. *Indian Rock Art of the Southwest*. Santa Fe, NM: School of American Research Press, 1980.

Schwarz, Maureen Trudelle. *Navajo Lifeways: Contemporary Issues, Ancient Knowledge.* Norman: University of Oklahoma Press, 2001.

Severance, Owen. "Prehistoric Roads in Southeastern Utah." In *La Frontera: Papers in Honor of Patrick H. Beckett* 25, edited by Meliha S. Duran and David T. Kirkpatrick. Albuquerque: Archaeological Society of New Mexico, 1999.

Shumway, A. Daniel. "The Mines on Old Highway 95." *Blue Mountain Shadows* 16 (Winter 1995): 79.

Shumway, Helen. "Trucking Ore: Adventures on San Juan County Roads." *Blue Mountain Shadows* 27 (Summer 2002): 80–81.

Smith, Anne M. *Ethnography of the Northern Utes.* Papers in Anthropology, Number 17. Albuquerque: University of New Mexico Press, 1974.

Stanton, Bette L. *Where God Put the West: Movie Making in the Desert.* Moab, UT: Canyonlands Natural History Association, 1994.

Steen, Charlie R. "The Natural Bridges of White Canyon: A Diary of H. L. A. Culmer, 1905." *Utah Historical Quarterly* 40 (Winter 1972): 56–87.

Tate, LaVerne. "Mining and Trucking." *Blue Mountain Shadows* 27 (Summer 2002): 67–73.

Thompson, Gerald. *The Army and the Navajo: The Bosque Redondo Reservation Experiment, 1863–1868.* Tucson: University of Arizona Press, 1982.

Till, Jonathan D., and Winston Hurst. "Trail of the Ancients: A Network of Ancient Roads and Great Houses in Southeastern Utah." Paper presented at 67th Annual Meeting of the Society for American Archaeology, Denver, Colorado, 2002.

Topping, Gary, ed. "An Adventure for Adventure's Sake Recounted by Robert B. Aird." *Utah Historical Quarterly* 62 (Summer 1994): 275–88.

Valle, Doris. *Looking Back Around the Hat.* Mexican Hat, UT: Self-published, 1986.
Vivian, R. Gwinn. "Chacoan Roads: Morphology." *Kiva* 62 (1997a): 7–34.
———. "Chacoan Roads: Function." *Kiva* 63 (1997b): 35–68.
Waters, Frank. *Book of the Hopi*. New York: Ballantine Books, 1963.
Wetherill, Louisa Wade, and Harvey Leake, ed. *Wolfkiller: Wisdom from a Nineteenth Century Navajo Shepherd.* Salt Lake City, UT: Gibbs Smith, 2007.
Wormington, H. M. *Prehistoric Indians of the Southwest*, Popular Series Number 7. Denver, CO: Denver Museum of Natural History, 1947.
Wyman, Leland C. *Blessingway.* Tucson: University of Arizona Press, 1970, 1975.
———. *The Red Antway of the Navajo.* Santa Fe, NM: Museum of Navajo Ceremonial Art, 1973.
———. *The Mountainway of the Navajo.* Tucson: University of Arizona Press, 1975.
Young, Darroll P. "Economic Impact of the Uranium Industry in San Juan County," *Blue Mountain Shadows* 16 (Winter 1995): 3–40.
Zolbrod, Paul G. *Diné bahane': The Navajo Creation Story.* Albuquerque: University of New Mexico Press, 1984.

Newspapers

Arizona Republic, 1986
Blue Mountain Panorama, 2007–2008
Canyon Echo, 1995
Cortez Herald, 1893
Deseret News, 1885–1888, 1980–1984
Durango Herald, 1893
Cincinnati Enquirer, 1915
Farmington Dailey Times, 1987
Grand Valley Times, 1904–1925
Indian Trader, 1995–1997
Mancos Times, 1893–1894
Montezuma Journal, 1907–1910
Salt Lake Herald Republican, 1915
Salt Lake Tribune, 1893
San Juan Blade, 1917–1918
San Juan Record, 1930–2008
The Times-Independent, 1923–1935
Washington Post, 1894

Index

C

D

E